THE
SHAKESPEAREAN
Imagination

THE
SHAKESPEAREAN
Imagination

NORMAN N. HOLLAND

Indiana University Press   *Bloomington and London*

SECOND PRINTING 1975

Library of Congress catalog card number: 63-15685
Manufactured in the United States of America

pa. ISBN 0-253-20114-4

TO THE BEST AUDIENCE:

Janie and Katy—

and John, Who Came in in the Middle.

PREFACE

REVERSING A CURRENTLY POPULAR PATTERN, THIS BOOK GROWS OUT OF A TELEVISION series, "The Shakespearean Imagination," and many, though by no means all, of its peculiarities stem from that swift and electronic origin. For one thing, the style: though I have translated the scripts from oral to written English, the language remains intractably more casual than the prose of literary criticism probably should be. The book, though it is about Shakespeare, is not aimed at the professional Shakespearean, but at the same audience as the television series, a course-for-credit. The audience, both those actually registered and the hitch-hikers, included a great variety of people: lawyers, housewives, teachers, nuns, engineers, sculptors, and one perceptive postman; the large number of high school students was surely balanced by the young lady cramming for her doc-toral examinations at a nearby university. In short, this is a book for that poltergeist of publishers, the intelligent general reader. My aim, in both book and series, is to enhance and enrich your perception and enjoyment of Shake-speare and, I hope, by a process of carry-over, literature in general. So ambitious a book should have been written at the end of a lifetime of teaching Shake-speare, and I can claim but a scant eight years. The opportunity to do such a series, however, both the subject matter and the new technique of teaching, was too good to miss. From the series the book inevitably grew.

I am, therefore, especially grateful to Dean Reginald Phelps of Harvard who originally approached me about doing the television course-for-credit for the Commission on Extension Courses. The staff, both desk and studio, of station WGBH (the Lowell Institute Cooperative Broadcasting Council) gave most generously of patience and effort at the beginning and end and all through those miles of video tape and the thirty long Thursdays of televising "The

Shakespearean Imagination." I owe a particular debt to Mr. Russell Morash who, in producing the series, gave me by precept and example a quite refreshing and unaccustomed respect for the director's art; and to Mrs. Bonnie Watts and her son Kevin who very graciously contributed their mutual time and energy to the preparation of the original scripts and telecasts. The series would not have been possible at all had it not been for the continued help of the actors and actresses who gave their performances; nor would the series have been much fun without the kindness of those in the audience who wrote encouragement.

Like the television series, the book has visuals. I am most grateful to the Folger Shakespeare Library for permission to reproduce the materials in Figs. 1, 3, 5, 13, and 15; to the Harvard College Library for Figs. 8, 10, and 11; to the Harry Elkins Widener Collection of the Harvard College Library for Fig. 12; to Mr. C. Walter Hodges and his publisher, Coward-McCann, Inc. for permission to reproduce his theater reconstructions in Figs. 2 and 6; and to the Marquess of Bath for Fig. 7. I am especially grateful to the Harvard Theatre Collection and the kindness of Miss Helen Willard for Figs. 9, 14, 16, 17, 18, 19, 20, 21, 22, 23, 24, and 25. Edwin Booth as Hamlet (Fig. 20) was painted from life by John Pope; the original is on view at the Loeb Drama Center and is the property of the Harvard Theatre Collection.

Both in the television series and in this book, alas, my debt to my fellow Shakespearean critics and scholars is very great and very ill paid, for I have made no attempt to enter credit for the various insights and ideas that follow. I can only plead that I have treated myself as stingily, making no effort to single out my own originations. Then, too, what I am formulating in this book is very largely the coin of current Shakespeare teaching: professionals will recognize my particular indebtednesses well enough; the amateur has no need to. I must acknowledge, however, a special debt to one fellow Shakespearean: Professor Max Bluestone, who was kind enough to read the manuscript and help me eliminate the most glaring *gaffes*.

My greatest source of help, hope, and harborage I have already mentioned in the Dedication.

NORMAN N. HOLLAND

Cambridge, Massachusetts
November, 1963

CONTENTS

ILLUSTRATIONS

THE
SHAKESPEAREAN
Imagination

SHAKESPEARE AND HIS
THEATER

PERHAPS THE BEST PLACE TO START AN INTRODUCTION TO SHAKESPEARE IS WITH THE one fact that most people *think* they know about Shakespeare, namely, that Shakespeare wasn't Shakespeare. The plays were actually written by some earl or spy or a committee of earls and spies hidden away in a cave and sending out secret messages in comedies and tragedies as though they were fortune cookies. These anti-Stratfordian theories, as they are called, came into being rather recently, outgrowths of nineteenth-century bardolatry. Shakespeare's contemporaries seem to have had no doubts he wrote the plays, nor did they idolize him. For a hundred years after his death, critics said sagely, "Shakespeare lacked art," meaning, a sense of classical restraint and craftsmanship. But in the nineteenth century, romantic spirits, rebelling against this kind of classicism, turned Shakespeare into a universal genius, lawyer, general, statesman, philosopher, and historian. At the same time, as a different kind of reaction against classicism, Romantic biographers turned him into a simple child of nature, "Avonian Willy," growing up among country scenes, unspoiled by bookish education, even illiterate. Finally, some other romantic spirits drew the obvious conclusion (given these peculiar premises): Avonian Willy could not have been the superlative lawyer, general, statesman, philosopher, and historian, who wrote the plays. There must have been a conspiracy to hush up the real author's name, which the anti-Stratfordian then produces—usually the type of person the particular anti-Stratfordian admires, intellectual, scientist, homosexual, aristocrat, or what you will. To back up these protean changes of identity, the facts of Shakespeare's life and times are tossed to the winds in favor of the shakiest kind of internal evidence. Romeo, for example—E-O stands for Earl of Oxford, so "Romeo" means E-O at Rome, and the tragedy becomes a secret allegory of the Earl of Oxford's visit to Rome.

This anti-Stratfordianism, of course, is just foolishness but, I suppose, really quite harmless and it does keep the people who figure it out off the streets and out of trouble. It is rather hard, though, on Shakespeare's reputation, and I can vouch from personal experience that it's hard on professors of Shakespeare when they are cornered by anti-Stratfordians at cocktail parties. The facts of the matter are that we have exactly the same kind of evidence that Shakespeare wrote these plays that we have for his contemporaries, in fact, the same kind of evidence of authorship that we would have for any modern writer (the writer of this book, for example). We have the book with the author's name on it, indeed, in Shakespeare's case, even his picture on it (see Fig. 1), and we have a couple of dozen references by contemporaries to Shakespeare as the author of his plays. Some of these references are by educated members of his audience, the scholar and clergyman, Francis Meres, for example, or the young lawyer, John Manningham. Others are by people like Ben Jonson or Francis Beaumont who actually worked in the world of the theater with Shakespeare, went drinking with him on Friday nights at the Mermaid Tavern and perhaps even talked over with him the problems of plays and playwriting. (Jonson at least seems to have done so.)

The whole anti-Stratfordian business rests on the completely false notion that the man Shakespeare was an unlettered peasant who could not have written these plays. The facts are that Shakespeare came from a solid, middle-class, even upper-middle-class, background, exactly the same background as most of the other Elizabethan popular playwrights, and that he was about as well educated as a modern college graduate, or, at least, as well educated as the people who say Shakespeare was an unlettered peasant.

Shakespeare was born in Stratford-on-Avon, a busy little market town in Warwick about eighty-five miles from London. The Elizabethans tended to care more about souls than bodies, so instead of recording birth dates they recorded baptisms. Shakespeare was baptized April 26, 1564, and the scholars have decided to give his birth date as April 23, for three reasons: first, it was customary to baptize children about two or three days after they were born; second, St. George is England's patron saint, April 23 is his day, and it is a Good Thing to have England's greatest poet born on St. George's day; third, Shakespeare died on April 23, and to have him be born and die on the same day makes a better story. Shakespeare's father, John Shakespeare, was a manufacturer of gloves, a dealer in agricultural commodities, and a leading citizen in Stratford. In fact, when young William was four years old, his father was elected Bailiff, the highest office in the town government, equivalent to a modern mayor. John and Mary Shakespeare first had two children who died in infancy, then William, so the poet was, in effect, like so many geniuses, an oldest child.

He was followed by a series of five younger brothers and sisters. Shakespeare most probably attended the Stratford Grammar School, where he would have received a quite good education. He learned, of course, to read and write, but, more important, he spent a lot of time studying rhetoric, how to write and speak well. He would have spent most of his time studying Latin, the classics of Latin literature, Roman history, and the Bible, and he would have had a little exposure to Greek. I wonder how many modern children—or, for that matter, how many modern Ph.D.'s—are educated that well. Of course, Shakespeare didn't study a lot of things that we think important. He didn't study mathematics or any foreign languages except Latin and Greek, and, as you can tell from the plays, he didn't study geography. Ben Jonson rather snidely pointed out, "Shakespeare, in a play, brought in a number of men saying they had suffered shipwreck in Bohemia, where there is no sea near by some hundred miles." And, of course, he didn't spend all his time studying. Judging from the language in the plays, we can guess young Shakespeare was very fond of sports and games; he uses a lot of figures of speech derived from sports like hunting, hawking, and bowling.

At eighteen, he became involved with one Anne Hathaway, a woman some eight years older than himself. They got married rather hastily and six months later Mistress Shakespeare was delivered of a daughter, Susanna. You can make of that what you will—and most people have. Two years later, when Shakespeare was twenty-one, they had a set of twins, and shortly after that, Shakespeare left for London. Legend has it—a most unreliable but persistent legend—that he had to get out of town because he was convicted of poaching.

In any case, once Shakespeare arrived in London, he eventually became an actor with one of the leading acting companies, the Lord Chamberlain's Men. In 1603 King James himself became their patron so the company then became known as the King's Men. Legend has it that Shakespeare got his start by holding horses outside the theater, but, anyway, by 1592, when he was twenty-eight, he had acquired enough reputation as an actor and playwright to elicit that surest indication of success—envy. We find a rival playwright, Robert Greene, making a highly uncomplimentary reference to him, as "an upstart crow beautified with our feathers . . . an absolute *Johannes factotum* . . . in his own conceit the only Shake-scene in a country," but then as time goes on, more and more compliments come his way, like Meres's remark, "The Muses would speak with Shakespeare's fine filèd phrase—if they would speak English." During the twenty years he lived in London, he seems to have kept his Stratford life and his London life more or less separate. Of course, there were occasional trips home, but no more children, and one of the twins, his only son Hamnet, died in 1596 when Shakespeare was thirty-two.

Then we begin to see the marks of success. Old John Shakespeare was apparently coming down the ladder as fast as his son William was coming up it. William begins to pay his father's debts. In 1596 he purchases a coat of arms for the family and the title of gentleman. In 1597 he buys the second biggest and fanciest house in Stratford. In 1599, at the age of thirty-five, he becomes what we would call a principal stockholder in his acting company. Shakespeare had achieved a social position and economic bracket very similar to that of Charlie Chaplin and Mary Pickford and Douglas Fairbanks when they founded United Artists in 1919. Most of what we hear of him after he became a principal stock-holder concerns investments and lawsuits—that was what the Elizabethans did for lack of television: they had lawsuits. About 1611, or when he was forty-seven, he retired from London and went back to live in his big, fancy house in Strat-ford, receiving visiting cronies from London, supposedly sitting around a mul-berry tree. Legend has it that, one April, two of his fellow playwrights came up from London, Ben Jonson and Michael Drayton. They all drank too much and Shakespeare fell into a fever that proved fatal. Be that as it may, he died on April 23, 1616, leaving his wife Anne his second-best bed, a not uncommon provision in the wills of the day.

That was Shakespeare's life in Stratford, and you can read about it in any edition of Shakespeare. What we really care about are those twenty years in London when he wrote what is purely and simply the greatest collection of plays in the world. The London that Shakespeare came to as a young man must have been a fascinating place. England had just beaten the Spanish Armada. She was now the greatest sea power in Europe, just beginning that age of colonization the effects of which we are still recovering from today. Along with empire came new scientific achievements, new voyages of discovery and colonization, new manners, new customs, and presiding over it all that wonderfully enigmatic, womanly un-woman, Elizabeth I.

She, like most of her Londoners, was terribly fond of the theater. At the height of Shakespeare's career there were nine theaters in that London of 160,000 people, the equivalent of 450 theaters in a city the size of New York. Most of those nine theaters could hold between 2,000 and 3,000 people, not counting standees, and on the holidays the theaters were packed tight. On a popular day, in other words, 16,000 people or 10 percent of the whole city could have been in the theater. It cost only an English penny to get in, about a twelfth of a skilled worker's daily wage. It wasn't, in short, at all like the modern theater. New York, the most theatrical city in America, doesn't have 450 theaters; it has about thirty. The Shakespearean theater was a truly popular medium and a modern analogy to the Elizabethan theater would not be today's legitimate theater, but the movies. You could find 450 movie theaters in a city the size of New York, and up until recently, anyway, you could find an admission price that was one-twelfth of a skilled worker's daily wage. No small part of Shakespeare's tremendous achievement stems from the fact that he was writing for what we would call today a mass medium, the movies or television. Don't be middle-brow, and turn up your nose at a popular art. Shakespeare didn't.

Specifically, there were four ways—at least four—that the popularity of the theater worked for Shakespeare. First, people do well what they do a lot of, and the English did a lot of theater toward the end of Elizabeth's reign and during James's. During the period from 1590 to 1625, the theater reached a height it has never attained since the theater became more specialized, less of a mass medium, appealing to the few instead of the many. Second, Shakespeare could count on his audience knowing a lot about what had been going on in the theaters. He could put in a character like Ancient (or Ensign) Pistol, who quotes a lot of garbled scraps from old plays and makes jokes that way. He could write a sequel basing one play on another because he could be pretty sure that his audience had seen the first. If *Part 1 of Henry IV* was successful, Shakespeare could write *Part 2* just the way we today have *Frankenstein, Son of Frankenstein, I was a Teen-Age Frankenstein,* and so on. Myths and legends and forms could grow this way. There are practically no sequels in the modern theater because it doesn't play to a large enough audience.

Third, and most important, Shakespeare had to write for all levels of the population, from the highest and fanciest critical or professorial taste to the very lowest, just as the modern moviemaker writes with one eye on the people who read *Screen Romances* and the other eye on the people who read *Cahiers du Cinéma*. Finally, there is a tremendous vitality in these recurring forms of the popular arts. Things like the Western, the gangster movie, or, in Shakespeare's day, the revenge play or the pastoral romance, such forms in a mass medium are constantly being improved and polished, given more appeal, and, ultimately, exhausted. Also, when you have such widely received forms, it means the writer doesn't have to invent so much. He knows what his audience expects in the way of conventions and plots and types of character, and he can concentrate his own attention on the subtleties.

There are a great many things about Shakespeare that will seem strange unless we keep in mind that he was writing for a popular art, a mass medium. The theater was quite an industry in Elizabethan London, and there couldn't have been half a dozen people in that industry who knew more about it than Shakespeare did. For more than twenty years, he worked in the theater, every day he could. If we let ourselves be a little speculative, a little more carefree with the evidence than perhaps we should be, we can imagine what one of Shakespeare's working days would have been like. It would have consisted of three parts, probably: writing a new play; rehearsing an old one with his acting company; then performing at the Globe Theater.

If, like many writers, Shakespeare did his writing in the morning, he would have gotten up at dawn, and after the standard Elizabethan breakfast of a piece of bread and a pint of ale (which no doubt stimulated his creativity) he would sit down to write. He would take a folio sheet of paper, a piece of paper about 14 by 17 inches, and fold it lengthwise three times so as to produce four pages, each divided into three columns. He could write the text of the play on the center of each page, on the left the speech tags, and on the right the stage directions and sound effects and the rest. (In fact, the few pages that survive of an Elizabethan playwright's manuscript were written this way.) Shakespeare used the older kind of handwriting, "secretary hand," it was called, which looks more like German script than the Italian or italic hand from which our modern handwriting, round hand, comes. Shakespeare's fellow actors tell us he never blotted a line, but Ben Jonson nastily says he wishes he had blotted a thousand.

Shakespeare turned out a play about every six months during his London career. He could have written them at the rate of fifty or a hundred lines a day without overstraining himself. He rarely had to collaborate with other writers the way most Elizabethan playwrights did, because he was himself a wealthy man. In Elizabethan times, as now, actors were paid very well, writers rather poorly, and Shakespeare made most of his money as an actor. Acting was a very skilled profession in Elizabethan times. It involved, like all Elizabethan professions, an extensive training, an apprenticeship. The actor had to know not only acting, but jumping and tumbling, dueling and singing, and all kinds of other necessary skills. Shakespeare apparently spent five years working up as an actor, and was known for his acting of older men. One tradition says he played Adam in *As You Like It,* another, that he may have played the Ghost of Hamlet's father (remember, Shakespeare had a son named Hamnet, who died).

At any rate, on this hypothetical day, about ten or eleven in the morning, either before or after dining, Shakespeare would cross the river to the Globe Theater which, like most of the theaters, was in the red-light district. Again, many things about Shakespeare will seem strange unless we recognize that he was writing for a theater which was very, very different from the modern theater. Shakespeare's theater was based on the simplest of stages, the kind that you will still see in use today in the primitive parts of the world or in circuses or carnivals (see Fig. 2). It consists simply of a platform with a place where the actor can change his costume and from which he can make his entrances and exits. There is no attempt to create an illusion of reality. In Shakespeare's lifetime strolling troupes of players would move these portable stages from inn to inn, setting them up in the innyards so that the inn served as an amphitheater to hold the audience.

In 1576, when Shakespeare was still a twelve-year-old boy in Stratford, the first permanent theater was built in London. It was a very simple arrangement. A man named James Burbage simply erected that innyard stage inside a standard Elizabethan amphitheater. The amphitheater was a round building with a large capacity and a round space in the middle, commonly used for that grand Elizabethan sport, bearbaiting, tying a bear up and letting a half-dozen or so dogs work him over. In fact, Shakespeare's fellow playwright, Ben Jonson, complained in one of his prologues that his grand, classical plays had to be performed in the middle of the stench left over from the previous day's bearbaiting. Visscher's seventeenth-century aerial view of the city shows what one of these theaters looked like from the outside (see Fig. 3). The names are confused but it doesn't matter much—you can see very little anyway except a few stray Elizabethans and the barest outline of the three-storey structure. The theaters were mostly open to the skies, although it was important to put a roof over the stage to protect from the rain not the audience, which you could replace, but the expensive costumes. What was inside that round or octagonal structure, though, is one of the greatest puzzles of modern scholarship. There survives a copy of a sketch by a Dutch tourist which shows a little of what an Elizabethan theater looked like from the inside (see Fig. 4). The sketch leaves out a lot of detail, but we can see that the stage is mostly a large platform, that there is no scenery, and that the audience is on three sides, perhaps four, of the action. Another drawing shows a so-called "private" theater, that is, one with a roof over it (see Fig. 5). Again, the stage is a simple platform stage with no scenery, no illusion of reality except possibly for the curtain or arras at the back.

Figure 6 shows one scholar's guess—I think the best one—as to what the inside of Shakespeare's theater looked like. The stage itself is simply a bare platform; in fact, Shakespeare speaks of it as "this unworthy scaffold," and it was exactly the same kind of scaffold that was used for another grand Elizabethan sport, executions. We know from a builder's contract the dimensions of this scaffold. It was $27\frac{1}{2}$ feet deep and 43 feet wide, an enormous playing area, a wonderfully fluid space on which action could be ending on one side at the same time that it was beginning on the other side. On three sides of this platform, the spectators stood on the bare ground and they were called "groundlings." More well-to-do spectators could go and sit on one of the three levels of benches by paying a penny or two pennies extra, and if you were a little short of cash you could go round and round that round theater while the man who collected the money tried to catch up with you to get the extra penny.

On so large a stage, one in the midst of its audience, most of the action must have taken place downstage, at the front edge of the platform. There was no curtain, so acts and scenes ran one after another with no interruptions. There may have been a small curtained recess (the "inner stage") at the back of the platform, but if it existed at all, it was small and used only for entrances, exits, and "discoveries," the actors moving out of the inner stage and downstage as quickly as possible. Sight lines to this inner stage would have been awkward, and to have played any extended action there would have left most of the spectators staring across 27½ feet of empty stage. The scaffold itself was covered with rushes instead of carpets, and the roof was made of straw. Two pillars supported the roof and they could be climbed or hidden behind if the action called for it. A trapdoor towards the front of the stage let down into the space underneath, a trapdoor being useful for raising ghosts, for disappearing acts, for people descending into hell or for other special occasions. There was an area (the "upper stage" or "the above") one storey above the platform that was used for those scenes in which one character on the main stage talks to a character "above," on the walls of a town, for example, or, like Juliet, on a balcony; but since "the above" was ordinarily filled with paying customers, it was better, if possible, not to use it at all. At the very top, two storeys above the platform, the roof, extending out over the main stage, was painted on its inside with stars and planets. "Look," says Lorenzo in *The Merchant of Venice,*

> how the floor of heaven
> Is thick inlaid with patens of bright gold.

And perhaps the musicians sat in a little room (the "heavens") right under that roof; if so, when Shakespeare speaks of "heavenly music," he means it quite literally. In any case, the star-painted roof over the stage, the trapdoor to hell below—is it any wonder Shakespeare said, "All the world's a stage"?

Within this theater played the King's Men, a repertory company made up year after year of approximately the same group of actors. The company would have been based on a capitalist, a real estate owner, the man who owned the theater. In Shakespeare's case, it was two brothers, Cuthbert and Richard Burbage, the heirs of James Burbage, who built the original permanent theater. Richard, fortunately, was not just a theater owner, but also an actor and therefore more sympathetic to the needs of the company than an ordinary real estate operator might have been. He was, in fact, the great tragedian of Shakespeare's company, the man for whom such parts as Hamlet, Othello, and Macbeth were written. Then the company would have included the sharers, as they were called (we would call them the principal stockholders), who were also the principal actors of the company. There would have been about ten of them, all growing rather fat and prosperous, and Shakespeare was one of these men. The sharers would hire some outside actors to play the minor parts, and usually a hired actor was expected to double in more than one minor part in a play. Of course, the hired actors didn't make as much money as the sharers and unemployment was a problem for them, so that they may have "stolen" a play by dictating it to a printer after they had memorized their parts (or so some scholars explain the early "stolen and surreptitious copies" of Shakespeare's plays). Then the company included the apprentices, boys learning the trade of acting, and they played the women's parts. No women were allowed on the public stage in Shakespeare's day, so that all his great parts for women—Lady Macbeth, Cleopatra, Juliet, and the rest—were meant to be played by boys about twelve years old. Finally, the company had its janitorial staff, the people who cleaned up the theater, put fresh rushes on the stage, and the gatherers, as they were called, who collected the money for admission. The janitorial staff was brought in when you needed an army or a crowd or a mob. As Shakespeare says in *Henry V*:

> Our scene must to the battle fly,
> Where—O for pity!—we shall much disgrace
> With four or five most vile and ragged foils,
> Right ill-disposed in brawl ridiculous
> The name of Agincourt.
>
> (IV. *Chorus*. 48–52)

Those "four or five most vile and ragged foils" are the janitorial staff.

Because he belonged to this repertory company, Shakespeare could work out his ideas in the theater, unlike the modern playwright. He knew the people he was writing for. He worked with them every day, he knew the kind of part they could play, and he, like other actors, probably took his turn directing. Shakespeare, then, may have directed his own works, like the modern writer-director of films. Rehearsals probably lasted about two hours at the Globe and then, around 1:30 in the afternoon, the actors would get ready for a performance. The janitorial staff would hoist the company's flag on top of the theater so that people all over the city would know there was a performance. On the Globe's flag was a picture of Hercules holding the earth, the Globe, on his shoulders, and underneath him the words *Totus mundus agit histrionem,* or, as Shakespeare put it, "All the world's a stage." After people had had time to come across the river to the theater, there would be three soundings of a trumpet. Finally, after the audience assembled and quieted down, on the third sounding of the trumpet, the Prologue in his traditional black cloak would come forward and speak his introduction and the play would start.

As we have seen from the drawings, there was no curtain, no fixed scenery and little movable; therefore there were no breaks for acts and scenes. One scene followed on another the way scenes in a movie do. The act-and-scene divisions you see in the texts of Shakespeare's plays today are a mere literary convention that has nothing to do with Shakespeare's own stage practice. No play of Shakespeare's printed during his lifetime was divided into acts and scenes. Similarly, the things you read in some editions of Shakespeare about "another room in the castle" or "another part of the battlefield"—all this was added by eighteenth-century editors and has nothing whatsoever to do with Shakespeare's stage. "Another part of the battlefield" was just another part of that empty 27½-by-43-foot stage. Similarly, there was no particular attempt to make the costumes realistic. Shakespeare's actors just wore very fancy but ordinary Elizabethan clothes for the most part, as you can see in what is apparently a sketch of a contemporary performance of *Titus Andronicus* (see Fig. 7). There were some conventionalized costumes for classical plays, but Shakespeare's Greeks and Romans didn't look very Greek or Roman. It wasn't until the end of the eighteenth century that people decided historically realistic costumes should be used. The idea of staging Shakespeare in "modern dress" isn't "modern" at all—that was the way he staged his plays himself. Similarly, the acting style in Shakespeare's day was apparently not very realistic. The actor did not set out to imitate a real human being but instead tended to be more ceremonial, more like an orator, more like a man reciting poetry.

Thus, the general thing to remember in reading Shakespeare's plays is that he was not writing for a so-called "naturalistic" theater, a theater which attempts to show real people in realistic situations like the late nineteenth- or early twentieth-century theater. Many of the excesses of nineteenth-century "character" criticism or modern "method" acting of Shakespeare's plays come about because people think of Shakespeare as telling realistic stories about realistic people. Shakespeare's theater was more abstract or stylized, more ceremonial than realistic—with one exception. The Elizabethans loved gore and the playwright was under an obligation to produce realistic beheadings and disembowelings and such episodes as the tearing out of Gloucester's eyes in *King Lear*. Shakespeare might have worked that, you see, with a peeled grape that would make a splat as Cornwall cries, "Out, vile jelly." "Upon these eyes of thine I'll set my foot." Trick tables made beheadings possible; and a sheep's bladder full of viscera could be hidden under a doublet for a disemboweling. But, except for that kind of episode, Shakespeare's plays were not done realistically. Even the history books of Shakespeare's day showed historical characters as though they were Elizabethans. An illustration from Holinshed's *Chronicles,* for example (see Fig. 12), shows the eleventh-century Macbeth and Banquo in sixteenth-century costume and the witches looking for all the world like three Elizabethan ladies out for a stroll. Perhaps, then, the best thing to think of when you try and think of the style of a Shakespearean play is a medieval painting with a blank background, showing the eternal, the universal part of man, lifted out of the bounds of a particular space and time.

Shakespeare speaks of "the two hours' traffic of our stage" in *Romeo and Juliet,* and because there were no intermissions and the scenes flowed one right after the other, he could indeed complete a play in two to two-and-a-half hours. In fact, he had to, in that outdoor theater, because he had to get his audience home before sundown. The play, even if it was a tragedy, was always followed by a "jig" or comic skit. For example, at the end of *Macbeth,* after Macduff has carried the tyrant's head all around that 27½-by-43-foot platform, perhaps with a little blood or catsup dripping from the neck onto the spectators nearest the stage, then three or four comic dancers would come out and do a jig to send the audience home across the river in a good mood. They were a good audience. Like most illiterate people, they were extremely sensitive to language and, all rumors to the contrary, they were apparently a quiet, attentive, and patient audience. Like every Shakespearean critic, I hope by my efforts to give Shakespeare another audience as good as his first. As Ben Jonson said of him, "He was not of an age, but for all time." He is our writer as much as theirs.

AFTER 1616

"NOT OF AN AGE, BUT FOR ALL TIME," WROTE JONSON; 'TIS TRUE, 'TIS PITY, AND pity 'tis, 'tis true. Each age since 1616 has had its own Shakespeare, and the story as a whole is one of the sadder illustrations of our perverse human ability to substitute superficials for essentials. Age after age has imposed on Shakespeare's life, gossip and idle backstairs fancies; on his work, the literary fads or venalities of the moment.

In fact, Shakespeare's troubles began, even before his death in 1616, with the so-called "bad" quartos. Copyright in Shakespeare's day offered an author little in the way of profit or protection, and authors usually sold their plays outright to an acting company (receiving from £6 to £10). The early copyright arrangements were particularly hard on the acting companies: once a play was printed, anybody could perform it. Companies such as Shakespeare's, therefore, tried to keep their plays out of print until they were no longer attractions in the theater. Printers, on the other hand, were not averse to turning a penny by pirating an edition of a play still being performed. Scholars differ as to just how this pirating was accomplished. Some hold that a man or men attended the performance to take the play down in one of the primitive shorthand systems of the day, but the more accepted view is that the printer connived with some of the actors who had been hired from outside the company to play minor parts: he got them to dictate what they could remember of the play to someone in the printer's shop. Here, for example, is the opening of *Hamlet* as it appears in one of the accepted texts (with modern spelling and punctuation):

Enter . . . two sentinels.

Bernardo.   Who's there?
Francisco.   Nay, answer me. Stand and unfold yourself.

Bernardo.   Long live the king!
Francisco.   Bernardo?
Bernardo.   He.
Francisco.   You come most carefully upon your hour.
Bernardo.   'Tis now struck twelve. Get thee to bed, Francisco.
Francisco.   For this relief much thanks. 'Tis bitter cold,
          And I am sick at heart.
Bernardo.   Have you had quiet guard?
Francisco.   Not a mouse stirring.
Bernardo.   Well, good night.
          If you do meet Horatio and Marcellus,
          The rivals of my watch, bid them make haste.

             Enter Horatio and Marcellus.
Francisco.   I think I hear them. Stand, ho! Who is there?
Horatio.   Friends to this ground.
Marcellus.   And liegemen to the Dane.
Francisco.   Give you good night.
Marcellus.   O, farewell, honest soldier.
          Who hath relieved you?
Francisco.   Bernardo hath my place.
          Give you good night.
                 Exit Francisco.
Marcellus.   Holla, Bernardo!
Bernardo.   Say—
          What, is Horatio there?
Horatio.   A piece of him.

This is the opening of *Hamlet* as it appears in the "bad" quarto of 1603 (apparently dictated by the actor playing Marcellus; notice how the text gets somewhat more accurate when Marcellus is on stage):

              Enter two sentinels.
Bernardo.   Stand: who is that?
Francisco.   'Tis I.
Bernardo.   Oh, you come most carefully upon your watch.
          And if you meet Marcellus and Horatio,
          The partners of my watch, bid them make haste.
Francisco.   I will. See—who goes there?

             Enter Horatio and Marcellus.
Horatio.   Friends to this ground.
Marcellus.   And liegemen to the Dane.
          O, farewell, honest soldier. Who hath relieved you?
Francisco.   Bernardo hath my place. Give you good night.
                 Exit Francisco.
Marcellus.   Holla, Bernardo!
Bernardo.   Say—is Horatio there?
Horatio.   A piece of him.

Often, after such a pirated text appeared, the acting company would try to recoup by bringing out its own good edition. In the case of *Hamlet,* after the "bad" quarto (Q1) appeared in 1603, 1604 saw the second quarto edition (Q2), "Newly imprinted and enlarged to almost as much againe as it was according to the true and perfect Coppie," a text apparently based on Shakespeare's own manuscript and the one from which modern texts of *Hamlet* are commonly taken.

Even with authorized quartos, though, the publishing of plays remained a fairly helter-skelter business. Shakespeare, for example, lavished considerable care on the publication at the beginning of his career of his two narrative poems, *Venus and Adonis* (1593) and *The Rape of Lucrece* (1594). Plays, however, were a fairly disreputable kind of writing, and Shakespeare seems never even to have watched his plays through the press, let alone written careful introductions to them as he did for the two poems. In fact, it seems possible that the world's greatest playwright may have expected his reputation as a writer to rest on these two good, but hardly outstanding, early poems. In 1616, however, Ben Jonson brought forth his plays in a large folio collection, somewhat pompously entitled *Works,* and playwrights began to take the publication of their plays more seriously. Here again, an analogy to the film is not out of place. Though, for a long time, screenplays have been published in an irregular sort of way, it was not until 1960 with the publication of *Four Screenplays by Ingmar Bergman* that there was a conscientious effort to bring out one man's work, more or less carefully edited, and closely associated with the author. Similarly, Jonson's *Works* started a trend and set other playwrights to publishing their collected plays. It is faintly possible that Shakespeare himself had begun editing his plays for the press when he died in 1616. He did leave, in his will, "to my ffellowes John Hemynge Richard Burbage & Henry Cundell xxvj^s viij^d A peece to buy them Ringes." Probably Shakespeare left them this bequest simply because they were the three surviving members of the old acting company; just possibly, though, he may have been rewarding them for taking the responsibility for seeing his plays through the press.

Burbage died shortly after Shakespeare ("Exit Burbage" went one epitaph for the great tragedian), but in 1623 John Heminge and Henry Condell brought out *Mr. William Shakespeares Comedies, Histories, & Tragedies. Published according to the True Originall Copies.* With this, the First Folio (F1), Heminge and Condell gave us, in effect, Shakespeare as we know him. It is difficult to imagine what we would know about the plays and the poet without these two men who worked, as they said, "without ambition either of selfe-profit, or fame: onely to keepe the memory of so worthy a Friend, & Fellow aliue, as was our SHAKESPEARE, by humble offer of his playes." Here are thirty-six plays (only *Pericles* has been added to the canon Heminge and Condell established), and for most of these plays, the Folio provides the authoritative texts. A somewhat elaborate volume, the Folio gives us our most authentic likeness of Shakespeare, the Droeshout engraving; it also contains a list of the "principall actors," which includes Shakespeare himself, and a scattering of tributes from London literary figures like Leonard Digges and Hugh Holland including probably the most eloquent tribute ever paid by one poet to a rival, Jonson's lines "To the memory of my beloued, The AUTHOR, Mr. WILLIAM SHAKESPEARE." Heminge and Condell themselves wrote an introduction, "To the great Variety of Readers," an important description of Shakespeare and his works, which contains also a useful admonition to critics and readers:

It had bene a thing, we confesse, worthie to haue bene wished, that the Author himselfe had liu'd to haue set forth, and ouerseen his owne writings; But since it hath bin ordain'd otherwise, and he by death departed from that right, we pray you do not envie his Friends, the office of their care, and paine, to haue collected & publish'd them; and so to haue publish'd them, as where (before) you were abus'd with diuerse stolne, and surreptitious copies, maimed, and deformed by the frauds and stealthes of iniurious impostors, that expos'd them: euen those, are now offer'd to your view cur'd, and perfect of their limbes; and all the rest, absolute in their numbers, as he conceiued the. Who, as he was a happie imitator of Nature, was a most gentle expresser of it. His mind and hand went together: And what he thought, he vttered with that easinesse, that wee haue scarse receiued from him a blot in his papers. But it is not our prouince, who onely gather his works, and giue them to you, to praise him. It is yours that reade him. And there we hope, to your diuers capacities, you will finde enough, both to draw, and hold you: for his wit can no more lie hid, then it could be lost. Reade him, therefore; and againe, and againe: And if then you doe not like him, surely you are in some manifest danger, not to vnderstand him. And so we leaue you to other of his Friends, whom if you need, can bee your guides: if you neede them not, you can leade your selues, and others. And such Readers we wish him.

With the First Folio, Shakespeare was left to the mercies of time. His plays were still performed, though cut to allow for the reduced playing time in the "priuat" theaters and changed a little (for example, song-and-dance scenes put into *Macbeth* to suit the growing demands of audiences for such things). In 1642, however, Puritan reformers finally succeeded in closing down the theaters, and Shakespeare was officially banished from the boards during the ensuing eighteen-year "dramatic interregnum." Unofficially, however, there were bootleg performances. Some of the more popular comic parts of the plays were excerpted and played as little "drolls" at country fairs and the like: the Bottom scenes from *Midsummer Night's Dream,* the Falstaff scenes from *I Henry IV,* and, oddly enough, the graveyard scene from *Hamlet.*

In 1660, when Charles II was restored to the throne and London theaters started up again, they opened to a changed audience, more aristocratic than the cross-section of society for which Shakespeare had originally written and more intellectual, their tastes influenced by French styles and the new, rationalist philosophy associated with Descartes and science. John Evelyn saw *Hamlet* in 1661 and liked it himself, but reported in his *Diary,* "Now the old plays begin to disgust this refined age, since his Majesty's being so long abroad." Samuel Pepys, indefatigable—if insensitive—playgoer and the great diarist of the day, found *Twelfth Night* "one of the weakest plays that ever I saw on the stage," and *Romeo and Juliet* "a play of itself the worst that ever I heard in my life." *Midsummer Night's Dream,* he said, was "the most insipid ridiculous play that ever I saw in my life," but (in the manner of an out-of-town buyer at a modern musical) "I saw, I confess, some good dancing and some handsome women, which was all my pleasure."

Accordingly, Restoration writers set about rewriting Shakespeare to suit the new tastes of their audience, much the way modern French plays are "adapted" to suit the needs and tastes of Broadway. First to go was the language—Shakespeare's "low" words were to be replaced by language more suited to the elevated and refined diction of the Enlightenment. Davenant's operatic version of *Macbeth,* complete with witches swinging about on wires like Peter Pan, provides samples aplenty of this "refinement." Where Shakespeare's Banquo, baffled at the witches' vanishing, had asked excitedly,

> Were such things here as we do speak about?
> Or have we eaten on the insane root
> That takes the reason prisoner?
>
> (I. iii. 83–85)

Davenant's Banquo genteelly inquired:

> Were such things here as we discours'd of now?
> Or have we tasted some infectious herb
> That captivates our reason?

Shakespeare's Lady Macbeth steels her courage for the murder:

> Come, thick night,
> And pall thee in the dunnest smoke of hell,
> That my keen knife see not the wound it makes,
> Nor heaven peep through the blanket of the dark
> To cry "Hold, hold!"
>
> (I. v. 48–52)

while Davenant's Lady Macbeth discreetly eschews "low" terms:

> Make haste, dark night,
> And hide me in a smoke as dark as hell,
> That my keen steel see not the wound it makes,
> Nor heav'n peep through the curtains of the dark
> To cry, "Hold, hold!"

Dr. Samuel Johnson (for all that he is the greatest of English critics and one of the most sensitive of commentators on Shakespeare) eighty years later applauded Davenant's substitution of "curtains" for "blanket" and suggested that the terror of the lines would be "weakened by the name of an instrument used by butchers and cooks in the meanest employments; we do not immediately conceive that any crime of importance is to be committed with a *knife*." Again, Macbeth, the real Macbeth, looks at his bloody hands and asks:

> Will all great Neptune's Ocean wash this blood
> Clean from my hand? No, this my hand will rather
> The multitudinous seas incarnadine,
> Making the green one red,
>
> (II. ii. 59–62)

while Davenant's Macbeth whimpers:

> Can the sea afford
> Water enough to wash away the stains?
> No, they would sooner add a tincture to
> The sea, and turn the green into a red.

Compare the lack of delicacy in: "The crow makes wing to th' rooky wood," with the refinement of: "The crow makes wing to the thick shady grove," or see how

> To-morrow, and to-morrow, and to-morrow
> Creeps in this petty pace from day to day
> To the last syllable of recorded time,
> And all our yesterdays have lighted fools
> The way to dusty death. Out, out, brief candle!
>
> (V. v. 19–23)

is so much better as:

> Tomorrow and tomorrow and tomorrow
> Creeps in a stealing pace from day to day,
> To the last minute of recorded time,
> And all our yesterdays have lighted fools
> To their eternal homes; out, out, that candle!

Davenant's *Macbeth* is at least easier, and Pepys did like it: "One of the best plays for a stage, and variety of dancing and musique, that ever I saw."

"Reforming" Shakespeare's language was only the beginning; the plots were next. Davenant's opera of *Macbeth*, for example, enlarged the role of the Macduffs to create the balance and symmetry the rationalist tastes of the age approved. Davenant also adapted *Measure for Measure* by using the main plot, but eliminating the "low" comedy of Elbow and Pompey and substituting for it the witty scenes from *Much Ado About Nothing;* the result, he called *The Law Against Lovers*. Davenant also collaborated with John Dryden to rework *The*

Tempest into a rather ribald and spectacular musical comedy. The plot which delighted an age discovering the "natural man" was the story of Miranda, the girl who has never seen a man, so Davenant added two more innocents, one of them a man who has never seen a girl; both plots afforded plenty of opportunity for the racy wit the Restoration favored. Thomas Shadwell turned *Timon of Athens* into an opera, and John Lacy rewrote *The Taming of the Shrew* into a more or less typical Restoration comedy featuring a comic servant with Scottish dialect and called *Sauny the Scot*. By 1710, most of Shakespeare's plays had been "improved," but of all these adaptations, the only one with any merit of its own is Dryden's *Antony and Cleopatra* which he called (one could scarcely ask for a more typical Restoration title) *All for Love;* it is certainly the best blank-verse tragedy written in English after 1642.

Surely the most extraordinary of the adaptations was Nahum Tate's version of *King Lear*. Tate eliminated Shakespeare's brilliant Fool, put in some love interest, and gave the tragedy a happy ending. At the end, Lear achieves a "blest Restauration" and Edgar marries Cordelia, pointing the moral demanded by the rule of "poetic justice":

> Thy bright example shall convince the World
> (Whatever Storms of Fortune are decreed)
> That Truth and Vertue shall at last succeed.

Indeed, the true Shakespeare has succeeded, and the adaptations serve today mostly to provide a few chuckles in scholarly circles. Nevertheless, they did have an astonishing durability. They replaced the real Shakespeare, some of them, for as long as a century and a half; Tate's version of *Lear,* for example, was being played in London well up into the nineteenth century. In fact, a few aspects of Colley Cibber's *Richard III* found their way into the recent film of that play.

Paradoxically, while some neoclassic authors were rewriting Shakespeare, others were valiantly trying to restore what he "really" wrote. If there is one feeling which characterizes the Enlightenment, it is: We know. Thus Davenant and others could "refine" and "improve" Shakespeare; and thus Nicholas Rowe, his first eighteenth-century editor, could pontificate: "I shall not undertake the tedious and ill-natur'd Trouble to point out the several faults he was guilty of" in not arranging his plays according to the supposed rules of Aristotle. "As *Shakespear* liv'd under a kind of mere Light of Nature, and had never been made acquainted with the Regularity of those written Precepts, so it would be hard to judge him by a Law he knew nothing of. We are to consider him as a Man that liv'd in a State of almost universal License and Ignorance: There was no establish'd Judge, but every one took the liberty to Write according to the Dictates of his own Fancy." Despite this "irregularity," Shakespeare's plays had gone through four editions in the seventeenth century, and Rowe took it upon himself to bring out a new one. His was the first illustrated edition of Shakespeare, the first to contain a biography, and the first to provide a complete set of act-and-scene divisions in the eighteenth-century manner. (Remember that on Shakespeare's stage the scenes followed one after the other without breaks; what act-and-scene divisions the First Folio has represent a literary, not a dramatic convention.) Unfortunately, Rowe based his text on the "latest edition" instead of turning back to early texts, and in doing so he set a precedent for Shakespearean editing that was to last nearly two hundred years.

Thus, when the poet Alexander Pope decided to bring out a correct edition of Shakespeare's works, "that of the late Mr. Rowe being very faulty," he worked from Rowe's text. Though Pope gave Shakespeare high marks for characterization, originality, "power over our passions," and "sentiments," "It must be own'd," he decided, "that with all these great excellencies, he has almost as great defects," and Pope set about to rescue him. In addition to *"Want of Learning,"* Shakespeare had leveled his plays to please "the *Populace"* and his audience "was generally composed of the meaner sort of people." "Not only the common Audience had no notion of the rules of writing, but few even of the better sort." Further, Shakespeare was a "player," and "They have ever had a Standard to themselves, upon other principles than those of *Aristotle*. Players are just such judges of what is *right,* as Taylors are of what is *graceful."* Consequently, Pope felt free to drop lines he did not like or bury them in footnotes or marginalia; he emended freely, flattening out Shakespeare's irregularities into the glassy slickness of eighteenth-century poetic diction. Pope's edition (1725) was a disgrace, and it prompted one Lewis Theobald to publish in 1726 a book, *Shakespeare Restored, or a Specimen of the many Errors as well Committed as unamended by Mr. Pope in his late edition of this Poet; designed not only to correct the said Edition, but to restore the true Reading of Shakespeare in all the Editions ever published."* Pope waspishly replied by immortalizing his opponent as "piddling Tibbalds" and making him the hero of the first version of the most delightful satire in English, the *Dunciad;* Theobald is made to apostrophize the Goddess of Dulness:

> For thee I dim these eyes and stuff this head
> With all such reading as was never read.

Theobald had indeed prepared himself for the study of Shakespeare by studying the sources from which Shakespeare took his stories, and when he retaliated by producing his own edition of Shakespeare, it proved far more satisfactory than Pope's. William Warburton, however, rallied to the defense of Pope and produced his own edition; at the same time both he and Pope attacked still another editor, Sir Thomas Hanmer.

All these warring editors, however, whether ridiculing or stealing one another's emendations, all assumed it was an editor's business to conjecture, where the text seemed difficult or unsatisfactory, what Shakespeare had "truly" written. An eighteenth-century satirist summed up the rights of editors: "He has a right to alter any passage, which he does not understand." "Where He does not like an expression, and yet cannot mend it, He may abuse his author for it." Rowe had set a procedure for future editing of Shakespeare which lasted well-nigh two hundred years: turn away from the early folios and quartos and substitute the cumulating wisdom of editors, adding emendation to emendation. Though later editions—in the eighteenth century, Edward Capell's, George Steevens' (who obtained for his edition commentary by Samuel Johnson), the great scholar Edmond Malone's edition, and subsequent variorums (editions which summarize the comments of other editors and scholars); in the nineteenth century, the *Cambridge Shakespeare* of 1863–1866—though these editions pruned the excesses of the warring editors, Rowe's principle of cumulating editorial wisdom remained largely intact.

Until our own century, the only radically new approach to editing Shakespeare was that of Thomas Bowdler who brought out, in 1818, *The Family Shakespeare* on the following editorial principle: "If any word or expression is of such a nature, that the first impression which it excites is an impression of obscenity, that word ought not to be spoken, or written, or printed: and if printed, it ought to be erased." Bowdler found to his pleasure "that the indecent words in [Shakespeare's] writings may, in almost every instance, be expunged, not only without injury, but with manifest advantage to the sense of the passage, and the spirit of the author." Accordingly, Bowdler improved Shakespeare by excluding from his edition "whatever is unfit to be read aloud by a gentleman to a company of ladies." "I can hardly imagine," wrote Bowdler, "a more pleasing occupation for a winter's evening in the country, than for a father to read one of Shakespeare's plays to his family circle"—indeed Bowdler's own father had done so, and so great was his father's skill in editing as he read, "that his family listened with delight to *Lear, Hamlet,* and *Othello* without knowing that those matchless tragedies contained words and expressions improper to be pronounced." The aim of Bowdler's *Family Shakespeare* was to enable other fathers, perhaps less skilled, to read to their family circles "without incurring the danger of falling unawares among words and expressions which are of such a nature as to raise a blush on the cheek of modesty, or render it necessary for the reader to pause, and examine the sequel before he proceeds further in the entertainment of the evening." Thus was Shakespeare improved, now, for the Victorians. "Here, ran Johnson's dagger through," quipped the *British Critic,* " 'see what a rent envious Pope has made,' and 'here, the well beloved Bowdler stabbed.' "

His plays were not of an age, but for all ages in the matters of editing and "improvements"; so also the man himself. Each age invented, as it were, its own image of the bard. "Shakespeare wanted art," said his friend Ben Jonson, that is, Shakespeare lacked that sense of technique which meant paying proper attention to the way the Greeks and Romans wrote plays and obeying the rules of Aristotle (which, of course, Aristotle himself did not invent; Renaissance commentators did). "His wit was in his owne power," said Jonson, "would the rule of it had beene so too," as he pointed out an absurd line in *Julius Caesar* (which apparently Shakespeare changed as a result of Jonson's scorn). This was to be the opinion of Shakespeare for a century and a half after his death, that he had a marvelous imagination but failed to control it well, "rule" it, because he "wanted art" or lacked learning. Thus Milton could write, some fifteen years after the playwright's death, of "sweetest Shakespeare, fancy's child," that is, imagination's favorite son, warbling "his native Wood-notes wild," and contrast Shakespeare's free flow of imagination with Jonson's "learned" style. So also Dryden in the Restoration found Jonson "the more correct poet, but Shakespeare the greater wit," that is, the man with greater imagination. The Restoration would speak of Shakespeare's "Artless beauty." " 'Twas well in spight of him what ere he writ," wrote an anonymous poet. We have already heard Pope's strictures in the early eighteenth century, and even Dr. Johnson in his magnificently sane and balanced "Preface to Shakespeare" (1765), though on balance he justified Shakespeare's style and judgment, relied in part on the Enlightenment's feeling that "The *English* nation, in the time of *Shakespeare,* was yet struggling to emerge from barbarity."

With the end of the century and the coming of Romanticism, the rules and "correctness" even the best minds of the Enlightenment had set such store by fell into disrepute. The conception of "artless" Shakespeare veered around—not to the correct view, that Shakespeare was a fairly well educated man—but to make of his supposed artlessness, not a vice, but a virtue. In the hands of the best Romantic writers, this view became a sound, even brilliant, corrective to the neoclassic clichés. Thus, Samuel Taylor Coleridge, greatest of the Romantic critics, said:

Let me now proceed to destroy, as far as may be in my power, the popular notion that he was a great dramatist by mere instinct, that he grew immortal in his own despite . . . [it] began in a few pedants, who having read that Sophocles was the great model of tragedy, and Aristotle the infallible dictator of its rules, and finding that the *Lear, Hamlet, Othello,* and other master-pieces were neither in imitation of Sophocles, nor in obedience to Aristotle . . . took upon them, as a happy medium and refuge, to talk of Shakspeare as a sort of beautiful *lusus naturae,* a delightful monster,—wild, indeed, and without taste or judgment. . . . In nine places out of ten in which I find his awful name mentioned, it is with some epithet of 'wild,' 'irregular,' 'pure child of nature,' &c.

The true ground of the mistake lies in the confounding mechanical regularity with organic form. The form is mechanic, when on any given material we impress a predetermined form, not necessarily arising out of the properties of the material;—as when to a mass of wet clay we give whatever shape we wish it to retain when hardened. The organic form, on the other hand, is innate; it shapes, as it developes, itself from within, and the fulness of its development is one and the same with the perfection of its outward form. Such as the life is, such is the form . . . and even such is the appropriate excellence of . . . our own Shakespeare.

In other words, Shakespeare's plays have the form which is right for Shakespeare's plays. It is nonsense to say he "wanted art."

In the hands of lesser men, however, Shakespeare was still supposed to be "Artless," uneducated, and this supposed lack of learning combined with the Romantic cult of the primitive and the "natural," the notion of the poet tutored only by nature, to produce a particularly tedious and confusing kind of sentimentality. This sentimentality had already begun at the Jubilee celebration at Stratford in 1769, presided over by David Garrick which greatly stressed the notion of "Avonian Willy":

> Ye Warwickshire lads, and ye lasses,
> See what at our Jubilee passes;
> Come revel away, rejoice, and be glad,
> For the lad of all lads was a Warwickshire lad,

went one of Garrick's songs. By the 1840's, Thomas Carlyle could speak in one breath of "the greatest intellect, who, in our recorded world, has left record of himself in the way of Literature" and in the next breath of "the Stratford Peasant." Even scholars were not immune to the image of a pastoral bard surrounded by "sweet English maidens," "pleasant country scenes," "Spring flowers," and, above all, "sheep-shearings." One of the finest scholars, Halliwell-Phillips, described in 1874 a Shakespeare "removed prematurely from school, residing with illiterate relatives in a bookless neighbourhood; thrown into the midst of occupations adverse to scholastic progress." Sidney Lee in 1898 found him "a village youth," "stagestruck."

Combined with this image of the "child of nature" was the most shameless kind of adulation. Jonson had said, "I lov'd the man, and doe honour his memory (on this side Idolatry) as much as any." Later, less reasonable souls have not stayed on the lee side of idolatry. Davenant, for all his "improvements," was willing to go a long way to link himself to the bard. Davenant's parents, notably his beautiful mother, had run the Crown Tavern in Oxford where (Davenant said) Shakespeare would stop over on his annual journeys to Stratford. "Now Sir William," a seventeenth-century antiquary reported of Davenant, "would sometimes, when he was pleasant over a glasse of wine with his most intimate friends . . . say, that it seemed to him that he writt with the very spirit that did Shakespeare, and seemed contented enough to be thought his Son. He would tell them the story as above, in which way his mother had a very light report, whereby she was called a Whore."

Davenant's willingness to sacrifice his mother on the altar of the Shakespeare cult was only a first step across the line of idolatry. It is rather striking, in fact, how often "bardolatry" (as it is called) soars into the language of religion. As early as 1765, an English writer had a Frenchman say: "A veneration for Shakespeare seems to be a part of your national religion, and the only part in which even your men of sense are fanatics," and Coleridge complained that Shakespeare was treated "as a sort of grand Lama, adored indeed, and his very excrements prized as relics." The citizens of Stratford were, to be sure, not slow in providing relics that the increasing throng of visitors to Stratford could purchase. Though the testy Reverend Francis Gastrell who purchased New Place cut down the mulberry tree the poet was said to have planted, indeed, razed the house, the tree was purchased by an aptly named Thomas Sharpe who fashioned from it a seemingly never-ending stream of cups, toothpick cases, and the like. "Perhaps," writes a kindly scholar, "it was, after all, a very big mulberry tree." At any rate, at the Jubilee, Garrick was given one of the cups and so moved to declaim:

> Behold this fair goblet, 'twas carv'd from the tree,
> Which, O my sweet Shakespear, was planted by thee;
> As a relic I kiss it, and bow at the shrine;
> What comes from thy hand must be ever divine.

Stratford was seeing the beginnings of the "Shakespeare industry." Edmond Malone, for example, wrote:

> In this retreat our Shakespeare's godlike mind
> With matchless skill surveyed all human kind.

The "retreat" began to realize some of the possibilities opened by the bard's growing reputation. Mrs. Hart, a distant descendant, sold off bits and pieces of the poet's chair. Anne Hathaway's descendants turned up with a beaded purse they said the poet had given his beloved and, even more exciting, an oak chair in which he sat during their courtship holding Anne on his knee. The succeeding owners of the Birthplace had, most surprising of all, Friar Laurence's lantern, but also produced what purported to be the poet's reading glass, pencil case, tobacco box, sword, baby chair, and easy chair (evidently, like the mulberry tree, selling off pieces of it had not diminished the original item).

The stream of relics from the shrine was equaled only by the stream of words from devout worshipers. All through the century, bardolaters were moved to massive apostrophes. There was De Quincey's (1823): "O mighty poet! Thy works are not as those of other men, simply and merely great works of art; but are also like the phenomena of nature, like the sun and the sea, the stars and the flowers; like frost and snow, rain and dew, hail-storms and thunder. . . ." Carlyle's (1840):

Here, I say, is an English King, whom no time or chance, Parliament or combination of Parliaments can dethrone! This King Shakespeare, does not he shine, in crowned sovereignty, over us all, as the noblest, gentlest, yet strongest of rallying signs. . . . We can fancy him as radiant aloft over all the Nations of Englishmen, a thousand years hence.

And on and on through the century, the paean swelled in all the orotundities of Victorian prose, culminating in Swinburne's effusions as he wound up his wit to consider the last plays: "And now, coming at length within the very circle of Shakespeare's culminant and crowning constellation, bathing my whole soul and spirit for the last and (if I live long enough) as surely for the first of many thousand times in the splendours of the planet whose glory is the light of his very love itself . . . what shall I say of thanksgiving before the final feast of Shakespeare?" Indeed, he would seem to have said all any reasonable man could.

By this time, Shakespearomania was not simply an English phenomenon but a European one. With the spread of Romanticism, the contempt for the rules of the Enlightenment, and the prizing of the "irregular" and "primitive," Shakespeare had conquered Europe as well as his native isle, and those who wished to could read in Goethe or Pushkin paeans in their native tongue, like this by Victor Hugo:

Shakespeare: what is he? You might almost answer, He is the earth. . . . In Shakespeare the birds sing, the bushes are clothed with green, hearts love, souls suffer, the cloud wanders, it is hot, it is cold, night falls, time passes, forests and multitudes speak, the vast eternal dream hovers over all. Sap and blood, all forms of the multiple reality, actions and ideas, man and humanity, the living and the life, solitudes, cities, religions, diamonds and pearls, dung-hills and charnel-houses, the ebb and flow of beings, the steps of comers and goers, all, all are on Shakespeare and in Shakespeare.

This kind of thing, while it expresses an admirable fondness for Shakespeare, can hardly be said to add to our understanding of his works, an understanding that was badly needed in the nineteenth century.

Bardolatry thrived on the fact that, then, little was known about the poet. Instead, the aura around the bard consisted largely of rather doubtful old stories. The Stratford citizens were no less slow in providing legends than they were in providing relics; and old actors who survived into the Restoration had added their dim recollections. Shakespeare "had been in his younger yeares a schoolmaster in the countrey" (though the records of such things do not show it). "His father was a Butcher, and . . . when he [Shakespeare] was a boy he exercised his father's Trade, but when he kill'd a Calfe he would doe it in a high style, and make a Speech." When he first came up to London, he held horses for the patrons outside of the theaters. He had died a Roman Catholic. He had written epitaphs for various Stratford figures (which the proud citizens then produced). He had died after a drinking bout with two fellow poets visiting from London, Jonson and Drayton (though Drayton was famous for his sobriety). He had played Adam in *As You Like It* and the Ghost in *Hamlet*. The most durable story of all was that Shakespeare had been persecuted by one Sir Thomas Lucy for poaching in his deer park and had lampooned Lucy as Justice Shallow in *The Merry Wives of Windsor,* giving Shallow twelve luces ("louses") in his coat of arms (the Lucys, however, had no deer park in the sixteenth century and a "luce" is a freshwater fish that appeared on many coats of arms in the period).

This intriguing, if rather fanciful, picture was further confused by forgery, and not just of mulberry wood and easy chairs. In the 1790's, William-Henry Ireland, inspired by the Stratford shrines and relics, "discovered" a mortgage deed. This first success, however, like the fatal glass of beer, led the young man on and on through receipts, portraits, letters, poems, manuscripts of plays, even a lock of the poet's hair, and finally to a hitherto undiscovered masterpiece, *Vortigern and Rowena*. This tragedy, in which Ireland took considerable pride, was actually produced—despite howls of laughter from a skeptical audience at the climactic line, "And when this solemn mockery is o'er." The nineteenth century produced a farrago of portraits, most of them truly Elizabethan, but probably none of them a portrait of Shakespeare. Even scholars were not immune from the mania for Shakespeareana, and one of the greatest of them, John Payne Collier, was carried away by the praise accorded his early discoveries of theatrical documents, praise which had made him the leading Shakespearean authority of his day. Haunted by heaven knows what strange visions of literary eminence, Collier "discovered" other diaries and documents of the period and finally came up with a whole set of marginalia in an early folio that purported to be corrections against Shakespeare's original manuscript. Even today, scholars are not entirely sure what in Collier's work can be relied upon. Other scholars of the nineteenth century, intent upon the further deification of the bard, became "disintegrators," that is, critics who insisted that such-and-such a scene or line was too inferior to be the poet's work—it must have been interpolated by somebody else. These "disintegrative" critics, in other words, simply brought Pope's thesis of the horrid actors up to date, and they, like Pope, did their bit to obscure the Shakespearean picture.

The combination of ignorance and idolatry is a dangerous one; it hardly makes sense to regard any man, even a Shakespeare, as on the one hand a universal genius and on the other an unschooled child of nature. It is not surprising that in all the confusion someone should ask could this "Stratford peasant" be the same man as "the greatest intellect who, in our recorded world, has left record of himself in the way of literature"? Someone, of course, did ask: Joseph C. Hart, in his *Romance of Yachting* (1848): "Ah, Shakespeare—Immortal Bard—Who were you?" Hart offered no solution, but Miss Delia Bacon did, in *The Philosophy of the Plays of Shakespeare Unfolded* (1857)—her namesake, Elizabeth's great jurist, Sir Francis Bacon. And in doing so, she opened the floodgates: out poured conjecture, speculation, codes, cryptograms, acrostics, anagrams,* and even conversations with the spirits of departed candidates for authorship—for, of course, Bacon's claim in time came to be regarded as no more valid than that of the "ignorant butcher's son." Since Delia Bacon's primitive efforts, we have been treated to cases for over twenty others, among them, the Earls of Derby, Rutland, and Oxford, Christopher Marlowe, Sir Walter Raleigh, Sir Edward Dyer, the Countess of Pembroke, a committee headed by Queen Elizabeth, and a nun named Ann Whateley (who exists solely as a clerk's error for "Hathaway").

In the days when bardolatry combined with a truly astonishing ignorance about Shakespeare and his theater (it was not, for example, until 1875 that a reasonable chronology for the plays was established), such an anti-Stratfordian cult is, in a way, not very surprising. What is surprising is that such a cult or cults should continue long after our ignorance of Shakespeare and his time has been cleared up. After all, we have inherited the achievements of nineteenth-century scholarship as well as its failures, and the documents proving the facts of Shakespeare's life and stage are now quite easily available to anyone willing to look at them. Shakespeare was not "a mean, drunken, ignorant and absolutely unlettered rustic," nor did his contemporaries find his plays particularly learned or aristocratic—in fact, quite the opposite. We can now see that the anti-Stratfordian cults are arguing (to put the notion in modern terms) that Chief Justice Warren—or Governor Rockefeller or Wernher Von Braun—has been secretly turning out screenplays at the rate of two a year leaving coded messages and allegories in them to prove his authorship when future ages shall have decided (two centuries hence) these movies were the work of a universal genius.

It would be pleasant to say that, while in the studies of the world, men were unmasking, forging, idolizing, bowdlerizing, "refining," "improving," and emending Shakespeare, on the stages of the world, this consummate dramatic

---

* Imagine, for example, the secret messages about authorship contained in a word like *honorificabilitudinitatibus* (for example, *hi ludi tuiti sibi, Fr Bacono,* which more or less says: these plays entrusted to themselves proceeded from Fr Bacon), though since Dante uses the word, too, the message must prove Bacon wrote *The Divine Comedy* as well as *Love's Labour's Lost*.

artist had remained pure, but such, alas, is not the case. On the stage, no less than in the study, each age has had its own special version of Shakespeare. Shakespeare had written his plays for a 27½-by-43-foot platform, surrounded on three sides by the audience, with little or no scenery, and no breaks between successive scenes. The popular theaters being open to the skies, there was no proscenium arch and no curtain. Such a simple stage obviously could not last long. Even in Shakespeare's lifetime, as the popular theaters faced various difficulties and the "priuat" or roofed, indoor theaters became increasingly important in the economics of the theater, his plays moved indoors with, apparently, some increase in scenery and breaks for musical intermissions.

After the dramatic interregnum, when the theaters were reopened, they were indoor theaters with a proscenium arch, curtain, and with a large part of the platform behind the arch. The purpose of increasing the area behind the arch was to provide space for scenery and other effects (space, for example, for the wires on which to hang Davenant's witches). The curtain meant breaks for act-and-scene divisions in the French manner, so that Rowe, in dividing the plays into acts and scenes, was simply following the theatrical practice of his day. No wonder Shakespeare seemed to lack "art"—the curtain would have been constantly going up and down for changes in scene.

In the eighteenth century, still more of the playing area moved behind the proscenium arch. Still more scenic effects were added, until what confronted the audience (now facing, not surrounding, the playing area) was essentially a modern picture-frame stage in which the proscenium arch frames what looks like a picture of the setting. It is at this time that editors begin adding those strange stage directions, "another room in the castle," "another part of the battlefield," when all there should have been was that grand scaffold 27½-by-43 feet.

What goes with the picture-frame stage is the "fourth-wall convention" in which the audience pretends, in effect, it is watching the action through the transparent fourth wall of a room. Such a stage calls for a more realistic, naturalistic style of acting. In Shakespeare's day, or at least just before his time, acting was more like recitation. Over the next two centuries, acting became more and more naturalistic, the greatest steps in that direction being taken by David Garrick in the third quarter of the century: "the illusions of imposing declamation" gave way, with Garrick's innovations, to "the just modulation of the words, and concurring expression of the features from the genuine working of nature." It would be no bad thing if modern actors and directors were more aware of the fact that Garrick's innovations were innovations. The theater has been a going concern for some three thousand years; only in the last 150 has naturalistic representation (which most modern actors and directors regard as the essence of the dramatic art) been considered important. Among the writers writing in the benighted ages before naturalism were Aeschylus, Sophocles, Euripides, Lope de Vega, Calderón, Molière, Marlowe, Jonson, Racine, Corneille, Congreve—and Shakespeare.

Naturalism, whether we regard it as a good influence or a bad one, came slow and late. As a matter of fact, it was only in Garrick's time that the custom ended of having the more well-to-do spectators sit on the stage, hardly an arrangement calculated to produce an illusion of reality. In Shakespeare's day, actors simply wore the clothes of their own time (with perhaps a few conventionalized garments that signaled they were playing Greeks and Romans). In what is apparently a sketch of a contemporary performance of *Titus Andronicus* (see Fig. 7), only the principals wear anything remotely like Roman costume; the guards wear Elizabethan clothes. This was indeed "Shakespeare in modern dress," and this approach lasted for two hundred years. Garrick, when he played Macbeth, "used to be dressed in a suit of scarlet and gold, a tail wig, etc., in every respect like a modern military officer" (see Fig. 9), and the witches wore "mittens, plaited caps, laced aprons, red stomachers, ruffs." Garrick's Hamlet looks simply like an eighteenth-century gentleman (see Fig. 17). It was Garrick's rivals, Aaron and John Hill and Charles Macklin, who introduced naturalism in stage dress. Macklin, wrote his biographer, "whose eye and mind were ever intent on his profession, saw the absurdity of exhibiting a Scotch character, existing many years before the Norman Conquest, in this manner [that is, as a modern military officer], and therefore very properly abandoned it for the old Caledonian habit." But his Shylock (see Fig. 14) wears eighteenth-century clothes.

At the same time, painters had begun painting what were called conversation pieces, that is, paintings that illustrated a line or scene from one of the plays. While some of these works were worthwhile in themselves, like Blake's engraving of the ghost of Caesar or Fuseli's painting of Lady Macbeth, they only confused readers of the plays as to what the plays were supposed to look like onstage. Increasingly, people began to regard a Shakespearean play not so much as a thing-in-itself but as a representation of something outside itself. People got the characters all mixed up with historical personages as though Shakespeare had been merely recording the doings of some actual people. The Stratford relic-works had come up with Friar Laurence's lantern, and if you go to Verona today, you will quite solemnly be shown the tomb of Romeo and Juliet, and Elsinore is always described as Hamlet's castle, though so far as anybody knows neither Romeo nor Juliet nor Hamlet ever actually existed.

In short, just as Shakespeare's plays were getting free of the alien critical standards the eighteenth century had imposed, the nineteenth century came up with an alien theatrical practice. By the end of the eighteenth century, theater people were slowly but surely getting rid of the Restoration "improvements" and adaptations. Garrick disposed of Hippolito (the young man who had never seen a woman in *The Tempest*), but he also dropped the gravediggers and Osric from *Hamlet*. Edmund Kean put the tragic ending back into *Lear*, but it was not until 1838 with William Macready that the tragedy regained its Fool and lost the romance between Edgar and Cordelia. By the mid-century, scholarly Samuel Phelps, working in the little suburban theater at Sadler's Wells, had finally played all but six of Shakespeare's plays substantially as they were written. The big London theaters, however, had so grown in size that for their audiences the plays had to be spectacles rather than the verbal dramas that Shakespeare actually wrote, and this need to turn the plays into pageants led to the next age's version of Shakespeare.

In the 1850's, Charles Kean began staging Shakespeare with a great to-do about archaeological accuracy. *Macbeth,* for example, had an enormous eleventh-century banquet hall complete with hundreds of retainers, roasted oxen being carried about, and all the rest. To move all that scenery, even to move around in it, takes time, and what was Kean to cut? Naturally—cut the language which is obviously of less importance than the roasted oxen. In *The Winter's Tale,* an obliging eighteenth-century editor had solved the problem of the nonexistent seacoast of Bohemia by assuring his readers that Shakespeare (that learned geographer!) had really meant "Bithynia," which made a nice savage contrast to the Graeco-Syracusan culture represented by the other scenes in the play. That was all Kean needed: "An opportunity is thus afforded," he wrote, "of reproducing a classical era, and placing before the eyes of the spectator, *Tableaux vivants* of the private and public life of the ancient Greeks." An awesome team of archaeologists reproduced with appalling accuracy chairs, harps, fountains, even a little go-cart which young Ellen Terry pulled about as she played Mamillius. Shakespeare's simple stage direction, "Here a dance of twelve Satyrs," became "the boisterous merriment of the Dionysia, a grand festival of the vintage, in honour of Bacchus, executed by an overpowering mass of satyrs, men, women, and children in wild disguises and with frantic energy. There must have been at least three hundred persons engaged in this revel. . . ."

Through the remainder of the century, Sir Henry Irving continued this style, staging a £30,000 *Henry VIII* complete with three stories of half-timbered Tudor houses crowded with citizens cheering the royal procession. *Hamlet,* Irving turned into a rather treacly love story, stressing Ophelia's touching madness at the expense of the murder and usurpation, and ending the play with the death of the hero: "The rest is silence"—if only it were! Beerbohm Tree continued Irving's ravages up to World War I, introducing, for example, into *King John* a spectacular dumb show of the granting of Magna Carta (though it contributed nothing to the play). His *Midsummer Night's Dream* had real grass with real rabbits hopping about on it. Finally, William Poel and Harley Granville-Barker led a successful revolt against this lush Victorian staging, and by producing Shakespearean plays under essentially Elizabethan conditions, gave a more satisfactory Shakespeare to audiences.

In essence, the nineteenth century's version of Shakespeare, then, not only in staging, but in criticism, was a picture or chronicle of something outside the play, historical personages in eleventh-century Scotland or Athens or Bithynia. We should probably see in this approach something of the influence of the novel, itself an outgrowth of a radical shift in thinking that took place in the eighteenth century. The classical world-view saw human nature as essentially unchanging, existing in timeless universals; the business of the artist was to bring out those enduring, unchanging aspects of the human situation, stripping off the irrelevant accidents of time and place. Shakespeare shared this view. He himself saw the past times he wrote about as in their important essentials very like his own day; hence, it was all right to dress the actors as Elizabethans even when they were playing Greeks and Romans, just as Italian Renaissance painters dress the characters of a crucifixion or Pietà in clothes of the Italian Renaissance. It was thirty years after Shakespeare's death before the word "anachronism" appeared in the English language. In the course of the eighteenth century, as society became more individualistic and capitalistic, as the hierarchical, all-embracing structure of Renaissance society broke up, people came to think of human nature as more particular and unique, different in different times and places. History ceased to be the record of an unchanging "nature," of fables for every age and clime, and became instead the analysis of individual and particular processes of cause and effect. The novel, with all its particularized details of name, date, place, or motive, replaced the theater as the great medium of popular art, and increasingly, audiences demanded from the stage realistic details such as those the novelist gave. Since Shakespeare is quite skimpy in such matters, Victorian directors supplied them by their staging (Kean's "placing before the eyes of the spectator *Tableaux vivants* of the private and public life of the ancient Greeks"). In short, we should not look on Victorian staging simply as a result of large theaters, but as a comprehensive view of Shakespeare's plays, indeed, a comprehensive view of nature and of art which applied to all writers. The Victorian view is no less false to Shakespeare's art, but it is not simply an empty theatricality.

In our own century, it would be nice to say Shakespeare is handled better. Modern producers do tend to stage Shakespeare in a simple set, often on a platform or arena stage, so that the play need not be cut to allow the curtain to go up and down and the sets to be moved. Recently, there has been more and more of a tendency to stage Shakespeare in whatever kind of costume seems best to bring out the values of the play, a trend set by Orson Welles's *Julius*

Caesar in the 1930's and continued, for example, in such productions as the Old Vic's of *Troilus and Cressida* in the military costumes of World War I (though perhaps future ages will find our staging of *Much Ado about Nothing* in the form of a Western as reprehensible as Beerbohm Tree's rabbits). We no longer rewrite Shakespeare, except for such special occasions as *Swingin' the Dream*, a 1939 version of *Midsummer Night's Dream* set in the New Orleans of the 1880's complete with three bands including the Benny Goodman Sextet and a cast of two hundred, among them Louis Armstrong as Bottom the Weaver. The lush Victorian tradition of staging has largely been left to the movies, a natural result of the difficulty of transferring to a highly visual medium a highly aural work like a Shakespearean play. Even in the films of Shakespeare, the best have left Shakespeare's language largely untouched, using the special techniques of the film to develop the central idea of the play (for example, Sir Laurence Olivier's *Henry V* abandons the usual naturalism of the film to produce a consciously "stagy" version, with an opening view of the Globe Theatre and backdrops flat as medieval paintings, thereby developing the play's central metaphor, the "stage" of history). The trouble with Shakespearean production in our age is our worship of the "original"—we are not content to have a good staging done over and over; we want a new one every time, and we are thus led into such absurdities as a production of *Hamlet* with three actors onstage at a time to play the one Prince and thus suggest the different sides of his character. "Original"? Certainly. But valuable?

Respect for Shakespeare's language—this, if anything, is what the twentieth-century approach to Shakespeare offers. In editing, for example, our age has abandoned the principle of cumulating editorial wisdom, the steady addition of emendations, in favor of closely following the original texts, except, of course, for spelling and punctuation. Modern bibliographers hold that the early quartos and the First Folio are our best sources for what Shakespeare "really wrote." Real knowledge of what copy was used to set up a given text (was it just a copy of another printed text, or did the printer turn back to a manuscript?), knowledge of the practices of Elizabethan printshops and of the kinds of mistakes an Elizabethan compositor was likely to make—these, say modern editors, are better guides to what Shakespeare wrote than a statement by even the most sensitive of editors that such-and-such a line makes no sense or doesn't "read right." One wonders, though, when reading an account of some industrious scholar tracing a particular broken "B" through the typefaces of the First Folio, whether the method of Pope does not have something to recommend it after all. The general reader, however, as against the scholar, need remember only two things about editions: first, what edition you read does matter—they vary considerably; second, you get closer to Shakespeare when you read a modern edition which follows the original quartos and the First Folio closely than when you read a nineteenth-century text full of emendations and conjectures.*

Above all, as reader, and as theatergoer, respect Shakespeare's own language. "Let us," he wrote of himself and his fellow actors, "on your imaginary forces work." "Piece out our imperfections with your thoughts." "Eke out our performance with your mind." No nineteenth-century spectacle with its elaborate illusions of reality is Shakespeare's real theater. Not even the Globe is his real theater, not after all these centuries. Shakespeare's real theater is what he called "the quick forge and working-house of thought," what we may call the theater in the mind.

---

* In this book, for example, I am quoting from the *Pelican* editions of the individual plays which are edited on modern principles. I have, however, reserved to myself an editor's privilege and altered punctuation.

3

THE THEATER IN
THE MIND

THE TWENTIETH CENTURY, IN SUCH MATTERS AS EDITING AND STAGING, DEVELOPED
a new respect for Shakespeare's language. In criticism (which we can define as
understanding and evaluating the plays—in that order), two schools of thought
have dominated: the "historical" critics and the so-called "new" critics. The historical critic holds, as his basic axiom, that the way to read a writer from the
past (like Shakespeare) is to put yourself in the position of his own original
audience: try to know what they knew, feel as they felt, think as they thought.
The "new" critic takes the opposite tack: the modern reader should put all
matters of biography, history, intention, evaluation, and background aside until
he has pondered the text by itself with all the twentieth-century care, intelligence, and feeling he can muster. These two approaches squarely contradict
each other in theory. In practice, however, they work out to much the same
thing: a historical critic tries to read with all the skill and imagination the new
critic would like him to use; the new critic (on the sly, as it were) corrects his
reading of the text in isolation by his (bootlegged?) knowledge of what an
Elizabethan play is likely to contain. Both schools of thought embody that most
distinctive trait of all twentieth-century thinking (not just Shakespeare criticism): concern for language. Both schools of thought recognize that Shakespeare's language creates the setting, the time and place of the action, the scenery
and costumes, the acting. In short, our minds responding to Shakespeare's language are his real theater.

As for language, Shakespeare wrote what is technically called "Modern
English" (as against Chaucer's Middle English or the Old English of the

Beowulf), but it is a rather different modern English from ours because we no longer think the way Shakespeare and his contemporaries did. Language and thought are interrelated; they cannot really be separated, for language determines thought and thought determines language. For example, some languages, say Bantu or Chinese, simply will not accommodate thoughts which are possible in English, and, vice versa, English cannot accommodate some thoughts possible in other languages. Language and thought each determine the other, and Shakespeare's language is different from ours because his thinking was different, specifically his thinking about the nature and order of the universe. The great contribution that historical criticism has made in our time to understanding Shakespeare's language is a knowledge of the Elizabethan world-view, the way men in the Renaissance saw the nature of the universe.

The Elizabethans believed in what is called the "great chain of being," an idea that had its first stirrings among the Greeks with Plato and Aristotle and which lasted until the eighteenth century. Compounded of Biblical lore, Greek philosophy, and a lot of farfetched natural history, "the great chain of being" stands as one of the most important and long-lasting ideas in the history of man. The idea is that the structure of the universe is an order or hierarchy like a chain or a ladder or a musical scale. Everything in and of the universe, from God at the top to the lowest stone at the bottom, every single created thing in the universe has its place in that hierarchy. Figure A, in effect, charts out this great chain of being. At the top is God, and it is God's love that flows through and sustains and holds together this whole system. A heavenly magnetism, God's love radiates down through the universe, and every created thing in turn gives back that love—had not the Psalmist said, "The heavens declare the glory of God: and the firmament sheweth his handiwork"? Immediately below God are the nine orders of angels—seraphim, cherubim, thrones, dominations, virtues, powers, principalities, archangels, angels. Each one of these groups is in charge of a particular heavenly or astronomical sphere. In order, they are the *primum mobile*—that is, the substance whose turning gives the heavens their motion—the stars, Saturn, Jupiter, Mars, the Sun, Venus, Mercury and the lowest of the planets, the moon—this, of course, is the old Ptolemaic or common-sense astronomy which said that the earth stood still and everything else moved around it.

Next in line comes Man, and he, too, finds himself in a hierarchy or an order: a political hierarchy, beginning with the Emperor, then the King, Duke, Marquis, Earl, Viscount, Baron, Baronet, Knight, Esquire, gentleman, then below the ranks of nobility the various professions and trades, lawyers, doctors, merchants, artisans, soldiers—then ordinary citizens, and, at the bottom, peasants, fishermen, then the lowest of human creatures, the beggar, and finally, almost subhuman, the Fool. The angels are characterized as "intelligences"—they know.

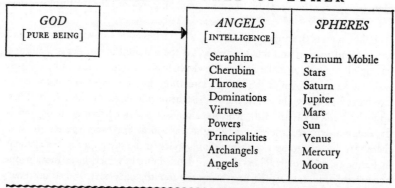

UNCHANGING WORLD OF ETHER

GOD [PURE BEING]	ANGELS [INTELLIGENCE]	SPHERES
	Seraphim	Primum Mobile
	Cherubim	Stars
	Thrones	Saturn
	Dominations	Jupiter
	Virtues	Mars
	Powers	Sun
	Principalities	Venus
	Archangels	Mercury
	Angels	Moon

CHANGING, "SUBLUNARY" WORLD COMPOSED OF FOUR ELEMENTS:

Fire *Air* (REGION OF DEVILS, ALSO IN NINE RANKS) *Water* *Earth*

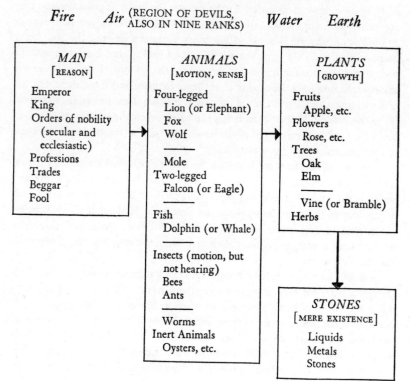

MAN [REASON]	ANIMALS [MOTION, SENSE]	PLANTS [GROWTH]
Emperor	Four-legged	Fruits
King	Lion (or Elephant)	Apple, etc.
Orders of nobility	Fox	Flowers
(secular and	Wolf	Rose, etc.
ecclesiastic)	———	Trees
Professions	Mole	Oak
Trades	Two-legged	Elm
Beggar	Falcon (or Eagle)	———
Fool		Vine (or Bramble)
	Fish	Herbs
	Dolphin (or Whale)	
	———	
	Insects (motion, but	
	not hearing)	
	Bees	
	Ants	
	———	
	Worms	
	Inert Animals	
	Oysters, etc.	

STONES [MERE EXISTENCE]
Liquids
Metals
Stones

Fig. A. The Great Chain of Being—a schematic diagram.

Man (except for the Fool) has the next best thing, reason; he can think matters out.

Below man is the order of the beasts, who lack reason, but have memory and hearing and motion and touch or sense. At the top are the four-legged animals having all these things: the lion or the elephant at the top, followed by the fox, wolf, snake, and down at the bottom something like the mole. Then come the two-legged animals, the birds, the highest being the eagle or the falcon. Then after the birds come the fish, who have motion but not hearing: at the top is the dolphin, which some people thought was a fish. For every species on land, there was thought to be a corresponding species in the ocean, a further element in harmony and order. Then there are land animals which have motion but not hearing, like insects, the bees being the top, the ants next, and so on down to the worms. Finally, there are animals which have sense or touch but no motion, for example, oysters or barnacles.

Below the animals come the plants which have only existence and growth, and they, too, have their order. At the top are the fruits, highest because they are made for man's needs, the highest of the fruits being the pomeroy, or *pomme royal,* the royal apple. After fruits come the flowers, the rose being highest. Then come the trees, the oak being highest, the elm, finally the bramble and, at the bottom, the herbs. All the way at the bottom of the scale are the minerals, having only the quality of existence in space and time; these, too, are ordered: first, there are the liquids, the most mobile; then the metals, with gold being the noblest, lead or brass being the basest; then the stones, the diamond being the noblest, then the rest of the jewels, the ruby, topaz, till finally we come to the common or garden-variety stone.

This created world is made out of the four elements which are, again running from higher to lower, fire—which is hot and dry; air—which is hot and moist; water—which is cold and moist; and earth—which is cold and dry. Corresponding to the four elements are the four basic fluids of the body: choler, blood, phlegm, and black bile; and these four fluids or "humours" determine the four basic personality types: the choleric man, the sanguine, the phlegmatic, and the melancholy.

In short, the "great chain of being" describes a tidy, finite universe, in which there is a place for everything and everything has its place. As long as everything stays in its place all goes well, but when someone or something tries to get out of line the whole order is wrenched or thrown into a state of mutiny or confusion. The first such wrenching came when Lucifer rebelled against God; the second when Adam sinned in the Garden of Eden. These wrenchings occur again whenever a son rebels against his father or a subject against his prince, or when the body falls into disease because one organ or humour has stepped out of line. This is what Shakespeare's Ulysses says in *Troilus and Cressida:*

The heavens themselves, the planets, and this centre,
Observe degree, priority, and place,
Insisture, course, proportion, season, form,
Office, and custom, all in line of order.

. . .

                    But when the planets
In evil mixture to disorder wander,
What plagues, and what portents, what mutiny,
What raging of the sea, shaking of earth,
Commotion in the winds, frights, changes, horrors,
Divert and crack, rend and deracinate
The unity and married calm of states
Quite from their fixture? O, when degree is shaked,
Which is the ladder of all high designs,
The enterprise is sick. How could communities,
Degrees in schools, and brotherhoods in cities,
Peaceful commerce from dividable shores,
The primogenity and due of birth,
Prerogative of age, crowns, sceptres, laurels,
But by degree, stand in authentic place?
Take but degree away, untune that string,
And hark what discord follows. Each thing meets
In mere oppugnancy. The bounded waters
Should lift their bosoms higher than their shores
And make a sop of all this solid globe;
Strength should be lord of imbecility,
And the rude son should strike his father dead.

                                        (I. iii. 85–115)

Notice the huge areas to which Ulysses applies the idea of degree or rank or
order: the planets, the fact that land stands above the sea, the winds, communities, commerce, schools, inheritance ("the due of birth"), the respect due to or
the "prerogative of age," all kinds of ranks—"crowns, sceptres, laurels," the
relationship of father and son (later in the passage, he ranks man's psychological faculties—reason, will, appetite). Notice, too, the images Ulysses uses for
degree, a ladder, a tuned string (the lengths of the string establish the order of
its scale), and, perhaps a little optimistically, "the *married* calm of states," re-
flecting the notion that the husband is higher on the scale than the wife. Earlier
in the passage, he had compared military order to the order in a beehive.

We should probably discount Ulysses' speech somewhat since Shakespeare
wants us to think of him as a pompous, even hypocritical, man. Nevertheless,
he does give us a classic statement of the Elizabethan world-view, the "great
chain of being." Naturally, not everyone held this view with equal vigor. The
young intellectuals of Shakespeare's day, interested in "new philosophy" or
science, were getting away from this idealizing of order that old conservatives
like Shakespeare's Ulysses went in for. This belief in order, however, did con-

stitute what Alfred North Whitehead termed a "climate of opinion," that is, a prevailing set of ideas which people either took for granted or took as a starting point for some other set of ideas, much the way twentieth-century Americans tend to assume rather automatically that science, in some sense, "has the answers."

There are three things to remember about this chain of being. First, it represents a belief in the *rightness* of order. What disturbs the order is wrong, like the fall of Lucifer or of Adam. For example, we look on the assassination of Julius Caesar as a nice sort of liberal, democratic thing to do, the way we rebelled against George III. For Shakespeare and his contemporaries absolute rulers were part of God's order, and the man who kills a king is as bad as Judas. This sense of order in the political and spiritual worlds is why so many of Shakespeare's plays deal with the problem of killing or deposing a king. Shakespeare is testing and probing, shaking, if you will, this universal order to see how it holds up. Drama, after all, demands conflict.

The second thing to notice about this chain of being is that it binds together fact and value. As in any hierarchical system, say the army or the academic world, the mere statement of what a thing is tells you also what its *value* is. An assistant professor is a bigger and better thing than a mere instructor but a far less grand thing than an associate professor. A lieutenant junior grade is a bigger and better thing than a mere ensign but less than a lieutenant senior grade. So in this great chain of being, if we know that such-and-such a thing is a whale, we know that, though it is the royal fish and outranks all other fish, it is, being a fish, less than a lion or an elephant or an eagle but more, on the other hand, than a bee or an ant. Mere events are emblematic; they symbolize moral values. To put it linguistically, "is" and "ought to be" are all mixed up together because of this hierarchical structure. The mere fact that the whale *is* tells us what it *ought to be,* where its proper place is in this chain of values.

The third thing to remember about this great chain of being is that it leads to a language which is primarily one of comparison and analogy. That is, the whole chain can fold up, as it were, like an accordion, into parallel pieces. Then the chain structure would produce a whole series of correspondences or parallel relationships among the angelic order; the planetary order; the human order, whether in the body politic or our physical bodies, in the family or in our minds; the animal order; and the mineral order (see Fig. B). Then, if you were looking for a way to describe a king, you might compare him to God, you might call him the "father" of his land or the "head" of his kingdom. You could compare him to the heart among the organs, to gold among the metals, to the sun among the planets, and so on. If you wanted to describe the body, you might compare it to the earth and call it, as Richard II does, "that small model of the barren earth which serves as paste and cover to our bones." If you wanted

PLANETARY ORDER	POLITICAL ORDER	FAMILY ORDER
Sun ——— ——— ——— Moon	King Nobility Citizens, etc.	Father Mother Eldest Brother, etc.

PSYCHOLOGICAL ORDER	BODY ORDER		ORDER OF ORGANS
Reason, Will, Understanding	Head Eye	Upper Region	Brain (Animal Spirits)
Memory, Fancy, "Common Sense"	Arm Trunk	Middle Region	Heart (Vital Spirits)
Five Senses	Leg Foot	Lower Region	Liver (Natural Spirits)

ANIMAL ORDER	FISHES	BIRDS
Lion (or Elephant) ——— ——— Mole	Dolphin (or Whale), etc.	Falcon (or Eagle), etc.

TREES	METALS	ELEMENTS
Oak Elm ——— ——— Vine	Gold Silver ——— ——— Lead	Fire Air Water Earth

Fig. B. Correspondences in the Great Chain of Being—a schematic diagram.

to describe a kingdom you might, as a courtier in *Coriolanus* does, compare it to the human body: you could speak of the "kingly-crowned head," you could compare the king's counsellors to the heart, the kingdom's soldiers to the arm, and so on. If you wanted to describe a kingdom another way you might compare it to a garden. As one of Shakespeare's gardeners says in Richard II's disordered kingdom:

> Why should we in the compass of a [fence]
> Keep law and form and due proportion,
> Showing as in a model, our firm estate,
> When our sea-walled garden, the whole land,
> Is full of weeds, her fairest flowers chok'd up,
> Her fruit trees all unprun'd, her hedges ruin'd,
> Her [plots] disordered and her wholesome herbs
> Swarming with caterpillars,
>
> (III. iv. 40–47)

that is, evil courtiers. If you wanted to describe the proper relation of a wife to her husband, you might compare the family to a kingdom. Thus, in *The Taming of the Shrew*, Katherine, the shrew who has been tamed, explains to wives how they should behave:

> Thy husband is thy lord, thy life, thy keeper,
> Thy head, thy sovereign.

(These were the days before "love, honor and obey" had been replaced by "love, honor and cherish.")

> Such duty as the subject owes the prince
> Even such a woman oweth to her husband;
> And when she is froward, peevish, sullen, sour,
> And not obedient to his honest will,
> What is she but a foul contending rebel
> And graceless traitor to her loving lord?
>
> . . .
>
> Why are our bodies soft and weak and smooth,
> Unapt to toil and trouble in the world,
> But that our soft conditions and our hearts
> Should well agree with our external parts?
>
> (V. i. 147–169)

Kate's phrasing suggests an important side effect of the Elizabethan world picture—it is the "external parts," the appearance of a thing that indicates what it is and where it belongs in the great chain of being. As Ulysses says, "Degree being vizarded," that is, the signs of authority being hidden, "Th' unworthiest shows as fairly in the mask," and degree is lost. Hence, in Shakespeare's plays, as we shall see, the ideas of seeming or, conversely, of perceiving appearances correctly become important.

The comparisons created by the chain of being show up visually in some pictures by Robert Fludd, a seventeenth-century cabalist. He shows (Fig. 8) the cosmos on a chain from God supported by bountiful, life-giving Nature and by man's Art (which imitates—"apes"—Nature). Within our world are all the intricate correspondences among animals, metals, plants, planets, and the rest. Figure 11 shows Fludd's diagram of the way the parts of the human body (the microcosm) correspond to the various elements and planets in the macrocosm. In Figure 10, Fludd shows the "music of the spheres"—the correspondences between the planets and elements and the notes of a musical scale tuned by God in Pythagorean proportions. Were we to look for a pictorial form of the way we think, as contrasted with the way the Renaissance thought, we would find it in one of those quasi-medical advertisements which show the body—the *inside* of the body, notice—as a glorified machine. For us, the heart is not the noblest of the organs, but a pump that pushes our blood around. We are the products of the scientific revolution of the seventeenth century. We can no longer say with Kate that our external parts describe what our condition should be, that our physical features fix our place in a universal order of values. Rather, we want today to probe into and look inside things. The order we find in the universe is not an order of things being higher and lower in value than other things but an order of cause and effect. The stomach does not "correspond to the aristocracy"; rather it is a kind of furnace for oxidizing Bufferin tablets and other foods. The brain is not the "throne of reason," but a series of electrical switches. There is no use expecting from Shakespeare the kind of cause-and-effect thinking that we do today. For him the heart is not just a pump, but the noblest of the organs. His language falls naturally into patterns of analogy and comparison. Ours does not.

John Dryden, writing at the end of the seventeenth century, is often called "the father of English prose." By that epithet, literary historians mean that Dryden is the first major writer to write the kind of English prose we admire: neat, spare, concise, businesslike—going straight to the point. Elizabethan prose (with a few exceptions) was no such thing, because it was written in the language appropriate to the Elizabethan world-picture, figurative language, that is, language having many figures of speech. Elizabethan writers prized long sentences developing rather involved analogies and comparisons. Similarly, Elizabethan poetry was richly metaphorical, while the poetry of the Restoration and eighteenth century became, like the prose, neat, balanced, more than a little abstract (just as the world-view of science is a series of generalizations and abstractions). In this sense, it was quite natural for men who valued this "scientific" language to find Shakespeare full of "quibbles," that is, puns and involved figures of speech; it was quite natural to rewrite him into the "refined" verse of, say, Davenant's *Macbeth*.

Again, Shakespeare's language turns out to be the crucial thing. The recogni-

tion of the Elizabethan world-picture (which is, to me at least, the great achievement of historical criticism in our time) enables us to see why Shakespeare
wrote the way he did, in verse, extremely rich verse, hardly a language real
men speak. Shakespeare's plays embody worlds like ours in many ways, but
different in some important respects: order is very important, and very good;
fact and value are each implicit in the other; the important relations between
things are those of likeness and difference, not those of cause and effect; exact
statement of psychological motives, of the timing or placing of events, is not
as important in a Shakespearean play as in most modern literature, notably the
novel. Rather, events are emblematic, symbolic, answering to moral rather than
literal truth. It is this kind of world a play of Shakespeare's creates; and this
is the world to which the historical critic's understanding of the Elizabethans'
world-view leads us.

The "new" critic also wants us to enter the world of the plays, but by a
different route. Nineteenth-century critics, when they were not exclaiming over
Shakespeare's plays, tended to think of the plays as representations of real situations in the real world, like photographs, if you will, or newspaper accounts
or like novels which give us accounts of people and events drenched in realistic
detail. As we have seen, nineteenth-century stagecraft, not finding those realistic
details in the plays, supplied them by reconstructing an elaborate archaeological
realism. In the same way, nineteenth-century critics supplied realistic details by
elaborate inferences from the text. As early as 1774, Maurice Morgann, in his
famous essay on the question of Falstaff's cowardice, wrote:

I affirm that those characters in *Shakespeare,* which are seen only in part, are
yet capable of being unfolded and understood in the whole. . . . If the characters of *Shakespeare* are thus *whole,* . . . it may be fit to consider them rather
as Historic than Dramatic beings; and, when occasion requires, to account for
their conduct from the *whole* of character, from general principles, from latent
motives, and from policies not avowed.

This kind of approach necessarily leads the critic away from the *actual words*
of the play into inferences and surmises about the *imaginary events described
by those words.* Thus, A. C. Bradley, whose *Shakespearean Tragedy* (1904)
was the culmination and final brilliant summary of this nineteenth-century
approach, goes into such questions as: Where was Hamlet at the time of his
father's death? Did Emilia suspect Iago? Did Lady Macbeth really faint? Inevitably, such an approach takes the critic away from the play as play into
considering the play as a fictitious record of events exterior to itself, almost like
a novel; inevitably, the critic's attention is drawn away from the language of
the play to the non-existent events.

The "new" critics of the 1920's and after turned their backs on this nineteenth-century kind of analysis, choosing instead to consider the plays more as

poems than as novels. Each particular play creates its own poetic world, a world in some respects like everyday reality, but in many respects different. Our business as readers is to enter, live in, and experience that special world, but we are bound to get mixed up if we apply notions from everyday reality unchanged to that contrived world of the play with its own special nature and its own interior, poetic logic. Rather, as readers, we need to accept the play as it is, not forcing it into a record of something like the real world. In the last analysis, the world of the play is the world it creates in our minds as we experience the play. On the stage, this "new critical" approach finds its expression in the nonrealistic sets of the modern performance of Shakespeare or such devices as costumes which are not historically accurate but which convey the flavor of the world of the play. To achieve the world of the play in the theater of our minds, however, calls for a fairly special kind of reading, something that goes beyond the ordinary kind.

At the age of six or thereabouts, most of us were taken by the hand and led to school where we were taught "how to read." More exactly, we were taught how to put letters together to form words and told we knew how to read. Essentially, what we learned to read was a sequence of words: a simple story or a progression of ideas. Reading literature or "seeing" literature in the form of a play or film, however, calls for something more. Good reading or good seeing, the "new" critic says, proceeds first and foremost by paying close attention to the work itself, putting aside value judgments and matters of biography or historical background until we have really understood the words themselves. There is a second basic principle of good reading—you might call it giving the author the benefit of the doubt: unless or until it is proved otherwise, assume that every detail in a work of literature serves a purpose, serves in one or more ways to add to the organic unity of the whole. Just as a child reads letters together to form words, so a more mature reader uses his skill and imagination to put details together to form an artistic totality.

Details act together in two basic ways: by likeness or difference, that is, by repetition or contrast, but there are literally myriads of possible variations. Key words can be repeated; the plot in a narrative may be echoed in a subplot, in "comic relief," or in figures of speech; characters may be presented in terms of symbols; even plot techniques (surprise, anticlimax, and the like) or methods of characterization (as by occupation or bodily detail) or the use of certain sounds in a poem or certain rhetorical figures, even these mere techniques can be used as meaningful elements. One can see these patterns only by looking at the work itself, keeping in mind the basic assumption that all these details probably will come together into an artistic wholeness. It is sometimes helpful to look first at what seems to fit in least well; because such elements are "farther away" from the center of a work, they often add most to it. For example, in a Shakespearean tragedy, the comic scenes often tell us most about the play as a whole. In every case, though, this kind of reading or seeing demands an imaginative effort to get the sudden intuitive understanding of likenesses that underlie seeming difference, the same kind of imaginative leap that any discovery requires. These imaginative graspings, these sudden awarenesses of the infinite variety of things "going on," are what give that marvelous sense of enlarging the mind and feelings which is the peculiar and special pleasure of literature.

A work of literature with a story (for example, a novel or a play or a film) makes a special, double demand on its audience because every element in it can serve in two ways. In a sense, one can think of literature-with-a-story as proceeding detail by detail, episode by episode, effect following cause, along the circumference of a circle. Each element of the work is related sequentially to the one before it and the one after it in the story. At the same time, each element is related to all the others at once by the shape or style of the curve in which they are all involved together. One can think of the center of the circle (though it is no part of the circle itself) as the thing which holds all these parts together, the essence or informing principle, the "point" of the work. Any given element in a narrative or dramatic work will thus serve both as a "story element" *and* as part of the overall unity of the work.

For example, in a story about a boy falling in love with a girl completely and wonderfully different from any he has ever known, it would nevertheless be a prosaic necessity for boy to meet girl. The writer could choose any one of a number of ways of getting the young man to his ladylove; he will, in fact, choose that way which adds most to the total effect of his story. For example, the young man might have to cross water (cross, in effect, from an old way of life to a new one) and pass a difficult test, as Bassanio does in *The Merchant of Venice*. The young man might very nearly die so as to be, in the Biblical phrase, "born again" to enter this new world, as Sebastian in *Twelfth Night* and Ferdinand in *The Tempest* are. The young man might have to disguise himself (indicating, in a way, he is leaving his former self behind), as Romeo wears a mask, hiding his Montague identity, when he meets Juliet, or as Prince Florizel dresses like a simple country swain to court Perdita in *The Winter's Tale*. In any case, something drastic is required. It would probably not be very effective to have the young man simply trot around next door to find such a transcendent love.

This coaction of events in both a realistic cause-and-effect way and a purely poetic way is what Aristotle had in mind when he said that fiction was "a more philosophical and a higher thing than history." History deals with particulars; fiction informs particulars with universal ideas. Oscar Wilde put it more whimsically when he complained, "Life is terribly deficient in form." A chronicler of life, such as a newspaper reporter, has little artistic choice; he is supposed to state the facts as directly as possible. A creative writer, on the other hand, shapes and chooses events to make a unity and coherence that the random happenings of everyday reality just don't have. It is because of this element of artistic choice that the "world" of a play (or novel or story or film) is not simply a copy of the everyday world (in which, for example, our young man achieving a transcendent love probably just met the girl in the college library). To enter the "world" of a work of art, the "theater of the mind," we need to pay attention to the way that world is shaped. We need to recognize that any given element in the story (if it is a good story) functions *both* to tell a coherent tale and to give a unity and "point" to the work as a whole.

This double demand that literature-with-a-story makes on its audience is particularly important in the plays of a verse dramatist like Shakespeare. If we think of *Macbeth* (for example) as simply a story of ambition and murder, the poetry of the tragedy will seem a mere chromium trim unnecessarily cluttering up a good yarn, making the play much inferior to the prosy, realistic, and deathless works of any Broadway season. When, for example, Banquo at II. iii. 122–123 wants to say, "After we get dressed," he comes out with:

> And when we have our naked frailties hid,
> That suffer in exposure. . .

Presumably, Shakespeare did not complicate matters for his own amusement; Banquo's more complex phrasing (thoroughly unnatural and unrealistic) has added something—poetry. And any real appreciation of the play involves understanding all of it, both story *and* poetry, more properly, story *as* poetry. One difference between "After we get dressed" and Banquo's poetic statement lies in the images (that is, sensations and ideas) brought in by such words as "naked," "frailties," "suffer," and "exposure." By these words (and thousands like them in *Macbeth*) Shakespeare builds up and emphasizes certain aspects of the essential action.

Imagery, narrowly defined, equals "similes plus metaphors" or "figures of speech." Broadly defined, however, imagery includes "any restatement of the essential," that is, any extra, not absolutely necessary, duplication of those things which are both necessary and of the essence. So understood, imagery becomes a very broad, far-reaching concept. It includes not only the language of a play, the relations among the plots, but the scenery, costumes, even the lighting. In a film, for example, the background of every shot represents a potential image which the director may or may not use. The best directors, of course, use backgrounds much the way Shakespeare used poetry, to establish the essential idea of the film. If we speak precisely, though, we cannot separate imagery from the play of which it is a part any more than one can separate the "background" in a film shot from the rest of what appears on the screen. If a work of art has organic unity, each of its parts is implicit in and involved with all the others. Nevertheless, we can—and will—talk about imagery separately, and precisely because of our broad definition of the concept.

If imagery "restates the essential," then a very good, direct way of getting at whatever is essential in a play would be to examine the imagery. For our test case (in this introduction and the next chapter), we will take *Macbeth,* useful for this purpose because it is both one of the shortest and one of the most familiar of Shakespeare's plays. As you read *Macbeth,* you will notice a great many references to procreation, parenthood, progeny, and their opposites. These images restate and remind us of important elements in the plot: the prophecy of kingship for Banquo's descendants, the fact that the Macbeths have no children, the murder of Macduff's children, the death of young Siward, and the like. In the list of characters, there are four sets of parents and children: Macduff and his son; Banquo and Fleance; Siward and young Siward; Duncan and his sons, Malcolm and Donalbain. All in all, procreation and parenthood would seem to be "essential" aspects of *Macbeth.*

In the tragedy as a whole, I find eighty-five images of procreation, parenthood, progeny, and their opposites:* enough to create a very strong impression in the mind of anyone seeing the play, let alone reading it. Some of these images are quite gratuitous: that is, Shakespeare could have put anything at all in their place or omitted them entirely. Others represent more limited choices, those that are called for by the plot or the situation (though, of course,

---

* This is a list of images of procreation, parenthood, and progeny in *Macbeth.* Those which are gratuitous, that is, not dictated directly by the plot, are asterisked.

I. iii. 58–59*	II. iii. 93–96	III. vi. 18–20
I. iii. 67	II. iii. 136	III. vi. 24
I. iii. 71		
I. iii. 86	II. iv. 4*	IV. i. 30–31*
I. iii. 118	II. iv. 25	IV. i. 55*
	II. iv. 34*	IV. i. 58–60*
I. iv. 25*		IV. i. 64–65*
I. iv. 28–29	III. i. 5–6	IV. i. 65–67*
I. iv. 38	III. i. 31	IV. i. 76 (*st. dir.*)*
I. iv. 48	III. i. 60–65	IV. i. 86 (*st. dir.*)*
	III. i. 70	IV. i. 86–89
I. v. 45–46*	III. v. 91*	IV. i. 102
	III. i. 135	IV. i. 111 (*st. dir.*)
I. vi. 8–9*		IV. i. 112–124
	III. ii. 37	IV. i. 152–153
I. vii. 21*		
I. vii. 54–59*	III. iii. 20*	IV. ii. 6
I. vii. 72*		IV. ii. 10–11*
	III. iv. 20	IV. ii. 27*
II. i. 1	III. iv. 29–31*	IV. ii. 30
	III. iv. 66*	IV. ii. 37–38
II. ii. 13*	III. iv. 106	IV. ii. 44
II. ii. 53*		
	III. vi. 5–10	
II. iii. 25–30*		

Shakespeare was free to change the plot had he wished to do so, and thus, in a sense, these images also embody choices). Notice that there is no question of "reading in" here. Such a tabulation is coldly factual. The inferences one draws from this complex of imagery (as it is called) may involve "reading in," but the images themselves are purely and simply "there."

There are other complexes of imagery for which similar lists could be made: images of animals, birds, blood, disease and medicine, domesticity (including eating, drinking, and sleeping), family life, night and darkness, public and political life, religion, shelter, seeds, plants, trees, and so on. There are, for example, twenty-five images of clothing or covering.* Though there are only a third as many of these images as those of procreation, many more of the clothing images represent "free" choices by Shakespeare, because clothing is not intricately tied in with the plot. Shakespeare seems to have gone out of his way to put these remarks about clothing in, and this fact suggests a corollary to our definition of imagery: the less necessary the image is, the more choice the writer has, and the more significant the image is likely to be. Thus, though there are in all fewer clothing images than images of procreation, since more are gratuitous, the clothing images are likely to be just as important as those of procreation. In general, though, one does not judge the importance of images simply by number. The importance of an image can lie in the degree to which

---

IV. ii. 59	IV. iii. 177	V. iii. 22–26
IV. ii. 62	IV. iii. 204	
IV. ii. 68	IV. iii. 211–212	V. vi. 3
IV. ii. 82–83*	IV. iii. 216	V. vii. 2–3
IV. iii. 5*	IV. iii. 218*	
IV. iii. 26		V. vii. 12–16
IV. iii. 61–63*	V. i. 66–67*	
IV. iii. 106		V. viii. 5–6
IV. iii. 108–110*	V. ii. 9*	V. viii. 14–16
IV. iii. 155*		V. viii. 31
IV. iii. 166*	V. iii. 3–4	V. viii. 37–38
	V. iii. 6	V. viii. 65*

* This is a list of images of clothing in *Macbeth;* the "gratuitous" images are asterisked:

I. ii. 54*	II. i. 107*	IV. iii. 33
	II. ii. 69*	IV. iii. 172*
I. iii. 40*		IV. iii. 208*
I. iii. 108–109*	II. iii. 12–13*	
I. iii. 145*	II. iii. 108–112*	V. i. 5
	II. iii. 122–123*	V. i. 57*
I. v. 51*	II. iii. 128*	
	II. iv. 38	V. ii. 20–22*
I. vii. 21*	III. ii. 47*	
I. vii. 34*		V. iii. 34*
I. vii. 36*	IV. i. 88	V. iv. 15*

it is "extra"; it can also lie in the prominence and distinctness of the image at important points in the play.

The images we have considered so far have been concrete. They have dealt with tangible things like clothing or children. Imagery, however, can be abstract, as, for example, the images of "shifting shapes" in *Macbeth*. These images would include not only the various hallucinations and apparitions in the play, but also the occasions, quite remarkable in number, in which someone expresses difficulty in seeing or understanding, the outstanding example being Macbeth's misunderstanding of the prophecies of "these juggling fiends,"

> That palter with us in a double sense,
> That keep the word of promise to our ear
> And break it to our hope.
>
> (V. viii. 19–22)

We can think of these as images of "uncertain perception." Another complex of abstract images clusters around the idea of "coming together" as in the striking image of:

> Two spent swimmers that do cling together
> And choke their art.
>
> (I. ii. 8–9)

or the very opening line of the play: "When shall we three meet again?" Abstract images can be just as important as the concrete ones, sometimes more important.

Where, however, do all these "complexes of imagery" leave the story of ambition and murder which is, after all, our first impression of *Macbeth?* The story is right where it was; the imagery has enriched it, interwoven with it, and brought out from the story its implications. To see these implications, we look back at those images and their contexts and see how they work together. For example, animals occur in *Macbeth* in two contexts: sometimes, like the "arm'd rhinoceros," they are violent, threatening; sometimes, as when the "mousing owl" (Macbeth) kills the "falcon, tow'ring in her pride of place" (Duncan), animals serve as symbols. This contrast matches other contrasts in the tragedy, for example, between man's frail nakedness and his civilized clothing; between bare facts and symbolic, ambiguous prophecies that cover them; between private, family life and public, symbolic, political life; perhaps in the largest sense between a nature red in tooth and claw and a symbolic nature impregnated with moral and religious, supernatural, order. *Macbeth,* then, though it begins in our minds as a story of one man's ambitions and murders, is ultimately a far bigger thing: a play about nature's way of growth and decay, an order in which supernatural and natural things mix and germinate in a man's mind and from there grow out into his acts, his family, and his commonwealth until finally their influence wanes and dies.

Only by being aware as we read Shakespeare of some such "informing principle," some such "essence" or "center" of each play, can we respond to the play in all its wholeness, its unity in variety; only that way can we experience the full pleasure of literature, feeling the massive oneness of the play implicit and powerful in its every moment. And only by all the play can we measure the genius of its author or enter the theater of his mind—or our own.

MACBETH

WE NO LONGER BELIEVE IN WITCHES, THOUGH PERHAPS WE ARE A LITTLE TOO QUICK to dismiss such matters out of hand. Anyone, I think, looking with an unbiased eye at such a scientific study of witchcraft as Joseph Glanvill's *Sadducismus Triumphatus* (1681) might find the evidence for witchcraft rather more impressive than schoolbooks lead us to believe. At any rate, because we no longer believe in witches, we no longer know very much about them, and many readers are rather puzzled by the witches in *Macbeth*. In some strange way they seem to preside over, even dominate, the action of the tragedy, and yet they do not actually *do* anything: Macbeth seems to create his own tragedy.

One school of thought holds that the witches are common or garden-variety Elizabethan witches, strange old women knowing a few tricks like fortune-telling, the kind of witch seventeenth-century believers in witchcraft were likely to burn, and so they appear in an illustration to Holinshed's *Chronicles* (see Fig. 12), the book from which Shakespeare developed the plot of *Macbeth*. Shakespeare, however, so freely altered the material he took from the *Chronicles* that he may well have altered the witches, too. There is no real reason to expect Shakespeare's witches to be the same kind of witches as Holinshed's. Another school of thought holds that the witches are the three Fates, the *moirai* or *Parcae* of Classical mythology, or the Norns of Norse mythology, the three nasty ladies who spin the thread of life, twist it, and then cut it off. Both Shakespeare and Holinshed refer to the three women Macbeth and Banquo meet as the "weird" or "weyard" sisters, and the old meaning of "weird" or "wyrd" was fate. In fact, Holinshed speaks of them as "the goddesses of destinie."

The best way, however, to decide who or what the witches in *Macbeth* are, what powers they have, and what influence they exert over Macbeth, is to look, not at Holinshed or even Elizabethan pastimes such as witch-burning, but at the play itself. To do that, it is necessary to take out three speeches that do not belong in Shakespeare's play. The text as we have it was evidently taken from an acting version of the play, one that was used as late as 1614, and in 1614, as today, actors and directors seem to have had an irresistible urge to "improve" Shakespeare's works. In *Macbeth* this took the form of putting in three speeches which we know don't belong in *Macbeth:* the so-called Hecate speeches, III. v. entire; IV. i. 39–43 and 125–132. The speeches were put in to introduce some songs and dances from *The Witch,* a play by Thomas Middleton. The Hecate speeches bring in a little musical comedy element to appeal to the tastes of an audience of 1614. You can see they don't belong. It's hardly likely that witches, having foretold Macbeth's utter failure, would then say:

> Come, sisters; cheer we up his sprites
> And show the best of our delights.
> (IV. i. 127–128)

With these Hecate speeches out, and the song-and-dance routines, the other powers of the witches become fairly obvious. Clearly, the witches can foretell the future. In the course of the play, every prophecy they make comes true. They predict that Macbeth will be made the thane, that is, the earl, of Cawdor, and he is. They predict that Macbeth will become king and he does. They predict that he should beware of Macduff and he should. They predict that "none of woman born shall harm Macbeth," and he is killed by Macduff who was "from his mother's womb untimely ripped." They predict that "Macbeth shall never vanquished be until Great Birnam Wood to high Dunsinane Hill shall come against him," and in the final, terrifying scenes of the play, Birnam Wood does indeed come against him. Finally they predict that Banquo will be father to a line of kings: "Lesser than Macbeth, and greater. . . . Thou shalt get kings, though thou be none," and Shakespeare's audience would have known that King James I of England, James VI of Scotland, claimed descent from that very same Banquo.

The fact that the witches can foresee the future, however, does not mean they control or cause that future. Their powers are sharply limited, as you can tell from Act I, scene iii, where one of the witches wants to revenge herself on a sailor's wife who would not give her any chestnuts. She is going to torment the sailor himself, but

> Though his bark cannot be lost,
> Yet it shall be tempest-tost.
> (I. iii. 24–25)

She can prophesy, she can torment the man, she can tempt him, but "his bark cannot be lost"—she cannot take his life. Neither can the witches take Macbeth's life, even through the agency of Macduff. The mere fact that the witches can see the future does not mean they cause it, any more than your seeing this book causes its existence, or any more than your knowing the weather will change causes it to change. The Elizabethans were familiar with this kind of distinction as an answer to a theological problem. That is, if God is omniscient, if he knows everything that is going to happen, then the future is determined, and man has no free will. If man has no free will, he is not responsible for his acts, but God holds him responsible. Theologians resolved this paradox by saying that God could foresee the future, but merely seeing the future did not make man act in any particular way: in a Christian scheme of things, man has —must have—free will.

And Macbeth does. He spends three scenes making up his mind to kill the King. As he writes to Lady Macbeth, what the witches gave him was knowledge: "I have learned by the perfect'st report they have more in them than mortal *knowledge*" (I. v. 2). In a Christian scheme, what Macbeth does with that knowledge is his own problem. As Banquo warns him,

> Oftentimes, to win us to our harm,
> The instruments of darkness tell us truths,
> Win us with honest trifles, to betray 's
> In deepest consequence.
>
> (I. iii. 123–126)

Macbeth was not forced to kill Duncan. As he says to himself,

> If chance will have me King, why chance may crown me
> Without my stir.
>
> (I. iii. 143)

He even decides not to kill Duncan, "We will proceed no further in this business," but then Lady Macbeth, who is a good deal better at witching than the professionals, eggs him on. Witches, both amateur and professional, tempt Macbeth and they betray him, but his destiny is his own doing. He chooses his fate with his own free will. They simply tell him the future. It is Macbeth's own idea that this represents a "supernatural soliciting."

In another sense, however, the witches do determine Macbeth's destiny in that they determine the tone and atmosphere of the play in which he exists. One can think of them as supernatural forces, or, perhaps, as some producers of *Macbeth* like to think of them, as dark forces in man's mind dredged up from some proto-Freudian nightmare, but basically, the feeling they give is one of uncertainty, bewilderment, a fear of the unknown. The world of *Macbeth* is a world in which shapes take form and shift and vanish in mysterious ways. The witches are themselves such a shape. As Macbeth writes his wife, "When I burned in desire to question them further, they made themselves air, into which they vanished." And Banquo says of them,

> Were such things here as we do speak about?
> Or have we eaten on the insane root
> That takes the reason prisoner?
>
> (I. iii. 83–85)

The witches are not the only things of which we might ask, Were such things here? Macbeth, on his way to murder King Duncan, cries out:

> Is this a dagger which I see before me,
> The handle toward my hand?
>
> (II. i. 33–34)

And then, after the killing itself,

> Methought I heard a voice cry 'Sleep no more!
> Macbeth does murder sleep.'
>
> (II. ii. 34–35)

Then there is the ghost of Banquo which Lady Macbeth names to her husband,

> O proper stuff!
> This is the very painting of your fear,
> This is the air-drawn dagger which you said
> Led you to Duncan.
>
> (III. iv. 60–63)

There are the apparitions the witches conjure up to state their second set of prophecies and so trigger the second great wave of action in the play: the armed head, the bloody child, and the child crowned with a tree in his hand. There is the dread vision of supernatural retribution closing in on Macbeth when Birnam Wood to high Dunsinane Hill comes against him. And then there are the two most famous apparitions in the play:

Yet here's a spot. . . . Out, damned spot! Out, I say! . . . What, will these hands ne'er be clean? . . . Here's the smell of the blood still. All the perfumes of Arabia will not sweeten this little hand.   (V. i. 29–48)

The tragedy is full of strange illusions and apparitions, stains that will not come out, trees that uproot themselves and move, mysterious voices, ghosts, hallucinations . . .

The tragedy has a fearful sense of uncertainty, and that uncertainty finds for itself a distinctive figure of speech which occurs again and again in the play. The technical name for this figure of speech is antithesis, the pairing of opposed ideas. The witches say, "When shall we three meet again?" and answer, "When the battle's lost and won." "Fair is foul," they say, and "foul is fair." And Macbeth's very first words echo them: "So foul and fair a day I have not seen." King Duncan says of the fallen Thane of Cawdor, "What he hath lost, noble Macbeth hath won." Banquo says to the witches,

> Speak then to me, who neither beg nor fear
> Your favors nor your hate.
>
> (I. iii. 60–61)

And the witches in turn say of Banquo, "Lesser than Macbeth, and greater," "Not so happy, yet much happier." "Thou shalt get kings, though thou be none." These antitheses are from only the first three scenes; but the figure of speech runs all through the play, harking back, of course, to those obscure and ambiguous prophecies. As Macbeth says,

> Be these juggling fiends no more believed,
> That palter with us in a double sense,
> That keep the word of promise to our ear
> And break it to our hope.
>
> (V. viii. 19–22)

In Macbeth's world, shapes shift, things appear and disappear, words lose their meaning and become their very opposites. It is, in short, a nightmare world, a world of moral disorder, in which heaven, "as troubled with man's act, threatens his bloody stage" (II. iv. 5–6). Order, for Shakespeare and his audience, meant that great chain of being in which every created thing had its proper place. In *Macbeth,* things don't stay put—they wander about in a thoroughly disconcerting way. As Macbeth says (somewhat petulantly, I think) when Banquo's ghost turns up:

> The time has been
> That, when the brains were out, the man would die,
> And there an end. But now they rise again,
> With twenty mortal murders on their crowns,
> And push us from our stools.
>
> (III. iv. 78–82)

(Things are getting pretty bad when the people you murder just won't stay murdered.) Not just the ghost, though, but everything in *Macbeth* is out of order. The subject rises against his anointed king just as, so two of the characters report:

> A falcon, tow'ring in her pride of place,
> Was by a mousing owl hawked at and killed.

> And Duncan's horses (a thing most strange and certain),
> Beauteous and swift, the minions of their race,
> Turned wild in nature, broke their stalls, flung out,

Contending 'gainst obedience, as they would make
War with mankind.

(II. iv. 12–18)

Other images for this moral disorder come in Macbeth's conjuration of the
witches when he calls on them for the second set of prophecies.

> I conjure you by that which you profess,
> Howe'er you come to know it, answer me.
> Though you untie the winds and let them fight
> Against the churches, though the yesty waves
> Confound and swallow navigation up,
> Though bladed corn be lodged and trees blown down,
> Though castles topple on their warders' heads,
> Though palaces and pyramids do slope
> Their heads to their foundations, though the treasure
> Of nature's germens tumble all together
> Even till destruction sicken, answer me
> To what I ask you.

(IV. i. 50–61)

The last is the most terrible curse of all, that the treasure of nature's "Germaine,"
genes, we would call them, tumble all together even till destruction sicken. It
is the curse of fallout, the tumbling together of all the seeds, the genes, that
guarantee that humans have human children, and not monsters made up out
of some mismatched collection of genes, half human, half animal.

Still another image for Macbeth's world of moral disorder is disease. To
the Elizabethans, disease was not just something you took pink pills for—
it was a psychosomatic condition of mental and physical disorder, a condition
in which the body's fluids fell into unbalance. The Macbeths are sick. They
eat their meals in fear. They cannot have children. They lack the season of all
natures, sleep. Lady Macbeth walks in the night repeating the dreadful words
of the murder scene. Her doctor says of her:

> Unnatural deeds
> Do breed unnatural troubles. Infected minds
> To their deaf pillows will discharge their secrets.
> More needs she the divine than the physician.

(V. i. 66–69)

Disease, in this metapsychosomatic sense, is not just something you take to your
neighborhood psychiatrist. This kind of disease goes deeper than medicine.
Macbeth himself asks that same doctor:

> Canst thou not minister to a mind diseased,
> Pluck from the memory a rooted sorrow,
> Raze out the written troubles of the brain,

> And with some sweet oblivious antidote
> Cleanse the stuffed bosom of that perilous stuff
> Which weighs upon the heart?
>
> (V. iii. 40–45)

and when the doctor says he cannot, Macbeth cries, "Throw physic to the dogs, I'll none of it." There is no remedy for Macbeth. Only true kings have holy powers, like the King of England, who we hear is himself a medicine:

> Strangely-visited people
> All swol'n and ulcerous, pitiful to the eye,
> The mere despair of surgery, he cures . . .
> and 'tis spoken,
> To the succeeding royalty he leaves
> The healing benediction. With this strange virtue,
> He hath a heavenly gift of prophecy,
> And sundry blessings hang about his throne
> That speak him full of grace.
>
> (IV. iii. 150–159)

The English King is the very opposite of Macbeth, the Scottish King, who creates not health, but death; who has no succeeding royalty; who must turn to witches for prophecy. In this same scene, Malcolm and Macduff join forces to attack Macbeth, as they say, to "Make us med'cines of our great revenge to cure this deadly grief" (214–215).

Disease is one image of the moral disorder of the Macbeths' Scotland; another is dismemberment. The last name we hear Macbeth called in the play is "this dead butcher," and, even at the beginning of the play, when he is still King Duncan's loyal warrior, when he finally faces the rebel Macdonwald, "he unseamed him from the nave to th' chops," that is, from the navel to the jaws, "and fixed his head upon our battlements." But the most famous instance of dismemberment is the witches' brew itself:

> Round about the cauldron go;
> In the poison'd entrails throw.
>   · · ·
> Eye of newt, and toe of frog,
> Wool of bat, and tongue of dog,
> Adder's fork, and blindworm's sting. . . .
>
> (IV. i. 4–16)

Macbeth is often called a "dark" tragedy. By that term, critics simply mean a lot of the tragedy's most important scenes take place at night; the murder of Duncan at midnight; the murder of Banquo just after twilight; the appearance of Banquo's ghost at an evening feast. Darkness usually connotes evil as light connotes goodness, but in this tragedy darkness is more specific.

It is a darkness that hides all these mysterious shifting shapes and forms. It is a darkness that enables the Macbeths not to look at the evil they do:

> Stars, hide your fires;
> Let not light see my black and deep desires.
>   (I. iv. 50–51)

In the very next scene Lady Macbeth says,

> Come, thick night,
> And pall thee in the dunnest smoke of hell,
> That my keen knife see not the wound it makes,
> Nor heaven peep through the blanket of the dark
> To cry 'Hold, hold!'
>   (I. v. 48–52)

And the day after the murder there is an unnatural darkness:

> By th' clock 'tis day,
> And yet dark night strangles the travelling lamp.
> Is't night's predominance, or the day's shame,
> That darkness does the face of earth entomb
> When living light should kiss it?
>   'Tis unnatural.
>   (II. iv. 6–10)

A clock in eleventh-century Scotland? When I was a schoolboy, we would pounce on such a blunder and come up baying like little hounds, "Anachronism!" No—Shakespeare does not think in such realistic terms. His half-medieval imagination has stepped beyond a realist's space and time into a world of values. This darkness in *Macbeth* is no ordinary darkness, but a moral darkness, a darkness that serves to hide evil, and it needs, to remedy it, a moral light, a light that serves to reveal evil. During the sleep-walking scene we learn of Lady Macbeth, "She has light by her continually. 'Tis her command" (V. i. 20). The light, in effect, is the light of her remorse, her sight of the evil in her own dark heart.

Not only is the atmosphere of the tragedy dark; it is also stifling, smothering, strangling. We hear of "thick night," "the fog and filthy air"; we are told of the opening battle, "Doubtful it stood, as two spent swimmers that do cling together and choke their art." In this stifling, smoky smog there are,

> Lamentings heard i' th' air, strange screams of death,
> And prophesying with accents terrible,
> Of dire combustion and confused events
> New hatched to th' woeful time.
>   (II. iii. 52–55)

Before Macbeth sets out to have Banquo killed, he cries,

> Light thickens and the crow
> Makes wing to th' rooky wood.
> Good things of day begin to droop and drowse,
> Whiles night's black agents to their preys do rouse.
> (III. ii. 50–53)

In this dark, stifling atmosphere we hear strange noises, but we see above all—blood. "Blood," "bloody," "bleeding," "bleeds," these words occur over forty times in this, the second shortest of Shakespeare's plays, or, if you like statistics, on average, about once every fifty lines. Lady Macbeth says, as coldly as any medical student, "Who would have thought the old man to have had so much blood in him?" (V. i. 36). The play has a whole river of blood, when Macbeth says,

> I am in blood
> Stepped in so far that, should I wade no more,
> Returning were as tedious as go o'er.
> (III. iv. 136–138)

Not just a river, there is even an ocean of blood, as Macbeth looks at his bloody hands and groans,

> Will all great Neptune's ocean wash this blood
> Clean from my hand? No, this my hand will rather
> The multitudinous seas incarnadine,
> Making the green one red.
> (II. ii. 59–62)

Blood fills the choking, stifling atmosphere of the play, an atmosphere that fills vast, empty, echoing spaces. As one of the noblemen says,

> I have words
> That would be howled out in the desert air,
> Where hearing should not latch them.
> (IV. iii. 193–195)

And Macbeth says of the king he is about to murder,

> His virtues
> Will plead like angels trumpet-tongued, against
> The deep damnation of his taking-off;
> And pity, like a naked new-born babe
> Striding the blast, or heaven's cherubin horsed
> Upon the sightless couriers of the air,
> Shall blow the horrid deed in every eye
> That tears shall drown the wind.
> (I. vii. 18–25)

Macduff says of Scotland,

> Each new morn
> New widows howl, new orphans cry, new sorrows
> Strike heaven on the face, that it resounds
> As if it felt with Scotland and yelled out
> Like syllable of dolor.
>
> (IV. iii. 4–8)

Macbeth himself calls on these vast, echoing, reverberating spaces when he says to Lady Macbeth's physician,

> If thou could'st, doctor, cast
> The water of my land, find her disease,
> And purge it to a sound and pristine health,
> I would applaud thee to the very echo,
> That should applaud again.
>
> (V. iii. 50–54)

At the same time that Macbeth's Scotland is a vast, empty, reverberating space, it is also a stage:

> Thou seest the heavens, as troubled with man's act,
> Threatens his bloody stage.
>
> (II. iv. 5–6)

Indeed it is a bloody stage on which Macbeth plays out what he calls "the swelling act of the imperial theme" (I. iii. 128–129). Those are playwright's terms, "act," "stage," "theme," and they suggest that life in this tragedy is treated as though it were a play or

> a poor player
> That struts and frets his hour upon the stage
> And then is heard no more.
>
> (V. v. 24–26)

The tragedy seems to say our actions cast shadows on a stage behind this stage, the stage of this world. Our actions here are but a play performed before heavenly judges. Vast as the world is, it is only a small part of a still vaster order. Even so, those heavenly judges, like an audience in a theater, do not change what transpires upon that "bloody stage." As Macduff moans when he hears his wife and children have been murdered, "Did heaven look on and would not take their part?"

Repeated references to stagecraft, to great, empty spaces, to blood, darkness, these constitute what we have called "complexes" or "clusters" of images. By "images," in a narrow sense, critics mean simply the sensations or pictures

called up by the figures of speech, the poetry of a Shakespearean play. In a
larger sense, though, images are a poet's way of stating the essence of what
he is writing about. Many people must have had the same experience I did
in school (at least, I get the impression from my students many people still
learn this kind of naturalistic *Macbeth*): "Macbeth is ambitious. Ambition
is his tragic flaw, the thing that makes him profound and interesting to us, but
also the thing that leads to his tragic fall. This is a tragedy of ambition." Well,
the statement is true enough, as far as it goes, but surely a man whose valet
is called Seyton (and pronounced like "Satan") has gone a little far to be
called simply "ambitious." Can we think simply of ambition when we hear
the magnificent words Macbeth speaks as he goes off to kill King Duncan?

> Is this a dagger which I see before me,
> The handle toward my hand? Come, let me clutch thee!
> I have thee not, and yet I see thee still.
> Art thou not, fatal vision, sensible
> To feeling as to sight? or art thou but
> A dagger of the mind, a false creation
> Proceeding from the heat-oppressèd brain?
> I see thee yet, in form as palpable
> As this which now I draw.
> Thou marshall'st me the way that I was going,
> And such an instrument I was to use.
> Mine eyes are made the fools o' th' other senses,
> Or else worth all the rest. I see thee still,
> And on thy blade and dudgeon gouts of blood,
> Which was not so before. There's no such thing.
> It is the bloody business which informs
> Thus to mine eyes. Now o'er the one half-world
> Nature seems dead, and wicked dreams abuse
> The curtained sleep. Witchcraft celebrates
> Pale Hecate's offerings; and withered murder
> Alarumed by his sentinel, the wolf,
> Whose howl's his watch, thus with his stealthy pace,
> With Tarquin's ravishing strides, towards his design
> Moves like a ghost. Thou sure and firm-set earth,
> Hear not my steps which way they walk, for fear
> Thy very stones prate of my whereabout
> And take the present horror from the time,
> Which now suits with it.

(II. i. 33–60)

Such a speech moves far beyond mere ambition in any usual sense; and the
speech reaches further because of its images: a darkness hiding "horror"; hallucinations like the "fatal vision"; mysterious noises, the very stones prating;
witchcraft; vast spaces like "the one-half earth"; antitheses such as "I see thee

still . . . There's no such thing"; disease, "the heat-oppressèd brain"; even "gouts of blood."

Because of its imagery, this speech, indeed all of *Macbeth,* hovers between nature and supernature, between the "sure and firm-set earth" and the "horror" of "the time," between the "fatal vision," "dagger of the mind," and "this which now I draw." In scene after scene, Shakespeare contrasts supernature and nature. Act I, scene i, gives us the supernatural disorder of witchcraft; Act I, scene ii, the natural disorder of the rebellions against King Duncan. The beginning of Act I, scene iii, gives us prophecies of honors to come to Macbeth, the throne to come to Banquo's heirs; the remainder of Act I, scene iii and scene iv show us the natural fulfillment of one of these prophecies, and we see King Duncan meting out rewards and punishments like the witches and, like them, predicting who shall inherit the throne. Scene v gives us Lady Macbeth tempting her husband as the witches had done; scene vi gives us Lady Macbeth, not as witch, but as gracious hostess. The next four scenes alternate between the Macbeths' castle as a scene of feasting, celebrations, and sleep, and that same castle as a "Hell" of treason and murder (the devil-Porter's phrase is "too cold for hell"). Act III, scene iv, shows us Banquo's ghost, an image of supernatural retribution; it is followed by III, vi, the suspicions of the courtiers, the beginnings of a naturalistic retribution. The unreal horror of the second interview with the witches (IV. i) gives way to the real horror of the slaughter of the Macduffs (IV. ii). It is through such imagery, such stagecraft, the poetic logic of juxtaposition, that common or garden-variety Elizabethan witches can become for us very "goddesses of destinie" *without* their actually controlling the fate of the characters.

The images we have considered so far are images of the supernatural, a supernatural conceived very much in the same shuddery forms that a child's fears of the dark might take: hallucinations and terrible dreams, shapes and shadows shifting and moving, witches and prophecies, stifling and smothering darkness, dismemberment, disease, strange echoing sounds, and blood, above all, blood. These are the images that take *Macbeth* beyond the schoolbook tragedy of "ambition," that make the play probe the dark bowels of the universe. Yet, balancing these images of supernature, there is a whole other mass of images, those that, in a way, support that schoolbook reading.

Macbeth is a moral tragedy and, like any moral problem, there are two ways of looking at it, from a supernatural point of view or from a natural. As always in Shakespeare, no matter how exotic and supernatural the action, it grows from a simple family situation. *Macbeth,* grand and tragic as it is, is, after all, a play about a husband and a wife, a wife we might meet in Suburbia as well as Glamis. Lady Macbeth is the proverbial ambitious wife, the wife pushing her husband ahead over his own hesitations and inhibitions. In fact, the first time we see Lady Macbeth, we find her in a classic wifely situation: her husband has invited the boss home to dinner practically without warning her—not only the boss, the whole board of directors. But like a good wife she manages a supper, indeed rather a feast; at least, everyone sleeps pretty soundly afterwards. We hear about food and beds; we hear about wine and drinking also: nightcaps and possets. In the course of the play we have not one, but two, feasts. In both these cases, however, the food and drink are perverted. The feasts are marred by murders, and the drinks, those cozy little nightcaps, are drugged. The home life of the Macbeths is—not to put too fine a point on it—sick.

We hear of the most homely of all substances, mother's milk, "the milk of human kindness." In Shakespeare's day, "kindness" did not simply mean benevolence. The word still had its original sense of "kin," as we use the word in "mankind," meaning all of us who are related, being man. When Lady Macbeth speaks of the "milk of human kindness," then, she means the milk we sucked in the first act of our common humanity. It makes her phrase all the more deadly,

> Yet do I fear thy nature.
> It is too full o' th' milk of human kindness
> To catch the nearest way.
>
> (I. v. 14–16)

Even more terrible is her curse,

> Come to my woman's breasts
> And take my milk for gall, you murd'ring ministers,
> Wherever in your sightless substances
> You wait on nature's mischief.
>
> (I. v. 45–48)

And again she says,

> I have given suck, and know
> How tender 'tis to love the babe that milks me:
> I would, while it was smiling in my face,
> Have plucked my nipple from his boneless gums
> And dashed the brains out, had I so sworn as you
> Have done to this,
>
> (I. vii. 54–59)

that is, the murder.

Sleep is another natural, homely thing that we see perverted and destroyed in this rather insomniac play.

> Methought I heard a voice cry "Sleep no more!
> Macbeth does murder sleep"—the innocent sleep,

> Sleep that knits up the ravelled sleave of care,
> The death of each day's life, sore labor's bath,
> Balm of hurt minds, great nature's second course,
> Chief nourisher in life's feast.

(II. ii. 34–39)

Later, as he is planning to murder Banquo, Macbeth cries out:

> Let the frame of things disjoint, both the worlds suffer,
> Ere we will eat our meal in fear, and sleep
> In the affliction of these terrible dreams
> That shake us nightly.

(III. ii. 16–19)

Food, wine, mother's milk, sleep—*Macbeth* is very much a family play, a play of domesticity, albeit perverted domesticity. A large part of this family life in *Macbeth* is fatherhood, and fatherhood is treated in the tragedy as a terribly important thing. A great deal of *Macbeth* is concerned with passing on one's inheritance to one's sons. This is the key issue between Macbeth and Banquo. As Macbeth recalls the witches' prophecies:

> When first they put the name of King upon me,
> . . . Then, prophet-like,
> They hailed him father to a line of kings.
> Upon my head they placed a fruitless crown,
> And put a barren sceptre in my gripe,
>
> . . .
>
> No son of mine succeeding.

(III. i. 58–64)

If I can put it in crude, naturalistic terms, the same crude terms in which Lady Macbeth becomes simply an ambitious corporation wife, the whole question in *Macbeth* is whether the son will inherit his father's business, or some interloper from outside will come in.

Still another way the play carries out the theme of domesticity is with birds, birds after all, being nest-building animals. "This castle hath a pleasant seat," says the innocent Duncan as he arrives at the Macbeths', and Banquo replies,

> This guest of summer
> The temple-haunting martlet, does approve
> By his loved mansionry that the heaven's breath
> Smells wooingly here. No jutty, frieze,
> Buttress, nor coign of vantage, but this bird
> Hath made his pendent bed and procreant cradle.
> Where they most breed and haunt, I have observed
> The air is delicate.

(I. vi. 3–10)

There is a fearful irony in associating with the hellish and sterile atmosphere of the Macbeths' castle, the innocence of a bird's nesting, the heaven's breath, a "temple," a "bed," a "procreant cradle," breeding, delicate air. We hear, though, not only of the procreant martlet, but the bird of death, the owl (twice), the rook, the chough, the goose, the kite, chickens—the killing of the Macduffs is told almost entirely in terms of birds—the wren, the vulture, the eagle, the sparrow. If we can enlarge the class, we hear also of the bat, the shard-borne beetle, and other flying creatures. Birds are important partly, I suppose, because they fly between heaven and earth; and for that reason they are like omens, like the witches' prophecies. Birds hover between heaven and earth even as the play itself does, and so remind us of the theme of supernatural intervention or Providence. "Are not two sparrows sold for a farthing? and one of them shall not fall on the ground without your Father," or, as Hamlet put it, "There is special providence in the fall of a sparrow." Birds, too, by flying from here to there, carry out the idea of shapes shifting and moving which is so important in *Macbeth*. Then, too, birds are the other two-legged animal—the other besides ourselves.

Birds make only one cluster among many, many animal images in *Macbeth*. For example, we hear about the hare, the lion, the serpent, the horse, the wolf, a whole list of dogs (hounds, greyhounds, mongrels, spaniels, curs, shoughs, water-rugs, and demi-wolves), "the rugged Russian bear, the armed rhinoceros or th' Hyrcan tiger"—in the witches' brew there is practically a whole menagerie, although in somewhat damaged condition: "eye of newt, and toe of frog," "lizard's leg and howlet's wing," among them the blood of a sow "that hath eaten her nine farrow" (talk about parenthood!). Sometimes animals are used to describe particular people. For example, Malcolm is called a sacrificial lamb, and Macbeth speaks of himself as a bear tied to the stake. In a more general way, though, these images of animals ask the question so much of the play asks: "What is a man?" As Lady Macbeth says when Macbeth hesitates before killing Duncan,

> What beast was't then
> That made you break this enterprise to me?
> When you durst do it, then you were a man;
> And to be more than what you were, you would
> Be so much more the man.
>
> (I. vii. 47–51)

One way man distinguishes himself from the animals is by clothing himself. Thus, in that very scene, Macbeth objects to his wife's urging,

> I have bought
> Golden opinions from all sorts of people,

> Which would be worn now in their newest gloss,
> Not cast aside so soon.
>
> (32–35)

And Lady Macbeth replies: "Was the hope drunk wherein you dressed your-self?" Clothes, like opinions and hopes, hide what's underneath them. Put another way, clothes, in this sense, are part of the hiding, disguising, obscuring imagery like the darkness or the fog and filthy air. Clothes also symbolize titles and honors. For example, when Macbeth is addressed as the thane of Cawdor, he replies,

> The thane of Cawdor lives; why do you dress me
> In borrowed robes?
>
> (I. iii. 108–109)

And Banquo comments,

> New honors come upon him,
> Like our strange garments, cleave not to their mould
> But with the aid of use.
>
> (I. iii. 144–146)

These clothes, titles, and honors, however, must be rightly won. Thus, at the end of the play we hear of Macbeth the tyrant,

> Now does he feel his title
> Hang loose about him, like a giant's robe
> Upon a dwarfish thief.
>
> (V. ii. 20–22)

Titles and honors are not enough, however, unless they come to pass in the rightful cycles of growth and inheritance, as Banquo, for example, is said to be "the *root* and father of many kings." To develop this notion of the cycles of growth and inheritance, the play uses a quite striking chain of images. It begins in Macbeth and Banquo's first scene with the witches, when Banquo asks them to "Look into the seeds of time, and say which grain will grow and which will not" (I. iii. 58–59). Then Duncan says to Macbeth, "I have begun to plant thee, and will labor to make thee full of growing" (I. iv. 28–29). Lady Macbeth tells her husband, "Look like the innocent flower, but be the serpent under it" (I. v. 63–64). When Malcolm and Macduff are gathering their forces in England, we are told, "Macbeth is ripe for shaking" (IV. iii. 237–238).

Macbeth's rise and fall is being compared to the growth and death of a plant. We hear of his fate first in connection with seeds, then as being planted, then as a flower, then as ripe for shaking, and finally he says of himself, "My way of life is fallen into the sear, the yellow leaf" (V. iii. 22–23). In fact, Macbeth's fate is identified with that of a tree—or a lot of trees—Birnam Wood: "Macbeth shall never vanquished be until great Birnam Wood to high Dunsinane Hill shall come against him." And Birnam Wood does indeed come against him. As part of their invasion, Malcolm and Macduff cut down branches and hold them up as "leavy screens" to conceal their numbers.

These "leavy screens" involve far more than just an early example of camouflage, something much more central to the significance of the tragedy as a whole. In the northern Europe of Shakespeare's youth, it was customary to celebrate the coming of spring with pageants and festivals, and a common ritual in these festivals was a meeting in the forest for games, dances, and other things. Then the celebrants would cut down green boughs and flowers and carry them before the townspeople as they marched back into the town from their gathering in the woods. Apparently, from this ancient ritual, came legends and stories of old and wintry kings besieged in their castles and defeated when an army comes marching toward them carrying the green boughs of the spring. One of these legends passed into Holinshed's *Chronicles* where Shakespeare found it and put it in the tragedy of *Macbeth*. When we take the episode of Birnam Wood, then, back into the mythological depths of the human mind, Macbeth is the king of a kind of Waste Land, a Scotland that "cannot be called our mother but our grave" where "good men's lives expire before the flowers in their caps" (IV. iii. 165-172). When he is overthrown, with God's help,

> (with Him above
> To ratify the work) we may again
> Give to our tables meat, sleep to our nights,
> Free from our feasts and banquets bloody knives,
> Do faithful homage and receive free honors—
> All which we pine for now.
>
> (III. vi. 32-37)

True food, drink, and sleep, true family life, in other words, will replace the perverted and sterile family life associated with the Macbeths. And, indeed, when this Waste Land is freed from its tyrant, the new, young king Malcolm sets out to do those things "which would be planted newly with the time" (V. viii. 65), and the cycle of the seasons is complete. The men carrying the green boughs have reestablished the natural, providential order of time and generation, harvest and inheritance, that the Macbeths violated. Oddly enough, one of those men carrying green boughs is himself an almost supernatural figure, Macduff, who was "from his mother's womb untimely ripped," a curious violation of that natural and sacred rhythm. Macduff himself at the end is childless, wifeless, almost like Macbeth, as though Macduff were his counterpart, his balance. Macduff is the instrument and manifestation of that larger, supernatural order that penetrates and probes the domestic and political tragedy of *Macbeth*.

> Macbeth
> Is ripe for shaking, and the pow'rs above
> Put on their instruments.
>
> (IV. iii. 237–239)

In the childless Macduff, the tragedy has closed its cycle, its two great movements of sin and retribution. The first wave of action (after the introductory scenes, supernatural and natural, I. i and I. ii) begins with the first set of prophecies, prophecies about benefits to come to Macbeth. Macbeth murders the fathers, Duncan and Banquo. Then the second set of prophecies, prophecies about the retribution to come, begins the second, the retributive, wave of action, in which the childless father, Macduff, kills Macbeth. The structure of the tragedy has a dualism, like so much of *Macbeth* with its two levels, supernatural and natural, its antitheses, its two criminals, its two revengers.

We have seen this dualism of *Macbeth* in terms of its images. There were the images of the real world, images of domestic life, of food, drink, sleep, mother's milk, marriage, procreation and parenthood, a real world, too, of animals and birds and plants, the real cycles of generation and inheritance, a world of Providential timing. Clothing, as it were, that real world, giving it an aura of significance, were images in which simple, natural things like animals or birds or plants acquired symbolic, emblematic value; images in which titles and honors and opinions were worn like clothing, distinguishing man from animals, raising him toward an order of being beyond that of the natural world. Also beyond the natural world were the images of "horrible imaginings," the witches, the hallucinations and terrible dreams, prophecies, moving shapes and shadows, strange noises, antitheses, in general, images of uncertain perception; images of disease and dismemberment as related to the theme of moral disorder; darkness hiding a nameless evil; stifling, smothering air filling vast, echoing spaces; and, above all, blood, blood with its double sense, natural and supernatural: a body fluid and divinely ordained lineage.

This is the world of *Macbeth,* and to see and hear and feel and savor the tragedy to the fullest, we must enter it like travelers to Cathay, taking that world on its own terms, understanding the people and events as they exist in that world. Only then can we feel the work of art as a whole, feel its central issues implicit, resonating, in every single part of it. Our memories, however, being such that we cannot hold the whole play in our minds at once, it is sometimes useful to state in a plain, bald, and maplike way the idea that informs the play and shapes its unique world. In this sense, we can say that *Macbeth* is a play about, first, the interpenetration of the supernatural and the natural; second, man as caught in that dualism and, at the same time, the uncertain, puzzled spectator of it; in short, *Macbeth* is the tragedy of our uncertainty about the way supernature penetrates nature. Given such an "informing principle" for the play, we are in a position to feel it whole, to feel the *Macbeth*-ness permeating every tiny aspect of the tragedy—even those parts which seem not very central to the action.

Take, for example, what is probably the most famous speech in *Macbeth,* though really a quite optional aside. Shakespeare could perfectly well have left it out, and it doesn't seem to have a great deal to do with the immediate occasion for the speech, Lady Macbeth's death. Note, however, how the speech builds on and adds to the elements that pervade and permeate the world of the tragedy: darkness, strange noises in the night, apparently meaningless words, and a rhythm of time, that fertile rhythm of the generations supported by God's love which in the hands of the Macbeths has become dried up, dusty, and sterile. The speech builds on the tragedy's sense that life is but action on a stage, that we act out our lives before a supernatural audience:

> To-morrow, and to-morrow, and to-morrow
> Creeps in this petty pace from day to day,
> To the last syllable of recorded time,
> And all our yesterdays have lighted fools
> The way to dusty death. Out, out, brief candle!
> Life's but a walking shadow, a poor player
> That struts and frets his hour upon the stage
> And then is heard no more. It is a tale
> Told by an idiot, full of sound and fury,
> Signifying nothing.
>
> (V. v. 19–28)

It is a famous speech, perhaps the most famous statement of disillusion in our language. And yet, though all of us have felt disillusion at one time or another, this speech gives the common emotion a distinctive *Macbeth*-ness. For one thing, the speech is full of darkness and uncertain perception (the walking shadow, the flickering candle). For another, the speech insists on a kind of dualism in the alliteration of such phrases as "petty pace," "day to day," "dusty death," "Out, out." The speech deals (as the whole tragedy does) with man as an actor playing out his part on the stage of the natural world, a natural world which is symbolic: syllables or "a tale." Yet they are meaningless noises, "sound and fury signifying nothing," as though Macbeth wished at this point to deny that connection with the supernatural which is the essence of his rise —and his fall.

This *Macbeth*-quality informs and permeates everything in the play, no matter how peripheral it may seem, for example, the famous comic speech of the Porter at the opening of Act II, scene iii, immediately after the most solemn moment of the tragedy, the murder of Duncan. It is a grandly obscene speech, and it seems grandly irrelevant. In fact, Coleridge, the greatest of Shakespeare's Romantic critics, said of it (rather snobbishly): "This low porter soliloquy I believe written for the mob by some other hand." And yet the speech echoes and reechoes the imagery of the rest of the play. The Porter compares the Macbeths' castle to hell, projecting it onto that supernatural level which is so essential to the tragedy. His speech is a long succession of perversions of such natural processes as growth and sexuality. He speaks of an "equivocator," a man who, like the witches, can make words shift and change their meanings into their very opposites. He speaks of French hose, false, foppish clothing like the false titles Macbeth wears. His discussion of lechery is one long series of the antitheses that we found to be a part of the mystery of the tragedy. And, as for the knocking that summons the Porter, as Thomas De Quincey, another Romantic critic, pointed out, it follows on the tragedy's most concentrated series of horrible imaginings: "Is this a dagger which I see before me?" "Had he not resembled my father . . ." "Didst thou not hear a noise?" "These deeds must not be thought . . ." "Methought I heard a voice cry . . ." "I am afraid to think what I have done." And after all these phantasms comes that solid, oh so solid, KNOCK, KNOCK: *

Porter.   Here's a knocking indeed! If a man were porter of hell gate, he should have old turning the key. (*Knock.*) Knock, knock, knock. Who's there, i' th' name of Belzebub? Here's a farmer that hanged himself on th' expectation of plenty. Come in time! Have napkins enow about you: here you'll sweat for't. (*Knock.*) Knock, knock. Who's there, in th' other devil's name? Faith, here's an equivocator, that could swear in both the scales against either scale; who committed treason enough for God's sake, yet could not equivocate to heaven. O come in, equivocator. (*Knock.*) Knock, knock, knock. Who's there? Faith, here's an English tailor come hither for stealing out of a French hose. Come in, tailor. Here you may roast your goose. (*Knock.*) Knock, knock. Never at quiet! What are you?— But this place is too cold for hell. I'll devil-porter it no further. . . .

Enter Macduff and Lennox.

Macduff.   Was it so late, friend, ere you went to bed,
That you do lie so late?

Porter.   Faith, sir, we were carousing till the second cock; and drink, sir, is a great provoker of three things.

* How rarely in stage performances of *Macbeth* is that knock given the solidity it demands. Far too often, it becomes simply a rattle and bang on a flat, giving an effect exactly the opposite of what is needed. So done, the knock becomes illusion topping illusion rather than, in De Quincey's words, making "known audibly that the reaction has commenced; the human has made its reflux upon the fiendish; the pulses of life are beginning to beat again . . . the re-establishment of the goings-on of the world in which we live, first makes us profoundly sensible of the awful parenthesis that had suspended them."

Macduff. What three things does drink especially provoke?
Porter. Marry, sir, nose-painting, sleep, and urine. Lechery, sir, it provokes, and unprovokes: it provokes the desire, but it takes away the performance. Therefore much drink may be said to be an equivocator with lechery. . . .

(II. iii. 1–28)

So far from being a spurious addition to the play, the comic speech carries on the very themes that constitute *Macbeth*-ness down to such miniscule details as the Porter's constant expletive, "Faith!" precisely what Macbeth has—and does not have.

Not only the great speeches and the so-called "comic relief," but also some of the puzzles of the play answer to the logic of the poetry, even where they do not answer to the logic of the story. For example, there is the puzzle of the third murderer. When in Act III, scene i, Macbeth plots the murder of Banquo, he deals with two assassins, but when in Act III, scene iii, the actual murder takes place, a third murderer appears. Who's he? Most critics say that the third murderer is Macbeth himself, and there is a little evidence for such a view. There is another way, though, of looking at such story-puzzles, namely, in terms of the play as a whole. Throughout the play, we see things coming together in twos and threes. In fact, the opening line of the play is, "When shall we three meet again?" Traditionally, two is the number of woman and three the number of man, for obvious anatomical reasons. Similarly, it is traditional that two is the number of earth and three the number of supernature. So in this play we have on earth the two Macbeths, a man and a woman coming together to kill together, and then die separately. Then there are the three witches, with their three sets of three prophecies each. This hovering ambiguity between an actual, earthly two and a mysterious, supernatural three is very much like the rest of the play hovering between nature and supernature so that perhaps a mysterious third murderer is not as mysterious as one might think. Perhaps, too, in the religious context of the play, there is a grim and horrible parody of that passage in the Bible which goes, "Where two or three are gathered together in my name, there am I in the midst of them."

There is another puzzle in this tragedy, perhaps the most famous question you can ask about *Macbeth:* How many children had Lady Macbeth? In Act I, scene vii, she says, "I have given suck, and know how tender 'tis to love the babe that milks me." The entire second half of the play, however, depends on the fact that the Macbeths have no children. Now perhaps the historical Lady Macbeth, the one in Holinshed, had been married before and had had a child by her first husband. But surely, had Shakespeare wanted us to think that, he would have told us. Critics used to think that this kind of omission was just sloppiness on Shakespeare's part, but really, critics ought to hesitate a little before they call the greatest dramatist the world has ever known, "sloppy." Shakespeare isn't simply telling a story, he is writing a poem, creating a world. Lady Macbeth's childless motherhood answers to a kind of poetic or psychological necessity. At the beginning of the play, she is stronger, crueler, more determined than Macbeth, who seems subordinate to her, like a son. She is conspiring with Macbeth against the fatherly Duncan upstairs. Thus, when she speaks of children, she is behaving like a mother, a seductive and horribly perverted mother, it is true, but a mother nevertheless. Later in the play, Macbeth becomes the fatherlike king and Lady Macbeth, now the childless Lady Macbeth, seems his wife, submissive and subordinate to him, fearful and remorseful as he had been earlier. When she is like a mother, she speaks of her children; when she is not like a mother, she has no children.

These little puzzles are minor points, of course, the kind of thing only specialists should discuss, but they suggest how seeing the play whole can give it a sense, a coherence, a feeling of oneness. *Macbeth* is not simply the story of an ambitious man. As a whole, *Macbeth* is the tragedy of how uncertain we all are about the ways supernature permeates nature, mixing and germinating in men's minds, spreading outward into their families and their commonwealths. *Macbeth* is not just some farfetched story about eleventh-century Scotland—it is our story and our world.

ROMEO AND JULIET

PEOPLE USUALLY SAY ABOUT *Romeo and Juliet* THAT IT IS A TRAGEDY OF YOUNG love, and so—in a way—it is. We should keep in mind, though, that there are many kinds of love in *Romeo and Juliet*. There is the love of parent for child, in this case, a somewhat misguided love as old Capulet tries to make Juliet marry the County Paris. There is religious love, the love of the Friar for his flock. There is political love, the Prince's care for the citizens of Verona. And we have unrequited love, Paris' love for Juliet, for example, and, even more important, the love of Romeo for that character whom even critics tend to forget, Rosaline. People apparently prefer not to remember that Romeo doesn't simply fall in love with Juliet. When we first see him at the opening of the play, he is pining away, not for Juliet, but for Rosaline, who has sworn that she will still live chaste. It isn't until the fifth scene of the play that Romeo meets Juliet and falls in love with her.

The tragedy has many different kinds of love. It also has hate and conflict, naturally enough, in a way, for the god of love is an archer and he shoots fatal arrows. We speak of the "victims" of love, of women "surrendering," or of love "conquering" all. At this point, I suppose, we stretch out our Freudian antennae, but the Elizabethans needed no psychoanalyst come from the couch to tell them how close love is to fighting. Shakespeare makes it very clear, very ribaldly clear, in the opening fight among the servants.

Sampson. I will push Montague's men from the wall and thrust his maids to the wall. . . . When I have fought with the men, I will be cruel with the maids—I will cut off their heads.

Gregory. The heads of the maids?

Sampson. Ay, the heads of the maids, or their maidenheads. Take it in what
        sense thou wilt.

                                                                (I. i. 15–25)

When this tragedy puts love and fighting side by side, it touches the oldest
and deepest part of our minds, and we should call *Romeo and Juliet* not a
tragedy of young love, but a tragedy of young love and old hate, a tragedy
of "the fatal loins."

   What people usually say about *Romeo and Juliet* is that it is a tragedy of
fortune, or as the Prologue at the opening of the play has it, the tragedy of "a
pair of star-crossed lovers." Now, most Elizabethans firmly believed in astrology, in the influence of the stars on human affairs. The stars were the agents
of fortune; as Romeo says after he has slain Tybalt, "Oh, I am fortune's fool!"
(III. i. 134), meaning he is fortune's plaything. As we saw, when we were
dealing with *Macbeth,* most Elizabethans believed in fortune, fate, and the
stars, but they were also Christian, and they believed in free will. Thus, though
a man's fate is predetermined, he determines it by choosing as he goes along.
God knows everything that is going to happen, but we make it happen.
Perhaps the best way of thinking of "the stars" in *Romeo and Juliet* is more
or less the way we think of luck. The stars, however, have an advantage over
luck in that one can use them to read one's fate, as by casting a horoscope. In
fact, this is more or less what Romeo does when, just before he first meets
Juliet, he has a foreboding of what is to come:

                                My mind misgives
            Some consequence, yet hanging in the stars,
            Shall bitterly begin his fearful date
            With this night's revels . . .

            But he that hath the steerage of my course
            Direct my sail!
                                            (I. iv. 106–113)

In effect, like a modern scientist, Romeo thinks of the stars as embodying and
revealing the laws behind physical events; they tell us what is going to happen.
Man chooses, as Romeo himself chooses to go to the Capulets' ball, but man
chooses to fulfill the course that has been plotted for him by God. In effect,
Romeo describes the stars as a way to *read* his future.

   There is a lot in this play about reading and books and the rules they can
teach you. For example, in Act I, scene ii, an illiterate servant comes to Romeo
to ask him to read the guest list that he is supposed to deliver for a party. The
second time that Romeo kisses her, Juliet says, "You kiss by the book,"
meaning he kisses politely, formally. (What a horrible thing to say to a young
man she's just kissed!) Mercutio, after he has been stabbed by Tybalt, complains

that he was stabbed by a villain "that fights by the book of arithmetic" (the two references to doing things "by the book" establish another parallel between loving and fighting).

The idea of doing things by the book runs all the way through the play; it's all part of *Romeo and Juliet*'s rather rigid and artificial style. *Romeo and Juliet* is a play with a great deal of formality in it, formality in its broadest sense as well as its narrowest. In a narrow sense, the style of *Romeo and Juliet* is formal. We find a great deal of rhyme in this play, as in most of Shakespeare's other early plays. And the rhyme is not wholly successful, as, for example, in the closing couplet of the play,

> For never was a story of more woe
> Than this of Juliet and her Romeo.

Not only do we have rhyme in this play, there are even whole little lyrics embedded in the dialogue. Juliet recites an epithalamium, or marriage song, as she waits for Romeo to climb her balcony the night after Friar Laurence has married them. After that wedding night, as the lovers watch the dawn break that will separate them, they recite another traditional kind of poem, an *aubade,* or a day-song as it is called, a poem in which trysting lovers lament the coming of day. The very moment they meet and declare their love, Romeo and Juliet speak an impromptu sonnet:

> *Romeo.* If I profane with my unworthiest hand
>   This holy shrine, the gentle sin is this;
>   My lips, two blushing pilgrims, ready stand
>   To smooth that rough touch with a tender kiss.
> *Juliet.* Good pilgrim, you do wrong your hand too much,
>   Which mannerly devotion shows in this;
>   For saints have hands that pilgrims' hands do touch,
>   And palm to palm is holy palmers' kiss.
> *Romeo.* Have not saints lips, and holy palmers too?
> *Juliet.* Ay, pilgrim, lips that they must use in prayer.
> *Romeo.* O, then, dear saint, let lips do what hands do!
>   They pray; grant thou, lest faith turn to despair.
> *Juliet.* Saints do not move, though grant for prayers' sake.
> *Romeo.* Then move not while my prayer's effect I take,
>
> (I. v. 93–106)

and he kisses her, after dutifully filling out the rhyme-scheme *abab cbcb dede ff.*

Romeo and Juliet was apparently written in the period when Shakespeare was more interested in writing poetry than plays. There is some evidence that he wrote *Romeo and Juliet* in 1591, at the very start of his career, and then revised it in 1596. In any case, Shakespeare wrote this play sometime in the first quarter of his career, the period when he wrote *Venus and Adonis* and *The Rape of Lucrece* and apparently began writing his sonnets, the greatest collection of sonnets in English. Shakespeare's imagination in *Romeo and Juliet* is lyric, rather than dramatic. Instead of the rich, complex metaphors of Shakespeare's middle style, *Romeo and Juliet* relies instead on mere word play, puns. Juliet, tormented by her nurse's delays, cries out,

> Hath Romeo slain himself? Say thou but 'I,'
> And that bare vowel 'I' shall poison more
> Than the death-darting eye of cockatrice.
> I am not I, if there be such an 'I' . . .
>
> (III. ii. 45–48)

and so on. Could Lady Macbeth have talked that way, expressing her emotions by a hail of puns? The puns get particularly thick in the battles of wits between the young men of the play, Romeo, Mercutio, and Benvolio. Romeo, for example, jokes about his pump, that is, his shoe, to Mercutio, and that worthy replies: "Follow me this jest now till thou hast worn out thy pump, that, when the single sole of it is worn, the jest may remain, after the wearing, solely singular." "O single-soled jest," Romeo comes back, "solely singular for the singleness!" And a modern audience sits on its hands.

Along with this interest in puns and poems and books, there is, naturally enough, a preoccupation with names, as in the famous, "A rose by any other name" (which should probably be "word"). The passage begins with Juliet asking, "Oh Romeo, Romeo! Wherefore art thou Romeo" (wherefore, of course, means why, not where, are you Romeo). Romeo goes on to answer and deny his name:

> My name, dear saint, is hateful to myself,
> Because it is an enemy to thee.
> Had I it written I would tear the word.
>
> (II. ii. 55–57)

And later, Romeo says to Friar Laurence:

> O, tell me, Friar, tell me,
> In what vile part of this anatomy
> Doth my name lodge? Tell me, that I may sack
> The hateful mansion.
>
> (III. iii. 105–108)

This interest in words and names extends even to the letters of the alphabet. At one point the Nurse has to deliver a message to Romeo, and she tells him of a poem Juliet has written based on the fact that Rosemary and Romeo both begin with the letter R. (Like many other things the Nurse says, this turns out to be rather a ribald remark if you know some Elizabethan slang.) Juliet herself plays on the letter "I" when she asks,

> Hath Romeo slain himself? Say thou but 'I,'
> And that bare vowel 'I' shall poison more
> Than the death-darting eye of cockatrice.
> I am not I, if there be such an 'I'
> Or those eyes' shot that makes thee answer 'I.'
>
> (III. ii. 45–49)

These two letters, R and I, are the initials of the two principal characters in the play, for the Elizabethans, like the Romans, used I for J when they felt like it as on the title page of the First Quarto text of this play (see Fig. 13). This careful playing around with the initials of the two lovers is just one such element in the very stylized and formal texture of this tragedy.

The tragedy also uses a number of the Elizabethan conventions about love. There is, for example, a great deal in *Romeo and Juliet* about eyes. Mercutio says of Romeo that he is "stabbed with a white wench's black eye," with a blonde's dark eye. Again, love and fighting, but this idea of stabbing with an eye also refers to an Elizabethan notion of optics. We say that when we see an object, light waves or photons or some mysterious thing from the object enters our eyes. The Elizabethan was much more humanistic, and he thought that when we saw something our eyes shot beams toward the object. Our theory is all very nice for physics; their theory explains how people fall in love. The girl looks at the boy, wiggles her eyelashes, and thus shoots darts into the pupils of his eyes which descend and stab him to the heart. Thus, when Juliet warns Romeo that her kinsmen will murder him he says, "Alack, there lies more peril in thine eye than twenty of their swords," one more case of that age-old link between love and fighting. And that link suggests that now we are beginning to see the essence of the tragedy of *Romeo and Juliet*.

The tragedy seems to be working itself out in a series of oppositions. We've already noticed Romeo versus Juliet, or, if you wish to generalize it, male versus female, in the delightful battle of love. Juliet says before her wedding night:

> Learn me how to lose a winning match,
> Played for a pair of stainless maidenhoods,
> (III. ii. 12–13)

as though love were a game between two opponents. Then there is the obvious opposition between the houses of Montague and Capulet, which is expressed in still another contrast: the Montagues are often called dogs; the Capulets are associated with cats, Tybalt, for example, being called "prince of cats" and "Good king of cats." A very important contrast in this tragedy plays off romantic love against physical love: romantic love as represented, say, by Romeo and Juliet themselves or by Romeo's idealizing of Rosaline; physical love as represented by Mercutio's ribald comments or those of Juliet's long-winded Nurse.

Romeo and Juliet, for all that it is supposedly a tragedy of young love, is one of Shakespeare's most obscene plays. For example, the Nurse in the process of taking thirty-odd lines to explain to us that Juliet is slightly less than fourteen years old recalls a time when she tripped and fell and her husband took up the child.

> 'Yea,' quoth he, 'dost thou fall upon thy face?
> Thou wilt fall backward when thou hast more wit;
> Wilt thou not, Jule?'
>
> (I. iii. 41–43)

Falling on one's face as against falling on one's back is only one in the play's long series of contrasts or oppositions. We have water as against fire when Romeo, in one of the poems embedded in the dialogue of this play, speaks of turning tears to fires. At one point one of his friends asks him, "What sadness lengthens Romeo's hours?" and Romeo replies "Not having that which having makes them short." Having and not having; long and short. At another point Juliet says to the Nurse:

> Though news be sad, yet tell them merrily;
> If good, thou shamest the music of sweet news
> By playing it to me with so sour a face.
>
> (II. v. 22–24)

The contrast is between good news and bad, sweet and sour. Again, Juliet cries out when she learns who Romeo is:

> My only love, sprung from my only hate!
> Too early seen unknown, and known too late!
>
> (I. v. 138–139)

Love and hate; unknown and known; early, late—this is the way Shakespeare's imagination is working in *Romeo and Juliet:* opposites juxtaposed. *Macbeth* has such contrasts, for example, "Fair is foul and foul is fair," and we said that Shakespeare's imagination was finding for itself a particular figure of speech in *Macbeth,* antithesis. In the case of *Romeo and Juliet,* there is also a characteristic figure of speech; it is oxymoron (a word particularly handy for crossword puzzles and cocktail parties). Like antithesis, oxymoron involves the joining of opposites, but joining them in a closer and more extreme way, often by coupling an adjective with a noun to which it cannot apply. We see this adjective-noun combination in such a statement as Juliet's cry of anguish when she learns that Romeo has killed her cousin Tybalt:

> Beautiful tyrant! fiend angelical!
> Dove-feathered raven! wolvish-ravening lamb!
> Despisèd substance of divinest show!

> Just opposite to what thou justly seem'st—
> A damnèd saint, an honorable villain!
>
> (III. ii. 75–79)

We hear the same kind of stuff when Romeo comes upon the scene of the fight with which the play begins. He translates the fight into an oxymoron for his own unrequited love for Rosaline:

> Here's much to do with hate, but more with love.
> Why then, O brawling love, O loving hate,
> O anything, of nothing first create!
> O heavy lightness, serious vanity,
> Misshapen chaos of well-seeming forms,
> Feather of lead, bright smoke, cold fire, sick health,
> Still-waking sleep, that is not what it is!
>
> (I. i. 178–184)

Oxymoron, of course, is a verbal figure of speech, but *Romeo and Juliet* has another kind of oxymoron, a visual oxymoron based on light. Light permeates this play, pervades almost every scene with all the ardor and warmth of young love—or old hate. The action of the play takes place in four days so that three times we see the dawn rise. As Romeo says, "More light and light —more dark and dark our woes" (III. v. 36). Light seems linked to love. On the first night of the action we go to Capulet's feast with its gay, sparkling torches. After the feast there is the balcony scene under the night sky studded with stars. The next day Romeo and Juliet are married and that night again there is a bright scene of love against the dark sky and then the dawn. The final scenes of the play take place in the darkness of the Capulets' tomb, lit by the troubled flickering of a lantern, and again the dawn, this time a reluctant gray dawn, breaks. Sometimes the light in *Romeo and Juliet* is like a brief flash against the darkness; we hear of lightning and the sudden flash of gunpowder. Friar Laurence moralizes,

> These violent delights have violent ends
> And in their triumph die, like fire and powder,
> Which, as they kiss, consume.
>
> (II. vi. 9–11)

More often, the light is a bright spot against a black ground, a torch or a lantern or a star, as in the phrase, "a pair of star-crossed lovers." Thus, Romeo, after he has met Juliet at the Capulets' ball, climbs over her garden wall and looks up at her balcony where suddenly she appears.

> But soft! What light through yonder window breaks?
> It is the East, and Juliet is the sun!
> Arise, fair sun, and kill the envious moon,

Who is already sick and pale with grief
That thou her maid art far more fair than she.

. . .

Two of the fairest stars in all the heaven,
Having some business, do entreat her eyes
To twinkle in their spheres till they return.
What if her eyes were there, they in her head?
The brightness of her cheek would shame those stars
As daylight doth a lamp; her eyes in heaven
Would through the airy region stream so bright
That birds would sing and think it were not night.

(II. ii. 2–22)

Juliet, too, sees Romeo in terms of a bright spot against a dark ground, day in night, snow on a raven's back, or stars against the night:

Come, night; come, Romeo; come, thou day in night;
For thou wilt lie upon the wings of night
Whiter than new snow upon a raven's back.
Come, gentle night; come, loving, black-browed night;
Give me my Romeo; and, when he shall die,
Take him and cut him out in little stars,
And he will make the face of heaven so fine
That all the world will be in love with night
And pay no worship to the garish sun.

(III. ii. 17–25)

This image of light against dark is, of course, not confined to stars; it can become the rather strange simile with which Romeo comments on his first sight of Juliet:

It seems she hangs upon the cheek of night
As a rich jewel in an Ethiop's ear—

. . .

So shows a snowy dove trooping with crows
As yonder lady o'er her fellows shows.

(I. v. 45–49)

That was his first sight of Juliet; we find the same image of light against darkness in his last sight. He has just killed his rival Paris and says to him:

I'll bury thee in a triumphant grave.
A grave? O, no, a lanthorn, slaught'red youth,
For here lies Juliet, and her beauty makes
This vault a feasting presence full of light.

(V. iii. 83–86)

The very grave becomes "a feasting presence full of light," a place of gaiety, even of love. Romeo speaks of it as the "bed of death" and then again as the "womb of death." When he buys the poison with which he commits suicide he says, "Well, Juliet, I will lie with thee to-night" (V. i. 34), thinking of dying together as an ecstasy of love.

Just as the opening scenes of the play bring together the act of love and the act of hate, sex and fighting, the closing scenes of the play bring together the place of birth and the place of death. These equations, love and hate, sex and dying, marriage and funeral, womb and tomb, such thoughts, modern psychologists are quick to tell us, occupy some of the oldest and deepest levels of the human mind. So, too, the strict and extreme contrasts of ideas are characteristic of our most primitive thinking, a child's feeling that things are either to be taken in the mouth or spat out. In fact, Friar Laurence puts this rigid, black-and-white pattern in images of food when he says:

> The sweetest honey
> Is loathsome in his own deliciousness
> And in the taste confounds the appetite.
> Therefore love moderately: long love doth so;
> Too swift arrives as tardy as too slow.
>
> (II. vi. 11–15)

It is Friar Laurence who, in one sense, is the spokesman for the play, who, if this were a modern play, we would call the *raisonneur,* the man who speaks for the author. At the intellectual center of the play stands Friar Laurence's speech about flowers. Throughout the play it is the love of Romeo and Juliet that has been called a flower. For example, Juliet in the balcony scene says,

> This bud of love, by summer's ripening breath,
> May prove a beauteous flow'r when next we meet.
>
> (II. ii. 121–122)

But the flower is struck by the chillness of death. Juliet dies and

> Death lies on her like an untimely frost
> Upon the sweetest flower of all the field.
>
> (IV. v. 28–29)

Life turning into death, the flowered Juliet into the poisoned Juliet, light into darkness, love into conflict, womb into tomb, bright spots fading against a dark ground—all these images and ideas come together in Friar Laurence's great tribute to nature and the dawn and the harmony of good and evil in the larger purposes of the universe:

> The grey-eyed morn smiles on the frowning night,
> Check'ring the Eastern clouds with streaks of light;
> And fleckèd darkness like a drunkard reels
> From forth day's path and Titan's fiery wheels.
> Now, ere the sun advance his burning eye

The day to cheer and the night's dank dew to dry,
I must up-fill this osier cage of ours
With baleful weeds and precious-juicèd flowers.
The earth that's nature's mother is her tomb.
What is her burying grave, that is her womb;
And from her womb children of divers kind
We sucking on her natural bosom find,
Many for many virtues excellent,
None but for some, and yet all different.
O, mickle is the powerful grace that lies
In plants, herbs, stones, and their true qualities;
For naught so vile that on the earth doth live
But to the earth some special good doth give;
Nor aught so good but, strained from that fair use,
Revolts from true birth, stumbling on abuse.
Virtue herself turns vice, being misapplied.
And vice sometime 's by action dignified.
Within the infant rind of this weak flower
Poison hath residence, and medicine power;
For this, being smelt, with that part cheers each part;
Being tasted, slays all senses with the heart.
Two such opposèd kings encamp them still
In man as well as herbs—grace and rude will;
And where the worser is predominant,
Full soon the canker death eats up that plant.

(II. iii. 1–30)

Two opposèd kings encamped in man—this is the vision *Romeo and Juliet* gives us of ourselves. In a later speech Friar Laurence, speaking over the supposedly dead Juliet, defines these two parts of man as the heavenly and the earthly.

Heaven and yourself
Had part in this fair maid—now heaven hath all,
And all the better is it for the maid.

(IV. v. 66–68)

As so often in drama and particularly in Shakespearean drama these two parts—the heavenly and the earthly parts of the principal characters—are projected outward onto the characters around them. There are, for example, two sets of parents in the play, the lovers' real parents and their spiritual parents. We see the real parents briefly, old Montague a little more conciliatory than his fiery opposite Capulet. We see the Capulets impetuously forcing Juliet to marry Paris. We hear at the end of the play that Lady Montague has died of grief. Behind these real parents are what we might call the spiritual parents of the lovers, a set of parents who project the most fundamental aspects of the lovers' characters. They are Friar Laurence, Mercutio, Rosaline, and the

Nurse. These four spiritual parents are in turn divided into heavenly and earthly parts. That is, Friar Laurence on the masculine side becomes a heavenly father. Mercutio, on the other hand, who seems almost an older brother to Romeo, is masculine but far more earthy. He seems to look only on the physical or sexual side of love, and when his imagination turns to spiritual things, it finds expression in paganism: the grand speech about Queen Mab and the fairies, or his conjuration of the hidden Romeo:

> The ape is dead, and I must conjure him.
> I conjure thee by Rosaline's bright eyes,
> By her high forehead and her scarlet lip,
> By her fine foot, straight leg, and quivering thigh,
> And the demesnes that there adjacent lie,
> That in thy likeness thou appear to us!
>
> (II. i. 16–21)

Rosaline, too, is pagan, but "She hath Dian's wit," that is, the temperament of the goddess of chastity. Rosaline herself projects another kind of spirituality: that hankering after the ideal, the absolute, which is so much a part of the young love of Romeo and Juliet. "She hath sworn that she will still live chaste." "She hath forsworn to love." Finally, at the opposite end of the scale from the holy father, Friar Laurence, is the profane mother, the Nurse. "Ancient damnation," Juliet calls her, "O, most wicked fiend." When she advises Juliet that, since Romeo has gone away, she might just as well marry Paris, Juliet rejects her evil parent and turns to the good one, saying, "I'll to the Friar to know *his* remedy." Figure C shows all these character relations in a kind of diagram—male-female; Christian-pagan; chaste-unchaste. There is another, rather curious justification for pairing the Friar and the Nurse this way: the Nurse has a helper, Peter; the Friar is associated with "St. Peter's Church."

This must seem very cold-blooded and schematic, but you should remember this is a very rigid and schematic sort of play. *Romeo and Juliet* is not just a tragedy of young love, but a tragedy of young love and old hate and that phrasing keeps us in mind of two of the dualities in the tragedy: love-hate, young-old. The whole tragedy, in a sense, depends on the contrast between the impulsive, hasty qualities of youth and the delays of old age. That is, Romeo and Juliet rush to get married; Mercutio and Tybalt rush into a deadly sword fight. On the other hand, old Montague, old Capulet, and the Prince delay —and have delayed for years—in trying to straighten out their quarrel.

We could put all these fragments of the play together by saying that the essence of *Romeo and Juliet,* the principle that informs and characterizes the play's distinctive world, is opposition: *Romeo and Juliet* is the tragedy of the way opposites are so close in this world. How often two and two-ness appear in the play, beginning with that crucial phrase of the prologue, "a *pair* of star-crossed lovers," and ending with the Prince's mournful comment at the tomb that he has "lost a *brace* of kinsmen." All through the imagery, we find opposites paired: virtue and vice; water and fire; long and short; quick and slow; sweet and sour; light and dark; bright spot and dark background; cat and dog; womb and tomb; birth and death; sex and fighting; but most of all, love and hate.

Not only are there sharp contrasts in the ideas and images, but also in

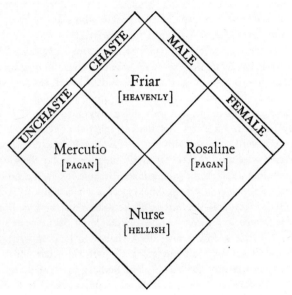

Fig. C. Character configuration in Romeo and Juliet.

the characters and action. Mercutio, Rosaline, the Nurse, and the Friar make up a pair of pairs, projections of the basic oppositions in the tragedy: chastity and unchastity; Christian and pagan; male and female. Throughout, the tragedy sets off the earthly aspects of people from the heavenly, just as the Friar separates medicine from poison in his flowers. The Friar himself, gathering medicines, bound to poverty, stands as a contrast to that poor apothecary from whom Romeo buys his poison. He contrasts, too, with Prince Escalus: the Prince wants to make peace between the two families by enforcing a political decree from *outside* the feud; the Friar wants to make peace by encouraging a spiritual decree (the marriage) that has grown up *inside* the feud. The humorous word battles begun by Mercutio contrast with the serious sword battles begun by Tybalt. Romeo and Juliet achieve a romantic, idealized love that contrasts with and transcends both the earthy, physical love so ribaldly described by Mercutio and the Nurse, and the chastity associated with Rosaline and the Friar. In the action as a whole, Juliet's wedding turns into a funeral; the lovers, in a hard irony, "die of love." In its essence, *Romeo and Juliet* is a *formal* tragedy. In the narrow sense of the word, it is a play much concerned with books, rules, conventions, poems, puns, words and names, and even letters of the alphabet. The play is formal, though, in a far broader sense, formal in this very quality of being composed of a series of sharp oppositions. *Romeo and Juliet* is the tragedy of two people who want to compromise, to marry, in a world where everything is black or white.

These opposites, this formality, typify Shakespeare's early style. "What early tongue," says Friar Laurence, "so sweet saluteth me?" *Romeo and Juliet* is indeed Shakespeare's early tongue and it is indeed sweet, maybe even a little too sweet. In the last analysis—and this may seem a horrible heresy to some —*Romeo and Juliet,* I think, is simply not a very good play. It is, of course, a great favorite with audiences, but that doesn't tell us whether it *should be* a great favorite with audiences. It's a great favorite with actresses, particularly aging actresses, who seem to have an irresistible urge to play the fourteen-year-old Juliet opposite a handsome young lover. Because it's such a great favorite, we ordinarily do include it among Shakespeare's major plays. If it is a major play, though, it is certainly the least of Shakespeare's major plays. But this, too, has its uses. *Romeo and Juliet* reminds us that even Shakespeare's hand can slip a little sometimes, and it gives us a chance to look at what we might call the lesser Shakespeare without going through the trials and tribulations of *Titus Andronicus* or the *Henry VI* plays. Perhaps most important, by seeing what *Romeo and Juliet* is not, we can see in high relief, as it were, what qualities we prize in the really great plays of Shakespeare. *Romeo and Juliet* gives us a chance to ask what we mean by greatness or goodness in a literary sense. Of course, this is a problem that has bothered all the philosophers of all the ages, and I do not mean to offer in the next few pages any real answer. Nevertheless, *Romeo and Juliet* does suggest some defects, some things that keep us from saying "this is great," which we can look out for in other Shakespearean plays or, for that matter, in any work of art.

For example, these rigid, sharp contrasts and oppositions—somehow they all seem a bit too easy, rather like the villain of the nineteenth-century melodramas who wore a black frock coat and a black stovepipe hat and would stalk around and twirl his moustache, foreclose the mortgage, and tie little Nell to the railroad track. We laugh at the villain of the nineteenth-century melodrama, and the reason we laugh, I think, is that we expect from a work of art some kind of complexity. We don't get it in the nineteenth-century melo-drama, and we don't get it in *Romeo and Juliet*. These sharp, rigid oppositions and contrasts are a little too easy: love-hate, light-dark, sweet-sour, cat-dog—it's like a word-association test. In this tragedy, the lovers are "good guys," and the parents are all "bad guys." Now, while there is a germ of truth in that, nevertheless, some of my best friends are parents and occasionally parents are right—but you would hardly know it from *Romeo and Juliet*.

The same thing holds true for the poetry. The figures of speech Shakespeare uses in *Romeo and Juliet* are not complex as they were in *Macbeth*, but simple, the ordinary stock-in-trade of any Elizabethan poet. Romeo, for example, says,

> Love is a smoke raised with the fume of sighs;
> Being purged, a fire sparkling in lovers' eyes;
> Being vexed, a sea nourished with lovers' tears.
> (I. i. 188–190)

These are trite, hackneyed figures of speech; you could find them in dozens of Elizabethan lyrics. At the end of the play, Juliet, wanting to commit suicide, grasps Romeo's dagger and cries: "This is thy sheath; there rust, and let me die." Old Capulet comes upon his stabbed daughter and says, "This dagger hath mistak'n, for, lo, his house is empty on the back of Montague," that is, the scabbard is empty, "And it missheathèd in my daughter's bosom." The figure of speech is that the dagger has been sheathed in Juliet's body instead of in its proper scabbard. Now this is surely a very small leap of the poetic imagination. Contrast the great passage in *Macbeth*, where Macbeth, who has murdered Duncan, describes the two grooms sleeping beside him whom he is accusing of the murder; he speaks of

> The murderers,
> Steeped in the colors of their trade, their daggers
> Unmannerly breeched with gore,
> (II. iii. 110–112)

of the daggers as wearing blood like breeches. It is a rather drastic figure of speech, but an effective one, unlike the much cruder idea in *Romeo and Juliet* that the dagger is sheathed in the body of its victim. The idea in the earlier play is too easy; it demands no complexity from us in our response. The figure of speech in *Macbeth*, on the other hand, does demand a complex response.

When critics speak of a too simple metaphor, they speak of it as relying on our "stock response." That is, crude works of art tend to use the way we would react anyway; you can see this trick any Sunday in the poetry columns of the Sunday supplements. We read a poem about a little boy who has died and gone to heaven and become an angel and we feel sad. Naturally enough. But it was not the poem that made us sad, but the thought of a little boy dying.

In other words, the poem used our stock response to gain its emotional effect. It cheated. The poem generated no emotion itself; it only tapped a preexisting emotion. The good poem or the good play, on the other hand, uses our stock response only a little bit, only somewhat, only as the start for something bigger and better. If it did not use our stock response at all, we would feel that it was foreign, strange to us, too complicated. We would complain, as many people do about some modern poetry and fiction, that it is too obscure, which, I take it, means simply that it is too far removed from the way we ordinarily think or feel, too far removed from our stock responses.

If, then, the great work of art uses our stock responses but is not subservient to them, we would expect to find a kind of peak or optimum point in the complexity which makes for great art, a point where there is neither too much complexity nor too little. Yet there seems to be no one level of complexity which automatically guarantees great art. That is, some great art is very complex, while other great art relies pretty heavily on our stock responses. For example, James Joyce's *Ulysses,* probably the greatest novel of our century, uses our stock responses relatively little. On the other hand, Spenser's *Faerie Queene* or the novels of Dickens or, in our century, the great Western movies such as *High Noon,* these build very heavily on our preexisting ideas of what constitutes good and bad. In other words, merely using or not using our stock responses is not itself a determining factor in literary value; we must also consider how our stock responses are used, either simply or complexly. Thus, in the case of *Romeo and Juliet,* not only does the play rely heavily on our stock responses about parents and children; it also uses those stock responses in a stock way. Contrast *Macbeth.* Surely our stock response to the man who assassinates his guest, kinsman, and king is that he is a bad man, but in the case of *Macbeth* this is complicated and enriched by the whole question of fate, the role of the witches, the role of Lady Macbeth, and the rest.

There is still another factor in the way a good work of art uses our stock or ready-built responses: it uses them always more or less at about the same level. For example, Juliet hears that Romeo is banished and she says,

> 'Romeo is banishèd'—to speak that word
> Is father, mother, Tybalt, Romeo, Juliet,
> All slain, all dead. 'Romeo is banishèd'—
> There is no end, no limit, measure, bound,
> In that word's death; no words can that woe sound.
> (III. ii. 122–126)

This is a sort of stock response, a young reaction. There is no end, no limit, no measure, no bound, in Juliet's response to the banishment. Romeo, on the other hand, when he speaks of his banishment to Friar Laurence, says,

> Hadst thou no poison mixed, no sharp-ground knife,
> No sudden mean of death, though ne'er so mean,
> But 'banishèd' to kill me—'banishèd'?
> O friar, the damnèd use that word in hell;
> Howling attends it! How hast thou the heart,
> Being a divine, a ghostly confessor,
> A sin-absolver, and my friend professed,
> To mangle me with that word 'banishèd'?
>
> (III. iii. 44–51)

Romeo is also saying that the word carries in it a kind of infinite death, but our response to his words is more complicated, more ironical. Romeo expresses his despair in religious terms, and those very religious terms suggest that he overstates his despair. After all, if we want to be cold-blooded and middle-aged—and religious—about it, the fact that Romeo has been banished from Verona is not the same as going to hell. Now one could make a play out of Juliet's response, somewhat crude and childish though it is; and one could make a play out of Romeo's response. But if a writer mixes these two attitudes in a single play, we get the feeling of an unevenness. It can be really disastrous if you mix these two different levels of response in a given speech. For example, at the beginning of Romeo's speech about being banished he cries,

> 'Tis torture, and not mercy. Heaven is here,
> Where Juliet lives; and every cat and dog
> And little mouse, every unworthy thing,
> Live here in heaven and may look on her;
> But Romeo may not. More validity,
> More honorable state, more courtship lives
> In carrion flies than Romeo. They may seize
> On the white wonder of dear Juliet's hand
> And steal immortal blessing from her lips.
>
> (III. iii. 29–37)

Suddenly the speech shifts from cats and dogs and little mice, soft, furry things, to a carrion fly and, at that, a carrion fly which is stealing immortal blessing from Juliet's lip. It's grotesque! Now it is possible, I expect, to write love poetry about a fly on one's beloved's lips—John Donne wrote a famous love poem about a flea biting first him, then his mistress—but it seems to me that it is probably not possible to write a love poem which starts out with little furry kittens and puppies and mice and then suddenly shifts to a carrion fly. The shift in tone is too sharp, too radical, and we simply don't go along with it. It doesn't succeed. In a good work of art, then, we ask for a certain consistency, a certain unity or evenness in the tone; not so even that it becomes monotonous, but not so disjointed that it becomes disturbing.

Another thing we ask for in a good work of art is a certain intensity or, if I can use a scientific word, density. In one of the great plays of Shakespeare's middle period, like *Macbeth,* in line after line and word after word, something new is happening, not just in the plot, in the action of the play, but in the language. It is constantly moving and involving itself. Contrast this speech from *Romeo and Juliet:* the Nurse is bewailing Juliet's supposed death:

> O woe! O woeful, woeful, woeful day!
> Most lamentable day, most woeful day
> That ever ever I did yet behold!
> O day, O day, O day! O hateful day!
> Never was seen so black a day as this.
> O woeful day! O woeful day!
>
> (IV. v. 49–54)

Now surely, if Shakespeare's hand ever slipped, it slipped there. We don't like that kind of poetry because nothing seems to happen in it. In six lines we learn only it is a black and woeful day. The lines lack intensity or density.

Finally, there is a fourth thing that we ask of a good work of art, namely, that everything in it contribute to the total effect. In *Macbeth,* for example, the Porter's speech, the one bit of comedy in that tragedy, contributes its own strange little bit to the effect of the whole. The Porter brings out in a different form the same themes and images that run through the larger aspects of the tragedy. He gives us a different perspective, a different attitude toward the play as a whole. He adds something. In *Romeo and Juliet* the scenes where Mercutio and Romeo match wits and engage in perfect volleys of puns, these work into the play as a whole. They don't add much, but they do add something to the general atmosphere of the play, the general tone of leisure or, if you prefer, delinquency. They suggest another attitude toward love besides Romeo's rather idealistic view, and often they develop particular words and themes from the main action. In the comic scene in Act IV, scene v, however, where Peter, the Capulets' servant, comes to the musicians who were supposed to play for Juliet's wedding and tells them now they must play for the funeral, these fifty lines contribute virtually nothing to the rest of the play. There is a good deal of talk about musicians being paid in silver because music has a silver sound, and this feeble witticism faintly echoes Romeo's remark in the balcony scene,

> How silver-sweet sound lovers' tongues by night,
> Like softest music to attending ears!
>
> (II. ii. 166–167)

It hardly adds much to the play, though, and in that sense, there are parts of *Romeo and Juliet* which do not contribute to the unity of the total artistic experience.

It may seem as though I am trying to shred *Romeo and Juliet,* but this calculated brutality has a purpose. We should not set Shakespeare up as a little tin god without fault or flaw. Shakespeare is no more perfect than other men, and *Romeo and Juliet* is one of the less perfect of his plays. In fact, by looking at some of the blemishes in *Romeo and Juliet* we can see better the virtues in the greater plays. We can see the importance of four things to the value we give a literary work:

1. The balancing of stock response and complexity.
2. Unity of tone.
3. Density.
4. Unity in general.

Note that these four criteria in no sense make up an invoice against which to check the work; we cannot simply pronounce a literary work good because it seems to deliver these four things. Such criteria as these really suggest only a certain way of reading, namely, looking for these four things we value: complexity, density, unity of tone, unity in general. We would read *Romeo and Juliet* differently had we set up other criteria, for example, realism in an absolute sense, instead of asking simply that a writer maintain a consistent degree of realism (part of the idea of unity of tone). In that sense, canons or criteria like these serve as a guide to our perception of a work rather than as a checklist of rules to be obeyed by writers.

In fact, by considering the flaws and virtues of *Romeo and Juliet* in terms of these four things, we can see that one thing in this tragedy which critics often call a flaw is not really a flaw at all. Aristotle, the wisest of literary critics, said that the best tragic effect is produced when the events come on us by surprise; the effect is heightened further when, at the same time, they follow as cause and effect. The tragic wonder, he said, will then be greater than if they happened of themselves or by accident. Now *Romeo and Juliet* falls woefully short of this standard. From the very prologue of the play, from the point where we first realize that these two young lovers are falling in love despite a family feud, I suppose we feel that things are not going to turn out well. Yet, while the family feud causes much of the trouble that leads to the lovers' deaths, there is a crucial link in the chain of cause and effect that is very weak indeed. It comes after Juliet has taken Friar Laurence's potion and apparently died. The Friar tries to send to Romeo to tell him that Juliet is not really dead, but the message is never delivered and therefore Romeo, when he comes back to Verona, thinks Juliet dead and commits suicide. Juliet, in turn, seeing him dead, herself commits suicide. Why wasn't the message delivered?

> *John.*   Holy Franciscan friar, brother, ho!

Enter [Friar] Laurence.

Laurence.   This same should be the voice of Friar John.
            Welcome from Mantua. What says Romeo?
            Or, if his mind be writ, give me his letter.
John.   Going to find a barefoot brother out,
            One of our order, to associate me
            Here in this city visiting the sick,
            And finding him, the searchers of the town,
            Suspecting that we both were in a house
            Where the infectious pestilence did reign,
            Sealed up the doors, and would not let us forth,
            So that my speed to Mantua there was stayed.
Laurence.   Who bare my letter, then, to Romeo?
John.   I could not send it—here it is again—
            Nor get a messenger to bring it thee,
            So fearful were they of infection.

                                              (V. ii. 1–16)

In short, Friar John could not deliver the message because he got stuck in quarantine. The catastrophe of *Romeo and Juliet,* then, is purely and simply accidental. In fact, Friar Laurence, when in the end he has to explain to friends what he has done, says, "He which bore my letter, Friar John, was staid by *accident."*

Yet if we look back at the reason the message failed to reach Romeo, there is a certain fitness to it. For one thing, Friar John got quarantined because he was looking for another friar with whom to associate himself. In other words, he was trying to make one friar into two. And as we have seen, the very essence of this tragedy is that it is involved with two warring houses, two cities, two star-crossed lovers. The very essence of the tragedy is that it deals with pairs of things, and it therefore makes a certain sense for the catastrophe to come about because friar number one went looking for friar number two. Then, too, that "infectious pestilence." It also makes a certain devious poetic sense. It serves as a symbol for the moral disorder that surrounds the love and harmony of the two lovers themselves. An "infectious" plague of hatred surrounds the lovers just as a black background so often in this tragedy surrounds and engulfs a bright spot of light. Here the single message which will save Romeo and Juliet is engulfed and surrounded by the blackness and darkness of the plague. In the same way, the weakness of the tragedy as a whole, its schematic and artificial style, its rigid use of opposites: womb, tomb; love, hate; light, dark; in short, its formality, makes up a background which engulfs the one great virtue of *Romeo and Juliet,* its kernel of psychological truth.

6

THE MERCHANT OF
VENICE

I am a Jew. Hath not a Jew eyes? Hath not a Jew hands, organs, dimensions, senses, affections, passions?—fed with the same food, hurt with the same weapons, subject to the same diseases, healed by the same means, warmed and cooled by the same winter and summer as a Christian is? If you prick us, do we not bleed? If you tickle us, do we not laugh? If you poison us, do we not die? And if you wrong us, shall we not revenge? If we are like you in the rest, we will resemble you in that.

(III. i. 51–59)

This, most people say, is the great speech of the play, because, supposedly, it shows Shakespeare's profound human sympathy and understanding transcending a play which at first glance seems in other respects thoroughly anti-Semitic. This speech, people say, shows Shakespeare breaking through the shell of prejudice to feel from inside the emotions of a persecuted Jew. We tend today to see *The Merchant of Venice,* not as a comedy, but as the tragedy of Shylock. We are sensitive about persecuting people of other races and religions, and rightly so, but wrongly so when we let that sensitivity twist and distort Shakespeare's comedy. This, like so many of the encrustations on Shakespeare, is an idea that began with an actor, Charles Macklin, who decided in 1741 to play Shylock as though Shakespeare wanted us to sympathize with him (see Fig. 14). Quite clearly, though, Shakespeare does not want us to sympathize with Shylock, as we can see if we look at the conditions surrounding Shylock's creation or even if we simply look at the play itself with an unbiased eye.

The Merchant of Venice is a comedy, and Shylock is that cruel, repressive father, which it is the business of comedians from Aristophanes to Ionesco to deceive and to laugh at and to put to scorn. When we hear Shylock's cries,

> 'My daughter! O my ducats! O my daughter!
> Fled with a Christian! O my Christian ducats!'
> (II. viii. 15–16)

we are supposed to laugh because we are watching a buffoon, a clown. Shylock is also a villain, perhaps a pitiful one, but a villain nonetheless. In Shakespeare's day, he would have been played in the red wig, red beard, and huge nose which the traditional Biblical plays assigned to Judas Iscariot. Shylock is a villain. Presumably, we need no external evidence to prove that any man who wants to cut a pound of flesh from another man's chest is a villain (be he Shylock or Gestapo doctor). If, however, we want external evidence, we can find it on the title page of the First Quarto of this play (see Fig. 15) where we see the title is "The Excellent History of the Merchant of Venice *with the Extreme Cruelty* of Shylock the Jew."

If, then, the play is not the tragedy of Shylock, is Shakespeare anti-Semitic? The answer, I think we must say from a look at the play as a whole, is, in a way, yes. In the first place, we should recognize that Shakespeare probably never knew a Jew. Edward I drove the Jews from England in the thirteenth century, and Jews did not return until Oliver Cromwell relaxed the discriminatory laws some forty years after Shakespeare died. There is some evidence there was a tiny Jewish community in London in Shakespeare's day, but it is unlikely the poet knew any Jews, and few in his audience would have. When Shakespeare drew Shylock, he was not drawing from life, but simply following a literary convention that dates back to the Middle Ages, for example, in the bloody tale told by Chaucer's gentle Prioress, the convention of the wicked Jew thirsting for Christian blood. Christopher Marlowe's play, *The Jew of Malta,* which had made quite a success some four years before *The Merchant of Venice,* was based on this same convention. The convention doesn't mean in any serious way that Jews are bad, any more than the modern Western movie means that people who wear black hats and ride black horses are bad. Second, even within this convention, Shylock's cruelty is something which is Shylock's own. We have two other Jews in the play besides Shylock, his daughter Jessica and his friend Tubal. Both of them are quite decent people, so it is quite fair to say that Shakespeare did not identify cruelty with Jewishness. Shylock is bad all by himself, regardless of his religion.

Third, even so, Shylock is treated rather badly in the play and he is treated badly because of his Jewishness, and in this limited sense, *The Merchant of Venice* is anti-Semitic. There is no need to attribute to Shakespeare the vicious sentiments of such young whelps of Venice as Solanio and Salerio (which are applied to the innocent Tubal as well as the guilty Shylock), but the play as a whole does attack Shylock and it does, in part, attack him because he is a Jew. Even the gentle Antonio spits at Shylock, calls him a cur. Partly, the reason is that *The Merchant of Venice* is an extremely religious comedy, a comedy permeated with Christian themes and Christian symbols. It makes its attack on Shylock as essentially a religious discrimination that would extend equally to Buddhists, Mohammedans, Hindus, or anyone else whom the Elizabethans would consider a pagan or an infidel or a heathen. If we paraphrase Shylock's great speech, using the word the play frequently applies to Shylock, perhaps you will sense the attitude the play takes:

I am an infidel. Hath not an infidel eyes? Hath not an infidel hands, organs, dimensions, senses, affections, passions?—fed with the same food, hurt with the same weapons, subject to the same diseases, healed by the same means, warmed and cooled by the same winter and summer as a Christian is?

Shakespeare's audience, I think, would have answered in its collective mind, "Yes, but. . . ." No one doubted that all men in an animal sense were the same, but in the Elizabethan mind the important part of man was not his animal nature but his soul, not his temperature, but his religious beliefs. So far as these are concerned in *The Merchant of Venice,* Shylock is a wicked infidel or heathen and as such he is to be abhorred. Even so, for an age when fire and sword were still fairly common ways of settling religious differences, Shylock is treated with a good deal of mercy. By attempting to cut the pound of flesh from Antonio, Shylock has forfeited both his life and his estate. Yet Antonio forgives him, allowing him to give his property as his daughter's dowry, provided he will become a Christian. That is the crux of the discrimination: whether or not one is a Christian. In this sense, the anti-Semitism of *The Merchant of Venice* is not the modern or country-club kind which runs to race. In the play, if the Jew will consent to accept Christ's sacrifice, he in turn is accepted into the Christian community. For example, Jessica, Shylock's daughter, adopts Christianity, and once she does, there is no discrimination against her. It doesn't seem very fair to us, but I'm sure to Shakespeare's audience it seemed more than fair. It seemed Christian mercy.

All this talk about Shylock, however, unbalances the play. *The Merchant of Venice* is an unusually complex and intricate work, and Shylock is only part of it. The play has in all five plots. Two are major. We can consider the first as the episodes in which Bassanio, looking for a rich wife, wins the heiress Portia by fulfilling the conditions of her father's will and choosing the correct one of three caskets, gold, silver, and lead. We can consider the second as the episodes in which the title character, the merchant of Venice (*not* Shylock, but Antonio), to finance Bassanio's wooing of Portia, borrows three thousand ducats from Shylock, promising to give a pound of his flesh if he fails to pay on time. We can consider as two lesser plots Lorenzo's eloping with Shylock's daughter, Jessica, and the problem of the rings: Portia gives Bassanio a ring when she marries him, and her maid, Nerissa, gives her suitor, Gratiano, a ring. When Portia dresses up as a young doctor of laws to save Antonio's life at the hands of Shylock, she demands the rings as payment (another money element). Finally, there are the doings of Launcelot Gobbo, Shylock's servant, if we can call them a fifth plot. For the most part all Launcelot does is crack the loutish jokes allotted to the Elizabethan clown, but in the course of the play, he does exchange his job with Shylock for a job with Bassanio.

These five plots in turn take place in two different worlds, one the world of Shylock's Venice, the other the world of Portia's Belmont (or, to translate the name, Beautiful Mountain). These two worlds are divided, ritually divided. To go from the one to the other, you must cross the seas, cross water (always a good, ritual thing to do). One world, Venice, is the harsh world of commerce and reality where fortunes are tempest-tossed upon the seas. The other world, Belmont, is a world of beauty, folktale, legend, and mythology. The whole plot associated with Portia's being courted by Bassanio is a kind of fairy tale. "Once upon a time there was a very rich man who had a beautiful daughter. When he died, he provided that she must marry the man who could guess correctly which one of three caskets held her picture. One casket was gold, one casket was silver, and one casket was lead." It could have come right out of Grimm or Andersen. It does, in fact, come out of that great medieval collection of folktales, the *Gesta Romanorum*. The story of Shylock and his pound of flesh is also a folktale going back to Roman times, but in Shylock's Venice the fairy tale becomes a harsh reality; in Portia's Belmont the fairy tale retains its shimmering, moonlit quality, issuing forth in music and feasting. In Shylock's Venice, people are mostly interested in whose fortunes are rising and whose are falling: "What news on the Rialto?" In Portia's Belmont, people are interested in myths and legends; they talk about them, about the Golden Fleece, for example, or Hercules, Troilus and Cressida, and many others.

Bassanio comes into Portia's world like the handsome prince out of a fairy tale to set free the imprisoned beauty. In fact, this fairy tale is much like the myth behind the Birnam Wood episode in *Macbeth*. Bassanio comes like a summer king, like the new spring, as Portia's messenger says of Gratiano when he comes to announce Bassanio:

> I have not seen
> So likely an ambassador of love.
> A day in April never came so sweet

To show how costly summer was at hand,
As this fore-spurrer comes before his lord.
(II. ix. 90–94)

Portia herself is a summer queen, still imprisoned by the winter past, or as the play says, "a living daughter curbed by the will of a dead father" (I. ii. 23). The fact that there are associated with Belmont three caskets, three rings and three brides, Portia, Nerissa, and Jessica, also has a mythological sound to it. Goddesses tend to come in threes in mythology: the three Fates, for example, or Paris' choice among Hera, Athena, and Aphrodite.

In Belmont, though, there are many myths besides the summer-king and the "triple goddesses," as they are called. In Belmont we hear of Alcides or, in his more usual name, Hercules, and in the beautiful scene between Lorenzo and Jessica at the opening of Act V, we hear a perfect garland of legendary lovers: Troilus and Cressida, Pyramus and Thisbe, Dido and Aeneas, Jason and Medea, and in talking of these old tales, Lorenzo and Jessica transfigure their own young love through a formalism of poetry into the very stuff of legend.

> *Lorenzo.* The moon shines bright. In such a night as this,
> When the sweet wind did gently kiss the trees
> And they did make no noise, in such a night
> Troilus methinks mounted the Troyan walls,
> And sighed his soul toward the Grecian tents
> Where Cressid lay that night.
>
> *Jessica.*   In such a night
> Did Thisbe fearfully o'ertrip the dew,
> And saw the lion's shadow ere himself,
> And ran dismayed away.
>
> *Lorenzo.*   In such a night
> Stood Dido with a willow in her hand
> Upon the wild sea banks, and waft her love
> To come again to Carthage.
>
> *Jessica.*   In such a night
> Medea gathered the enchanted herbs
> That did renew old Aeson.
>
> *Lorenzo.*   In such a night
> Did Jessica steal from the wealthy Jew,
> And with an unthrift love did run from Venice
> As far as Belmont.
>
> *Jessica.*   In such a night
> Did young Lorenzo swear he loved her well,
> Stealing her soul with many vows of faith,
> And ne'er a true one.
>
> *Lorenzo.*   In such a night
> Did pretty Jessica, like a little shrow,

Slander her love, and he forgave it her.

(V. i. 1–22)

Lorenzo and Jessica go on to pay Shakespeare's most exquisite tribute to music, for Portia's Belmont is a world not only of legend but also of harmony.

How sweet the moonlight sleeps upon this bank!
Here will we sit and let the sounds of music
Creep in our ears; soft stillness and the night
Become the touches of sweet harmony.
Sit, Jessica. Look how the floor of heaven
Is thick inlaid with patens of bright gold.
There's not the smallest orb which thou behold'st
But in his motion like an angel sings,
Still quiring to the young-eyed cherubins;
Such harmony is in immortal souls,
But whilst this muddy vesture of decay
Doth grossly close it in, we cannot hear it.

. . .

For do but note a wild and wanton herd
Or race of youthful and unhandled colts
Fetching mad bounds, bellowing and neighing loud,
Which is the hot condition of their blood:
If they but hear perchance a trumpet sound,
Or any air of music touch their ears,
You shall perceive them make a mutual stand,
Their savage eyes turned to a modest gaze
By the sweet power of music. Therefore the poet
Did feign that Orpheus drew trees, stones, and floods;
Since naught so stockish, hard, and full of rage
But music for the time doth change his nature.
The man that hath no music in himself,
Nor is not moved with concord of sweet sounds,
Is fit for treasons, stratagems, and spoils;
The motions of his spirit are as dull as night,
And his affections dark as Erebus.
Let no such man be trusted. Mark the music.

(V. i. 54–88)

And who is that man that hath no music in himself nor is not moved with concord of sweet sounds—he is, of course, our old enemy, Shylock, who late in the play makes some nasty remarks about the effects of bagpipes, and earlier says:

What, are there masques? Hear you me, Jessica:
Lock up my doors; and when you hear the drum
And the vile squealing of the wry-necked fife,
Clamber you not up to the casements then,

. . .

But stop my house's ears—I mean my casements;
Let not the sound of shallow fopp'ry enter
My sober house.

(II. v. 27–35)

Neither harmony nor legend has charms for him.

Shylock's Venice is a man's world. Virtually all the characters we see in Venice—Antonio, Bassanio, Solanio, Salerio, Gratiano, the Gobbos, both father and son—are men. Indeed, of the three women we see in Venice, all three disguise themselves as men while they are there: Jessica to elope with Lorenzo, Portia and Nerissa to play the young doctors of laws in the courtroom scene. Portia's Belmont, on the other hand, is a world dominated by women. Men come there only as suitors and wooers, worshipers at the shrine of love. The props we find in that moonlit, legendary land are rings and caskets, symbols, as Freud so tactfully put it in his essay on this play, of "the essential thing" in woman. The props for Venice, on the other hand, are bags with coins in them and that knife that Shylock so gleefully whets upon the sole of his shoe.

The male world of Shylock and Venice runs on a scarcity economy. Everything has its price; nothing is given away (except by Antonio, who, as we shall see, is a very special case). The world of Shylock's Venice is sad: in the opening line of the play, Antonio wonders, "I know not why I am so sad." His friends suggest it is because "Antonio is sad to think upon his merchandise," but that, he says, is not the reason, nor do we ever learn why Antonio is sad. Portia, too, in her opening line, says she is sad: "My little body is aweary of this great world." Her maid, however, points out, "They are as sick that surfeit with too much as they that starve with nothing." In other words, the sadness in Portia's Belmont is a kind of lovesick melancholy, a sadness of surfeit; the sadness in Shylock's Venice is a sadness of scarcity, a taxing worry—we moderns would call it anxiety or insecurity. Solanio and Salerio imagine the merchant's state of mind:

> *Solanio.*   Believe me, sir, had I such venture forth,
> The better part of my affections would
> Be with my hopes abroad. I should be still
> Plucking the grass to know where sits the wind,
> Peering in maps for ports and piers and roads;
> And every object that might make me fear
> Misfortune to my ventures, out of doubt
> Would make me sad.
> *Salerio.*   My wind cooling my broth
> Would blow me to an ague when I thought
> What harm a wind too great might do at sea.
> I should not see the sandy hourglass run
> But I should think of shallows and of flats,
> And see my wealthy *Andrew* docked in sand . . .

> . . . Should I go to church
> And see the holy edifice of stone
> And not bethink me straight of dangerous rocks. . . .
>
> (I. i. 15-31)

In that divisive, anxious Venice, we hear Shylock calculate the rate of interest, and even Antonio's friends count off one by one Antonio's ships as they supposedly sink, leaving him to the harsh justice of Shylock.

In Venice, things divide and fragment. In Belmont, however, things multiply and grow. As Portia says, when Bassanio guesses the right casket:

> You see me, Lord Bassanio, where I stand,
> Such as I am. Though for myself alone
> I would not be ambitious in my wish
> To wish myself much better, yet for you
> I would be trebled twenty times myself,
> A thousand times more fair, ten thousand times more rich,
> That only to stand high in your account,
> I might in virtues, beauties, livings, friends,
> Exceed account.
>
> (III. ii. 149-157)

Everything multiplies in Belmont. In fact, Portia's love for Bassanio doubles itself on the spot, when Gratiano, his companion, immediately proposes to Nerissa, Portia's companion. That is the magic of love, that it can somehow multiply, make nothing into everything. Even division in Belmont becomes a kind of multiplication, as when Portia speaking to Bassanio makes a slip of the tongue:

> Beshrow your eyes!
> They have o'erlooked me and divided me;
> One half of me is yours, the other half yours—
> Mine own, I would say; but if mine, then yours,
> And so all yours!
>
> (III. ii. 14-18)

Shylock's Venice is the court of hard justice, the law of the talon, an eye for an eye, a tooth for a tooth. Into that harsh court about to divide Antonio's body, comes Portia, in the guise of a doctor of laws, bringing Belmont's loving, bountiful, multiplying mercy:

> The quality of mercy is not strained;
> It droppeth as the gentle rain from heaven
> Upon the place beneath. It is twice blest;
> It blesseth him that gives and him that takes.
> 'Tis mightiest in the mightiest; it becomes
> The thronèd monarch better than his crown.
> His sceptre shows the force of temporal power,
> The attribute to awe and majesty,

Wherein doth sit the dread and fear of kings;
But mercy is above this sceptred sway;
It is enthronèd in the hearts of kings;
It is an attribute to God himself,
And earthly power doth then show likest God's
When mercy seasons justice.

(IV. i. 182–195)

Critics sometimes say that that speech, Portia's speech on mercy, is the heart of the play, that *The Merchant of Venice* is a play about justice and mercy, and so it is. But it is also a play about division and multiplication, about man against woman, about scarcity against plenty, or as Lorenzo says, "Fair ladies, you drop manna in the way of starvèd people." As Lorenzo's image of food suggests, you might sum it all up by saying the two worlds of Venice and Belmont correspond to two ways of using our mouths. Shylock's mouth bites. He snaps out phrases, mouthing them over and over compulsively as:

I'll have my bond! Speak not against my bond!
I have sworn an oath that I will have my bond.
Thou call'dst me a dog before thou hadst a cause,
But since I am a dog, beware my fangs.

. . .

I'll have my bond. I will not hear thee speak.
I'll have my bond, and therefore speak no more.

. . .

I'll have no speaking; I will have my bond.

(III. iii. 4–17)

Shylock bites and gnashes. Repeatedly he is called a cur and a dog with teeth and fangs. He himself brings in the image of a rat gnawing in the bowels of a house. To Antonio he says, "Your worship was the last man in our mouths," and of Antonio's flesh he demands it "to bait fish withal. If it will feed nothing else, it will feed my revenge." Twice in Venice feasts are planned, once for Portia as the young doctor of laws, but she must rush away; once as a way of getting Shylock out of his house so that Jessica and Lorenzo can elope. The feasts of Venice are false or they are broken. In Belmont, by comparison, the play abounds in feasts, a feast for the prince of Morocco, a feast for Bassanio, a feast for Lorenzo and Jessica. In a very real sense, the beautiful mountain of Belmont is the bountiful mother feeding her dependents, while Shylock in Venice is the harsh, threatening, and stingy father.

That harsh father hates and his hate creates hate, and also penury, hunger, and loneliness. The bountiful mother, Portia, as freely as the rain, gives mercy and love and money. Love and money—90 percent of modern anxieties, a psychologist once told me, come from love or money—they are the things of life as well as plays, and perhaps the juxtaposing of love and money is what makes *The Merchant of Venice* so much more intricate, so much more satisfying as a play than *Romeo and Juliet* with its simple black-and-white contrasts of love and fighting. The two worlds in which the comedy's five plots take place, do, of course, contrast, but they contrast in a rich, dynamic way, the harsh man's world of Venice and price and scarcity as against the bountiful woman's world of riches and plenty, Belmont.

Distinguishing the two contrasting worlds of the play, however, does not tell us what binds together its five plots. The answer to that question depends in turn on the issue of usury. To us, usury means excessive or illegal interest on money borrowed or lent. In Shakespeare's day, usury (or "usance," the word the play uses) referred to any interest at all, excessive or not excessive, on money borrowed or loaned. All through the Middle Ages and well into Shakespeare's time it was both a deadly sin and a crime to charge or give any interest whatsoever. To us, who, for better or for worse, have become wedded to mortgages and installment plans, this is a very strange arrangement. Indeed, it was necessary for the statutes against usury to be repealed for the economy of Western Europe to move into what it's now fashionable to call the "take-off" stage, that is, to become a modern credit economy. Even in Shakespeare's day, the statutes against usury or charging interest were being evaded, but in the popular morality of the theater (like the morality of movies or television today), old values were loudly trumpeted inside the theater, even when they were not being practiced outside.

The question we need to answer, then, is why was it so horrendous to do such an ordinary thing as charge interest? *The Merchant of Venice* tells us the answer in Act I, scene iii, when Antonio signs with Shylock the fateful bond. Shylock says of Antonio, "I hate him for he is a Christian; but more, for that in low simplicity he lends out money gratis and brings down the rate of usance here with us in Venice." In other words, Antonio is unwilling to commit the sin of usury. By refusing to take interest, Antonio drives down the rate of interest that Shylock can charge, so that, in part, Shylock's hatred of Antonio is a commercial hatred, the hatred of a business rival. As Antonio says, "I neither lend nor *borrow* by taking or by *giving* of excess," for giving interest was as sinful as taking it. More to the point, Antonio asks, "When did friendship take a breed for barren metal of his friend?" This is the key to the crime and sin of usury, *a breed of barren metal.* It was Aristotle who decided that interest was unnatural. The Greek word for interest on money was *tokos,* which means offspring. In other words, the man who lends money makes the money breed more money. Thus, Dante, in *The Divine Comedy,* put usurers in the same circle of hell as sodomites, both being sinners who distort the natural processes of breeding. It is unnatural to make money breed, because money, being metal, is at the bottom of the great chain of being. Breeding belongs only to plants or animals or man.

Thus, in this same scene (I. iii), Shylock tries to justify his charging of interest by quoting the totally inapposite case of Jacob and Laban and the spotted sheep in the Bible, inapposite because breeding animals is not the same thing as breeding money. The story of Jacob and Laban has nothing at all to do with the question of charging interest, as Antonio immediately points out:

> This was a venture, sir, that Jacob served for,
> A thing not in his power to bring to pass,
> But swayed and fashioned by the hand of heaven.
>
> (I. iii. 87–89)

And he asks, "Is your gold and silver ewes and rams?" to which Shylock cynically replies, "I cannot tell; I make it breed as fast."

The essence, then, of the sin of usury is making metal breed metal, money, money. It is no sin, however, as Antonio points out, to make money from money provided some other factor, a factor of risk or "venture," enters in, as when Antonio himself sends cargoes out upon the sea. The word Antonio uses is "venture," that is, taking a chance, taking some kind of risk. To put it in modern terms, it would be ethical to buy common stocks or even preferred stocks, but not bonds. Common stocks involve an element of risk or venture; bonds (in theory, at least) do not.

This contrast between breeding and multiplying money and venturing it underlies the Shylock-Antonio plot. The same idea, however, underlies all the plots. We have seen that Portia herself involves a kind of creating and multiplication:

> For you
> I would be trebled twenty times myself,
> A thousand times more fair, ten thousand times more rich . . .
>
> (III. ii. 152–154)

When she hears of Antonio's trouble, she promises Bassanio, "You shall have gold to pay the petty debt twenty times over." Portia, wealthy and womanly, seems to embody in her very self a living process of multiplication—a contrast to the dead multiplication of usury practiced by Shylock. Portia's kind of multiplying is tied to a risk or venture: "the *lottery* that he [Portia's father] hath devised in these three chests of gold, silver and lead." To win Portia, a suitor must take the chance of never marrying at all, should he guess wrongly; and the winning casket itself, the leaden one, has written on it, "Who chooseth me must give and *hazard* all he hath."

Bassanio brings together these ideas of doubling and adventuring (or hazarding) in a speech which is very close to the intellectual center of the play. He is apologizing to Antonio in the opening scene for the moneys that he has borrowed of him in the past. He suggests that Antonio lend him some more in the hopes of getting the first back. He puts it in terms of shooting a bow:

> In my schooldays, when I had lost one shaft
> I shot his fellow of the selfsame flight,
> The selfsame way, with more advisèd watch,
> To find the other forth; and by adventuring both
> I oft found both. I urge this childhood proof
> Because what follows is pure innocence.
> I owe you much, and like a willful youth
> That which I owe is lost; but if you please
> To shoot another arrow that self way
> Which you did shoot the first, I do not doubt,
> As I will watch the aim, or to find both
> Or bring your latter hazard back again
> And thankfully rest debtor for the first.
>
> (I. i. 140–152)

By adventuring both to find both—this is Bassanio's venture. He goes on to explain to Antonio that his venture or voyage is to marry the wealthy Lady Portia. Now this sounds very suspect to us; it sounds as though Bassanio were the crudest kind of gold-digger. When we think this way, however, we betray our nineteenth-century romantic heritage. We feel that love must be irrational, that our emotions must be unsullied by any touch of reason. We find matches where one party is rich and the other poor romantically attractive, romantically interesting, a proof, as it were, that love triumphs over reason. The Elizabethans, however, were much more realistic about these things. A man's estate, or a woman's, was just as much a part of them as the color of their hair or the sound of their voice. Bassanio and several other heroes of Shakespeare's comedies are being quite romantically correct in ascertaining the lady's financial status before wooing her. Even in our own vocabulary, love and financial status are not as far apart as we might think. After all, "dear" means expensive as well as beloved, as many a husband with a "dear" wife can testify, and when we speak of a person's "worth," it is not always clear whether we mean his intrinsic value as a human being or his net worth in an accountant's sense. In this very play, Antonio says to a friend, "Your worth is very dear in my regard" (I. i. 62). We hear of Bassanio as "costly summer," Jessica's "unthrift love," and Lorenzo's "stealing her soul." Portia herself expresses to Bassanio a wish "to stand high in your account." So do not misunderstand Bassanio when he says,

> In Belmont is a lady richly left;
>
> . . .
>
> Her name is Portia, nothing undervalued
> To Cato's daughter, Brutus' Portia;

Nor is the wide world ignorant of her worth,
For the four winds blow in from every coast
Renownèd suitors, and her sunny locks
Hang on her temples like a golden fleece,
Which makes her seat of Belmont Colchos' strand,
And many Jasons come in quest of her.
                                        (I. i. 161–172)

Indeed, she is just exactly the golden fleece in Bassanio's quest and venture. After she is won, Gratiano, Bassanio's companion, cries gleefully, "We are the Jasons, we have won the fleece," and Salerio, who brings news of Antonio's bad fortunes, links the Portia plot to the Shylock plot when he says of Antonio, "I would you had won the fleece that he hath lost!" (III. ii. 241–242). In other words, Bassanio has ventured to win Portia and he has won; Antonio ventured with his ships and he has lost.

The other three plots are also linked by a common idea of venturing, both in love and money, though a little less clearly than the Portia and the Shylock plots. When Jessica elopes with Lorenzo, a very dangerous thing for a proper young Elizabethan lady to do, she, in effect, ventures herself and she links her love to money. When she elopes she carries away with her a casket of jewels, and she and Lorenzo scatter the money riotously. As the thrifty Tubal remarks, somewhat shocked, to Shylock, "Your daughter spent in Genoa, as I heard, one night fourscore ducats" (III. i. 96). Lorenzo and Jessica, too, have won love's riches by venturing themselves.

Venturing lies behind the fourth of the five plots, too. Portia and her maid, Nerissa, give rings to their new husbands, Bassanio and Gratiano. These rings are the tokens of their love and are never to be given away. They, in effect, venture or risk their husbands' love in the form of these rings, and they apparently lose their venture, when in Venice Bassanio and Gratiano give up the rings as rewards to the young doctor of laws, Portia in disguise, and her clerk, Nerissa in disguise. Then, when the husbands come home to Belmont, Portia and Nerissa, no longer in disguise, quarrel with them for having given the rings away. As Portia says,

I will become as liberal as you;
I'll not deny him anything I have,
No, not my body, nor my husband's bed.
                                        (V. i. 226–228)

The rings, like the other moneys of the play, are metal made into living flesh. Like the other moneys, they, too, are linked to love, and with the forgiveness at the end when the secret of the rings is told, this love multiplies and breeds when we find that Portia is really two persons. This love multiplies at the very moment when we learn that Antonio's ships have come to harbor safe, indeed "are richly come to harbor." The success of Antonio's venture and voyage coincides with Bassanio's.

Finally, the idea of risking or hazarding underlies the fifth and least of the five plots, that of Launcelot Gobbo. Launcelot does very little in the play although, as we shall see, he is more important than he seems. All he does is cease being Shylock's servant and become Bassanio's, or as Bassanio puts it, "Leave a rich Jew's service to become the follower of so poor a gentleman" (II. ii. 135-136). Gobbo, too, takes a chance, and he, too, wins.

Love and money, risk and venture, lawful breeding and unlawful, the multiplying of living creatures as opposed to the multiplying of dead, lifeless metals, these are the themes that bind together the five strands of *The Merchant of Venice*. That distinction that underlies the sinfulness of usury, the distinction between people and objects, between the certainty we associate with dollars and cents, numbers, and things of all kinds and the chanciness we associate with life, this distinction seems to run all through *The Merchant of Venice*. Throughout the comedy, people are treated as objects. Portia, for example, is the subject of a lottery, and when we first see her, she is numbering over her suitors as though they were so many head of beef. The three suitors whom we see choose the three caskets—the ones who choose wrong—seek a certainty life does not have. The golden Prince of Morocco chooses the golden casket seeking certainty in "what many men desire." Silver Aragon hopes to win by choosing "as much as he deserves," and he feels pretty certain he deserves Portia: "I will assume desert." But there are no certainties in life; one must "give and hazard all he has," as the leaden casket says. When he chooses correctly, Bassanio contrasts to the other suitors' other-directedness:

> So may the outward shows be least themselves;
> The world is still deceived with ornament.
> In law, what plea so tainted and corrupt,
> But being seasoned with a gracious voice,
> Obscures the show of evil? In religion,
> What damnèd error but some sober brow
> Will bless it and approve it with a text,
> Hiding the grossness with fair ornament?
> There is no vice so simple but assumes
> Some mark of virtue on his outward parts.
>
> (III. ii. 73-82)

There is, in short, no certainty in human affairs, because things are seldom what they seem: "Ornament is but the guilèd shore to a most dangerous sea."

> Look on beauty,
> And you shall see 'tis purchased by the weight,
> Which therein works a miracle in nature,
> Making them lightest [i.e., least chaste] that wear most of it:

So are those crispèd snaky golden locks,
Which maketh such wanton gambols with the wind
Upon supposèd fairness, often known
To be the dowry of a second head,
The skull that bred them in the sepulchre.

(III. ii. 88–96)

In this grim simile of the beautiful woman wearing a wig made of a dead woman's hair, we have what must be the ultimate in ornament, in making people over into objects. The certainty we associate with things has no place in the world of people. How horrid is Shylock's cry, "Oh, my daughter! Oh, my ducats!", as though the two were the same order of being, or his later curse, "I would my daughter were dead at my foot, and the jewels in her ear! Would she were hearsed at my foot, and the ducats in her coffin!" The essence of Shylock's crime against Antonio is that he is treating him like a thing, an object, not a human being, just as in his usance he breeds dead moneys as though they lived. But Shylock is not the only guilty one. In the courtroom scene he accuses the merchants of Venice of committing the same crime as his by their owning slaves:

You have among you many a purchased slave,
Which like your asses and your dogs and mules,
You use in abject and in slavish parts,
Because you bought them.

(IV. i. 90–93)

The law itself is involved with treating people as objects, for law is an effort to bring into the chanciness of human affairs the certainty of natural laws. To the layman, it always seems hard that the law insists on applying its general rules in particular cases. Lawyers themselves have a saying that hard cases make bad law, or as Portia puts it when Bassanio asks that the law be twisted a little bit to let Antonio escape:

'Twill be recorded for a precedent,
And many an error by the same example
Will rush into the state. It cannot be.

(IV. i. 218–220)

When today we praise "a government of laws, not men," we are praising laws that apply to high and low, rich and poor, Jew and Christian, all alike, erase the distinctions among people, treat human beings impersonally as though they were so many interchangeable objects. Portia, however, though she recognizes the need for such laws, defeats them, because they turn out to be the justice without mercy that only a Shylock would endorse.

Religion, as well as law, has a way of turning people into things or, at least, playing with the distinction between the numerical certainties of inanimate things and the venture of life. In this context, Shylock, by demanding interest, a return on his money without any element of risk or venture, is demanding a sinful certainty—he is unwilling to take a chance on life. In a religious sense, he lacks faith. There is a wry paradox, then, in the repeated comparisons of Shylock to a dog, for the dog was the traditional Christian emblem of faith (in fact, the nickname "Fido" comes from the Latin, *fides*). In this atmosphere contrasting the numerical certainties appropriate to objects and the risks and hazards flesh is heir to, it is rather striking that the resolution of the Shylock-Antonio plot hinges (in part) on the arithmetical calculation of human flesh; Portia says to Shylock:

> If thou tak'st more
> Or less than a just pound, be it but so much
> As makes it light or heavy in the substance
> Or the division of the twentieth part
> Of one poor scruple—nay, if the scale do turn
> But in the estimation of a hair—
> Thou diest, and all thy goods are confiscate.
>
> (IV. i. 324-330)

How often in the New Testament Christ's parables hinge on the counting of money, of talents, and how often the point of the parable is that the kingdom of the spirit transcends the kingdom of numbers. Indeed, the central action of *The Merchant of Venice* involves the word made flesh, commercial paper made into the precious pound of Antonio's flesh. As Bassanio says,

> Here is a letter, lady,
> The paper as the body of my friend,
> And every word in it a gaping wound,
> Issuing lifeblood.
>
> (III. ii. 263-266)

The word is made flesh to bait fish withal, to feed Shylock's revenge, as though Antonio were saying, "Take, eat; this is my body." There is a fabulous irony in that Shylock, who does not accept the sacrifice of Christ's flesh and blood, nevertheless does "rather choose to have a weight of carrion flesh than to receive three thousand ducats." Antonio likewise gives or, at least, lends his body for Bassanio, "I once did lend my body for his wealth," and so buys for Bassanio what Jessica calls "the joys of heaven here on earth." Antonio is in effect the sacrificial lamb of a vengeful father, Shylock the Jew, almost the hard Jehovah of the Old Testament. In fact, Antonio calls himself a sheep, "I am a tainted wether of the flock, meetest for death," and perhaps here we have the secret of Antonio's mysterious sadness. "I hold the world but as the world," he says, "A stage where every man must play a part, and mine a sad one." Christ's part, indeed, was a sad one, the sacrificial "lamb of God." Again, it is striking that the resolution of the Shylock-Antonio plot depends on the distinction between the sacrificial victim's body and his blood:

> This bond doth give thee here no jot of blood;
> The words expressly are 'a pound of flesh.'
> Take then thy bond, take thou thy pound of flesh;
> But in the cutting it if thou dost shed
> One drop of Christian blood . . .
>
> (IV. i. 304–308)

There is a hidden meaning here in that Shylock, very much a creature of the Old Testament, is denied the blood. In Christ's words, "This is my blood of the new testament." It is almost as though the unleavened bread of the Passover, the flesh, precisely measured, not allowed to rise, were being contrasted with the transubstantiated wine, the blood, of the Christian communion ceremony. Even if this seems too fancy, at least we can see, I think, Christian imagery and symbolism permeate the Shylock-Antonio plot, like so many other folktales of the Middle Ages.

There are similar religious overtones in, of all things, the comic episode of Launcelot Gobbo. Shakespeare's comic scenes, because they are the freest acts of his imagination, often tell us most about the play. The careful reader does not neglect them. In the little scene between Launcelot and his father (II. ii), Launcelot begins by debating with the devil whether or not he should "stay with the Jew, my master, who, God bless the mark, is a kind of devil." His old father appears and Launcelot plays on his father the trick that Jacob played on Isaac. He pretends to be a hairy man and obtains his father's blessing. In medieval times and even in Shakespeare's day, every story of the Old Testament was allegorized as a foreshadowing of the new. The story of Jacob and Esau, in which the younger son steals the birthright of the older, foreshadowed, the interpreters said, the way the Jews, who were the older chosen people, would lose their birthright, the blessing of God, to the younger order of Christians. That is exactly what Launcelot Gobbo is doing: he is leaving "a rich Jew's service to become the follower of so poor a gentleman." What I'm hinting at—and only hinting—is that around Launcelot Gobbo, as around Antonio, there are faint overtones, a nimbus, as it were, of Christ who, by venturing his body, made the transition from the Old Testament, Jewish dispensation to the New Testament, Christian dispensation.

It is enough, though, to say simply that *The Merchant of Venice* is an intricate and beautiful play, based on no simple pattern of blacks and whites as *Romeo and Juliet* is. The play gives us two worlds: Shylock's Venice, daylit, masculine, realistic, a stingy world of harsh law subject to storms and tempests; then there is Portia's Belmont, a magical moonlit world of love and legend, a world of plenty, a world in which things double and treble. This seems to be the core of the comedy, the contrast between lawful multiplication and unlawful, the breeding of living creatures as against the breeding of money. The bridge between these two worlds seems to involve turning people into objects, into sacrificial victims, prizes in the hazard, the quest, the risk, the venture, the lottery of life itself. Antonio is such a prize, Bassanio, Portia herself, even Shylock, who is converted at the end, and even Launcelot Gobbo, even Christ; and since this is a play about Christians and Jews, perhaps the allegory of God's risking or venturing his only Son is not so farfetched after all.

HENRY IV, PART I

BY THE TIME OF *1 Henry IV*, 1597, SHAKESPEARE HAD REACHED THE HEIGHT OF HIS powers. In *1 Henry IV*, we are dealing with a fully developed playwright. Critics and scholars usually divide Shakespeare's writing career into four parts, each representing a different stage in his development. When the Victorians did so, they would give the parts flowery names like "In the Workshop" or "On the Heights." Our age, for better or for worse, is more tough-minded, and while we have the same four periods (more or less), we drop the names. The first period, which is usually dated from 1590 to 1595, is a period of experimentation, a period in which Shakespeare wrote in a variety of ways, imitating other writers (most notably Christopher Marlowe), trying to find a style of his own. In this first period, Shakespeare wrote all three kinds of plays: tragedies like *Titus Andronicus* or *Romeo and Juliet;* comedies in different styles like *The Comedy of Errors* in the Roman manner or the Italianate *Love's Labour's Lost* or the pastoral *Midsummer Night's Dream;* and histories, the three parts of *Henry VI, Richard III,* and *King John.*

A history play, by the way, was simply a play that chronicled the events in the reign of some English or Scottish king within recorded history. Thus, *Part 1* of *Henry IV* is a history play; *King Lear* and *Macbeth,* however, though they deal with English and Scottish kings respectively, deal with legendary history, and therefore Shakespeare's first editors, Heminge and Condell, called these plays tragedies, not histories. Both the *Henry VI* and *Henry IV* histories are titled in parts—Parts 1, 2, and 3 of *Henry VI,* Parts 1 and 2 of *Henry IV.* The "part," of course, does not mean that when you go to a theater to see *Part 1* of *Henry IV* you are only going to see half a play. Rather, the *Henry IV* plays are part of a series of four plays which professional Shakespeareans call the Lancastrian Tetralogy because these four plays deal with the fortunes of the house of Lancaster. The four plays are *Richard II, Part 1* of *Henry IV, Part 2* of *Henry IV,* and *Henry V.* Sometimes scholars treat these four plays as though they were one long story. In a way, they are. The events follow in sequence and the characters, some of them, carry over from one play to the next. But Shakespeare conceived and wrote each play to be performed by itself in the theater, perhaps followed the next day by its sequel. Each play is a two-hour entity, not a fraction of some gargantuan eight-hour play. The conceptions and themes of the four plays are rather different, and even the characters change a bit from play to play so that the Falstaff we see in *Part 2* of *Henry IV* is somewhat different from the Falstaff we see in *Part 1.* The word "part" in the title really only refers to the fact that *Part 1* of *Henry IV* deals —in a loose-jointed sort of way—with events in the first part of the reign of Henry IV, and *Part 2* of *Henry IV* deals with events in the second half of the reign of Henry IV. We are not dealing with *The Perils of Pauline* where each episode depends upon the last. From a dramatic or artistic point of view, *Part 2* of *Henry IV* is not so much a continuation of *Part 1* as an imitation of it, perhaps written to capitalize on the theatrical success of the earlier play.

At any rate, Shakespeare wrote the *Henry IV* plays during the second period of his writing career, a period in which he seems to have concentrated on comedy. In fact, these histories often seem as much like comedies as like the histories of his first period. In the *Henry IV* plays, moreover, he created perhaps the greatest comic character in all literature, Falstaff. The third period of Shakespeare's career, from 1600–1607, is associated with the great tragedies, though we should not forget he also wrote four or five comedies in this period. Beware of saying Shakespeare went through some period of despair—remember the gaiety of *Twelfth Night,* which he probably wrote after the tragic *Julius Caesar* and *Hamlet.* The fourth period, from 1607–1613, is associated with the late plays, the romances, as they are called, comedies which are set in faraway, exotic places, which deal with the relationship of parent to child, and whose themes are forgiveness and reconciliation. As you can see, it is very tempting to be biographical about all this, to say that Shakespeare went through a happy period and then sank into the depths and then passed on to a period of parental wisdom. But all that glitters in the scholarly eye is not the gold of truth. One must take into account the changing tastes of Shakespeare's audience, the conventions of his theater, and many other factors.

Nevertheless, there are some generalizations we can make. In the early period, for which *Romeo and Juliet* (1591, revised 1596?) served as an example, there is a good deal of interest in poetry for its own sake. There were, for instance, separable, discrete lyric poems embodied or embedded in *Romeo and Juliet*. Another characteristic of this early period is that Shakespeare tended to think in sharp black-and-white contrasts. As we go on toward the second period, however, in the *Merchant of Venice* (1596), the poetry becomes more relaxed, more plastic, closer to a language real people might speak. There is also an increasing use of prose. Shakespeare's dramatic conceptions become more complex, more subtle, more intricate. As we saw in the *Merchant of Venice* he used five separate strands in the play each to probe the others. Finally, and this brings us to *Part 1* of *Henry IV*, we find Shakespeare not only using multiple plots but also becoming more and more skilled at making *transitions* from one plot to the next.

In *1 Henry IV*, Shakespeare uses two large plots, each to comment on the other. One is the action around Falstaff; the other is the action around Harry Percy (or, as he is called in the play, Harry Hotspur). Both Falstaff and Hotspur are—in their quite different ways—rebels and robbers. Hotspur plans a rebellion to rob King Henry IV of his crown, while Falstaff robs the King's exchequer on the King's highway. Hotspur is the very spirit of chivalry; Falstaff is the very spirit of low roistering. And young Prince Hal must somehow choose or find a golden mean between these two extremes.

The scenes of the play alternate between the high plot dealing with Hotspur's rebellion against King Henry IV and the low plot dealing with the exploits of Falstaff and his friends. Act I, scene i shows us the disorder in King Henry IV's kingdom, while scene ii shows us the disorder in Prince Hal, who has been hanging around with Falstaff and other low types. Scene i ends with King Henry telling Westmoreland to "come yourself with *speed* to us again." Three lines later, scene ii opens with Falstaff saying, "Now, Hal, what time of day is it, lad?" And Prince Hal goes on to explain that time means nothing to Falstaff. These contrasting attitudes toward time make a transition from Act I, scene i, to Act I, scene ii. Again, still in the first act, scene ii deals with planning a robbery, and this robbery is matched in scene iii, which deals with the planning of the rebellion-robbery. Scene ii plans a robbery of the King's highway; scene iii deals with robbing the King of various ransoms to which he is entitled. In scene ii, Falstaff speaks of himself and his fellow robbers as being governed "by our noble and chaste mistress, the moon." In scene iii, we hear Hotspur say:

> By heaven, methinks it were an easy leap
> To pluck bright honor from the pale-faced moon.
> (201–202)

Again, in Act I, scene ii, Falstaff asks Hal, "Shall there be gallows standing in England when thou art king?" In Act I, scene iii, Hotspur speaks of his uncle's having played the hangman to Henry IV. These pairs of references to robbery, to the moon, to hanging, carry us along in Act I, from scene ii to scene iii.

The next scenes, Act II, scenes i and ii are the robbery on Gad's Hill. First Falstaff, Peto, and Bardolph rob the travelers; then the Prince and Poins, who have hidden themselves, rob the robbers as a kind of practical joke. In Act II, scene iii, we find Hotspur plotting his rebellion, and just as in the robbery on Gad's Hill, some of the conspirators apparently back out. There is a still further irony. If you know your English history as Shakespeare's audience did, you would know that Henry IV "robbed" Richard II of the throne, and you would see in Hotspur's plan to take Henry's crown another form of the robber-robbed theme that the Gad's Hill episode plays with. A good deal of the humor in the Gad's Hill episode comes about because Falstaff's horse has been hidden so that "Falstaff sweats to death and lards the lean earth as he walks along." Then in the next scene we see Hotspur calling for his horse— a comparison of the low robber on foot to the high robber on horseback. Falstaff's name has in it a *staff,* something you use when you're on foot, walking. Hotspur has in his name a *spur,* something you use when you ride on horseback. This comparison continues when in Act II, scene iii, we see Hotspur say farewell to his wife Kate, the woman of the high plot; then in Act II, scene iv, we see the woman of the low plot, Mistress Quickly.

Act II, scene iii shows us cowardice among the rebels; Act II, scene iv shows cowardice among the robbers, as Falstaff lies about the number of men who attacked him. In Act II, scene iv, a tavern scene, Hal plays a joke on Francis, a drawer (or, as we would call him, a waiter); Hal has Poins go offstage and pretend to call for service while he, Hal, keeps Francis talking. Francis is thus torn between two alternatives, just as in the preceding scene Hotspur was torn between the conspiracy on the one hand and the demands of his wife on the other. At the end of this scene Hal gets a paper, a tavern reckoning, out of Falstaff's pocket. Five lines later, but in the next scene, Hotspur remarks, "A plague upon it! I have forgot the map." "No, here it is," says Glendower, finding a paper. (Were I directing this play on a stage similar to that simple, bare scaffold on which Shakespeare worked, with scenes running one right after the other, as in a movie, I would have Hal throw down the piece of paper in Act II, scene iv, and Glendower pick it up in Act III, scene i, to establish the parallelism, using the same piece of paper for Falstaff's reckoning and for the rebels' reckoning. But that's pretty fancy and I suppose it's just as well I'm a critic and not a director.) The point is simply that all through the play, scenes alternate so as to build up the relationship between the high plot and the low, at least up till the end of the play when both the plots blend together in the final battle scenes.

This combination of the high plot and the low gives us, in effect, a father with two sons and two sons with two fathers. In a passage very near the opening of the play, King Henry (one of the fathers) complains

> that my Lord Northumberland
> Should be the father to so blest a son—
> A son who is the theme of honor's tongue,
> Amongst a grove the very straightest plant;
> Who is sweet fortune's minion and her pride;
> Whilst I, by looking on the praise of him,
> See riot and dishonor stain the brow
> Of my young Harry. O that it could be proved
> That some night-tripping fairy had exchanged
> In cradle clothes our children where they lay,
> And called mine Percy, his Plantagenet!
> Then would I have his Harry and he mine.
>
> (I. i. 79–90)

Northumberland's Harry—Harry Hotspur—is the "theme of honor's tongue," while King Henry's own son, Harry Plantagenet—Prince Hal—spends all his time carousing about the Boar's Head Tavern in Eastcheap. One son is the very soul of honor, the other of dishonor. Henry, in effect, has two "sons," one good, one bad. Hotspur himself has, in effect, two fathers, one good, one bad. Henry IV is his king and master, a father-surrogate. His real father, Northumberland, and his uncle Worcester coalesce, as it were, into a single father-figure, a bad father who tricks and betrays his son until he is killed: Northumberland withholds his help in the rebellion; Worcester bears false intelligence between the King's forces and Hotspur's.

The other son, Prince Hal, also has two "fathers," one good, one bad. Henry IV is his real father and essentially a good father, as fathers go. Old Falstaff, whom he emulates, with whom he spends all his time, is his corrupting father or, if you prefer, his "false" father. Shakespeare makes Falstaff's role as a father abundantly clear, when he has Falstaff actually pretend to be King Henry IV in the tavern scene. In this scene, which begins with the drawer trying to answer conflicting calls, a "scene of alternatives," Hal and Falstaff put on a play-within-the-play, one of the most exquisite bits in all Shakespeare. First Falstaff pretends to be King Henry, giving Hal a stiff talking-to (in a delicious parody of some of the theatrical writing styles of the day). The "King" concludes his advice to his son with:

And yet there is a virtuous man whom I have often noted in thy company, but I know not his name. . . . A goodly portly man, i' faith, and a corpulent; of a cheerful look, a pleasing eye, and a most noble carriage; and, as I think, his age some fifty, or, by'r Lady, inclining to threescore; and now I remember me, his name is Falstaff. . . . Him keep with, the rest banish.

(II. iv. 397–409)

At this point, Hal, outrageously amused, changes places with the "King" (that action itself is an epitome of the action of the *Henry IV* plays as a whole). Falstaff steps down to the role of a son, where again he defends the man whom this new "King" calls, "That villainous abominable misleader of youth, Falstaff, that old white-bearded Satan":

> That he is old (the more the pity), his white hairs do witness it [says Falstaff-as-Hal]; but that he is (saving your reverence) a whoremaster, that I utterly deny. If sack and sugar be a fault, God help the wicked! If to be old and merry be a sin, then many an old host that I know is damned. If to be fat be to be hated, then Pharaoh's lean kine are to be loved. No, my good lord: banish Peto, banish Bardolph, banish Poins; but for sweet Jack Falstaff, kind Jack Falstaff, true Jack Falstaff, valiant Jack Falstaff, and therefore more valiant being, as he is, old Jack Falstaff, banish not him thy Harry's company, banish not him thy Harry's company. Banish plump Jack, and banish all the world!
>
> [*A knocking heard.*]
>
> *Prince.* I do, I will.
>
> (II. iv. 444–457)

Clearly enough, Falstaff is a kind of father to Hal. Hal's problem is to choose between alternatives (remember Francis) so as to become like his real father, not his false one; and when he says, "I do, I will," that is the turning point of the play—ever after that Hal acts more like a true prince.

Shakespeare juggled history quite shamelessly to bring out this father-son parallel between Falstaff and Henry IV, Hotspur and Hal. In the sources from which he worked, King Henry was a man in the prime of life: Shakespeare chose to show him as an old man. The Hotspur of history was older than King Henry; but Shakespeare turns him into a young man and so sets him off against Prince Hal. This can be a very instructive thing, looking back from the plays to the sources from which Shakespeare worked. Often a comparison of a play with its source will tell you more about the play than anything else. In this case, Shakespeare's changes from Holinshed's *Chronicles* and the old history play called *The Famous Victories of Henry V* point up very clearly the fact that *Part I* of *Henry IV* is very much a play about fathers and sons.

Realizing that this is a play about fathers and sons should lay to rest the idea that somehow the Falstaff scenes in this play are "comic relief." The whole idea of comic relief is a fairly silly one. It has never seemed particularly relieving or soothing to me, at least, in the middle of a serious drama to have a clown appear and make a series of outrageous puns. We are not, after all, dealing with *Abbot and Costello Meet the Wolfman* in which, after the monster appears, the two comics come on and "relieve" us by making jokes.

The idea of comic relief, I suspect, was devised by teachers at a loss for an explanation—the only one comic relief relieves is the English teacher who has no other way of explaining the presence of the comic scenes. Throughout history, all the great critics have cried out against this mixing of serious and comic. Aristotle, for example, said it was improper to mix high and low personages. The French critics have always been puzzled by this thing in Shakespeare, this mixing of low farce and high tragedy. English critics in Shakespeare's day and for a hundred years after his death thought it highly improper to mix comic and tragic elements. Later playwrights, as we have seen, felt it necessary to rewrite the plays, removing the comic parts. Nowadays, I hope, we are wiser, and we recognize that we are not dealing with comic "relief" but comic reinforcement. The comic parts of a Shakespearean play are a way of reinforcing the main action, creating a radical perspective on it, as the Macbeths' Porter or Launcelot Gobbo do. In *Part 1* of *Henry IV,* we have seen that Hotspur's rebellion against the King parallels Prince Hal's rebellion against his father. Hotspur's treacherous father is mirrored in Hal's false father, Falstaff.

There are still other relations between the serious plot and the comic plot. Most of the comic scenes are concerned with the Gad's Hill episode, which we can think of as "the robbers robbed." As Poins explains the plan to the Prince at the end of Act I, scene ii: "I have a jest to execute that I cannot manage alone. Falstaff, Bardolph, Peto, and Gadshill shall rob those men that we have already waylaid. Yourself and I will not be there; and when they have the booty, if you and I do not rob them, cut this head off my shoulders." And indeed, that is what happens: Falstaff and his friends rob the merchants; then the Prince and Poins, who have been hiding, rob Falstaff and the robbers.

Exactly the same thing happens in the serious plot, in the contrast between Hal and Hotspur. Hotspur has been "robbing" honors from other people in the course of his chivalric activities, and Prince Hal in turn robs him of these honors, just as he robbed Falstaff of his booty. The Prince, when he promises his father he will reform, spells this out quite exactly. He compares Percy or Hotspur to a factor, that is, a purchasing agent, who has been engrossing, that is buying up, glorious deeds. He promises his father,

> For every honor sitting on his helm,
> Would they were multitudes, and on my head
> My shames redoubled! For the time will come
> That I shall make this northern youth exchange
> His glorious deeds for my indignities.
> Percy is but my factor, good my lord,
> To engross up glorious deeds on my behalf;
> And I will call him to so strict account
> That he shall render every glory up,

> Yea, even the slightest worship of his time,
> Or I will tear the reckoning from his heart.
>
> (III. ii. 142–152)

When Hal and Hotspur meet for their final battle, Hotspur, mindful of the little honor he will buy by defeating the Prince, says, "Would to God thy name in arms were now as great as mine!" The Prince replies,

> I'll make it greater ere I part from thee,
> And all the budding honors on thy crest
> I'll crop to make a garland for my head.
>
> (V. iv. 70–72)

Hotspur's pathetic words as he dies, the death of a man whose life has been devoted to taking honors (you can almost think of him as a gunfighter out of a Western movie), sigh out the same idea:

> O, Harry, thou hast robbed me of my youth!
> I better brook the loss of brittle life
> Than those proud titles thou hast won of me.
> They wound my thoughts worse than thy sword my flesh.
>
> (V. iv. 76–79)

In other words, in the Falstaff scenes, the Gad's Hill robbery, we are dealing not with comic relief, but with comic reinforcement of one of the basic ideas of the play, the robber robbed. Falstaff, the robber of money; Hotspur, the robber of honors, both these Prince Hal robs in turn. Only one robber cannot be robbed, King Henry IV, who robbed a kingdom from Richard II.

There is still another way the comic action mirrors the serious action, through the idea of excess, excessive size in particular. Prince Hal stands over the dead body of Hotspur and pronounces his epitaph:

> Fare thee well, great heart.
> Ill-weaved ambition, how much art thou shrunk!
> When that this body did contain a spirit,
> A kingdom for it was too small a bound;
> But now two paces of the vilest earth
> Is room enough. This earth that bears thee dead
> Bears not alive so stout a gentleman.
>
> (V. iv. 86–92)

A delightful irony, for Hal turns from Hotspur to an exceedingly stout gentleman, Falstaff, lying down on the earth, pretending to be dead. The great bulk of Falstaff's body matches the great bulk of Hotspur's spirit, for which a kingdom was too small. As for Falstaff, "Could not all this flesh keep in a little life? Poor Jack, farewell!" Both Falstaff and Hotspur have, in the modern phrase, gotten too big for their breeches, Hotspur figuratively, but Falstaff quite literally.

Falstaff's size brings us naturally enough to the bulk of his character. When we come to the character, though, I feel I should post a warning. It seems to me very suspect to treat literary characters as though they were the equivalent of real people. It is true, a literary character is in part the illusion of a human being, but that does not mean that he will necessarily behave with the same consistency as a human being. Rather he will do what it is necessary for him to do in the logical and meaningful reality of the work of art. Falstaff, for example. Is he a coward? How much critical ink has been spilled on that question! At Gad's Hill, in the robbery, he runs away most ignominiously. But in the real battle, Shrewsbury, we always find him in the thick of the fight. The answer to this apparent inconsistency is that the character Falstaff does what the play demands, which may or may not be what a real human being would do. The whole point of Gad's Hill is to have Falstaff play the robber robbed; he must run away, and not unsurprisingly he does. On the other hand, in the battle scenes, we have to see Falstaff compared to Hal's true father, the King, so necessarily Falstaff must be in the thick of the battle. Rather than ask what kind of human being this illusion of a human being is, it makes more sense to ask what this literary character contributes to the world of the play in which he exists: why do we react to this figure as we do?

Dr. Johnson confronted Falstaff (what a mighty weighing-in of literary avoirdupois was that!), and the result was a rare apostrophe:

But *Falstaff* unimitated, unimitable *Falstaff,* how shall I describe thee? Thou compound of sense and vice; of sense which may be admired but not esteemed, of vice which may be despised, but hardly detested. *Falstaff* is a character loaded with faults, and with those faults which naturally produce contempt. He is a thief, and a glutton, a coward, and a boaster, always ready to cheat the weak, and prey upon the poor; to terrify the timorous and insult the defenceless. . . . Yet the man thus corrupt, thus despicable, makes himself necessary to the prince that despises him, by the most pleasing of all qualities, perpetual gaiety, by an unfailing power of exciting laughter. . . . The moral to be drawn from this representation is, that no man is more dangerous than he that with a will to corrupt, hath the power to please.

Freud was another giant who undertook to explain Falstaff's appeal:

The grandiose humorous effect of a figure like that of the fat knight Sir John Falstaff rests on an economy in contempt and indignation. We recognize him as an undeserving gormandizer and swindler, but our condemnation is disarmed by a whole number of factors. We can see that he knows himself as well as we do . . . besides this, his physical misproportion has the effect of encouraging us to take a comic view of him instead of a serious one, as though the demands of morality and honour must rebound from so fat a stomach. His doings are on the whole harmless, and are almost excused by the comic baseness of the people he cheats. We admit that the poor fellow has a right to try to live and enjoy himself like anyone else, and we almost pity him because in the chief situations we find him a plaything in the hands of someone far his superior. So we cannot feel angry with him and we add all that we economize in indignation with him to the comic pleasure which he affords us apart from this.

Freud's answer, I think, is correct. We enjoy Sir John because we need not condemn him (and Dr. Johnson is the exception that proves the rule). I think, though, we can find a no less psychological, but more literary answer.

The place to look for that answer is, of course, in the language. In all the plays we have considered so far, we have found a distinctive figure of speech or trope. In *Macbeth* it was antithesis: "Fair is foul, and foul is fair." In *Romeo and Juliet* it was oxymoron: "Feather of lead, bright smoke, cold fire, sick health." In *The Merchant of Venice,* it was Shylock's habit of repeating himself: "I'll have my bond." In this play it is Falstaff's way of using "if."

If I travel but four foot by the squire further afoot, I shall break my wind.

(II. ii. 12-13)

If the rascal have not given me medicines to make me love him, I'll be hanged.

(II. ii. 17-18)

If manhood, good manhood, be not forgot upon the face of the earth, then am I a shotten herring.

(II. iv. 120-121)

If I fought not with fifty of them, I am a bunch of radish.

(II. iv. 175-176)

If reasons [raisins] were as plentiful as blackberries, I would give no man a reason upon compulsion, I.

(II. iv. 227-228)

If to be fat be to be hated, then Pharaoh's lean kine are to be loved.

(II. iv. 449-450)

If I be not ashamed of my soldiers, I am a soused gurnet.

(IV. ii. 11-12)

If your father will do me any honor, so; if not, let him kill the next Percy himself.

(V. iv. 137-139)

And so on, and so on. One could multiply examples almost indefinitely of Falstaff's "if" clauses followed by some vivid imagining. You should remember too that the Elizabethans had another conjunction for "if," namely "an" or "and," and that leads to even more examples:

An 'twere not as good a deed as drink to turn true man and to leave these rogues, I am the veriest varlet that ever chewed with a tooth.

(II. ii. 21-23)

An I have not ballads made on you all, and sung to filthy tunes, let a cup of sack be my poison.

(II. ii. 41-43)

An I have not forgotten what the inside of a church is made of, I am a pepper-corn, a brewer's horse.

(III. iii. 6–8)

It is as though Falstaff were constantly changing his own identity, "I am a 'peppercorn,' 'a brewer's horse,' 'a soused gurnet,' and so on." He seems to live in a play world, an imaginary world of visions, where his own identity constantly changes.

This habit of speech, I think, suggests the real source of Falstaff's appeal. He suggests to us a world in which we (or Hal) are freed of our responsibilities; we no longer have to live up to what our "fathers" want us to be. Instead, we enter a world of play and foolery and the gratification of every kind of pleasure in which our "father" is not like a father at all but an irresponsible child. Perhaps, then, this is the relationship between the "immoral" Falstaff and the "immortal" Falstaff: that he is the embodiment of an immortal—and immoral—wish, a wish for a father like Falstaff, a father full of fun and games as irresponsible as the child himself. This Falstaff-wish, then, is an immortal wish that goes on from generation to generation without being satisfied—except in comedies like *1 Henry IV*.

Falstaff's "iffy" habit of speech suggests still another relationship between the serious plot and the comic plot. The character with whom Falstaff shares this trick of speech is, oddly enough, Hotspur:

An if the devil come and roar for them,
I will not send them [the prisoners].

(I. iii. 125–126)

Zounds, an I were now by this rascal, I could brain him with his lady's fan.

(II. iii. 20–21)

An if we live, we live to tread on kings;
If die, brave death, when princes die with us!

(V. ii. 85–86)

Hotspur, too, seems to live in a world of imaginings. After his interview with the King in Act I, scene iii, Hotspur becomes so excited that it takes his father and his uncle a hundred lines of poetry to calm him down to the point where he will listen to them. As Worcester says, "He apprehends a world of figures here, but not the form of what he should attend." You could say the same of Falstaff. Both he and Hotspur seem to spend their time in a world of figures of speech, imaginings, games, play. Each holds out his different world of visions to Hal as an alternative. Yet each of these worlds is wrong, one seriously, one comically. And in each of them the father is false, again, one seriously, one comically. As against these two imaginary worlds, the play holds up the real relationship of Henry IV to Hal, of real king to real prince, of real father to real son.

So far, in considering *1 Henry IV,* our procedure has for the most part been to try and grasp the play as a whole, to look for the larger patterns of repetition and contrast within it. Sometimes it's useful to proceed the other way, taking a small passage and looking for the links that bind it to the rest of the play. This binding is what critics mean by the organic unity of art, the idea that the whole work of art is implicit in each small part. With a writer as great as Shakespeare, in every speech, in almost every line or word, are implicit the themes and ideas which are central to the imaginative conception of the play as a whole. A useful example is Hal's last dialogue with Falstaff before the battle of Shrewsbury. At this point, Hal has become very princely indeed, offering himself in single combat against Hotspur to save the lives of the others. Falstaff, of course, is the same irresponsible child that he always is:

Falstaff.   Hal, if thou see me down in the battle and bestride me, so! 'Tis a point of friendship.
Prince.   Nothing but a colossus can do thee that friendship. Say thy prayers, and farewell.
Falstaff.   I would 'twere bedtime, Hal, and all well.
Prince.   Why, thou owest God a death.   [*Exit.*]
Falstaff.   'Tis not due yet: I would be loath to pay him before his day. . . .

(V. i. 121–128)

and Falstaff goes into his famous discussion of the visionary nature of honor, one more example of the imaginations and visions held out before Hal as a temptation. In fact, the very first line of this little passage reminds us of "if," the "iffy" elements in this play—or, if you prefer a technical term, its enthymematic quality.

The word "bestride" also has links to the rest of the play, for example, the association of Falstaff with fighting on foot, lowly, as against the mounted Hotspur. The low image of Hal's bestriding Falstaff contrasts with Hotspur's high words in the next scene: "An if we live, we live to tread on kings." Notice, too, the episode in Act V, scene iv, lines 25 and following, in which the King, alone on the battlefield, is suddenly confronted by the rebel Douglas. The stage direction reads, *"They fight. The king being in danger, enter Prince of Wales."* Hal engages the Douglas in combat and apparently succeeds because the stage direction reads, *"They fight. Douglas flieth."* Now these are very meager stage directions, as almost all of Shakespeare's are (the reason, I suppose, is that since he worked every day in the theater with his actors, he did not need to write his stage directions out, except in the form of a short memorandum to himself). Were I directing this action, I would have the Douglas' fighting make the King fall down. Then Hal enters and bestrides the King, taking on the Douglas, and fights him off. The King perhaps could rise then and join Hal in the fight, and then as the Douglas flees, father and son shake hands. There is no particular warrant in the stage directions for this bit of business, the King's falling down and Hal bestriding him, but it would bring out that parallelism between Falstaff and King Henry IV which we have already seen. Where Falstaff had said, "If thou see me down in the battle and bestride me, so!" a director could make the action itself take place with the King, and thus contrast Hal's real father with his "iffy" father. And, of course, having the King fall down would produce a more exciting bit of stage business. There is a little textual evidence for such a bit of business: at line 52, Hal says to his father, "I might have left alone the insulting hand of Douglas over you." The notion that Douglas' hand was *over* the King suggests that the King was down. As I've said before, though, it's probably just as well that I'm not a director, just a critic.

The word "point" in our little passage is a fairly common word in this play, occurring nine times and mostly referring to the points of swords. The scene immediately following this dialogue between Hal and Falstaff ends with Hotspur's wonderful speech before the battle to his troops, presumably a parallel to Hal's and Falstaff's final words before the battle:

> O gentlemen, the time of life is short!
> To spend that shortness basely were too long
> If life did ride upon a dial's point,
> Still ending at the arrival of an hour.
>
> (V. ii. 81–84)

Hotspur's point is a "dial's point," a thing of time, and time is an important theme in this play. Falstaff's "point" has another overtone, one that is lost to us in the passage of time. In Shakespeare's day, the *oi* in point would have been pronounced approximately *aie,* so that Falstaff's line would sound " 'Tis a [pint] of friendship," like the "cup of kindness" in "Auld Lang Syne." It needs no critic to tell us that by and large Falstaff and his world of Eastcheap are associated with pints and drinking, as well as food and sex, unlike Hotspur's world which is the world of chivalry. Blunt Hotspur, moreover, is a man of few words and many deeds, while Falstaff is a man of many words and few deeds. Just as Hotspur abuses his deeds with his rebellion, so Falstaff abuses his words with puns, like *point* and *pint.*

To return to our little dialogue, Hal responds to Falstaff's pun with the inevitable joke on his size—"Nothing but a colossus" could bestride so fat a knight. As we have already seen, both Falstaff and Hotspur represent excesses of size. Hal's speech over their bodies at the battle makes the parallelism clear: Falstaff is big of body; Hotspur is big of spirit. Each in his own way is a grotesquely outsized individual.

Hal's conventional phrase, "Say thy prayers," sounds a religious note, and

1 Henry IV is a very religious play indeed, at least in the sense that the characters talk a good deal about religion. The play opens, for example, with Henry IV's wishing to go on a crusade. The rebellion of the Percys is identified with the devil; we hear about "that fiend Douglas, that spirit Percy, and that devil Glendower." Practically a whole scene is devoted to Glendower's supposed ability to deal with the devil.

Falstaff's rueful, "I would 'twere bedtime, Hal, and all well," recalls again time, one of the important ideas of the play. In particular, there is a contrast between the way Hotspur thinks of time and the way Falstaff does. Hotspur is always in a hurry, always wanting to do things before he should. As he says, "O, gentlemen, the time of life is short." On the other hand, the very first words we hear Falstaff say in the play are: "Now, Hal, what time of day is it, lad?" and the Prince replies,

> Thou art so fat-witted with drinking of old sack, and unbuttoning thee after supper, and sleeping upon benches after noon, that thou has forgotten to demand that truly which thou wouldest truly know. What a devil has thou to do with the time of the day? Unless hours were cups of sack, and minutes capons, and clocks the tongues of bawds, and dials the signs of leaping houses, and the blessed sun himself a fair hot wench in flame-colored taffeta, I see no reason why thou shouldst be so superfluous to demand the time of day.
>
> (I. ii. 2–11)

Falstaff, in other words, seems to live in a world where time does not matter, where life is only leisure, and the only actions in time, vices.

In our passage, however, it is not just time to which Falstaff refers, but "bedtime." This, too, refers to a recurring contrast in the play. Falstaff and his friends are, in the Greenwich Village phrase, night people—Falstaff calls them, "Diana's foresters, gentlemen of the shade, minions of the moon." Hotspur, too, is a creature of the moon. As he says,

> By heaven, methinks it were an easy leap
> To pluck bright honor from the pale-faced moon.
> (I. iii. 201–202)

The scene (III. i) in which he and his friends take leave of their wives takes place at night. "The moon shines fair; you may away by night," says Glendower. It is typical of Hotspur's impetuosity that he wants to fight the very night he arrives where the King's army is: "We'll fight with him tonight."

Henry IV, on the other hand, and Hal and his friends (to the extent they are associated with the King) are associated with daylight and the sun. The King speaks of "sunlike majesty," and Sir Richard Vernon describes the Prince of Wales and his friends before the battle as

> Glittering in golden coats like images;
> As full of spirit as the month of May

> And gorgeous as the sun at midsummer.
> (IV. i. 100-102)

Hal in his interview with his father, when he promises to reform, tells him,

> I will redeem all this on Percy's head
> And, in the closing of some glorious day,
> Be bold to tell you that I am your son.
> (III. ii. 132-134)

(The juxtaposition of "son" with "day" makes us think of *sun*.) At any rate, at the end of the play we see the closing of such a glorious day when the King says:

> Rebellion in this land shall loose his sway.
> Meeting the check of such another day.
> (V. v. 41-42)

And in that key speech at the end of the first scene between Falstaff and Hal, when Hal in soliloquy promises us, the audience, he will reform, he promises in an image of the sun:

> Yet herein will I imitate the sun,
> Who doth permit the base contagious clouds
> To smother up his beauty from the world,
> That, when he please again to be himself,
> Being wanted, he may be more wond'red at
> By breaking through the foul and ugly mists
> Of vapors that did seem to strangle him.
> (I. ii. 185-191)

And similarly, when Falstaff is playing the part of King Henry IV in the tavern scene, he says to Hal, "Shall the blessed sun of heaven prove [a truant] and eat blackberries? A question not to be asked. Shall the son of England prove a thief and take purses? A question to be asked." Again, that pun sets off the son (sun), royal Hal, against the moon, associated with Falstaff and Hotspur, the night people.

To return to our passage, after Falstaff's wry wish for bedtime, Hal twits him, "Why, thou owest God a death," a pun on *debt,* which Falstaff answers in his next line, "Tis not due yet." The pun brings us to a major complex of imagery, commercial images, images of money, accounts, debts, reckonings, coins, and trades. They run all through the play, and insofar as there is a single idea which holds the play together, we can think of it as *reckoning.* For example, the parallel between the Gad's Hill robbery of the low plot and the battle of Shrewsbury in the high plot—in both cases, we have a reckoning, a set of robbers robbed. At Gad's Hill, Falstaff and the minor comic characters rob the travelers; then the Prince and Poins rob Falstaff. At the battle of Shrewsbury, Hotspur has been robbing honors from all sorts of people;

then Hal crops "all the budding honors on thy crest"—another robber is robbed.

As Hal had said, "Percy is but my factor," my purchasing agent. Hotspur, the good chivalric knight, himself treats honors as a part of his trade, as a kind of commodity which he buys up and exchanges with others. He wins honors by killing men. In a way, then, we could say that men and honor in this play are treated like money, and there are two cases where some men— and honor—are quite literally coined into money. One is Falstaff's use of the Elizabethan selective service, or, more properly, the King's press: he confesses, "I have misused the King's press damnably." What he has done is to threaten to draft someone, and then accept a payment of money from that individual for not forcing him to go to war. "I have got, in exchange of a hundred and fifty soldiers, three hundred and odd pounds," he says. This is exactly the low counterpart of the high situation the play opens with, when in Act I, scene i, Henry demands that he be given the prisoners that Hotspur has won. The prisoners, in effect, are a commodity; they are worth so and so many pounds in ransom.

When Hotspur and the rebels begin to plan their conspiracy, Hotspur says, "No! Yet time serves wherein you may *redeem* your banished honors." The word "redeem" is a commercial word. Again, Hotspur speaks

> Of this proud king, who studies day and night
> To answer all the debt he owes to you
> Even with the bloody payment of your deaths.
>
> (I. iii. 184–186)

(This is exactly the same pun that Falstaff and Hal make in their speech just before the battle, "Thou owest God a death.") Hotspur's speech abounds in commercial words. In Act II, scene iii, as he is preparing to leave for the battle he cries out to his wife,

> We must have bloody noses and cracked crowns,
> And pass them current, too.
>
> (89–90)

A crown was the name of a five-shilling coin, and Hotspur puns on cracked —defective—crowns, that is, the crowns of heads, which he is going to make pass as good common currency. In Act III, scene i, we see a sort of directors' meeting among the rebels where they speak of their "indentures," their "business," their "bargain," all mercantile terms. These are commercial images only in the high plot.

Needless to say, there are even more in the low. The whole Gad's Hill episode is concerned with the stealing of money, and in Act II, scene i, we even see two carriers, men who transport goods for trade. The people in the low plot make jokes about money, as when the Prince asks, "Why, what a pox have I to do with my hostess of the tavern?" and Falstaff slyly replies, "Well, thou hast called her to a reckoning many a time and oft." The Prince tops the joke with, "Did I ever call for thee to pay thy part?" (I. ii. 44-48). Act II, scene iv, the scene in which Falstaff tells us how brave he was at the robbery on Gad's Hill, constitutes a kind of reckoning, a paying back of Falstaff for his boasting. Indeed, at the end of the scene, the Prince tells us, "The money shall be paid back again with advantage." In fact, even as he says that, he is looking at a "reckoning," Falstaff's account at the tavern.

Such words, then, as "money," or "reckoning," or "account," "coin," "crown," "angel" and "royal" (both names of coins) are key words in *1 Henry IV*. "Current" is another of these words, and the play has a recurring pun on "metal" and "mettle," one referring to what goes into coins, the other what goes into brave or honorable men. There is a reason for all this concern with coins. Then, as now, English coins bore the image of the monarch. When the Douglas, for example, in the battle scenes, speaks of the "counterfeits" that are wearing the clothes of the King, the word is peculiarly appropriate. Indeed, we could say that the whole question of this play is whether or not Prince Hal will turn out to be a counterfeit coin or a true image of his kingly father.

There are, in this highly commercial play, a number of references to cloth and clothmaking, which was the most important trade in Shakespeare's England. We hear about "sarcenet," or "gummed velvet," "dowlass" and "holland," which is a kind of linen. Surprisingly enough, it is the knightly and chivalric Hotspur whose speech is full of the names of cloths and trades, crude, low images born from a commercial world that such a knightly fellow as he should sneer at.

> I had rather be a kitten and cry mew
> Than one of these same metre ballet-mongers.
> I had rather hear a brazen can[dle]stick turned
> Or a dry wheel grate on the axletree,
> And that would set my teeth nothing on edge,
> Nothing so much as mincing poetry.
>
> (III. i. 127-132)

(Remember, in *The Merchant of Venice,* what Shakespeare had to say about people who did not like music and poetry.) It is almost as though Shakespeare were saying, by Hotspur's choice of images, that Hotspur's kind of knighthood and chivalry is low and tradesmanlike. Prince Hal, for example, speaks of Hotspur's "ill-*weaved* ambition." Certainly, Shakespeare is saying that killing men is a trade to Hotspur, just as robbing them is a trade to Falstaff.

All this business imagery seems, however, a little odd in a play about monarchy and chivalry. Yet, not so. In Hal's famous soliloquy at the end of his first scene with Falstaff, he tells the audience that he is going to reform:

> So, when this loose behavior I throw off
> And pay the debt I never promisèd,
> By how much better than my word I am,
> By so much shall I falsify men's hopes;
> And, like bright metal on a sullen ground,
> My reformation, glitt'ring o'er my fault,
> Shall show more goodly and attract more eyes
> Than that which hath no foil to set it off.
> I'll so offend to make offense a skill,
> Redeeming time when men think least I will.
>
> (I. ii. 196–205)

"Redeeming time" is a commercial image and perhaps the key to the play. Hal will pay the debt he never promised, and perhaps we can say that that is the central idea of the play—the sense of debt, the idea of obligation. In a way, *1 Henry IV* is the literary form of Nietzsche's contention that all sense of moral obligation stems from the concept of the money debt. The issue of the play is: Will Hal pay the debt of kingship? Will he behave like a true prince and not a counterfeit? Hotspur has promised the debt: he has promised allegiance to Henry IV but he refuses to pay his debt. Likewise, Falstaff is unwilling to assume any kind of obligation. In short, the play sets off against each other two kinds of childishness or irresponsibility, Hotspur's chivalry and Falstaff's hedonism. It is up to Hal to find a middle road.

That seems to be the central issue of the play, though we have managed to derive it from only a half-dozen lines.

Falstaff. Hal, if thou see me down in the battle and bestride me, so! 'Tis a point of friendship.
Prince. Nothing but a colossus can do thee that friendship. Say thy prayers, and farewell.
Falstaff. I would 'twere bedtime, Hal, and all well.
Prince. Why, thou owest God a death.
Falstaff. 'Tis not due yet: I would be loath to pay him before his day.

> (V. i. 121–128)

That odd procedure, though, may be useful in itself, as a way of suggesting how, with an artist as great as Shakespeare, the central imaginative conception of the play will permeate and pervade even its smallest part. Essentially, Hal stands at the center of the play in a position of choice (see Fig. D). He must choose toward the high and right way of behaving, represented by his kingly father. He has before him two ways of falling short of that ideal. One is to continue his riotous play with Falstaff and his friends. The other is to become another Hotspur, which his father would like him to do. Hal himself finds Hotspur a little ridiculous, as, I think, we in the audience must. The images of the play distinguish among these three possibilities. "Grace," for example, is associated with monarchy as opposed to "fortune" which is associated with the rebels or the robbers. The legitimate king is associated with daylight and the sun-son while the rebels and the robbers are associated with night and the moon.

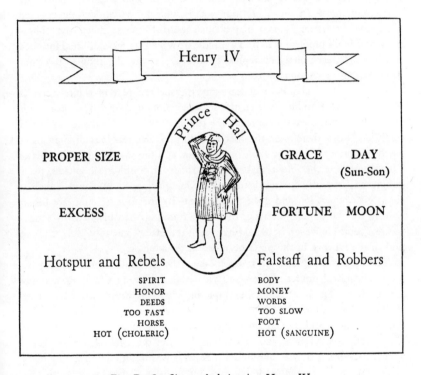

Fig. D. Conflicts and choices in 1 *Henry IV.*

Henry IV seems to be associated with proper size and timing whereas Falstaff is associated with an excess of body and Hotspur with an excess of spirit. Hotspur tends to do things too fast in time, Falstaff, too slow in time. Hal's problem is to "redeem" time. Then the play establishes likenesses and differences between these two ways of failing to meet one's debts and obligations, Hotspur's and Falstaff's. Hotspur is concerned with debts of honor; Falstaff is concerned with debts of money. Both concerns are treated as tradesmanlike. Just as Hotspur's deeds are false, so Falstaff's words are very often "counterfeits" or puns. Hotspur is associated with his horse repeatedly while many jokes are made about Falstaff's having to go on foot. Their names, Hot*spur* and Fal*staff*, are associated with going on horse and on foot respectively. The Elizabethan would have recognized that Hotspur was a particular character type, the choleric or angry man: his body-state is hot and dry. Falstaff, too, is an equally recognizable type, the sanguine man, the man fond of wine, women, song, and good food. Blood is the dominant fluid in his body, and his body-state is hot and moist. In short, Hotspur and Falstaff form two sharply opposed alternatives. *1 Henry IV* is a play about choosing so as to meet your obligations, and Hal's problem is to find a middle between two ways of life, Hotspur's and Falstaff's, each of which represents a different way of failing to pay your debts, failing to respond correctly to time.

In any play of choice, or at least any Elizabethan play of choice, there is likely to be some influence from the so-called morality plays. The theater for which Shakespeare wrote was really the fusion of two quite different theatrical traditions. First, there were the folk arts: the popular religious dramas, plays based on episodes from the Bible, saints' lives, and the so-called morality plays. Then there was the intellectual tradition shaped from classical sources, plays performed primarily for academic audiences, plays with humanistic themes about good education and good government. By the time Shakespeare began writing for the popular theaters, these two traditions had blended. In Shakespeare's youth, however, he would have seen the "pure" morality plays, and we find their influence in the plays he wrote as an adult.

The idea of a morality play was to show the Christian's soul standing between allegorical figures of vices and virtues and choosing rightly or wrongly among them. The most famous example in English is *Everyman,* whose hero at first chooses Good Fellowship, Goods, and other characters who stand for things of this world. Everyman is finally rescued from death by Knowledge, Confession, Good Deeds, and so on. The Vice, in these morality plays, came to be a trickster, a clown—like Falstaff. Now, it was traditional in the morality plays (not in *Everyman,* as it happens, but in others) for the Vice, that is, the character representing vice, to make his final exit carrying off the body of a condemned soul or a convenient devil, on his back to hell. Curiously, this is an exit Falstaff makes at the end of the play when he carries Hotspur's body off on his back, and Hotspur is called a "spirit"—by Falstaff. Another attribute of the Vice was that he carried a dagger of lath, that is a false dagger, a wooden sword which he would use the way a clown in a circus uses a slapstick. And, curiously, Falstaff threatens Hal, "If I do not beat thee out of thy kingdom with a dagger of lath, I'll never wear hair on my face more." We are also told, albeit in jest, that Falstaff has sold his soul to the devil. Indeed,

Poins says, "Thou soldest [it to] him on Good Friday last for a cup of Madeira and a cold capon's leg." To sell one's soul on Good Friday! for a cup of wine and a cold capon's leg!—is there something in the air of a black mass? a parody of the flesh and blood of Christ? Another aspect of the Vice was his capacity for deception, and this trickiness is one of the things Shakespeare stresses about Falstaff, his witty roguery and his "iffy" way of conjuring up imaginary worlds. In short, Falstaff shows a number of the attributes of a Vice, and to cap this suggestion, Prince Hal actually calls him one, "That reverend Vice," "That villainous abominable misleader of youth, Falstaff, that old white-bearded Satan."

We can think of Prince Hal, then, as the Christian hero of a morality play, overcoming both the Vice (Falstaff) and the devils ("that fiend Douglas, that spirit Percy, and that devil Glendower"). Just as Elizabethan drama as a whole represents a fusion of the intellectual, academic, political tradition with the religious, popular tradition, so in *Henry IV* we find traces of both. This is a political play, but it is told us in terms of religion and the trades of Shakespeare's homely audience. Hotspur is a political rebel but also a religious devil. Hal is the young Prince in a political and educational way, but he is also the Son in a religious sense, who will at the end of his career become the archetype of the Christian King. And Falstaff, whether or not he is a coward, is, in part at least, a Vice out of a medieval morality play. Beware of treating Shakespeare's characters as though they were real people. What a striking action it is for Falstaff to carry Hotspur off on his back, but it tells us nothing about his personality; it tells us only that he is a creation out of a quite traditional form of drama.

1 Henry IV shows how a great writer draws upon, and is influenced by, his tradition. Shakespeare's imagination, like every artist's imagination, is in part shaped by the kind of play he is trying to write; the kind of play he is trying to write is in turn determined by what his audience is used to and what it expects. We should notice, too, that Shakespeare is drawing on a *popular* tradition. The morality play is by modern standards surely a very crude (if gratifying) form of art. The fact that Shakespeare could draw on it and transmute it into so wonderful a thing as *1 Henry IV* should serve as an admonition to all of us not to snub the popular arts. The popular arts have a kind of vitality, a recurring appeal, that any artist ignores at his peril, while a purely intellectual art can become a very dull and arid thing when it is cut off from the wisdom of ordinary people. In no small part, Shakespeare's great achievement grows out of the fact that his imagination, as in this play of choice, worked within a theater which combined into one harmonious whole a popular and an intellectual tradition.

JULIUS CAESAR

OUR WHOLE AMERICAN CULTURAL TRADITION PULLS US, IN EFFECT, INTO A MIS-understanding of this play. To us, kings and dictators are bad. To us, liberty is good. To Shakespeare and his audience, however, the word "liberty" could be quite a doubtful virtue, particularly when shouted this way:

> *Cinna.*　Liberty! Freedom! Tyranny is dead!
> 　　　　　Run hence, proclaim, cry it about the streets!
> *Cassius.*　Some to the common pulpits and cry out
> 　　　　　'Liberty, freedom, and enfranchisement!'
>
> (III. i. 78–81)

Liberty, in that tone of voice, meant something close to what we know as license or anarchy. America began with a revolution, and we tend, at least initially, to look on revolutions with favor, but recent history (Castro? Nasser? Tito?) has made us a little wary.

> *Brutus.*　　　　　　　　　　　　Stoop, Romans, stoop,
> 　　　　　And let us bathe our hands in Caesar's blood
> 　　　　　Up to the elbows and besmear our swords.
> 　　　　　Then walk we forth, even to the market place,
> 　　　　　And waving our red weapons o'er our heads,
> 　　　　　Let's all cry 'Peace, freedom, and liberty!'
>
> (III. i. 105–110)

Is this the noble Brutus, smeared with blood, shouting slogans like a Middle Eastern or Latin American revolutionary? We have become a little more distrustful than we used to be of men who rush at us with bloody swords announcing peace, freedom, and liberty.

The Elizabethans reacted with more than just a little distrust. Shakespeare and his audience were horrified by the assassination of Julius Caesar, for to the

Elizabethans a king (or natural leader) was a good thing, a part of the rightful, providential order. Democracy, to most Elizabethans, would have seemed a mob rule, an unnatural situation in which the natural leader is forced to submit his will to those who are not natural leaders. Notice the way the citizens behave in this play, particularly the way they are so easily swayed by orators. First, Brutus makes his noble speech, explaining he killed Caesar to keep them all free citizens of a republic, not subjects of a king—they reply with, "Let him be Caesar!" "Caesar's better parts shall be crowned in Brutus!" Then Antony's speech turns the citizens right around into trying to lynch Brutus. Shakespeare is not being a snob. If you consider his plays as a whole, you will find that he always treats the common people with a measure of respect rather unusual among Elizabethan playwrights. But he treats them with respect as individuals; he has no use for them at all as a ruling class.

Notice, too, that in this play, which follows its historical source (Plutarch's *Lives*) fairly closely, the assassination of Caesar leads to civil war. Few things in the realm of political action were quite so appalling to the Elizabethans as civil war. They were still fairly close to the bloody Wars of the Roses, and they were exceedingly grateful for the rule of the Tudors, which put a stop to them—even at the expense of establishing what we would call today a dictatorship, albeit a fairly mild dictatorship. To the Elizabethans, in a general sense, kingship was the rightful way of organizing men into political groups. The assassination of Caesar just as he was about to achieve a monarchy was a terrible, tragic wrong, a wrong against the natural order of things. The omens the night before Caesar is killed, for example, are the same kind of omens as those the night Duncan is killed in *Macbeth,* and we need to think of Brutus as just as wrongheaded a killer as Macbeth was.

The curious thing is that Brutus himself seems to show a kind of glimmering awareness of the Elizabethan belief that a kingdom is the natural order not only for a political body, but for the planets, the mind and body of man, the animal "kingdom," indeed, the entire universe.

> *Brutus.* Between the acting of a dreadful thing
> And the first motion, all the interim is
> Like a phantasma or a hideous dream.
> The genius and the mortal instruments
> Are then in council, and the state of a man,
> Like to a little kingdom, suffers then
> The nature of an insurrection.
>
> (II. i. 63–69)

Brutus seems instinctively drawn to a kingdom as the image for the natural order of things and to an insurrection or civil war, such as he himself is planning, for disorder. Caesar, too, seems to have that same faint awareness:

These couchings and these lowly courtesies
Might fire the blood of ordinary men
And turn preordinance and first decree
Into the lane of children. Be not fond
To think that Caesar bears such rebel blood
That will be thawed from the true quality
With that which melteth fools—I mean, sweet words.
(III. i. 36–42)

He speaks of "preordinance and first decree," "the true quality"; he speaks of flattery (a most pernicious vice to Elizabethans) as trying to overthrow his kingly mind with *rebel* blood (a political image). In short, Shakespeare's Romans seem to have a glimmering of what the Elizabethans regarded as truth, the rightness of a natural, monarchical order.

Only a glimmering, though, and this partial awareness leads to another factor in the Elizabethan attitude toward the Romans, which needs to be taken into account to understand *Julius Caesar* as Shakespeare's audience did. The Romans, for all their brave humanistic and political achievements, were heathens. Unaware of the Christian dispensation, these pagans could do terribly wrong things—such as the suicides of Portia, Brutus, and Cassius. These are terrible sins, but they are committed in ignorance, because the Romans had no Christian revelation to supplement what they could learn by the glimmering light of reason. Because of this Elizabethan attitude, the tragedy has most of Shakespeare's rare references to philosophy. Brutus is evidently a Stoic; Cassius tells us that he himself was an Epicurean. Yet the events of the play, which are ordered in a Christian way, whether Brutus and Cassius know it or not, prove them wrong and, before they die, both Brutus and Cassius abandon their philosophies. Both seem to gain some faint awareness of what Brutus calls, "The providence of some high powers that govern us below."

No small part, then, of the attitude the play takes toward its Romans is that they are purely and simply wrongheaded. In all three of Shakespeare's important Roman plays, *Julius Caesar, Antony and Cleopatra,* and *Coriolanus,* he portrays the Romans in the same way. He draws them as so preoccupied with political and military affairs that they are unable to live their private lives, to love their children and their wives, to enjoy the simple creature comforts of this world in a reasonable way. Maybe Shakespeare was striking back at the Stratford Grammar School for all that Roman history he had to read from dawn to dusk and be birched for if he got it wrong. Perhaps that is why he makes his Romans all Hotspurs, leaving their wives behind to run after some crazy ambition. In *Julius Caesar,* for example, Caesar overrules his wife's wish that he stay home, and Brutus neglects his wife in favor of his enterprise; he leaves Portia to swallow fire and die alone.

Of course, Brutus is not a villain in any crude, moustache-twirling sense. He is, however, in the context of the play, profoundly and deeply wrong-headed, as wrongheaded as Shakespeare's other tragic mistakers, Macbeth, Lear, or Othello. For not accepting monarchy, he is mistaken in a political sense; but he is also mistaken in a far deeper way. Dante—and Dante is a good deal closer to Shakespeare than we are—put Brutus and Cassius in the ninth circle of hell, in the very mouth of Lucifer himself. Their sin was the worst sin of all, ingratitude. Sir Thomas Elyot, a sixteenth-century writer on education (and ancestor of T. S. Eliot), used Brutus and Cassius as the classic examples of ingratitude. In Shakespeare's source, Sir Thomas North's translation of Plutarch's *Lives,* the word this Elizabethan Englishman uses for Caesar's death is always "murder." And Shakespeare himself, in his early plays, wrote such lines as:

> Great men oft die by vile besonians.
>
> . . .
>
>   Brutus' bastard hand
> Stabb'd Julius Caesar.
>   (2 *Henry VI,* IV. i. 134-137)

or:

>   O traitors! murderers!
> They that stabb'd Caesar shed no blood at all,
> Did not offend, nor were not worthy blame,
> If this foul deed were by to equal it.
>   (3 *Henry VI,* V. v. 52-55)

In *Julius Caesar* the very omens themselves give a cosmic validation of this Elizabethan attitude toward the murder of Julius Caesar, that it was a terrible deed of regicide and ingratitude. A writer named John Weever may have been commenting on an actual performance of Shakespeare's *Julius Caesar* when he wrote this quatrain:

> The many-headed multitude were drawne
> By *Brutus* speach, that *Caesar* was ambitious,
> When eloquent *Mark Antonie* had showne
> His vertues, who but *Brutus* then was vicious?

It's not very good poetry, but it does suggest the Elizabethan attitude; Brutus was simply wrongheaded—"vicious."

His reasons for killing Caesar (a man who loved him, whom he supposedly loved) are almost unbelievably abstract. In a key soliloquy, he works them out for himself: (1) "I know no personal cause to spurn at him." (2) However, he wants to be crowned. (3) Even so, I have not known him to abuse power. (4) However, were he crowned, he might then begin to abuse his power. (5) "Then lest he may, prevent."

> It must be by his death; and for my part,
> I know no personal cause to spurn at him,
> But for the general. He would be crowned,
> How that might change his nature, there's the question.
> It is the bright day that brings forth the adder,
> And that craves wary walking. Crown him that,
> And then I grant we put a sting in him
> That at his will he may do danger with.
> Th' abuse of greatness is, when it disjoins
> Remorse from power. And to speak truth of Caesar,
> I have not known when his affections swayed
> More than his reason. But 'tis a common proof
> That lowliness is young ambition's ladder,
> Whereto the climber upward turns his face;
> But when he once attains the upmost round,
> He then unto the ladder turns his back,
> Looks in the clouds, scorning the base degrees
> By which he did ascend. So Caesar may.
> Then lest he may, prevent.
>
> (II. i. 10–28)

In other words, *if* Caesar were crowned, and *if* that changed his nature, he *might* prove dangerous.

> And since the quarrel
> Will bear no color for the thing he is,
> Fashion it thus: that what he is, augmented,
> Would run to these and these extremities.
>
> (28–31)

And on the basis of this conditional, abstract, imaginary reasoning, Brutus resolves to kill a man who loves him, whom he himself will later call "my best lover." *Et tu, Brute,* indeed!

All through *Julius Caesar,* the characters announce their love. Cassius, even as he is luring Brutus into the conspiracy, smiling to himself over his cleverness, tells Brutus he is "your friend that loves you." Antony, at the moment when he is taking the first steps in his revenge on the conspirators, says to them, "Friends am I with you all, and love you all." Most terribly, Brutus tells the crowd of citizens, "I slew my best lover for the good of Rome." And on and on —the citizens "loved" Pompey, but now love Caesar; Caesar loves the citizens, loves Brutus, loves Antony; Antony loves Caesar; Cassius loves Brutus; Brutus loves Cassius, and so on. The tragedy is full of people who talk a great deal of love, but do very little loving. All this talk of love coupled with the failure to make it gives the play a cold, stuffy, almost air-conditioned, chilliness.

This chilliness comes out in the language. The characters seem unable to talk to one another without making speeches. The very opening line of the play is the beginning of a street-corner oration: "Hence! home, you idle creatures, get you home! Is this a holiday?" Cassius, when he sets out to persuade his supposedly dearest friend Brutus to murder, does it as though he were wooing an audience. He starts with a question purely for rhetorical effect:

> Cassius. Tell me, good Brutus, can you see your face?
> Brutus.   No, Cassius; for the eye sees not itself
>   But by reflection, by some other things.
> Cassius. 'Tis just.
>   And it is very much lamented, Brutus,
>   That you have no such mirrors as will turn
>   Your hidden worthiness into your eye.
>   (I. ii. 51-57)

Cassius uses a more or less irrelevant "gimmick" to get Brutus involved, much like the beginning of a television commercial. We find the same kind of formal rhetoric even between wife and husband. Portia finds her husband walking troubled in the night. He says he is sick, and how does she reply?

> Brutus is wise and, were he not in health,
> He would embrace the means to come by it.
>   (II. i. 258-259)

Again,

> Is Brutus sick, and is it physical
> To walk unbracèd and suck up the humors
> Of the dank morning? What, is Brutus sick,
> And will he steal out of his wholesome bed
> To dare the vile contagion of the night,
> And tempt the rheumy and unpurgèd air,
> To add unto his sickness? No, my Brutus.
> You have some sick offense within your mind
>   (II. i. 261-268)

—a play of rhetorical questions and answers. She says she loves him; he says he loves her; but they seem unable to talk to each other without speechifying. All through *Julius Caesar,* we find faulty love. All through the language of the play, the characters seem to use the ways of *public* speech to try to express their *private* emotions; they show the flaw in love so very characteristic of *Julius Caesar*—people in that Rome seem unable to translate their *private* love into *public* action.

Julius Caesar is the most rhetorical of all Shakespeare's plays. It contains, of course, the two great speeches of persuasion, Brutus' address to the citizens and Antony's. It is Brutus' speech that most clearly shows this failure to bridge the gap between private man and public man, and notice, too, how he twists and distorts the real issue:

> Romans, countrymen, and lovers, hear me for my cause, and be silent, that you may hear. Believe me for mine honor, and have respect to mine honor that you may believe. Censure me in your wisdom and awake your senses, that you may the better judge. If there be any in this assembly, any dear friend of Caesar's, to him I say that Brutus' love to Caesar was no less than his. If then that friend demand why Brutus rose against Caesar, this is my answer: Not that I loved Caesar less, but that I loved Rome more. Had you rather Caesar were living, and die all slaves, than that Caesar were dead, to live all freemen? As Caesar loved me, I weep for him; as he was fortunate, I rejoice at it; as he was valiant, I honor him; but—as he was ambitious, I slew him. There is tears for his love; joy for his fortune; honor for his valor; and death for his ambition. Who is here so base that would be a bondman? If any, speak; for him have I offended. Who is here so rude that would not be a Roman? If any, speak; for him have I offended. Who is here so vile that will not love his country? If any, speak; for him have I offended. I pause for a reply.
>
> (III. ii. 13-33)

Not unsurprisingly, the citizens do not rush forward to proclaim their desire to be slaves or their dislike of Rome. The real matter at issue is: Were Brutus and the rest right in killing Caesar? By the end of his speech Brutus has twisted this issue into: Do you want to be a slave? Do you love your country? Any politician, indeed, any writer of television commercials, would be proud of such a speech. Like most of Brutus' discourse, his oration is full of abstract terms like "my cause," "mine honor," "valor," "fortune," "ambition." His whole justification is one of abstract principle—he killed a man he loved because he "loved Rome more." Brutus' appeal is a cold, stern, patrician appeal. He tells the citizens, in effect, he is an honorable man; therefore, they should trust him. "Believe me for mine honor, and have respect to mine honor, that you may believe."

Antony turns this appeal around on Brutus himself. Limited by his promise to the conspirators that he will not in his speech "blame" them, he resorts to irony. He turns Brutus' patrician appeal around by using the phrase "honorable man" (or "men") as an ironic refrain in his own oration. Seven times he repeats the phrase, all five flowing syllables of it, "ho-no-ra-ble men," until the crowd finally calls out, "They were traitors! Honorable men!" Antony uses the same trick to introduce the idea of mutiny in the citizens' mind by insisting that that is what he does not want to do:

> O masters! If I were disposed to stir
> Your hearts and minds to mutiny and rage,

> I should do Brutus wrong, and Cassius wrong,
> Who, you all know, are honorable men.
>
> (III. ii. 121–124)

Where Brutus spoke in cold prose, Antony's speech is in ringing verse. Contrast Brutus' opening words, "Romans, countrymen, and lovers," with the one-two-three-syllable march of Antony's far more effective, "Friends, Romans, countrymen."

There are far too many rhetorical effects in Antony's oration to analyze them all (like Brutus, he too ignores the real issue in favor of an irrational pleading); but there is a basic and sound appeal in Antony's words that Brutus' lacked. Antony accuses Brutus quite correctly of ingratitude.

> For Brutus, as you know, was Caesar's angel.
> Judge, O you gods, how dearly Caesar loved him!
> This was the most unkindest cut of all.
>
> (III. ii. 181–183)

Where Brutus showed ingratitude, Antony speaks love. He assures the citizens at length that Caesar greatly loved them, indeed, left them each a legacy in his will (though, right after this speech, Antony schemes to avoid the expenditure of actually paying the legacies in the will). Antony pleads his own love for the people: "You are not wood, you are not stones, but men." (These words contrast squarely with those of the two patricians in the opening scene of the play: "You blocks, you stones, you worse than senseless things!") In short, where Brutus and the other patricians look down on the people and appeal to them in terms of principle, Antony appeals to them in terms of love. And in the magnificently dramatic peak of his oration, having shown the citizens Caesar's pierced and bloody mantle, Antony makes the most direct appeal of all, the appeal to the body, as he throws the mantle back to reveal Caesar's pierced and bloody corpse.

It all comes back to Caesar. The ways we react to Brutus, to Cassius, to Antony depend on our reaction to Caesar. In school, I was taught to recite dutifully that Caesar is (1) superstitious, (2) pompous, and (3) weak. If he were all these things, then Brutus might rightfully object to his being king. But he is not.

Is Caesar superstitious? By modern standards, he is, of course. He believes in omens and auguries; he believes dreams are prophetic. He is superstitious by modern standards, but so is the play as a whole. The night before Caesar is killed, there are gliding ghosts; men all in fire walk up and down the streets,

> And yesterday the bird of night did sit
> Even at noonday upon the market place,
> Hooting and shrieking.
>
> (I. iii. 26–28)

And, as matters turn out, Calpurnia's dream that she saw the statue of Caesar spouting blood proves quite prophetic indeed. In fact, the most intelligent character in the play, Cassius, just before he dies, rejects the scientific view and says, "Now I change my mind and partly credit things that do presage."

In short, Caesar *in the context of the play* is quite correct in believing omens and auguries (and to believe what is correct is not "superstitious"). In fact, Caesar is wrong when he does *not* pay sufficient heed to Calpurnia's fears and the soothsayer's warning about the Ides of March. The only evidence the play gives us that Caesar is more superstitious than makes sense in the world of the play comes from Cassius, who tells us Caesar "is superstitious grown of late," but Cassius himself adopts "superstition" in his final wisdom. Cassius' opinion is seconded only by that doubtful character Decius Brutus, a most suspicious type, the character in Shakespeare who seems nearest to a true literary critic—notice the way he takes Calpurnia's dream and twists it subtly around by his interpretation to make it mean what he wants it to mean. The issue of Caesar's superstition represents one more case where we will distort the play if we pull the characters out of it and look at them in isolation. A play is a world, and to enjoy the play we need to enter that world. In the case of *Julius Caesar* (like *Macbeth*) it is a world of ghosts and prophecies, omens and auguries, and our modern notions of superstition simply do not apply.

Is Caesar pompous? Perhaps, but as the ruler of the entire civilized world perhaps he has a right to be. The thing that gives us the impression he is pompous, I think, is the fact that he usually speaks of himself in the third person: "Shall Caesar send a lie?" "What is now amiss that Caesar and his Senate must redress?" But Shakespeare as a boy had suffered through Caesar's *Gallic Wars,* and he knew that all through that book Caesar spoke of himself in the third person. Furthermore, not only Caesar, but Brutus and Cassius often speak of themselves in the third person or by their own names. Shakespeare is simply following here what he takes to be a Roman mannerism, just as his kings in the English history plays often speak of themselves as "the king" or "we" or "England."

Is Caesar a weak man? We do hear of several of his physical defects. Brutus reminds us that Caesar had the falling sickness or, as we would call it, epilepsy; and every schoolboy would have known how quick Caesar was to take advantage of that Roman kindness which allowed their bald ruler to wear a laurel wreath. Caesar himself reminds us that his left ear was deaf in a speech which illustrates quite clearly how he balances the public and private man in himself. He looks at Cassius and remarks to Antony,

> Yond Cassius has a lean and hungry look.
> He thinks too much. Such men are dangerous.
>
> (I. ii. 194–195)

He continues:

> He reads much,
> He is a great observer, and he looks
> Quite through the deeds of men. He loves no plays
> As thou dost, Antony; he hears no music.
> Seldom he smiles . . .
>
> (201–205)

and he takes these characteristics to illustrate to his protégé Antony, the younger politician, what a ruler can expect from such men, and, as matters turn out, his observation is deadly accurate:

> Such men as he be never at heart's ease
> Whiles they behold a greater than themselves,
> And therefore are they very dangerous.
> I rather tell thee what is to be feared
> Than what I fear; for always I am Caesar.
> Come on my right hand, for this ear is deaf,
> And tell me truly what thou think'st of him.
>
> (208–214)

There, in a sense, is the whole range of Caesar. He is the public man maintaining order in the state, instructing his successor; he is also the private man with his physical infirmities.

These physical infirmities do not of themselves make Caesar weak. What does is Caesar's seeming indecision and vacillation on the morning of the murder, when he decides not to go to the Senate, because Calpurnia has had a portentous dream. Then that doubtful Decius Brutus comes, and by a series of specious arguments persuades him to go. Here again, Shakespeare is stressing the dual nature of the ruler. He is a private man with a wife, whom he must humor—indeed, Caesar is far kinder to Calpurnia than Brutus is to Portia. At the same time, the purely private acts of the ruler, staying home one day, for example, have a public consequence. All through that scene (III. ii), Shakespeare very carefully shows us Caesar distinguishing between, for example, the reason he will give in public for staying home, and his private reason. True, he is swayed by Decius' argument, but who would not be swayed when a crown is at stake? Furthermore, this is a small, private matter in which he allows himself to be ruled by Decius. When it comes to public matters, he tells us (in a burst of pride the moment before the conspirators stab):

> But I am constant as the Northern Star,
> Of whose true-fixed and resting quality
> There is no fellow in the firmament.
> The skies are painted with unnumb'red sparks,
> They are all fire, and every one doth shine;

> But there's but one in all doth hold his place.
> So in the world: 'tis furnished well with men,
> And men are flesh and blood, and apprehensive;
> Yet in the number I do know but one
> That unassailable holds on his rank,
> Unshaked of motion; and that I am he.
>
> (III. i. 60–70)

He has stated what, to the Elizabethans, a monarch should be, the pole star among stars. His very phrasing, "I am he," suggests the balancing of public and private man which is the essence of the successful ruler.

Caesar, in short, is not superstitious, not simply pompous or weak. Perhaps, however, by answering these views, we have come to the center of the tragedy: the relationship between the public and the private man. That was an important theme in the great history plays, in *Richard II* or the *Henry IV* plays or *Henry V*, the theme of the public ruler and the private man, both embodied in the King. Now, when Shakespeare's imagination turns to tragedy he uses the same theme, embodied in the public and private aspects of Julius Caesar. This, the first of Shakespeare's great tragedies, represents a bridge between the history plays (which tend to concentrate on the public aspects of their heroes) and the tragedies (which tend to concentrate on the private). Thus, Shakespeare moves from plays which stress the explicitly political to plays which stress the interior and eternal problems of private men. Julius Caesar, then, is not just a political leader but a man who epitomizes something all of us have: the quality of being both private man and public. Caesar was on the one hand friend and husband; on the other, ruler and public leader. His very name contains these two sides: "Julius," his family name; "Caesar," that word that has dominated the European imagination even into such modern survivals as "Kaiser" and "Czar." He was both private and public man, physical body and almost holy spirit. The tragedy of Brutus and Cassius—for this is a joint tragedy like *Romeo and Juliet* or *Antony and Cleopatra*—their tragedy lies in their partial attitudes toward this totality.

This division into body and spirit occurs in the very opening scene, in which the two tribunes, Flavius and Marullus, berate some citizens for turning out to give Caesar a hero's welcome. In the very first speech of the play, Flavius says,

> What, know you not,
> Being mechanical, you ought not walk
> Upon a laboring day without the sign
> Of your profession?

The public man, wearing the sign of his profession; the private man on holiday. The cobbler, to whom Marullus speaks, makes a series of puns ending with the idea that he is a mender of bad soles, the sole of the shoe and the soul of the spirit. And in that rather crude pun, "sole" and "soul," lies the central theme of the tragedy; Caesar the sole, private man; Caesar the spirit, the "soul" of Rome.

To Brutus, Caesar seems primarily a public man. The crucial speech in which Brutus decides to kill Caesar is a soliloquy, and the convention of a soliloquy is that it is the truth as far as the character knows it. He may be deceiving himself, but he is not deceiving the audience. In other words, Brutus is saying what he truly believes when he says, "For my part, I know no personal cause to spurn at him, but for the general." He speaks of what Caesar *may* become. "Then lest he may, prevent." "Since the quarrel will bear no color for the thing he is, fashion it thus: that what he is augmented would run to these and these extremities." In other words, Brutus rejects his personal, private feeling for Caesar in favor of the public cause. Not only that, but he defines that public cause in the most abstract and conditional terms possible. Later, he says to Cassius and the other conspirators,

> We all stand up against the spirit of Caesar,
> And in the spirit of men there is no blood.
> O that we then could come by Caesar's spirit
> And not dismember Caesar! But, alas,
> Caesar must bleed for it!
>
> (II. i. 167–171)

Just as he decides to kill Caesar because *if* he were crowned, he *might* abuse his power, so here, he wishes to get only at the man's spirit without killing the man (a touchingly idealistic wish). Brutus seems to walk in a world of abstractions and ideals, as in his abstract oration to the mob. He speaks to the conspirators of their "cause," and later, when he quarrels with Cassius, he says:

> Did not great Julius bleed for justice sake?
> What villain touched his body that did stab
> And not for justice?
>
> (IV. iii. 19–21)

It is, however, a peculiar notion of justice that leads to murder. As Antony accuses this pious idealist,

> In your bad strokes, Brutus, you give good words;
> Witness the hole you made in Caesar's heart,
> Crying 'Long live! Hail, Caesar!'
>
> (V. i. 30–32)

There is a terrible irony in Antony's words over Brutus' body at the end:

> This was the noblest Roman of them all.
> All the conspirators save only he

> Did that they did in envy of great Caesar;
> He, only in a general honest thought
> And common good to all, made one of them.
>
> (V. v. 68–72)

It is precisely the generality of Brutus' "general honest thought" that enables
him to stab his "best lover" for a "cause." Brutus' thought, if honest or noble,
is terribly abstract. Of Caesar the public and private man, Brutus separates out
and sees only the public or symbolic side, the "spirit of Caesar."

Cassius is just the opposite. He sees Caesar almost entirely as simply another
individual like himself,

> A man no mightier than thyself or me
> In personal action, yet prodigious grown.
>
> (I. iii. 76–77)

Caesar is exactly right when he says of Cassius,

> Such men as he be never at heart's ease
> Whiles they behold a greater than themselves,
> And therefore are they very dangerous.
>
> (I. ii. 208–210)

In Cassius' great speech where he defines his motives, he makes it quite literally
true that he would "as lief not be as live to be in awe of such a thing as I
myself." He sees Caesar primarily in body terms, as a man in a bodily sense
no different from Cassius, and here Shakespeare is psychologically very wise,
for we all see the world the way we see ourselves. Cassius sees himself—and so
Caesar—as "a thing":

> I cannot tell what you and other men
> Think of this life; but for my single self,
> I had as lief not be as live to be
> In awe of such a thing as I myself.
> I was born free as Caesar; so were you.
> We both have fed as well, and we can both
> Endure the winter's cold as well as he.

He describes a swimming-match between himself and Caesar, a bodily contest,
which Caesar lost; and he bitterly complains,

> And this man
> Is now become a god, and Cassius is
> A wretched creature and must bend his body
> If Caesar carelessly but nod on him.
> He had a fever when he was in Spain,
> And when the fit was on him, I did mark
> How he did shake. 'Tis true, this god did shake.
> His coward lips did from their color fly,

And that same eye whose bend doth awe the world
Did lose his luster. I did hear him groan.
Ay, and that tongue of his that bade the Romans
Mark him and write his speeches in their books,
'Alas,' it cried, 'give me some drink, Titinius,'
As a sick girl! Ye gods, it doth amaze me
A man of such a feeble temper should
So get the start of the majestic world
And bear the palm alone.

(I. ii. 93-131)

To Cassius, Caesar is nothing but another body: "Upon what meat doth this our Caesar feed that he is grown so great?" And when he is about to stab Caesar, he cries out, "As low as to thy foot doth Cassius fall," showing that same sense of his own lowness, which makes him hold Caesar also in contempt, which makes him see Caesar only as a body.

Where Brutus was an idealist, Cassius is a realist. After the assassination, Antony enters; Brutus holds out to him friendship, "all kind love, good thoughts, and reverence." Cassius, however, says, "Your voice shall be as strong as any man's in the disposing of new dignities." In other words, he promises Antony his share of the spoils. Brutus and Cassius are opposites. Cassius, if you like, is the party politician; Brutus is the reformer. Brutus is the idealist, Cassius the realist. Cassius sees only the body of Caesar; Brutus sees only the spirit of Caesar—indeed, it is only to Brutus that the spirit, the ghost, of Caesar appears.

Not just in Brutus and Cassius, though, but all through the tragedy, in its incidents and imagery, the division between body and spirit, private and public, appears. There is the actual bodily assassination as opposed to the omens, portents, and auguries from the world of spirits. There is the cobbler's disgraceful pun on the "soul" as opposed to the "sole" of the foot. There is the little incident in which Caius Ligarius, a man with a cold in his head, comes to see Brutus and join the conspirators, in "a piece of work that will make sick men whole," and make whole men sick.

There is Brutus' abstract oration as opposed to Antony's concrete appeal to the body of Caesar. We hear about Caesar's epilepsy and his deafness; we hear about Calpurnia's barrenness and Portia's inflicting on herself a voluntary wound in her thigh. We see, but do not hear about, Antony's body stripped for the race run on the feast of Lupercal. (This is a favorite device of Shakespeare's when he is stressing the idea of the physical body, to show us on the stage a stripped body.) Cassius tells us that Caesar "doth bestride the narrow world like a Colossus, and we petty men walk under his huge legs." And Caesar says of Cassius in the famous line, "Yond Cassius has a lean and hungry look."

We hear of eyes, as when Cassius begins his temptation of Brutus by asking him, "Can you see your face?" And Brutus replies, "No, Cassius. For the eye sees not itself but by reflection, by some other things." It is a perfect image for the relation between Brutus and his opposite, Cassius—they are like opposed reflections of each other. The eye image recurs when Brutus cries out as he sees the ghost of Caesar, "I think it is the weakness of mine eyes that shapes this monstrous apparition." And again, in the final battle when Cassius commits suicide under the mistaken impression that Brutus has lost his half of the battle, Cassius says, "My sight was ever thick." In other words, he was nearsighted. The eye acquires a kind of symbolic value; it stands for the faulty split perception of the natural order that leads Brutus and Cassius into the murder, that makes Cassius see Caesar only as a body and Brutus see him as a "monstrous apparition."

Blood, too, is another part of the body that acquires a symbolic status. We hear of Caesar's blood spouting from his statue in Calpurnia's dream and of a rain of blood upon the Capitol the night before the murder. Brutus insists that the conspirators bathe their hands in Caesar's blood as a symbolic gesture. Antony shows Caesar's bloody garment to the crowd in his oration. Similarly, the heart acquires a symbolic value. Caesar's heart burst at Brutus' ingratitude, and Cassius offers to give Brutus his heart instead of gold. In the Elizabethan world-picture, the heart is the highest of the organs, and on that fateful morning of the Ides of March, when the augurers open the beast and find its body has no heart, it is as if to say that the political body, the state, will soon lack its highest organ, Caesar. Indeed, after his death, Antony standing over his body murmurs a frightful pun:

> Pardon me, Julius! Here wast thou bayed, brave hart;
> Here didst thou fall; and here thy hunters stand,
> Signed in thy spoil, and crimsoned in thy lethe.
> O world, thou wast the forest to this hart;
> And this indeed, O world, the heart of thee!
>
> (III. i. 204–208)

Not only the parts of the body, however, take on symbolic values; natural objects do, also. This play repeatedly speaks about animals, which in turn stand for the characters. That is, Caesar, we are told, is like a serpent, a lion, an adder, a stricken deer. Brutus is a lamb, and Cassius is a horse. Lepidus, poor Lepidus, is an ass. Other natural objects tend to acquire a symbolic value. For example, there is a symbolic value given the Northern Star which serves as an emblem when Caesar compares himself to that unmoving pole. Brutus speaks of the *ladder* of ambition and the *kingdom* of man. In another famous speech, he says:

> There is a tide in the affairs of men
> Which, taken at the flood, leads on to fortune;

> Omitted, all the voyage of their life
> Is bound in shallows and in miseries.
> On such a full sea are we now afloat,
> And we must take the current when it serves
> Or lose our ventures.
>
> (IV. iii. 218–223)

Other characters tell us of a symbolic significance in the setting sun. In short, over and over again in this play, the literal events of everyday life are given a symbolic or emblematic significance. That should come as no surprise, for when everything is in a great chain of being, a fixed hierarchy, as in the Elizabethan world-picture where fact and value are each implicit in the other, everything in reality has a symbolic value. Perhaps, then, the eighteenth-century critics were right when they complained that Shakespeare's Romans were insufficiently Roman. They are not Romans at all, really, but Elizabethans, and the world they describe to us is a world of Elizabethan values, not Roman. In the Elizabethan universe, represented here as Rome, literal events are emblems of cosmic ones; the acts of our bodies reach for a spiritual consequence. Body and spirit are one.

So is the play. Sometimes people say this play is wrongly titled *Julius Caesar* because it really is the tragedy of Brutus. Brutus appears throughout the play, they say, while Caesar is somewhat forcibly dropped out of sight in Act III, scene i. This is not so at all: Julius Caesar dominates this tragedy from beginning to end. We hear about the body of Caesar from the opening scene (his "images" decked with trophies) until the assassination. It is the spirit of Caesar that dominates the second half of the play. Indeed, Brutus himself recognizes it:

> Oh, Julius Caesar, thou art mighty yet!
> Thy spirit walks abroad and turns our swords
> In our own proper entrails.
>
> (V. iii. 94–96)

The point of transition from the first movement of this tragedy, concerned with Caesar's body, to the second movement, concerned with Caesar's spirit, comes in Antony's soliloquy just after the assassination. Antony has pretended to make his peace with the rebels. They in turn have left him alone with Caesar's body as Brutus goes out to address the crowd. The speech moves from Caesar's body, which has dominated the first half of the play, to his spirit, which will dominate the second half of the play.

> O, pardon me, thou bleeding piece of earth,
> That I am meek and gentle with these butchers!
> Thou are the ruins of the noblest man
> That ever livèd in the tide of times.
> Woe to the hand that shed this costly blood!

Over thy wounds now do I prophesy
(Which, like dumb mouths, do ope their ruby lips
To beg the voice and utterance of my tongue),
A curse shall light upon the limbs of men;
Domestic fury and fierce civil strife
Shall cumber all the parts of Italy;
Blood and destruction shall be so in use
And dreadful objects so familiar
That mothers shall but smile when they behold
Their infants quarterèd with the hands of war,
All pity choked with custom of fell deeds;
And Caesar's spirit, ranging for revenge,
With Atè by his side come hot from hell,
Shall in these confines with a monarch's voice
Cry, 'Havoc!' and let slip the dogs of war,
That this foul deed shall smell above the earth
With carrion men, groaning for burial.

(III. i. 254–275)

Antony is unlike Caesar's other two sons, if I may call them that. He is unlike Brutus, who could see Caesar only as a spirit and as an abstraction, and unlike Cassius, who could see him only as a body, as a private man like Cassius himself. Antony sees *both* the body *and* the spirit of Caesar. And in his speech, moving from Caesar's body to his spirit ranging for revenge, we have the culminating image of all those occasions in the tragedy when physical, natural objects beget spiritual consequences.

We have come very close to the central tragic conception of *Julius Caesar*. The play gives us a world in which body and spirit, real things and symbolic, are all bound up together. This ordered universe Brutus and Cassius tear apart into civil war by separating the body and spirit of Caesar, by killing him. As in *Macbeth,* we have a joint tragedy, a tragedy of two people who kill together and die separately. They are totally different, hopelessly mismatched, yet each needs the other. Their tragedy lies in the fact that they are two and not one. Brutus, we have seen, is the idealist, the man of spirit. Cassius is the practical, positivistic realist, the man of body. Each of our two villains, for that is what they are, reflects a separate aspect of Caesar, one his spirit, the other his body. Each is terribly mismatched with the other, as we see in their famous quarrel scene. The quarrel comes about because of a man who is condemned by Brutus for having taken bribes. Cassius has spoken for leniency, because the man has a certain amount of pull with him. Cassius, the political realist, points out quite accurately, "In such a time as this it is not meet that every nice offense should bear his comment." But Brutus gets all huffy and stuffy and idealistic and replies with pious utterances about "justice," none of which are particularly helpful in the matter at hand. The same hopeless mismatch shows in Cassius'

Mr. WILLIAM

SHAKESPEARES

COMEDIES,
HISTORIES, &
TRAGEDIES.

Published according to the True Originall Copies.

Martin Droeshout sculpsit London.

LONDON
Printed by Isaac Iaggard, and Ed. Blount. 1623.

Fig. 1. Title page of the First Folio (1623).

Fig. 2. An innyard stage (reconstruction by C. Walter Hodges).

Fig. 3. The Globe Theatre as shown in Visscher's View of London (1616).

The Globe

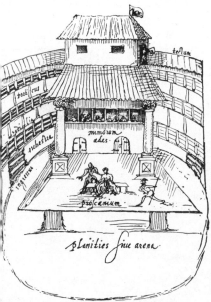

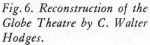

Fig. 4. Inside the Swan Theatre (c. 1596). A copy by Arend Van Buchel of a drawing by Johannes de Witt.

Fig. 5. Frontispiece from Francis Kirkman's The Wits *(1672).*

Fig. 6. Reconstruction of the Globe Theatre by C. Walter Hodges.

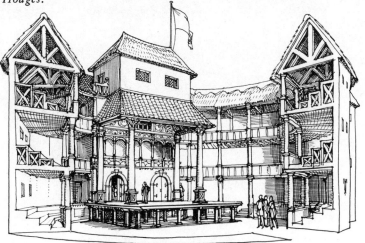

Fig. 7. *Drawing attributed to Henry Peacham of a scene from* Titus Andronicus *(c.1594).*

Fig. 8. *The Cosmos— a drawing from Robert Fludd's* History of the Greater and Lesser Worlds *(1617).*

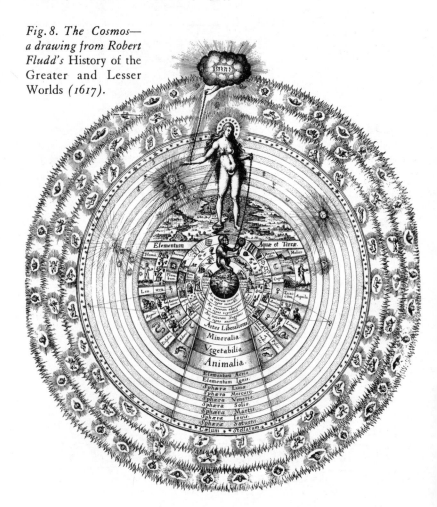

Fig. 9. Painting by Zoffany of David Garrick and Mrs. Pritchard in Macbeth (1776).

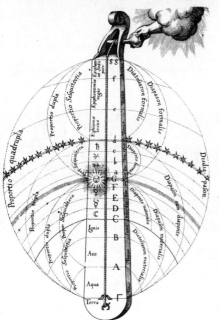

Fig. 10. The Music of the Spheres—from Fludd's History (1617).

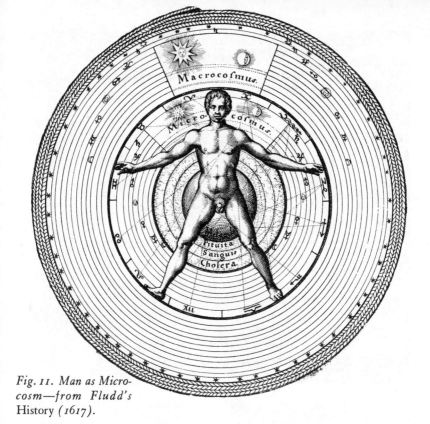

Fig. 11. Man as Micro-
cosm—from Fludd's
History (1617).

Fig. 12. Macbeth and Banquo meet the witches—from
Holinshed's Chronicles (1577).

AN
EXCELLENT
conceited Tragedie
OF
Romeo and Iuliet.

As it hath been often (with great applause)
plaid publiquely, by the right Ho-
nourable the L. of *Hunsdon*
his Seruants.

LONDON,
Printed by Iohn Danter.
1597

Fig. 13. Title page of the First Quarto of Romeo and Juliet.

Fig. 14. Charles Macklin (c.1697-1797) as Shylock (1741).

The most excellent
Historie of the *Merchant*
of Venice.

VVith the extreame crueltie of *Shylocke* the Iewe
towards the sayd Merchant, in cutting a iust pound
of his flesh: and the obtayning of *Portia*
by the choyse of three
chests.

As it hath beene diuers times acted by the Lord
Chamberlaine his Seruants.

Written by William Shakespeare.

AT LONDON,
Printed by *I. R.* for Thomas Heyes,
and are to be sold in Paules Church-yard, at the
signe of the Greene Dragon.
1 6 o o.

Fig. 15. Title page of the First Quarto of The Merchant of Venice.

Fig. 16. Thomas Betterton (c. 1635-1710) as Hamlet.

Fig. 17. A Sketch by John Nixon of David Garrick (1717-1779) as Hamlet (1775).

Fig. 18. John Phillip Kemble (1757-1823) as Hamlet.

Fig. 19. Henry Irving (1838-1905) as Hamlet.

Fig. 20. Edwin Booth
(1833-1893) as Hamlet.

Fig. 21. Maurice Evans
as Hamlet.

Fig. 22. *John Barrymore (1882-1942) as Hamlet.*

Fig. 23. *Leslie Howard (1893-1943) as Hamlet.*

Fig. 24. Sir Laurence Olivier in the film Hamlet.

Fig. 25. John Gielgud as Hamlet.

strange soliloquy, after he has persuaded Brutus to join the cause. Brutus, he says, is honorable, while he, Cassius, is not, and therefore can bend and twist him. "Therefore it is meet that noble minds keep ever with their likes; for who so firm that cannot be seduced?"

Their tragedy is that, mismatched as they are, yet they each need the other. Brutus is an idealist, a philosopher, a man of thought, not action. It is Cassius, the realist, the practical man, who begins the enterprise. But precisely because Cassius is the practical realist, people do not respect him. He must have Brutus because "That which would appear offense in us, his countenance . . . will change to virtue and to worthiness." Yet once he gets Brutus, the supposed figurehead for the conspiracy, the figurehead takes over, and Brutus promptly proceeds to make the four mistakes that doom himself and Cassius to failure.

Cassius suggests that they get Cicero into the conspiracy, but Brutus refuses: "He will never follow anything that other men begin." In other words, I, Brutus, am the figurehead for this conspiracy; we don't need another. But, oh, as matters turn out, they did so desperately need an orator. Cassius suggests that it would be no bad thing to murder Antony while they're murdering Caesar, but Brutus refuses:

> Antony is but a limb of Caesar.
> Let's be sacrificers, but not butchers, Caius.
> (II. i. 165–166)

("Sacrificers but not butchers"—the kind of nice distinction that so satisfies an idealist like Brutus, particularly when he is committing a murder.) After the assassination, Antony asks if he can make a little speech over Caesar's body and Brutus very piously agrees. Cassius, who is wiser, says, "Brutus, a word with you," and he warns him that this is a rather risky thing to do. But Brutus replies: "By your pardon—I will myself into the pulpit first and show the reason of our Caesar's death." And we all remember how splendidly Brutus' oratory turns the trick. The final mistake that Brutus forces on Cassius comes out of that splendidly abstract and general speech, "There is a tide in the affairs of men." He insists that they must fight at Philippi right away. Cassius reluctantly agrees, Octavius and Antony crow, "Our hopes are answered," and the conspirators lose and die.

The tragedy of Brutus and Cassius, then, is that these two, the realist and the idealist, both need the other yet both defeat the other; they cannot succeed because they are two and not one. So separated, the idealism defeats the realism instead of fulfilling it. This split is nicely imaged in the strategy of the final battle, an episode, by the way, where Shakespeare altered history to make his point. Cassius and Brutus divide their armies into two parts, an image for that separation which dogs them to their downfall. Brutus wins over

Octavius, while Antony wins over Cassius. Yet all was not lost, "it is but change," a draw. Then, precisely because of their separateness, they lose. Cassius, who was thick of sight, nearsighted, mistook matters and thought that Brutus had been defeated when actually Brutus had won. Cassius then committed suicide, and all was indeed lost. This, then, is the essence of the tragedy of Brutus and Cassius: they are each but half a Caesar. Had both their qualities been in one man, there would have been no tragedy. They were, in fact, in one man, namely, Caesar.

This idea of the separation of body and spirit occurs in still another central image of the play—the day. The opening line of the play is, "Hence! home, you idle creatures, get you home! Is this a holiday?" The very last words of the play are "this happy day." We are told in advance about the day of the assassination, "Beware the Ides of March" and when the conspirators meet at Brutus' they make small talk by debating how close it is to daybreak and where the sun will rise. Just before Brutus and Cassius separate for the battle at Philippi, Brutus notes, "This same day must end that work the Ides of March began." "Oh that a man might know the end of this day's business ere it come! But it sufficeth that the day will end, and then the end is known." And Cassius' death, too, carries out this image of the day. Cassius dies on the very day he was born (even as Shakespeare did—though I suppose he had no way of knowing that at the time he wrote the play). As Cassius says:

> This day I breathèd first. Time is come round,
> And where I did begin, there shall I end.
> My life is run his compass.
>
> (V. iii. 23-25)

Titinius' speech spells out the story:

> Cassius is no more. Oh setting sun,
> As in thy red rays thou dost sink to night,
> So in his red blood Cassius' day is set!
> The sun of Rome is set. Our day is gone.
> (V. iii. 60-62)

The rest of the image of the day is, of course, night, night when the body and the spirit are separated, when we dream, when the world of spirit manifests itself in omens and auguries. There was the fearful night before the assassination with its strange, fiery omens. It was at night that Caesar's ghost appeared to Brutus. The innocent man sleeps at night. As Caesar wisely says, "Let me have men about me that are fat, sleek-headed men, and such as sleep a-nights." Brutus sees the innocent servant, the boy Lucius, sleeping as Brutus and the conspirators meet; sleeping again even as Brutus sees Caesar's ghost. It is a sign of the moral disorder of Brutus and Cassius that we never see them sleep a-nights. (Remember, "Macbeth shall sleep no more.")

Brutus and Cassius have violated and broken the normal rhythm of night and day. They have thrust night, the time of dreams, when body and spirit separate, into the day of Rome. They have plunged Rome into the darkness of civil war and murder, as indeed the omens before Caesar's assassination foretold: "The bird of night did sit even at noonday upon the market place, hooting and shrieking." Brutus and Cassius have violated the day as well, the day when a man's spirit and his body should walk together. Instead, in the form of Brutus and Cassius themselves, they walk as two men.

This, then, is why *Julius Caesar* is a tragedy of separateness, the separating of body and spirit, private and public, fact and symbol. Those qualities, which joined in one man made the kingly Caesar, when split into two men in Brutus and Cassius, make a pair of wretched murderers. These murderers violate and wrench the normal rhythm of day and night in which body and spirit separate and come together, separate and come together, with all the regularity and rhythm of life itself.

9

HAMLET

THERE ARE FOUR SUBJECTS ON WHICH MORE BOOKS ARE WRITTEN THAN ANYTHING else in the world—or so have I heard, and do in part believe it. The first three are: Christ, Napoleon, and Shakespeare; the fourth is *Hamlet*. While all these books about *Hamlet* are rather a trial and tribulation to the professional Shakespearean, they do serve to prove that *Hamlet* is a play which dazzles the imagination, a play which piques and puzzles us until we project upon it—ourselves. *Hamlet,* these books say, is an enigmatic play, and its enigma is: Why does Hamlet delay? As we shall see, this is an odd and perhaps downright wrong way of trying to grasp the tragedy. It is, though, the one most people take, and far be it from me to spurn anything so useful as a jumping-off place.

Why does Hamlet delay? That is the question. By the end of Act I, the Ghost has spoken to Hamlet and ordered him to revenge his foul and most unnatural murder. But it is not until four acts and almost three thousand lines later (*Hamlet,* by the way, is the longest of Shakespeare's plays), that Hamlet gets around finally to carrying out his father's command. In the meantime, he has been going through a great deal of fuss and feathers. He has played mad, and while his antics amuse and intrigue his audience, they contribute nothing to his revenge. He has meditated upon skulls in the graveyard. He has cajoled some actors into putting on a play for his uncle, his father's murderer, but he has not revenged his father. By the time he finally does revenge his father, no less than seven extra people are murdered in the process: the old dotard Polonius; the Bobbsey twins, Rosencrantz and Guildenstern; the innocent Ophelia; her choleric brother, Laertes; Hamlet's mother, Queen Gertrude (his father had warned him, "Leave her to heaven"), and finally, of course, Hamlet himself. Surely, Hamlet is the most magnificent failure the world has ever known, and he fails because he delays.

Why does Hamlet delay? There are three common answers to this question. The first is that Hamlet really doesn't delay at all. One group of critics argues that Hamlet acts as fast as he can be expected to act under the circumstances. If he were to rush right out and kill Claudius, these critics say, he would be killed himself; he might expose his mother's guilt, which he is supposed to keep quiet; Claudius' guards might kill Hamlet and so make revenge impossible; and so on. But this line of reasoning, I think, will simply not hold up.

First of all, there is something peculiar in this conditional talk about a play. A play, or any work of art, is finished; it is complete, given; nothing in it can be any different. When we say *if* Hamlet were to do so-and-so, *then* such-and-such would happen, then we are not talking about Shakespeare's play; we are talking about some other play in which "so-and-so" and "such-and-such" happen, not Shakespeare's *Hamlet*. It is a logical error to create a hypothetical play *Hamlet* in which some other set of events takes place and then measure Shakespeare's *Hamlet* against that hypothetical un-*Hamlet*. Furthermore, the facts of the play simply will not bear out the idea that Hamlet acts as fast as he can under the circumstances. Consider the timetable. There are three references in the play which fix for us the times the critical events take place. In Act I, scene ii, Hamlet bemoans the fact that his mother's affection shifted so suddenly from his father:

> Why she would hang on him
> As if increase of appetite had grown
> By what it fed on, and yet within a month—
> Let me not think on't; frailty, thy name is woman—
> A little month. . . .

> (I. ii. 143–151)

"she, even she . . . married with my uncle." He is speaking the morning after we in the audience have first seen the Ghost. A few lines above these words, Hamlet says his father is "But two months dead, nay, not so much, not two."

So far, we have this much of a timetable: Hamlet's father died; one month later, his mother married his uncle; two months (or less than two months) after Hamlet Senior's death, the Ghost began to appear. Now, in Act III, scene ii, just before the play-within-the-play, Hamlet is clowning about with Ophelia, and he rather snidely says, "Look you how cheerfully my mother looks, and my father died within's two hours." Ophelia corrects him: "Nay, 'tis twice two months, my lord," and her words fill in the rest of the timetable. It is twice two months, four months, since Hamlet's father died: there have been two months between his death and the appearance of the Ghost, so that two months or more have elapsed since the Ghost gave the command to revenge. In that time Hamlet has done nothing but play mad, insult Ophelia, amuse himself with the actors, and set up the play-within-the-play. For two months or more, Hamlet has done nothing or, for all practical purposes, nothing to further his revenge.

Now, it is true that Hamlet has a problem about that Ghost: as he says,

> The spirit that I have seen
> May be a devil, and the devil hath power
> T'assume a pleasing shape; yea, and perhaps
> Out of my weakness and my melancholy,
> As he is very potent with such spirits,
> Abuses me to damn me.
>
> (II. ii. 584–589)

Perhaps the Ghost is a devil in disguise trying to trick Hamlet into committing the mortal sin of murder. But Hamlet says this the night before the play-within-the-play. In other words, he has waited two months or more before taking any step to check the Ghost's veracity—he still delays. Contrast this two-month lag with his words to the Ghost when he saw him:

> Haste me to know't, that I, with wings as swift
> As meditation or the thoughts of love,
> May sweep to my revenge,
>
> (I. v. 29–31)

or to Horatio at that time:

> Touching this vision here,
> It is an honest ghost, that let me tell you.
>
> (I. v. 137–138)

For all this eagerness, Hamlet waits two months before taking the first step in his revenge, validating the Ghost.

Even more important, though, than this timetable, which, resting on only a few lines, could well slip by us in an actual performance, is the fact that Hamlet himself says he delays. He says it best in the famous "Hecuba" soliloquy—after listening to an actor passionately deliver a speech about Queen Hecuba's misery at the fall of Troy, he cries,

> What's Hecuba to him, or he to Hecuba,
> That he should weep for her?
>
> (II. ii. 543–544)

and wonders to himself how the actor can so work himself up over a fictitious cause, while he, Hamlet,

> for a king,
> Upon whose property and most dear life
> A damned defeat was made,
>
> (554–556)

can seem to do nothing:

> Yet I,
> A dull and muddy-mettled rascal, peak
> Like John-a-dreams, unpregnant of my cause,
> And can say nothing.
>
> (551–553)

Further, not only Hamlet himself, but also the Ghost accuses him of delay. When he breaks into Hamlet's interview with his mother, Hamlet says, guiltily,

> Do you not come your tardy son to chide,
> That, lapsed in time and passion, lets go by
> Th' important acting of your dread command?
> (III. iv. 107–109)

And the Ghost replies,

> This visitation
> Is but to whet thy almost blunted purpose.
> (111–112)

Still a further answer to those people who say that Hamlet acts as quickly as he can under the circumstances lies in the fact that neither Hamlet nor the Ghost ever mentions an external reason for Hamlet's delay. They do not say, as the critics do, that Claudius' guards will kill Hamlet, that Hamlet's mother's guilt will be revealed, or that Hamlet himself might be killed in the action. In short, we cannot assume that Hamlet acts as quickly as he can under the circumstances, because Hamlet never refers to those circumstances; nor does he himself think that he is acting as quickly as he can; nor does the Ghost.

There is a third and final answer to the notion that Hamlet does not delay: Laertes. Laertes, too, has had a dear father murdered, and he, like Hamlet, holds Claudius responsible. Hamlet himself points out the parallel when he remarks, "By the image of my cause I see the portraiture of his," that is, Laertes'. But where Hamlet, for two months or more, plays mad, reads books, insults his girlfriend, and directs plays, Laertes acts immediately. A messenger comes to Claudius, crying out,

> The ocean, overpeering of his list,
> Eats not the flats with more impiteous haste
> Than young Laertes, in a riotous head,
> O'erbears your officers.
> (IV. v. 99–102)

No sooner has he returned from France, than Laertes has stirred up a mob, begun a revolution, and he is ready to assassinate Claudius on the spot. How can we say, then, that Hamlet, whose cause is the same as Laertes', acts as quickly as one could under the circumstances? Hamlet *does* delay.

Why does Hamlet delay? We come back to the question, and to the second of the customary answers to it: Hamlet delays because Shakespeare had to make the play last five acts. As an anonymous eighteenth-century critic put it: "Had Hamlet gone naturally to work, as we could suppose such a prince to do in parallel circumstances, there would have been an end of our play. The poet therefore was obliged to delay his hero's revenge; but then he should have contrived some good reason for it." In our own day, the most famous expositor of this point of view is T. S. Eliot. He concludes that "Hamlet [the man] is dominated by an emotion which is inexpressible because it is in excess of the facts as they appear." And Mr. Eliot concludes, "So far from being Shakespeare's masterpiece, the play is most certainly an artistic failure." I suppose it would be cruel of me to point out that Mr. Eliot was twenty-nine when he wrote this, and there is no denying that one way for a rising young poet to call attention to himself is to call perhaps the world's greatest play an artistic failure. Even so, Mr. Eliot has never recanted, and, oddly enough, I think he is right. Of the three reasons for Hamlet's delay, this is the one, silly as it sounds, I would agree with—not, of course, in the form that Shakespeare simply had to make his play last five acts. On the contrary, he could have had Hamlet kill Claudius in the second act, as Macbeth kills Duncan, but that would have been a different play. Yet it is true, I think, that we do not see in the play, considered realistically, sufficient reason for Hamlet's delay, and when we have felt the artistic and emotional sense behind that omission, we will have grasped the play.

Finally, though, we come to the third customary explanation of Hamlet's delay. The first was: he doesn't delay at all. The second was: no reason is given for his delay. The third approach, by all odds the favorite among critics and scholars, is to find something in Hamlet's character which explains his delay. It is a curious thing about the character, Hamlet, that, as each century takes its look at Hamlet, it seems to find there—itself. As Hamlet—the real Hamlet, the one in the play—says of acting, "the purpose of playing . . . [its] end, both at the first and now, was and is, to hold, as 'twere, the mirror up to nature, to show virtue her own feature, scorn her own image, and the very age and body of the time his form and pressure." And that is exactly what has happened. The actors, the critics, the scholars, look at Hamlet and they seem to find there—themselves.

Thomas Betterton (see Fig. 16), the greatest actor of the latter half of the seventeenth century, played *Hamlet,* and Sir Richard Steele, the essayist, wrote of Betterton's 1709 performance, "He acted youth; and by the prevalent power of proper manner, gesture, and voice, appeared through the whole drama a young man of great expectation, vivacity, and enterprise." The seventeenth and eighteenth centuries tended to see Hamlet as a young man of considerable promise, a rationalist, a prince, almost a philosopher-prince, very much as Ophelia describes him; and this young man of great expectations, what reason does he have for delay? Well, none, really, and perhaps this is one reason why many eighteenth-century critics did not think too highly of *Hamlet*. Their view of the character Hamlet gave no reason, no motive, for his delay, and that troubled the critics—though not the audiences, those people that the intellectuals of the eighteenth century would have called, "the multitude." They loved the tragedy of Hamlet. But a number of eighteenth-century critics objected to the tragedy, complaining how typical it was of the barbaric tastes of their forefathers that Shakespeare had not invented a proper reason for Hamlet's delay.

As we move further into the eighteenth century, Hamlet becomes a more complicated figure, as set forth, for example, by Aaron Hill, a minor dramatist: "The characteristic distinction that marks the temper of Hamlet is a pensive, yet genteel, humanity. He is by nature of a melancholy cast, but his polite education has illuminated the sable and like the sun, through a wet May morning, mixed a gleam, with his sadness." Hamlet, in other words, has become an eighteenth-century gentleman, albeit a somewhat melancholy one, rather in the style of the so-called "graveyard" school of poetry which was coming into popularity—Gray's "Elegy" is the most famous example. It was out of this conception of Hamlet as a gentlemanly but melancholy prince that David Garrick, perhaps the greatest of all Shakespearean actors, created his interpretation (see Fig. 17). Drawing on Garrick's performance, Thomas Wilks, a minor critic, decided in 1759 that Shakespeare "has drawn this prince of a reserved, cautious turn, arising from a melancholy stamped on him by his father's untimely death, and some consequent misfortunes." "Of a reserved, cautious turn"—we begin to hear the first signs of that interpretation of Hamlet which was to dominate the nineteenth century. Indeed, Johnson's Boswell enthusiastically recorded how his friend Thomas Sheridan "made it clear that Hamlet, not withstanding of his seeming incongruities, is a perfectly consistent character. Shakespeare drew him as the portrait of a young man of a good heart and fine feelings who had led a studious contemplative life and so become delicate and irresolute. . . . His timidity being once admitted, all the strange fluctuations which we perceive in him may be easily traced to that source." "Timidity"—it is only a short step from Boswell's friend's remarks in 1763 to the nineteenth-century Hamlet.

It was Goethe, the most magnificent of the Romantic poets, at the end of the eighteenth century who created him, the Romantic Hamlet, the one who haunts our stages even today. "To me," his Wilhelm Meister proclaims, "it is clear that Shakespeare meant, in the present case, to represent the effects of a great action laid upon a soul unfit for the performance of it." "A lovely, pure, noble and most moral nature, without the strength of nerve which forms a hero, sinks beneath a burden which it cannot bear and must not cast away." And he summarized his idea in a beautiful, if somewhat fanciful, image: "There is an oak-tree planted in a costly jar, which should have borne only pleasant flowers in its bosom; the roots expand, the jar is shivered." Now all this has a great deal to do with Goethe, at least the Goethe who wrote *The Sorrows of Young Werther,* but can we really speak of Shakespeare's Hamlet as a delicate jar, that man who stabs Polonius and then says, "I'll lug the guts into the neighbor room"? Goethe forgets how Hamlet fights off Horatio and two soldiers to talk to the Ghost. Goethe forgets that Hamlet is a skilled fencer, almost a national champion. Goethe forgets, in short, that Hamlet has plenty of nerve, that he is very much a man capable of bloody action.

Nevertheless, Goethe's Hamlet was to be Hamlet for at least another century. Coleridge, the greatest of the English romantic critics, said Shakespeare "intended to portray a person in whose view the external world, and all its incidents and objects, were comparatively dim and of no interest in themselves, and which began to interest only when they were reflected in the mirror of his mind." At another point, Coleridge speaks of "great, enormous, intellectual activity, and a consequent proportionate aversion to real action, with all its symptoms and accompanying qualities."

Notice that something odd has happened at this point. Goethe and Coleridge are both talking about Hamlet, not as though he were a character in a play, but as though he were a real person. In the romantic period and after, there seems to have been a feeling that the ultimate fact in the human world is history, the most important product of this feeling being Karl Marx and the dialectic interpretation of history. History was felt as an ultimate and ruling set of laws, "the dictatorship of history." Plays, therefore, were increasingly treated as though they were simply dramatizations of actual historical events. Thus, we begin to get Hamlets like that of John Philip Kemble (see Fig. 18). The actor wears plumes to create the effect of a man out of some archaeological past. He wears the Sacred Elephant, a Danish medal, and another effort at literal historical correctness. This, then, was the nineteenth-century Hamlet: a figure out of history, and a delicate, willowy poetic type, unable to act in the trying circumstances in which he finds himself. The key lines in the play become, "The time is out of joint. Oh, cursèd spite that ever I was born to set it right!" And out of this tradition come most of the great Hamlets: Edwin Booth, America's Hamlet of the nineteenth century (Fig. 20); Sir Henry Irving, the great Victorian actor-producer (Fig. 19); John Barrymore (Fig. 22); Leslie Howard (Fig. 23); Maurice Evans (Fig. 21); John Gielgud (Fig. 25); Sir Laurence Olivier (Fig. 24)—these are all, give or take a little bit, Hamlets in the tradition of Goethe and Coleridge. They are all really nineteenth-century

Hamlets, delicate flowers, who cannot bring themselves to commit the bloody business; they show, in Coleridge's nicely turned phrase, Hamlet's "continually resolving to do, yet doing nothing but resolve" (except fence, wrestle, and defy, as well as murder, Polonius, Rosencrantz-and-Guildenstern, and the King).

As long as we have just been looking at these nineteenth-century Hamlets, it should be pointed out that not one of them looks like Hamlet. This is the kind of thing that makes the professional Shakespearean like myself a little annoyed with actors and directors. How many portrayals of Hamlet have we illustrated here—ten, eleven?—not one, *not one,* beginning with Betterton, shows Hamlet as the play tells us he physically is. We are told three things about the physical figure of Hamlet. First, like any self-respecting Elizabethan courtier, he has a beard. In his Hecuba soliloquy, Hamlet cries,

> Who calls me villain? breaks my pate across?
> Plucks off my beard, and blows it in my face?
> (II. ii. 557–558)

Plain as day, yet not one of our actors plays Hamlet with a beard.

The second thing about Hamlet—and Shakespeare seems almost to go out of his way to tell us this—is that he is thirty years old. In the graveyard scene, Hamlet asks the sexton, "How long hast thou been a grave-maker?" and the man replies that he began his work "the very day that young Hamlet was born." And then a few lines later, he says, "I have been sexton here, man and boy, thirty years." Yet actors persist in playing Hamlet as though he were eighteen or nineteen, a kind of overgrown Romeo.

The third thing we know about the physical figure of Hamlet, and this is perhaps the hardest to take, is that he is a mesomorph. The Queen, his mother, says of him during his duel with Laertes, "He's fat and scant of breath." Now the word "fat" did have other meanings in Shakespeare's day: it could mean simply "pleasingly plump"; it could mean "soft," that is, "out of shape"; it could mean "oily" or "sweaty." But Shakespeare used the word more than seventy times with its usual meaning, while he uses the word "fat" to mean "sweaty" just once, and the other suggested meanings—not at all. No one would dream of saying that the word "fat" when applied to Falstaff meant simply "having difficulty in breathing." And yet the hold of that poetic, nineteenth-century Hamlet on our imaginations is so strong, that we are all, I suppose, tempted to keep our Hamlet slim by picking an odd meaning for a simple word like "fat." Further, if philology is inconclusive, stage history is not. Remember that Shakespeare wrote that part for Richard Burbage, the Globe's star tragedian, who played Macbeth, Othello, Lear; no one suggests *they* were frail, willowy types. This, then, is the physical Hamlet: thirty years old, bearded, fat, and still going back to the University. If you want to lift him out of the play, you can see him as a recognizable type that you might find around, say, New Haven or Harvard Square: the perpetual graduate student.

At any rate, each critic and each historical period seems to find itself in Hamlet. The eighteenth century found in Hamlet a melancholy gentleman; the nineteenth century found a delicate poet in the manner of Bunthorne. In our own century, Hamlet is a man with an Oedipus complex. We are perhaps most familiar with this conception from Sir Laurence Olivier's film version of *Hamlet*, where it was larded in very thickly indeed. Of course, people get very upset when you mention psychoanalysis, but there is nothing so shocking in all this. We have all seen Oedipus complexes in action; you can find it quite adequately described in most instruction books for raising children. Lo, the well thumbed Spock: "Boys become romantic toward their mother, girls toward their father," so runs the black-letter of section 507 in which Dr. Spock discusses the problems of young boys about four.* "By the time he is four, he is apt to insist that he's going to marry his mother when he grows up. He isn't clear just what marriage consists of, but he's absolutely sure who is the most important and appealing woman in the world." And then further on,

When a human male, old or young, loves a woman very much, he can't help wanting her all to himself. He can't help feeling jealous of the love that exists between her and some other man. And so, of course, the boy of 3 and 4 and 5, as he becomes more aware of his possessive devotion to his mother, also becomes aware of how much she already belongs to his father. . . . At times he secretly wishes his father would get lost, and then he feels guilty about such disloyal feelings.

And so on. The child wishes his father would just go away for good, and he could have his mother all to himself. The child's imagination is somewhat more lurid than Dr. Spock—and I—are willing to say, but that is the essence of it, and there is plenty of scientific evidence for this fact, and also evidence in your own experience, and mine.

Now what do critics mean when they say that Hamlet cannot act because of his Oedipus complex? The argument is very simple, very elegant. One, people over the centuries have been unable to say why Hamlet delays in killing the man who murdered his father and married his mother. Two, psychoanalytic experience shows that every child wants to do just exactly that. Three, Hamlet delays because he cannot punish Claudius for doing what he himself wished to do as a child and, unconsciously, still wishes to do: he would be punishing himself. Four, the fact that this wish is unconscious explains why people could not explain Hamlet's delay.

It is worth adding, as a little historical footnote, that it was not Freud who brought the Oedipus complex to Hamlet, but Hamlet who brought the Oedipus

* Dr. Benjamin Spock, *Baby and Child Care* (Duell, Sloan, and Pearce).

complex to Freud. In the very letter of October 15, 1897, in which Freud wrote, "I have found love of the mother and jealousy of the father in my own case too, and now believe it to be a general phenomenon of early childhood," it is in that letter that Freud produces this interpretation of *Hamlet* and also of *Oedipus Rex*. It is as though *Hamlet* and *Oedipus Rex* had been guiding him in his thinking. In fact, in later life, Freud said, "Not I, but the poets discovered the unconscious."

At any rate, it seems to me that the logic of this scientific reading is unimpeachable. The reading is correct, and settles the question—except that the question was wrongly asked in the first place. The psychoanalytic reading, in other words, makes the same mistake as all these literalistic readings of Hamlet's character, beginning with Goethe's. They lift Hamlet out of the play and treat him as a living person. It was Edgar Allan Poe, of all people, who put his finger on the mistake:

> In all commentating upon Shakespeare, there has been a radical error. . . . It is the error of attempting to expound his characters—to account for their actions —to reconcile his inconsistencies—not as if they were the coinage of a human brain, but as if they had been actual existences upon earth. We talk of Hamlet the man, instead of Hamlet the *dramatis persona*—of Hamlet that God, in place of Hamlet that Shakespeare created. If Hamlet had really lived, and if the tragedy were an accurate record of his deeds, from this record (with some trouble) we might, it is true, reconcile his inconsistencies and settle to our satisfaction his true character. But the task becomes the purest absurdity when we deal only with a phantom.

This is the real answer to people who try to find a reason for Hamlet's delay in Hamlet's character. Hamlet is not a living person, but a part of a play. He delays because that is part of the play. And it is not fair to look only at those parts of the play which deal with the quite appealing figure of Hamlet. We have to look at the play as a whole.

When we look at the play as a whole, I think Hamlet's delay may seem a little less enigmatic to us. We do not need to turn to costly jars with oak trees in them or, for that matter, to psychoanalysis to see why Hamlet delays. He delays because we all delay. We all plan things, project things, and do they ever come out as quickly or as well as we think they should? Certainly, our approach to *Hamlet* through the question, Why does Hamlet delay? has not. Perhaps another question will serve us better, and I shall offer this one: Why *both* Rosencrantz and Guildenstern? Why do we need two of them —wouldn't one do? These two characters, I am told by actors, are so indistinguishable that they are known in the theater as Knife and Fork—I always think of them as the Bobbsey twins, particularly at the point where the King says, "Thanks, Rosencrantz and gentle Guildenstern," while the Queen says,

"Thanks, Guildenstern and gentle Rosencrantz." Why do we need two of them?

Silly as it may seem, the question at least has the virtue of leading us into the play as a whole, not just to one character. And when we look at the tragedy as a whole, we find that *Hamlet* has the same structure as *Macbeth. Macbeth,* we have seen, consists of two waves of action, one of crime and one of retribution. The beginning of each wave in *Macbeth* is marked for us by the witches' prophecies, and then there was an initial, introductory appearance of the witches, when they did not appear to Macbeth. So in *Hamlet,* there is an initial, introductory appearance of the Ghost; then there is a first wave of action set off by the Ghost's first appearance to Hamlet, followed by a second wave of action set off by the Ghost's second appearance to Hamlet.

In *Macbeth,* the two waves of action involved first, the crime, second, the retribution for the crime. The two waves in *Hamlet* consist of first, words, second, actions. The first wave begins with the Ghost's command to Hamlet to "Revenge his foul and most unnatural murther." Hamlet responds by playing mad, saying a lot of odd words; in fact, he says, "Words, words, words." The King responds to Hamlet's madness by setting on him first Rosencrantz and Guildenstern, then Ophelia, to find out what's wrong with Hamlet. Again, a verbal action. Hamlet produces the play-within-the-play. Again, words. The King tries to purge himself of his crime by prayer. Again, words. Hamlet speaks words like daggers to his mother. Finally, this verbal wave of action culminates in the false killing, the "play" killing of Polonius, that creature of words who had served as the King's ally and Hamlet's foil in the first wave.

Then, in Hamlet's scene with his mother, the Ghost appears again, to whet Hamlet's "almost blunted purpose." The Ghost's second appearance marks the beginning of the second wave of action, in which the King's ally and Hamlet's foil is the man of action, Laertes. Laertes returns and immediately whips up a revolution. Ophelia drowns herself. Hamlet and Laertes wrestle in Ophelia's grave. There is a sea battle offstage. The King and Laertes set up and carry out the crooked fencing match. In that last, bustling scene, murders fairly abound: Laertes, the Queen, Claudius, finally Hamlet himself—"Such a sight as this becomes the field, but here shows much amiss." And with the turbulent ending of the play, the second wave, the wave of action, subsides.

Just as *Hamlet* the tragedy is a play first of words and then of action, so is Hamlet the character. When we look at Hamlet, not in isolation, but in his play, we find that he, too, has two parts. He is a man of words—clearly. He puns with a virtuosity any modern comic might envy. He speaks exquisitely of the nature of human character, of destiny, of philosophy, of the life after death—a whole series of abstract topics such as would fascinate a graduate student at Wittenberg. He is very much the intellectual the nineteenth-century critics wished to find him. But he is also and equally clearly a man of action. We see him fighting off Horatio and two soldiers to speak to the Ghost alone; brusquely, carelessly stabbing Polonius; sending Rosencrantz-and-Guildenstern off to their collective doom with scarcely a backward glance; scrapping with Laertes—remember, too, that Hamlet is a fencer fit to compete in national championships.

In short, Hamlet is, in that horrible phrase of the educationists, a "whole man." This is Ophelia's description of him:

> O, what a noble mind is here o'erthrown!
> The courtier's, soldier's, scholar's, eye, tongue, sword,
> Th' expectancy and rose of the fair state,
> The glass of fashion, and the mould of form,
> Th' observed of all observers . . .

(III. i. 150–154)

Admittedly, the young lady's vision is colored by the fact that she is in love with the man; even so, she is describing a Renaissance ideal: the courtier, soldier, scholar combined; the man of eye, tongue, sword; the expectancy of the state. Her words embody the seventeenth- and early eighteenth-century view of Hamlet, Hamlet as the Prince, Hamlet as the young man of all the moral and social virtues. Ophelia is describing Hamlet as portrayed by the Restoration actor, Betterton, "a young man of great expectation, vivacity, and enterprise." We probably ought to give considerable weight to this seventeenth-century Hamlet, if for no other reason than that, chronologically and spiritually, the seventeenth century was a lot closer to Shakespeare's *Weltanschauung* than we are. In fact, Betterton claimed that his performance of Hamlet had been approved by Shakespeare himself, and while the evidence for this approval is quite shaky indeed, chronologically, it is a faint possibility, and even a faint possibility of a word from Shakespeare deserves attention.

Hamlet is, according to Betterton and Ophelia, a man of action and also, clearly enough, a man of thought. Yet, as in the play as a whole, we find his thoughts and words primarily in the first wave of the play, his actions primarily in the second. He seems unable to bring them together. He can talk beautifully, and he can act on impulse, but he seems unable to formulate a verbal plan and then bring it into being by action. In the first wave of the play, his culminating achievement is a verbal one, the play-within-the-play, the "talk of the poisoning." Once he has returned from his sea voyage, that is to say, once he has taken the journey-and-return, the symbolic death-and-rebirth so favored by mythic heroes, he explicitly rejects the idea of planning action:

> Rashly,
> And praised be rashness for it—let us know,
> Our indiscretion sometime serves us well

When our deep plots do pall, and that should learn us
There's a divinity that shapes our ends,
Rough-hew them how we will.

(V. ii. 6–11)

Hamlet seems to be saying that there is no point in planning action, because there's a divinity that decides these things; man should be, in his word, "rash." And again, a short time later, when Horatio suggests that he need not enter the duel with Laertes unless he wishes to, Hamlet brushes him off: "Not a whit, we defy augury. There is special providence in the fall of a sparrow. If it be now, 'tis not to come; if it be not to come, it will be now; if it be not now, yet it will come. The readiness is all." In effect, Hamlet is saying, "Don't plan, just act on impulse; let yourself rest in the hands of Providence or Divinity."

Isn't this, then, the central problem of *Hamlet,* the problem of putting together words or thoughts on the one hand and actions on the other? Hamlet seems to be able to act, and he seems to be able to plan, but he cannot do them together. And this is true of the play as a whole with its two great movements marked off by the appearances of the Ghost. The two waves follow one on the other; they do not occur together. This split is the enigma of *Hamlet,* but now, seen in terms of the play as a whole, rather than simply in a part, the character of Hamlet. Somehow, we do not seem to be able to put words and action together.

There is another side to this relationship between words and action: not only do we seem to be unable to put them together; when we do put them together, each seems to corrupt the other. We can see this in Laertes' dying words:

The foul practice
Hath turned itself on me.

(V. ii. 306–307)

As Hamlet says, " 'Tis the sport to have the enginer hoist with his own petar," that is, blown up with his own bomb. And at the very end of the play, Horatio sums up the action, and concludes with this phrase, "Purposes mistook, fall'n on the inventors' heads."

In this tragedy, thought and action seem each to recoil on the other. Claudius seizes the throne, and this deed preys on his thoughts. Polonius gives himself over to the service of the King and is killed instead of the King. Laertes tries to kill Hamlet, but kills himself at the same time. Action seems to turn around and strike back at the man who thought it up. Thought, on the other hand, seems to inhibit action. As Hamlet says,

> Thus conscience does make cowards of us all,
> And thus the native hue of resolution
> Is sicklied o'er with the pale cast of thought,
> And enterprises of great pitch and moment
> With this regard their currents turn awry
> And lose the name of action.
>
> (III. i. 83–88)

The healthy color of action is turned into the sick pallor of thought. It is almost as though thought and action together make a kind of disease, in which each corrupts the other.

Just as the characters' actions and thoughts have this quality of each recoiling on the other, so does the play as a whole. It consists of a first wave (of thought) followed by a second wave (of action) which recoils on and corrupts the first. In the first wave, Hamlet knows a secret, something the people around him do not know; on the basis of that secret, he tries to affect the society around him. The second wave turns the first, as it were, inside out: Claudius knows that Hamlet knows, and now Hamlet, when he is not absent, is relatively passive, resigned, and the society around him in the persons of Claudius and his agents tries to affect Hamlet. Just as the first wave of action ends with the play-within-the-play and the killing of Polonius, which Hamlet treats as a game ("Dead for a ducat, dead!" "Hide fox, and all after"), so the fencing match at the end of the second is a kind of "play"—in fact, that is the word the play customarily uses for it. Both waves of action, Hamlet trying to affect Claudius, Claudius trying to affect Hamlet, these "mighty opposites," both end in mere "play." "Play" itself seems to lie between thought and action, as does "the play," both the "play" of *Hamlet* and the "play" we play on this stage, the world. As the King says in his prayer, in heaven "there the action lies in his true nature," whereas, "in the corrupted currents of this world" action can shuffle and evade law and justice; thought and action are fragmented, broken apart.

Shakespeare dramatizes this fragmentation in *Hamlet* by a device called "character splits" or, to vary a term of Henry James, "reflectors." That is, minor characters are used to reflect certain aspects of the major character, in this case, Hamlet. And the two major aspects of Hamlet are, of course, thought and action. These two aspects of Hamlet are split off into two characters, so that we can see the two principles of Hamlet separately in their pure forms.

The two characters are Horatio and Fortinbras. Horatio, as Hamlet's confidant, reflects to us the thinking Hamlet. The soldiers say to Horatio in the first scene, "Thou art a scholar," and indeed he is. He is Hamlet's fellow student from Wittenberg. He is the man to whom Hamlet says,

There are more things in heaven and earth, Horatio,
Than are dreamt of in your philosophy.

(I. v. 166–167)

If Horatio is the thinking side of Hamlet, then Fortinbras is the acting side. He is, like Hamlet, a revenging son. His father was killed by Hamlet's father on the very day young Hamlet was born, and in a long speech in the opening scene, Horatio tells us the history of this episode as he explains to the watchmen why the kingdom of Denmark is preparing for war. Fortinbras' father challenged Hamlet's father to single combat, in which Hamlet's father won, and as a result Fortinbras forfeited his lands. Young Fortinbras has gathered together an army—Horatio says, "Sharked up a list of lawless resolutes"—and he is going to try to recover those lands from Denmark, "by strong hand." That phrase "strong hand" is curious, because Fortinbras' name means, more or less, "strong arm," just as Horatio's name seems related to the Latin word *oratio,* speech. Even in their names, these two characters suggest the two poles of the play, words and action, and also in their occupations: one the scholar, the man of thoughts and words; one the soldier, the man of deeds.

These two characters, Horatio and Fortinbras, also bracket the whole action of the play. That is, they are the first important people (as opposed to ghosts) we hear about, and they are the two important characters left in the end on that very bloody stage. The opening is one of the finest things in *Hamlet:* in just a few lines, it sets up this whole theme of words as against action. The setting of the scene sums it up: we find ourselves in the midst of an elaborate military preparation against some real, physical, armed invasion from outside, and we see the invader, too, the Ghost, but the Ghost is not from outside; he is a native Dane, and though he wears armor, his invasion is not a physical, military one, but an invasion of conscience. As so often in *Hamlet,* the action and the preparation for action are misdirected. We see a Denmark involved with military preparation, but plagued by the walking conscience of the land. Into this situation, poised between conscience and action, comes Horatio, the man of thought, the man of words. And what does he tell us? He tells us of Fortinbras, the man of action, the revenging son, preparing to dominate Denmark with his strong hand.

This is the beginning of the action, and the end of the play is also dominated by Horatio and Fortinbras. As Hamlet dies, he performs two acts. First, he asks Horatio to live on after him "to tell my story." He asks, in other words, that Horatio perform a deed of language. And then Hamlet casts his vote for Fortinbras for the new king, "He has my dying voice." Hamlet dies, and Fortinbras takes over. Horatio promises that he will speak to the yet unknowing world how these things came about. And Fortinbras, never a man to miss a trick, says,

I have some rights of memory in this kingdom,
Which now to claim my vantage doth invite me.
(V. ii. 378–379)

—as long as I happen to be here, I might just as well take over. And at the end of the play, there they stand, the man of words and the man of action, each successful in his own way. Between them lies the body of a man who was both a man of words *and* a man of action, who failed, tragically failed.

Horatio and Fortinbras are the two big "reflectors" in the tragedy; there are also two lesser reflectors, two characters who reflect the central action of the play, but in a lesser way. They are Laertes and Ophelia. Hamlet does two things in the course of the play: he pretends to be mad, and he makes his fitful efforts to revenge his father's death. These are the two aspects of Hamlet we find in Laertes and Ophelia. Their actions begin when Hamlet kills Polonius, their father. After that, Ophelia goes mad and Laertes revenges his father. But where Hamlet is only pretending to be mad, "playing," Ophelia's madness is real, and it ends in her death. Similarly, where Hamlet only makes fits and starts toward revenging his father, "plays" the revenging son, Laertes really revenges his father, but that, too, ends in his death. It is as though Shakespeare were saying through this splitting of Hamlet's madness and his revenge into Ophelia and Laertes, that all action, whether it is real or just pretended action, "play," ends in the grave.

The ideas of "playing" and the grave bring us to the third pair of reflectors of the central action: the actors and the gravediggers. By juxtaposing these two kinds of people, the play puts us in mind of that haunting image, the dying actor: we see it today over and over again in the films of Ingmar Bergman, and we see it in Shakespeare's plays over and over again in the image of man as "a poor player that struts and frets his hour upon the stage and then is heard no more." But those are lines from *Macbeth,* and the image of death and the actor are bound together. In *Hamlet,* death and the actor, like so many other things in *Hamlet,* are fragmented, broken apart, decomposed. The actors are associated with words, with words instead of action, words leading only to a kind of play-action. The actor, as Hamlet points out to us in his instructions to the players, is preeminently a man who has a plan, a script, a part he must play to the letter, and yet what he does issues in no *real* action. Hamlet says,

The play's the thing
Wherein I'll catch the conscience of the king.
(II. ii. 590–591)

And, indeed, he does catch the King's conscience and send him off to his prayers, but his *conscience* is all he catches; the play-within-the-play leads to no real action, no real revenge, only a verbal revenge. As Hamlet says in what is, to me, the greatest soliloquy of the play, the Hecuba soliloquy:

> O, what a rogue and peasant slave am I!
> Is it not monstrous that this player here,
> But in a fiction, in a dream of passion,
> Could force his soul so to his own conceit
> That from her working all his visage wanned,
> Tears in his eyes, distraction in his aspect,
> A broken voice, and his whole function suiting
> With forms to his conceit? And all for nothing,
> For Hecuba!
> What's Hecuba to him, or he to Hecuba,
> That he should weep for her? What would he do
> Had he the motive and the cue for passion
> That I have? He would drown the stage with tears
> And cleave the general ear with horrid speech,
> Make mad the guilty and appal the free,
> Confound the ignorant, and amaze indeed
> The very faculties of eyes and ears.
> Yet I,
> A dull and muddy-mettled rascal, peak
> Like John-a-dreams, unpregnant of my cause,
> And can say nothing.
>
> (II. ii. 534–554)

"Can *say* nothing"—what an irony there is in that phrase! Hamlet calls upon himself to *do* something, but ends up criticizing himself that he "can *say* nothing." And indeed, his resolution in this Hecuba speech issues only in the play-within-the-play, a "play" revenge.

Yet, curiously, though the play-within-the-play and the actors are the most fictional part of this tragedy, they are also the most real. When Hamlet discusses the actors with Rosencrantz and Guildenstern in Act II, scene ii, the two courtiers tell him about the war of the theaters in London. All of a sudden we have vanished from Denmark in the—what shall we say? ninth, eleventh century? Suddenly we hear three young men, three young theater buffs, talking about current London theatrical affairs: the rivalry between the private theaters with their boy companies and the public theaters with their adult companies. Now, curiously, this very same kind of breakthrough takes place in the graveyard scene. The sexton has been chatting with a clown or bumpkin, making riddles and games with him, and finally says, "Go, get thee to Yaughan and fetch me a stoup of liquor." "Yaughan," as far as anyone knows, is Johann, the name of a local tavern keeper, so that, in effect, the sexton is saying, "Look, step down to McSorley's, will you, and get me a glass of beer." * Again, there

---

*"Yaughan" appears only in the Folio text. (Does this suggest "Yaughan" started doing business sometime after 1605? Or that "Yaughan's" was near, not the Globe, but the Blackfriars where the company played much of the time after 1608?)

is a sudden breakthrough from the graveyard in Denmark to the London of the audience. By breaking up the dramatic illusion, Shakespeare says, in effect, "See? Every play is your play, every grave is your grave."

Indeed, the grave is the other side of this stage, the world, and we see that other side in the graveyard scene, where the two clowns laugh and joke, tell riddles, sing love songs, even as they are surrounded with skulls and bones. All of it, all the jokes, the riddles, the songs, the logic, it all ends in the grave. Hamlet holds up a skull and points out that it could have been a politician, a courtier, a beautiful woman, a lawyer, a tanner (his hide will keep out the water longer), a jester, a king. We bright moderns don't like to think about death very much, and the chromium-plated propaganda of our morticians is all designed to cover up the fact that death is a physical thing. Elizabethans knew about death, cared about it—it was not uncommon for an attack of the plague to carry off a tenth of the population. Many an Elizabethan kept a skull on his desk to remind him, no matter how grand man is, he ends up in the grave. A skull is, after all, a sobering thing. In the hollow round of a skull there were thoughts; a man loved and hated and lived. The skull once had eyes like mine or yours, a nose, cheeks. "Here hung those lips that I have kissed I know not how oft." We moderns do not like to think about death, but when we see *Hamlet,* we must. The end of all action, play action or real action, is death. It is no accident that the gravedigger scene opens with a discussion of what an action is, and the clown with his chop-logic says, "An act hath three branches, it is to act, to do, and to perform." And none of them can Hamlet accomplish. When he does, "will he, nill he," accomplish his act, he dies.

"To act, to do, and to perform"—everywhere we turn in this tragedy, we find this sense of fragmentation, splitting, decomposition. We find it in one of the tragedy's two characteristic figures of speech: hendiadys, which means expressing a single idea by two nouns or adjectives paired by a conjunction: "the sensible and true avouch of mine own eyes," "the gross and scope of mine opinion," "well ratified by law and heraldry," "food and diet to some enterprise," "by strong hand and terms compulsory," "this posthaste and romage in the land," "the sheeted dead did squeak and gibber," "the extravagant and erring spirit," and so on. These are all from just the opening scene—is it any wonder that as we read and see *Hamlet,* we get a sense of fragmentation, division?

We find this division in the language, in the character of Hamlet himself, but also in the pairings of the minor characters as well. Ophelia, for example, seems young and sweet and also very passive, in this respect, the polar opposite of her choleric brother. We see her passivity dominated and corrupted by her father and her king when she is made to serve as a spy against the man she loves. Nevertheless, in the prevailing atmosphere of the play, that atmosphere of corruption and decomposition, Ophelia suggests a kind of vegetable purity. Repeatedly, she is linked to flowers: to a rosebud, to a primrose, to violets; Polonius calls her a "green girl"; Laertes cries, "O rose of May!" When she is mad, she brings in herbs and flowers, rosemary, pansy, fennel, columbine; she decks herself in fantastic garlands and drowns by "a willow grows askant the brook." "Too much of water hast thou, poor Ophelia," weeps her grieving brother, and, indeed, she does. We first see her bidding her brother farewell for his sea journey; we last see her drowning, "like a creature native and indued unto that element." She seems almost a goddess of the spring, a life force, here rudely drowned in her own life-giving element. Yet, even in that lovely description of Ophelia's drowning, Gertrude manages to sound the distinctive *Hamlet* note, to give the coarsening touch. Among the flowers in Ophelia's garlands we find,

> long purples,
> That liberal shepherds give a grosser name,
> But our cold maids do dead men's fingers call them.
>
> (IV. vii. 168–170)

Gertrude, too, is a kind of life force; she seems almost an older Ophelia, passive, worked upon first by Claudius, then by Hamlet. Yet in Gertrude that sense of vegetable growth and vitality has aged into animality: crude, gross, physical, sensual love:

> Why, she would hang on him
> As if increase of appetite had grown
> By what it fed on.
>
> . . .
>
> O most wicked speed, to post
> With such dexterity to incestuous sheets.
>
> (I. ii. 143–157)

Over and over again, she is associated with animals, with sensuality, lust. Gertrude, Ophelia, the only women of the play are alike in being associated with physical reality, in being like life forces; they seem to hold in themselves what Horatio calls "the womb of earth." Yet the innocence of Ophelia has aged, decayed into the sensuality of the older woman:

> Rebellious hell,
> If thou canst mutine in a matron's bones,
> To flaming youth let virtue be as wax
> And melt in her own fire.
>
> (III. iv. 83–86)

Laertes and Polonius show the same kind of decay and decomposition, though they are associated with, not earthy reality, but verbal reality. Laertes is preoccupied with the shows and forms of the world. He seems almost as annoyed that his father didn't get a proper funeral, as he is that the old man was killed:

> His means of death, his obscure funeral—
> No trophy, sword, nor hatchment o'er his bones,
> No noble rite nor formal ostentation—
> Cry to be heard.
>
> (IV. v. 211–214)

He is put into a rage by the fact that Ophelia's funeral is not what he thinks it should be; twice he cries, "What ceremony else?" Twice in the play he seems willing to refer his charges to public, formal arbitration. Claudius puts him off his swift revenge by suggesting,

> Go but apart,
> Make choice of whom your wisest friends you will,
> And they shall hear and judge 'twixt you and me.
>
> (IV. v. 201–203)

Hamlet, put into a rage by the "bravery of his grief," its showiness, insults Laertes, who agrees to accept his apology—

> I am satisfied in nature,
>
> . . .
>
> But in my terms of honor
> I stand aloof, and will no reconcilement
> Till by some elder masters of known honor
> I have a voice and precedent of peace,
> To keep my name ungored.
>
> (V. ii. 233–239)

In other words, though he is about to engage in the foulest treachery, he has to check out Hamlet's apology with some expert referees in honor.

Polonius, like Laertes, is concerned with erecting ostentations and ceremonies. He had been an actor in his youth; he is interested in Hamlet's love-poetry, criticizing it for a vile figure of speech. He is fond of drawing careful and somewhat meaningless verbal distinctions, as in his famous speech;

> Be thou familiar, but by no means vulgar.
>
> . . .
>
> Give every man thine ear, but few thy voice;
> Take each man's censure, but reserve thy judgment.
>
> . . .
>
> Neither a borrower nor a lender be,
>
> (I. iii. 61–75)

and so on. His distinctions soar as he describes Hamlet's decline:

> He, repellèd, a short tale to make,
> Fell into a sadness, then into a fast,
> Thence to a watch, thence into a weakness,
> Thence to a lightness, and by this declension,
> Into the madness wherein now he raves.
>
> (II. ii. 146–150)

But they do not reach their peak until his elaborately precise description of the actors: "The best actors in the world, either for tragedy, comedy, history, pastoral, pastoral-comical, historical-pastoral, tragical-historical, tragical-comical-historical-pastoral" (talk about fragmentation!).

Polonius, however, goes a step beyond Laertes. Where Laertes is preoccupied with erecting formalities, Polonius not only wishes to conceal himself in shows, but also to probe through the masks of others—to hunt "the trail of policy," political scheming, "With windlasses and with assays of bias, by indirections find directions out." There is a quite apt irony in Hamlet's sword probing through the show, the arras, behind which Polonius has concealed himself to penetrate Hamlet's disguise: "Thou find'st to be too busy is some danger," is the epitaph Hamlet gives him,

> Indeed, this counsellor
> Is now most still, most secret, and most grave,
> Who was in life a foolish prating knave.
>
> (III. iv. 214–216)

Ophelia and Gertrude constitute a pair of characters, "reflectors," focused on physical, earthy reality; Laertes and Polonius constitute another pair, focused on verbal reality, formalities, and shows. Finally, those mighty opposites, Claudius and Hamlet, constitute still another pair, focused not simply on one kind of reality or the other, but on the tension between external and internal reality. Claudius seems all mask, easy, gracious, friendly, smiling (as Hamlet tells us several times). He strikes an amiable balance between the ceremonial King and the inner man, speaking of himself sometimes as "I," sometimes ceremonially, royally, as "we." His figures of speech are drawn from the ceremonial world of law, or from the world of personal, physical pleasure. Claudius likes his liquor and his sex; he is also a skillful, successful king, if we can judge from his brisk handling of *l'affaire norvégienne*. Yet he has won only an uneasy balance; an aside will break through:

> How smart a lash that speech doth give my conscience!
> The harlot's cheek, beautied with plast'ring art,
> Is not more ugly to the thing that helps it
> Than is my deed to my most painted word.
>
> (III. i. 50–53)

And his prayer reveals the same tension between inner man and external manifestation: "My words fly up, my thoughts remain below."

Hamlet, too, suffers in this tug-o'-war between physical reality and verbal abstractions. He is preoccupied with the low, physical details of death: skulls, bones, worms, rotting corpses. He is preoccupied, too, with the physical facts of sex, with "reechy kisses" or "country matters," to use the obscene pun he makes to Ophelia. He speaks steadily of disease and food, particularly rotting food. One half of Hamlet is bound up in this distaste for the world of physical reality. The other half, the reaction, is the meditative, philosophical Hamlet, the Hamlet of words. He loves to play with words, to parody a Polonius or an Osric; he loves to repeat phrases: "Well, well, well." "Words, words, words." "Except my life, except my life, except my life." The effect is to probe and lay open the inner meanings of language. Even more, Hamlet is a punster. The first words we hear him say are a pun, "A little more than kin and less than kind," and he dies on a pun: "The rest is silence"—"rest" as either "repose" or "remainder."

Just as Hamlet and Claudius are pulled in this tension between words and deeds, between thought and actions, between mind and body, between the exterior and the inward man, between mental abstractions and dirty, physical reality, so is the play as a whole; so is man as a whole. And as man responds by questioning, so *Hamlet* is a play of questions. The very opening words of the play are, "Who's there?" but there are others, many others, that fly out from the puzzling, enigmatic world of the play:

> What, has this thing appeared again tonight?

> Is it not like the King?

> Whither wilt thou lead me?   Speak.

> Murder?

> Do you not come your tardy son to chide,
> That lapsed in time and passion lets go by
> Th' important acting of your dread command?

These are questions about the Ghost. There are others: parents questioning their children:

> But now, my cousin Hamlet, and my son—

> How is it that the clouds still hang on you?

> What is't, Laertes?

> What is it, Ophelia, he hath said to you?

There are questions about love:

> Have you a daughter?
>
> Lady, shall I lie in your lap?
>
> Why would'st thou be a breeder of sinners?

There are questions about death:

> What have you done, my lord, with the dead body?
>
> How long will a man lie i' th' earth ere he rot?
>
> Why may not imagination trace the noble dust of
> Alexander, till 'a find it stopping a bunghole?

And then there are simply questions: "To be or not to be—that is the question."

    Hamlet is a play of questions; indeed, Horatio seems to call it "this bloody question." In incident after incident, we see the characters questioning, probing, testing, spying. We see Polonius set his man Reynaldo to spy on his son's behavior in Paris. We see Polonius, as he so quaintly puts it, "loose" his daughter to Hamlet, and the King, no less, hide behind a curtain to spy on them. We see Polonius spy on Hamlet's interview with his mother. We see the King and Gertrude setting Rosencrantz-and-Guildenstern to spy on Hamlet. And we see Hamlet spy on the King at prayers. We see him lure Claudius with the play-within-the-play to a fatal revelation.

    That fatal revelation is the disease, the rottenness, at the core of the play. Early on, Hamlet speaks of the tragic flaw that a man may have: he calls it "the dram of e'il," "some vicious mole of nature" and later he calls the Ghost "old mole." Indeed, the Ghost is the walking blemish of the land, the figure who proves by his very presence that "Something is rotten in the state of Denmark." The Ghost turns this blight, this disease, onto Hamlet himself, so that Hamlet becomes, in the words of the King, "the quick of the ulcer," the living, growing part of the disease. The King regrets that he did not purge himself of Hamlet earlier,

> But, like the owner of a foul disease,
> To keep it from divulging, let it feed
> Even on the pith of life.
>
>   (IV. i. 21–23)

Hamlet spreads the disease to his mother, accusing her in her remarriage of such an act, that

>   takes off the rose
> From the fair forehead of an innocent love,
> And sets a blister there.
>
>   (III. iv. 43–45)

"Oh, Hamlet," she cries,

> Speak no more.
> Thou turn'st mine eyes into my very soul,
> And there I see such black and grainèd spots
> As will not leave their tint.
>
> (89–92)

Then the Ghost appears. Hamlet tells his mother not to delude herself into thinking that he is mad because he has seen the Ghost and she has not:

> Lay not that flattering unction to your soul,
> That not your trespass but my madness speaks.
> It will but skin and film the ulcerous place
> Whiles rank corruption, mining all within,
> Infects unseen.
>
> (146–150)

The disease spreads on from Hamlet to Claudius ("like the hectic in my blood he rages"); and from Claudius the disease kills Gertrude through the poisoned cup. The disease is the disease of life itself—or death—in which

> The native hue of resolution
> Is sicklied o'er with the pale cast of thought.
> (III. i. 84–85)

The world of *Hamlet* is a world of diseases; it is also a world of food, a world in which food is being transformed, changing, rotting, a world in which

> The funeral baked meats
> Did coldly furnish forth the marriage tables.
> (I. ii. 180–181)

Food is transformed, as Hamlet says, so that "a king may go a progress through the guts of a beggar." "A man may fish with the worm that hath eat of a king, and eat of the fish that hath fed of that worm." "Your fat king and your lean beggar is but variable service, two dishes, but to one table—that's the end." That is the end: death, the worm.

Food is thought of, too, in terms of appetite, as when the Ghost says of his erstwhile wife,

> So lust, though to a radiant angel linked,
> Will sate itself in a celestial bed
> And prey on garbage.
> (I. v. 55–57)

Love in this tragedy becomes such things. At another point, when Hamlet is again describing the lovemaking between his mother and his uncle, he speaks of letting "the bloat King tempt you again to bed." He speaks of

> a pair of reechy kisses,
> Or paddling in your neck with his damned fingers.
>
> (III. iv. 185–186)

In that same terrible scene, he describes them as living

> In the rank sweat of an enseamèd bed
> Stewed in corruption, honeying and making love
> Over the nasty sty.
>
> (III. iv. 93–95)

Not only Gertrude comes in for this, but even the sweet Ophelia. Perhaps out of too much experience of the coeds at Wittenberg, Hamlet snarls at her,

I have heard of your paintings too, well enough. God hath given you one face, and you make yourselves another. You jig and amble, and you lisp; you nickname God's creatures, and make your wantonness your ignorance. Go to, I'll no more on't; it hath made me mad.

> (III. i. 142–146)

He goes on to tell her to "get thee to a nunnery," which was, in Elizabethan slang, a cant term for a brothel. Hamlet makes obscene jokes to Ophelia just before the play-within-the-play, and when she, poor thing, goes mad, she suddenly delivers herself of a series of ribald ballads.

Love in this tragedy is lust, physical, filthy; food is garbage; bodies are rotten with disease and caked with cosmetics. As Hamlet says in his first, great soliloquy:

> O that this too too sullied flesh would melt,
> Thaw, and resolve itself into a dew,
> Or that the Everlasting had not fixed
> His canon 'gainst self-slaughter. O God, God,
> How weary, stale, flat, and unprofitable
> Seem to me all the uses of this world!
> Fie on't, ah, fie, 'tis an unweeded garden
> That grows to seed; things rank and gross in nature
> Possess it merely.
>
> (I. ii. 129–137)

Hamlet, tortured by his personal situation, can find only disgust and filth in his physical self. And, as we have seen, in the Elizabethan imagination, the body was an image for the world's body, so that this disease is a disease of the macrocosm as well as of the microcosm. Thus, the corruption spreads, grows, until it rots the whole universe, which becomes "an unweeded garden that grows to seed."

"Things rank and gross in nature possess it merely"—these are, among other things, the animals we hear so much about in the play. We hear of woodcocks, the porcupine, the mole, fish, maggots, dogs, crabs, hawks, herrings, asses, kites, ravens, deer, the rat, the mouse, the toad, a tomcat, an ape, the adder, the fox, the horse, the water-fly, the lapwing, and, above all, worms—or, below all, worms, the lowest thing on the animal scale, that yet seems to triumph over all the others. "Here's fine revolution an we had the trick to see't." Man, though, is more than these animals, for he has reason. And yet, to Hamlet, his own mother has behaved like "a beast that wants discourse of reason."

The world of *Hamlet,* Hamlet the character or *Hamlet* the play, seems to poise against all this physical animality the purity of abstract thought and speculation. Over and over again in this tragedy, the characters turn away from the situation at hand, to deliver some set of remarks on a general and universal level. For example, in the opening scene, after the Ghost appears, Horatio and the soldiers follow with an abstract discussion of ghosts and portents, their significances and their habits. In Act I, scene ii, the first scene in the court, when Claudius tries to get Hamlet to stop grieving, he does it by a general discussion of condolences and mourning, a discussion on a very universal level,

> 'Tis a fault to heaven,
> A fault against the dead, a fault to nature,
> To reason most absurd.
>
> (I. ii. 101–103)

And after they have left him alone, Hamlet goes off into a meditation on "all the uses of this world." In the next scene, when Laertes wants to caution his sister against Hamlet's advances he goes into a general discussion of youth and princes, of "nature crescent." Polonius, instead of simply saying goodbye to his son, gives him a whole series of abstract rules culminating in the most abstract rule of all, "This above all, to thine own self be true." In the scene after that, when Hamlet comes to see the Ghost, Horatio comments on the King's rather curious custom of firing off a cannon every time he takes a drink, and this remark leads Hamlet into a totally general discussion about the nature of the tragic flaw in a given man. Even the Ghost, whose time, heaven knows, is limited, breaks into his hurried explanation of his death to give us some general remarks on virtue and lewdness. These are abstract discussions from only the first act, the play goes on and on with them, always poising them against the particular situation, the physical, dirty, grimy fact.

This tension between the physical and the abstract gives rise to one of the play's two distinctive figures of speech: metonymy, which we can define as translating abstract entities into concrete things: "the table of my memory," "death, the undiscovered country," "the slings and arrows of outrageous fortune," "murder, though it have no tongue, will speak." These are from Hamlet's speech, but the other characters talk the same way, notably Claudius:

"Offense's gilded hand may shove by justice." "O, my offense is rank, it smells to heaven." "We will fetters put about this fear." The play receives a continuing coloration from these juxtapositions of abstract and concrete, spiritual and animal, heavenly and earthly. Another way the play sets up man's reason as an opposite to his animality is by its interest in words. Think of all the different kinds of language in the play. We have Polonius' babbling on and on, taking forever to say anything, a habit always good for a laugh in the theater. We have Hamlet's "wild and whirling words." We have the jokes and riddles in the graveyard. We have the language of the play-within-the-play, or the "Pyrrhus" speech, in a blank verse that Shakespeare, with great skill, distinguishes from the blank verse of the rest of the play. And toward the end of the play we have that "water-fly," Osric, the ridiculous fop who comes, like some grotesque angel of death, to announce to Hamlet his fate, and to announce it in the strangest and most distorted language of all, a language which Hamlet gleefully parodies. It is a language, Hamlet tells us, by which Osric tries to set himself off from ordinary mortals.

Language, words, reason: these are the things that lift man above his animal level. Thus we find in *Hamlet* an interest in nationalities. We hear about Denmark, Poland, Norway, England, France, and "the most high and palmy state of Rome, A little ere the mightiest Julius fell." All these countries are fat and prosperous (as fat as an affluent America), and they suffer from it; they suffer

> th' imposthume of much wealth and peace,
> That inward breaks, and shows no cause without
> Why the man dies.
>
> (IV. iv. 27–29)

Just as he has nationality, man has trades and occupations which depend on language and which set him above the animals. There is a great deal of interest in the play in occupations and trades, and we hear in the course of the action about shipwrights, armorers, watchmen, pastors, brokers, bawds, the pioneer (we would say the "miner"), a fishmonger, beggars, a judge, a falconer, a barber, the harlot, the anchorite, the dicer (or "gambler"), the slave, cutpurse, engineer, pilgrim, steward, shepherd, gardener, ditcher, mason, carpenter, politician, lawyer, peasant, and that tanner whose dead hide will keep out water "a great while." These are the trades we hear about in the poetry, but we also see trades in the characters before us on the stage. We see Fortinbras the soldier, a pirate with a message from Hamlet, a priest, Horatio the scholar, two ambassadors, and we see such courtiers as Osric or Rosencrantz-and-Guildenstern. But most of all we see those two strange professions, the actor and the gravedigger. The one puts up a show, a ritual, a ceremony of words; the other digs and probes in the dirtiest dirt of physical reality. The one lives in the world of plays; the other lives in the world of the harshest fact of all, death. By our words, by our reason, we seek to rise above that death, into a world of ritual, of play. And just as the play is preoccupied with trades, so its figures of speech turn again and again to "play," sports and games like falconry, bowling, hunting, cockfighting—to say nothing of "play" in theaters or swordplay.

And yet, this godlike reason of nations, trades, and play is still tied to our physical selves, our bodies. Language must still enter an ear. As if to remind us of that fact, the word "ear" occurs in this play more than in any other of Shakespeare's, particularly in the sense of words penetrating our ears; words do our ears "violence," "take prisoner" the ear, "cleave" the ear, "split" the ear, "infect" the ear—Hamlet's mother says,

> O, speak to me no more;
> These words like daggers enter in my ears;
> No more, sweet Hamlet!
>
> (III. iv. 95–97)

And when we think of ears, in *Hamlet,* at any rate, we need to think of poison and disease, for example, the Ghost's telling us how Claudius,

> in the porches of my ears did pour
> The leperous distilment,
>
> . . .
>
> a most instant tetter barked about
> Most lazar-like with vile and loathsome crust
> All my smooth body.
>
> (I. v. 63–73)

When Claudius was frightened by the play-within-the-play, he rushed out "upon the *talk* of the poisoning." Words, which seem man's highest attribute, lead us back only to man's fleshy mortality. They probe our ears, they penetrate us, they dig into us to show us our own mortality.

The actor and the gravedigger: the man of words and the man of action, the man of play, the man of reality, the man of heaven and the man of earth. In the sick and rotting state of Denmark, this is the way man appears to us; confronted by a set of alternatives, men are, in Claudius' phrase, "to double business bound." To be or not to be. Man faces in *Hamlet* three sets of tensions. First, he stands between angel and beast: in Hamlet's words, "What should such fellows as I do crawling between earth and heaven?" Second, man the player stands between thoughts and action, between abstraction and reality. As Hamlet says, "The hand of little employment hath the daintier sense." Third, and most deadly, we are all condemned to what the gravedigger tells us is Adam's profession, to dig. We try to penetrate the shows and ceremonies of the world to find what Hamlet calls, "that within which passeth show." And yet we fear to find it—for it is ourselves.

Throughout the play, Hamlet's search for revenge is a search for truth, the truth of action and the truth of words. And, irony of ironies, he finds that truth, as he tells us in his dying words,

> You that look pale and tremble at this chance,
> That are but mutes or audience to this act,
> Had I but time—as this fell sergeant, Death,
> Is strict in his arrest—O, I could tell you—
> But let it be. Horatio, I am dead;
> Thou livest; report me and my cause aright
> To the unsatisfied.

(V. ii. 323-329)

When he says "you that look pale," he doesn't mean the supers, those other actors standing around on the stage; he means the actors in the audience, you, me. He has found his answer, but death prevents him from telling us. Instead, he says, in effect, "Let Horatio tell the story, for in Hamlet's story is the truth he had found." And what is that truth?

Is it that Hamlet is a young man of great expectations? or a willowy poet? or the victim of an Oedipus complex? The truth of *Hamlet* is the creation of a world, more properly, the creation of certain feelings in us about the world. Above all, we feel fragmentation, splitting, decomposition. We feel it in Hamlet's delay, his inability to bring together thoughts and deeds into a coherent plan. We feel it, too, in the two waves of the play, first words, then actions, but not at the same time; one delayed; both split off from each other. We feel it in the play's characteristic figures of speech: metonymy and hendiadys. We feel it in Hamlet himself, split as he is into Horatio, the man of thought, and Fortinbras, the man of action; Ophelia's madness and Laertes' revenge; playing and digging. And now perhaps we feel why there has to be both a Rosencrantz and a Guildenstern; we had to have two of them because everything in *Hamlet* is fragmented and broken into pairs.

We have seen splits in Shakespeare's work before. In *1 Henry IV*, for example, Hotspur and Falstaff were two figures competing for the soul, as it were, of Prince Hal. There, though, the central character himself was not split up; he only had to choose between alternatives. In *Julius Caesar,* we found the fragmenting of spirit and body, but there, too, it was different from *Hamlet*. At the end of the tragedy, the spirit of Caesar was laid to rest, and the day came full circle to its close. *Hamlet* is more of a tragedy; it leaves us with a sense of division as the ultimate fact of life. At the end of the play, the man of thought and the man of action stand, facing each other, separated, divided;

between them lies the man who was both, a failure precisely because he was both.

There is something final and rotten in this state of division. The world of *Hamlet* is a world of disease, garbage, filthy animals, obscenity, a world from which the rational and sensitive man retreats into abstract speculation. Digging, probing, splitting things to find their core, we find something is rotten in the state of Denmark. It is as though the very state of schism were decomposition; we long, metonymically, for the abstract, the pure, the speculative, but it comes to us only as the raw, physical grime of reality. In a religious sense, *Hamlet* is a play about original sin, or primal crime that endowed man with his sinfulness, his mortality. If we wish to be modern, we can say that the Oedipus complex is itself that primal fall, that shadow, that imposes itself on the godlike world of childhood. However we describe it, it is this flaw, this hidden imposthume that defines the world of *Hamlet*. It is in this sense, I think, that T. S. Eliot can tell us more about *Hamlet* than anyone—not in that passage in his criticism, where he says Hamlet is an artistic failure, but in the ending of his poem "The Hollow Men": *

> Between the idea
> And the reality
> Between the motion
> And the act
> Falls the Shadow

The rest is indeed silence.

---

* T. S. Eliot, *Collected Poems* (Harcourt, Brace, and World).

TWELFTH NIGHT

"THIS IS ILLYRIA, LADY"—AND THE VERY NAME CONJURES UP VISIONS OF ITS QUALITY: an Elysium, a lyric world, a world of legend and music, like Portia's Belmont, a world dallying with the innocence of love as in the golden age. Above all, though, Illyria is a world of illusion. *Twelfth Night, or, What You Will*—now, there's a title to confound critics. I can just picture Shakespeare sitting there, saying craftily to himself, "Wait till the critics hit this one. It doesn't mean a thing, just 'what you will.'" But when we look at the play, at this charming world of foolery, we find that that is precisely what the play means, "What you will."

There are really three plots. At the top, that is, among the high-ranking characters, Orsino and Olivia play out a little drama of thwarted love. At the opening of the play Orsino is mooning about, listening to music as a modern lover might play the blues, to console himself for his unrequited love for Olivia. She keeps rejecting his offers of love, until Viola appears on the scene. She has been shipwrecked, and she disguises herself as a boy, named Cesario, to whom Orsino takes a sudden and unaccountable fancy. He sends Cesario to woo Olivia for him, a quite conventional Renaissance procedure. But Olivia, alas, suddenly falls for Cesario, this girl disguised as a boy. Naturally, this leads to complications until Sebastian, Viola's twin brother, also shipwrecked, turns up, and evens the balance so that everything can end happily: Olivia marries Sebastian and Orsino marries Viola.

The second plot concerns Malvolio, Olivia's steward, who tries to keep some order in her household despite her jolly and drunken relative, Sir Toby Belch, and his assorted friends: Maria, the maid, and Sir Andrew Aguecheek, the marvelously inept wooer that Sir Toby has imported to court his niece, Olivia.

These clowns get very angry at Malvolio for trying to cut down the noise at their midnight revels, and they play a joke on him. Maria leaves, where he will find it, a letter which enables him to believe that Olivia is in love with him. Ah, such dreams of glory! " 'Some are born great, some achieve greatness, and some have greatness thrust upon them.' " And Malvolio tries to take Olivia up on the letter, with the result that everyone thinks he is mad. He is locked in a dark room (a standard Renaissance cure for madness), and he ends up the play being very indignant at everybody, "I'll be revenged on the whole pack of you!" In this century, we rather like the idea of a steward marrying his mistress. It's a good democratic thing to do, rather like marrying the boss's daughter. To the Elizabethans, though, this kind of romance tended to twist that great chain of being out of order. Malvolio, they would have said, is being terribly, terribly presumptuous. In this century, some producers of *Twelfth Night* tend to make it over into the tragedy of Malvolio, but this is surely to deform the play. Malvolio is an extremely stuffy and tiresome individual, and we in the audience should take great delight in seeing that he gets what's coming to him.

The third plot—you could scarcely call it a plot—concerns the clowns, Sir Toby, Maria, and Sir Andrew. It is rather vestigial, but they do do a lot of fooling around, Sir Toby does end up marrying Maria, and he does bawl Sir Andrew out for having gotten Sir Toby's head battered through his cowardice.

Finally, presiding over it all, is that wonderfully enigmatic, legendary spirit, the Fool, or, as he is called in this play, Feste.

Now, what holds all these plots together? That is the central question in any Shakespearean play, as we have already seen in *The Merchant of Venice* or *Part I* of *Henry IV* or, for that matter, *Hamlet*. Just because this play is a comedy, we cannot avoid the same question: What holds it all together? You could say, in a way, that all these plots are in the same boat, because *Twelfth Night* is an extraordinarily sloshy play, much concerned with liquids, fluids, and one thing flowing into another. All through the play we hear about many, many different kinds of fluids: the sea, tears, liquor, urine, blood, ink, water, ale, gall, aqua vitae, the humors of the body, and so on. Most of these images are really quite gratuitous—that is, they are not demanded by the action—as when Malvolio says of Viola-Cesario: " 'Tis with him in standing water, between boy and man." Or, when Sir Toby wishes to challenge Sebastian to a duel: "I must have an ounce or two of this malapert blood from you."

Contrasted with fluids, dryness seems to suggest barrenness or lack of fertility. Maria tells us that Sir Andrew Aguecheek's hand is a dry hand. It was an old idea that a moist hand betokened a warm, we might even say sexy, heart; Andrew's hand is just the opposite, and that tells us something about Sir Andrew. In the same vein, Sir Toby says of Malvolio in a wonderful line, "Dost thou think, because thou art virtuous, there shall be no more cakes and ale?"

Malvolio is a sour, dried-out kind of person, one who is not associated with the fluid of ale or any other liquor, for that matter. Again, early in the play, Olivia, his mistress, tells the Fool he is a "dry fool," that is, a fool who lacks the fluidity or fertility of invention. Then Malvolio tells him he is a "barren rascal." These insults the Fool takes to heart: he resolves to prove his fertility, and he helps cause Malvolio and Olivia all that trouble. As against this connection of dryness with sterility, any fluid, even salt tears, is fertile. In fact, Viola actually speaks of "fertile tears."

Far and away the biggest fluid in *Twelfth Night,* however, is the sea. Both Viola and Sebastian are nearly drowned in the sea, and miraculously they are thrust up out of it in almost an act of birth. There are two sea captains. And one of them, Antonio, stands in peril of his life because of his activities in a sea battle against Orsino's forces. The sea in *Twelfth Night* is vast, hostile, and devouring, but, oddly enough, it is to be associated with love. In the first lines of the play Orsino sighs,

> O spirit of love, how quick and fresh art thou,
> That, notwithstanding thy capacity,
> Receiveth as the sea: nought enters there,
> Of what validity and pitch soe'er
> But falls into abatement and low price
> Even in a minute.
>
> (I. i. 9–14)

Orsino is saying that love can take, absorb everything else and render it of little value, just as the most precious cargoes are of low price when still subject to the risks and hazards of the sea. Later on, talking to Viola-Cesario, he comes back to the same image; his love, he says,

> is all as hungry as the sea
> And can digest as much.
> (II. iv. 99–100)

Viola herself, when she first begins to hope that Sebastian may still be alive, cries out, "Tempests are kind, and salt waves fresh in love!" (III. iv. 364). Antonio, the sea captain, describes himself as having redeemed Sebastian "From the rude sea's enraged and foamy mouth" (V. i. 72). The sea is always in *Twelfth Night* thought of as devouring, swallowing, digesting. And at the same time it seems to be mixed up with love and death, risk and value.

People in love are described as voyaging over the devouring and digesting sea. It is as though the sea were the spirit of love in a broad and universal sense, while the particular lover makes his risky voyage. Sebastian's friend Antonio, the sea captain, speaks of his love to Sebastian, as such "As might have drawn one to a longer voyage." After Sir Andrew Aguecheek has missed a wooing opportunity, he is told, "You are now sailed into the North of my lady's opinion, where you will hang like an icicle on a Dutchman's beard." Maria speaks of Viola-Cesario's embassy to her mistress Olivia as a voyage, and tries to dismiss Viola by saying, "Will you hoist sail, sir? Here lies your way." And Viola replies, "No, good swabber, I am to hull here a little longer." Feste, the Fool, tells the lovesick Duke, "I would have men of such constancy put to sea, that their business might be everything, and their intent everywhere; for that's it that always makes a good voyage of nothing." And the Duke muses,

> For such as I am all true lovers are,
> Unstaid and skittish in all motions else
> Save in the constant image of the creature
> That is beloved.
>
> (II. iv. 16–19)

In effect, the Duke is describing himself as like a voyager on the sea, unstaid and skittish in all motions, ever moving, floating, flowing, constant only in the fact that he always sees the sea, the beloved, the spirit of love. In the lovely words of the Fool's song,

> Trip no further, pretty sweeting;
> Journeys end in lovers meeting.
>
> (II. iii. 39–40)

The sea is the big fluid in *Twelfth Night;* but there are some littler fluids, too, the body fluids or humors, as the Elizabethans called them. These were four fluids, the balance of which determined personality and mood. Usually, in *Twelfth Night,* humor is used to refer to a whim or sudden fancy, as though one of these humors were suddenly asserting itself. Malvolio speaks of himself as having suddenly "the humor of state," meaning, he will suddenly want to talk like a man of importance with political business. Sir Toby hiding in the bushes watches Malvolio pick up the fateful letter and says, "The spirit of humors intimate reading aloud to him!" in other words, give him a whim to read aloud. Some of Orsino's attendants comment on the suddenness of Viola-Cesario's popularity with the Duke. She says, "You either fear his humor or my negligence that you call in question the continuance of his love." In other words, you are treating this as a mere whim, if you think he won't continue to love me. And Sir Andrew, that grand philosopher—Toby asks him, "Does not our lives consist of the four elements?" in this context, the four humors, and Andrew replies, "Faith, so they say; but I think it rather consists of eating and drinking," another fluid. This is one of the significances of Malvolio's madness—his humors, his liquids, have gotten out of balance.

A whole mass of the play comes together when Olivia asks the Fool, "What's a drunken man like, Fool?" And Feste answers, "Like a drowned man, a fool, and a madman." Just in these two lines we see four of the characters of the play, a drunken man, Sir Toby; a drowned man, Viola-Cesario-Sebastian, this peculiar androgynous figure thrust up from the sea; a fool, Feste; and a madman, Malvolio. "What's a drunken man like, Fool?" "Like a drowned man, a fool, and a madman. One draft above heat makes him a fool, the second mads him, and a third drowns him." In other words, all these four characters, drunken man, drowned man, madman, and fool, they are all to be associated with a fluid and different amounts of a fluid.

A lot of Feste's wit has this same fluid quality, running on from word to word or idea to idea, often by a kind of question-and-answer process. For example, the first time we see Feste he opens with a curious, flowing dialogue with Maria, then the same kind of thing with his mistress Olivia. She complains he is a "dry fool" and he says, "Give the dry fool drink, then is the fool not dry." He says he will mend, that is "amend," get better, and proceeds by a kind of, as he says, "catechism," to prove his mistress a fool. He describes this kind of wit himself: "To see this age! A sentence is but a chev'ril glove to a good wit. How quickly the wrong side may be turned outward!" Chev'ril was a very elastic and flexible kid leather, easily stretched, and stretch is exactly what Feste does with words. In fact, he insists to Viola that he is not Olivia's "fool, but her corrupter of words." Not only Feste, though, but all the characters to some extent have this interest in making words flow into one another, getting ideas to merge and blend as in mixing a drink. In his opening speech, Duke Orsino describes the line of music he likes,

> O, it came o'er my ear like the sweet sound
> That breathes upon a bank of violets,
> Stealing and giving odor.
>
> (I. i. 5-7)

He starts out talking about music coming over his ear like a sweet sound, but suddenly it flows into a wind blowing upon a bank of violets and giving, not sound, but odor.

Orsino's words bring us to music, music, music. The play is full of it. In the course of the play we hear four songs, three of which are among the loveliest in Shakespeare: "Oh Mistress Mine," "Come Away, Come Away, Death" and "I am Gone, Sir." Then there is that lovely, ambiguous song with which the play closes, "When that I was and a little tiny boy." The play not only ends with music, it begins with music. "If music be the food of love, play on." And all through the fooling with Sir Toby, Sir Andrew, and Feste, we hear little scraps and fragments of ballads and songs. We hear about dancing, too, when Sir Andrew says, "I would I had bestowed that time in the tongues that I have in fencing, dancing, and bear-baiting." He tells us he thinks he has the back trick (we would say, the "dip"), "simply as strong as any man in Illyria." And Sir Toby says, "Wherefore are these things hid? . . . Why dost thou not go to church in a galliard and come home in a coranto? My very walk should be a jig. I would not so much as make water but in a sink-a-pace," all names of dances—plus one fluid.

Fluids, tears, drinks, the sea and voyaging in the sea, the flow of music and dancing, this whole play is full of different kinds of flowing. This is how Viola describes her difficult predicament, being in love with Orsino, and being sent by Orsino to woo Olivia for him:

> My master loves her dearly;
> And I (poor monster) fond as much on him;
> And she (mistaken) seems to dote on me.
>
> (II. ii. 32–34)

It is the eternal triangle, and as Viola says, "What will become of this?" "O Time, thou must untangle this, not I." Indeed it is, as Feste says at the end of the play, "the whirligig of time" that straightens out the situation; and perhaps the flow of time is the ultimate flowing in *Twelfth Night*. The triangle of crossed lovers, the whirligig of time—now I think we are in a position to say what is binding the three plots of *Twelfth Night* together.

All three plots present their characters with some sort of fluid, ambiguous object; then the comic victims see in that object what they wish to find there. The modern psychological word for this is "projection," that is, the act of attributing to external reality something that is really only a desire in our own minds. *Twelfth Night* shows us a world rather like the psychiatrist's ink blots, except that the ink isn't blotted—it's still sloshing around. In the lowest plot, Sir Andrew plays the ambiguous, epicene figure, and on him Sir Toby projects his wishes for money and fun. In the middle plot, Malvolio finds what Maria calls "some obscure epistles of love." On this peculiar letter with its riddling anagrams and puns, Malvolio projects his secret wish, namely, that Olivia will love and marry him, thus raising him in rank. In the high plot, the ambiguous hermaphroditic or androgynous figure is Viola-Sebastian. These mysterious twins are thrust up out of the sea in what is virtually an act of birth, and on them Olivia and Orsino project what they would like to love. Reality, in *Twelfth Night,* is such a fluid: the sea, tears, ink, wines, even music and dancing, or some ambiguous, flowing, shifting thing like Feste's foolery or a plot of crossed lovers. Man, in *Twelfth Night,* is man the projectionist, man who imagines into the flow of reality what he wants to find there and then finds it. "Prove true, imagination, O prove true!" cries Viola as she first comes to suspect her brother may be alive.

"Projection" is a modern word—Shakespeare's equivalent is "fancy" or "fantasy" or "imagination," that is, image-making, delusive imaginings, the ability to make up shapes and forms as in the famous passage from *A Midsummer Night's Dream:*

> Lovers and madmen have such seething brains,
> Such shaping fantasies, that apprehend
> More than cool reason ever comprehends.
> The lunatic, the lover, and the poet
> Are of imagination all compact.
> One sees more devils than vast hell can hold:
> That is the madman. The lover, all as frantic,
> Sees Helen's beauty in a brow of Egypt.
> The poet's eye, in a fine frenzy rolling,
> Doth glance from heaven to earth, from earth to heaven;
> And as imagination bodies forth
> The forms of things unknown, the poet's pen
> Turns them to shapes, and gives to airy nothing
> A local habitation and a name.
> Such tricks hath strong imagination
> That, if it would but apprehend some joy,
> It comprehends some bringer of that joy;
> Or in the night, imagining some fear,
> How easy is a bush supposed a bear!

> (V. i. 4–22)

We have no poets in *Twelfth Night,* but lovers and madmen galore. Our principal lover, Orsino, spells out this contrast of apprehension and comprehension, "fancy" as against "capacity," rational mental power:

> O spirit of love, how quick and fresh art thou,
> That, notwithstanding thy capacity,
> Receiveth as the sea: nought enters there,
> Of what validity and pitch soe'er,
> But falls into abatement and low price
> Even in a minute. So full of shapes is fancy
> That it alone is high fantastical.

> (I. i. 9–15)

Fancy alone deserves the name "high fantastical," a form grotesquely imagined, because of the way it contains every imaginable image and turns from one to another "even in a minute."

"Fancy," "fantasy"—the words come from a Greek verb meaning "to make visible"—they are ocular things and hence closely linked to whatever it is that makes us fall in love either in Elizabethan terms or in those of the modern cosmetics ad; that is, we fall in love through sight:

> O, when mine eyes did see Olivia first,
> Methought she purged the air of pestilence.

> (I. i. 20–21)

And Orsino asks Viola-Cesario:

> My life upon't, young though thou art, thine eye
> Hath stayed upon some favor that it loves.
>
> (II. iv. 22–23)

And Olivia falls for that same Viola-Cesario with her eyes:

> Methinks I feel this youth's perfections
> With an invisible and subtle stealth
> To creep in at mine eyes.
>
> (I. v. 282–284)

All through the play, people speak of being drawn by their eyes. We see it most clearly in the little scene (III. iii) between Viola's twin, Sebastian, and his rescuer, the sea captain Antonio (for whom it is death to enter Illyria). Antonio says, despite the danger, he had to follow his young friend into town for "love to see you" and for "jealousy," apprehension of what might happen to one entering an unknown place—itself another kind of projection or fancy. Sebastian makes a classic statement of tourism:

> I pray you let us satisfy our eyes
> With the memorials and the things of fame
> That do renown this city.
>
> (III. iii. 22–24)

Antonio replies:

> I will bespeak our diet,
> Whiles you beguile the time and feed your knowledge
> With viewing of the town.
>
>   .   .   .
>
> Haply your eye shall light upon some toy
> You have desire to purchase.
>
> (40–45)

These passages speak as though our eyes led our appetites (hence Antonio's food imagery). Actually, though, as the rest of the play shows, the process is just the other way round—our appetites give rise to our projections onto the outer world, and we then see or fancy what we desire.

Conversely, if we wish to be desired, fancied, the recipe is to make ourselves mysterious, ambiguous, so as to draw in the fancy of the viewer. Thus, Olivia by wearing her mourning veil draws Orsino even more tightly into the toils of love. She tries the same trick when Viola-Cesario first comes to call on her, putting a veil over her face, turning herself into an ambiguous thing onto which men will project their desires—the effect is not unlike the sunglasses movie stars wear.

Twelfth Night makes much of one specific kind of projection—we can call it entertainment. The comedy abounds in music, dancing, songs, jokes—it even has a professional clown in it. And perhaps we can see the relation of this entertainment to the idea of projection or fancy from a picture which the professional clown mentions (II. iii. 16), the picture of "We Three." It showed two fools or mules and then, you, the audience, looked at the picture and saw the caption, "We Three"—you making the third. Entertainment in *Twelfth Night* creates rather the same relation between audience and object of entertainment as the picture of "We Three." The business of the entertainer seems to be to give his audience an ambiguous thing on which they can project their desires and hungers and so be drawn in to the entertainment by their fancy—as in the opening lines of the play:

> If music be the food of love, play on,
> Give me excess of it, that, surfeiting,
> The appetite may sicken, and so die.
> (I. i. 1–3)

The entertainer presents—or even becomes—an ambiguous mystery which his audience can "fancy." Viola, for example, dressed up as a boy, becomes an ambiguous figure and thinks of herself as an entertainer:

> I'll serve this duke.
> Thou shalt present me as an eunuch to him;
> It may be worth thy pains. For I can sing
> And speak to him in many sorts of music
> That will allow me very worth his service.
> (I. ii. 55–59)

But the example *par excellence* of the entertainer as one who offers his ambiguous self as the object of our fancies is, of course, Feste: "Bonos dies, Sir Toby; for, as the old hermit of Prague, that never saw pen and ink, very wittily said to a niece of King Gorboduc, 'That that is is.' " You can make of *that* what you will. Sir Andrew sums it up: "In sooth, thou wast in very gracious fooling last night, when thou spok'st of Pigrogromitus, of the Varians passing the equinoctial of Queubus. 'Twas very good, i' faith. I sent thee sixpence. . . ." And Feste replies:

> I did impeticos thy gratillity, for Malvolio's nose is no whipstock. My
> lady has a white hand, and the Myrmidons are no bottle-ale houses.
> *Andrew.* Excellent! why this is the best fooling, when all is done.
> (II. iii. 25–29)

And so it is—in a way—for surely the best fooling is: What you Will.

In short, then, *Twelfth Night* is a play about "what you will," a play which offers its characters—and its audience—a fluid, ambiguous reality which they

—and we—can fancy. Then, in a second movement, that fluid turns on us and overwhelms us, leaving us splashing about, drunk, mad, or drowned. Sir Toby gets his head battered in by Sebastian as a result of his trying to entice Sir Andrew, one ambiguous, epicene figure, into a duel with the other ambiguous, epicene figure, Viola-Sebastian. Olivia is made ridiculous by falling in love with a woman. Orsino is shown how sillily he has behaved in pursuing someone who does not love him and neglecting someone who has humbly served him out of love. Malvolio is thought mad and locked up in a dark room to keep his eyes from leading his fancy astray again. The comedy shows us one fluid situation after another onto which the characters project their wishes and are thereby maddened and, figuratively, drowned. "What's a drunken man like, Fool?" "Like a drowned man, a fool, and a madman. One draught above heat makes him a fool, the second mads him, and a third drowns him." This theme of fancying and being engulfed in fancy not only holds all three plots together but the imagery such as the sea and other fluids, music and dancing, seeing and hungering, and also the idea of entertainment. For, after all, that is what we are watching when we see *Twelfth Night,* an ambiguous, flowing entertainment in which we find—"what you will." The play, in other words, names itself.

Entertainment has another special sense in this comedy. *Twelfth Night* is the twelfth night after Christmas, January 6, the feast of the Epiphany, and in many places in Europe the time when Christmas festivities are celebrated after a carnival period. We now know that this festival derives from an old Roman holiday called the Saturnalia. The Saturnalia took place at the same time of year but it was a fertility festival, a festival celebrating the sowing of crops, and, I suppose, with all the lovemaking going on in *Twelfth Night,* fertility is not wholly inappropriate. The Saturnalia was a time of general festivity, indeed, license, a time for gift-giving, and a time when the normal rules of rank, say, as between master and slave, were thrown away. These customs, rather like those of a modern Mardi Gras or carnival, carried over into the *Twelfth Night* games and customs of Shakespeare's England. Presiding over the Saturnalia was a mock king called the *festus,* and he survives in Shakespeare's play as Feste, the Fool, who is, in a sense, the spirit who presides over the play, the Lord of Misrule, to use the Elizabethan term for him. In Shakespeare's day, these mockery kings often took the role of priests as our Feste does. It was customary, too, to sacrifice the Festus in a ritual or symbolic way, and Feste, by being left alone on the stage at the end to sing his strangely bittersweet song, is, in one way, sacrificed. He is sacrificed another way: where the other characters are allowed to give themselves over to folly, he may not. He must play to the flowing mood or whim or humor of the people with whom he jests; he cannot be guilty, as the wise man can, of taking an ambiguous situation and projecting the wrong thing on it:

He must observe their mood on whom he jests,
The quality of persons, and the time;
Not, like the haggard, check at every feather
That comes before his eye. This is a practice
As full of labor as a wise man's art.

(III. i. 60–64)

In other words, what is a carnival or holiday for the others, is not for the professional fool.

Further, in *Twelfth Night,* as in a carnival or Saturnalia, we find the normal relations of rank overturned in the general fluidity of it all. The sea captain, Antonio, who brings Viola's brother Sebastian ashore—there could hardly be a more authoritarian figure than a sea captain—nevertheless cries out to Sebastian, "If you will not murder me for my love, let me be your servant." Olivia says to Sebastian "Would thou'dst be ruled by me!" and Sebastian replies, dutifully, "Madame, I will." In this comedy, it is the women who rule the men; the men are, in the idiom of the old style of courtly love, their servants. For example, Olivia, who is below the Count Orsino "in degree, estate, years, and wit," nonetheless rules his heart. That strange poem which Olivia is supposed to have written to Malvolio begins "I may command where I adore." At the end, when the Duke Orsino accepts Viola as his wife, he gives her a rank she did not have, "his fancy's queen":

Your master quits you; and for your service done him,

.   .   .

And since you called me master for so long,
Here is my hand; you shall from this time be
Your master's mistress.

(V. i. 311–316)

Naturally, the word "mistress" doesn't have its modern or tabloid connotation —it's simply the feminine form of "master." Thus, Olivia is Malvolio's "mistress," though they have nothing to do with each other in the way of love. At least not really. Of course, there is that letter that reaches Malvolio which begins, "If this fall into thy hand, revolve," that is, have a revolution, overturn the natural relationship of master and servant. All through the comedy that natural relationship is overturned, as part of the Saturnalian, ritual quality of the *Twelfth Night* festival.

On January 6, 1662, that is, Twelfth Night, 1662, Samuel Pepys, the famous diarist, wrote, "After dinner to the Duke's house, and there saw *Twelfth Night* acted well, though it be but a silly play and not related at all to the name or day." "Not related to the name or day"—I fear Pepys was as wrong in this as in most of his other dramatic judgments. Twelfth Night is the Feast of the Epiphany, and the word "epiphany" means a "showing forth" (in fact, it comes from the same root as "fantasy" and "fancy"). The Feast of the Epiphany celebrates the time when the miraculous Christ Child was shown to the Wise Men. But, lo and behold, we look at *Twelfth Night* and what do we find but this peculiar miracle-working child, this androgynous, hermaphroditic young thing, Viola-Sebastian, who is shown in the play not to Wise Men but to fools and folly. The Feast of the Epiphany is the time in many parts of Europe when Christmas gifts are given. The custom comes from folk etymology, as it's called. Illiterate people, puzzled by the word "epiphany," decided it referred to a spirit named Befany in England or Befana in Italy, where the legend starts out, and they invented a story to explain the giving of gifts at the Feast of Epiphany. There was an old woman, Befana, who was supposed to accompany the Wise Men to see the Christ Child, but, like so many women starting out on trips, she ran back in her house for one last thing. The Wise Men, wiser than most husbands, got tired of waiting around and went off. Ever since, this old woman is condemned to go around on Twelfth Night giving presents to all the children because she didn't give one to the Christ Child. It's a charming story, but what does it have to do with *Twelfth Night?* For one thing, just as the Wise Men had to travel and travel to find the Christ Child, so in this play people are constantly traveling: Viola and Feste travel back and forth between Orsino's house and Olivia's, Viola and Sebastian and Antonio travel over the seas; finally, the climax of the play comes when Olivia travels to Orsino and Viola and Sebastian show themselves in the same place at the same time.

Also, all through this *Twelfth Night,* people are giving one another tips and presents of different kinds. In particular, the Fool, Feste, manages to get tips from Viola, from the Duke, from Sir Toby and Sir Andrew; he is one wheedler of gifts and a kind of miraculous child. But everyone else gets and gives gifts, too. We know that Toby has been wheedling money out of Sir Andrew. Olivia sends Viola a ring; Orsino sends Olivia a jewel; Olivia sends Sebastian a pearl. Throughout the play, this play of love, love is treated as a kind of wealth (much the way it was in *The Merchant of Venice*). Thus Orsino speaks of the love he *owes* to Olivia, as though it were a debt. Earlier he complains, when Olivia is mourning for her brother, that she is paying the debt of love to her brother, and he wishes she would pay the same debt to him. This money, these jewels and gifts passing back and forth, are part of the imagery in the play of things flowing and moving. They are also associated with our basic theme, the theme of projection. We pay, in effect, for the privilege of projecting our hopes and our wishes, what Orsino calls our "love thoughts," onto another person. This is the role of the entertainer in our lives; and he is precious indeed, and we pay him very highly for it.

Even if Samuel Pepys didn't think so, the comedy *Twelfth Night* has a good deal to do with the feast, Twelfth Night. Is it not possible to think of the Christ Child as some sort of ultimate entertainer, an ambiguous person, half human, half divine, a god-man on whom we project our wishes, to whom we pay rich gifts and love, whose kingdom is one of universal love in which there are no masters, no servants? And is he not the ultimate *festus* sacrificed to pay for our folly? Be that as it may, *Twelfth Night* is a Twelfth Night revel, a party, an entertainment in a very formal, literal way, complete with songs, dances, music, and entertainment, gift-giving, mockery king, and the rest.

This revel takes place, as it were, at the edge of the sea. There is a bittersweet tone to this play. We are always aware in it, that Illyria is a fanciful world, and somehow on the edge of Illyria is waiting the real world, the world of storms and drownings and pirates. We see it best in the clown's final song with its refrain, "For the rain it raineth everyday." I have read of a performance of this play in which at the end Feste, left alone on the stage to sing his half-jolly, half-sad song, sang it, laid down his lute, and took from his costume the rose he had been wearing all through the performance and laid it on the strings, making a final chord with which the play ended. This little bit of sentimental business captures the mood perfectly, the sense of revel and entertainment, a little island of revelry in a world where the rain it raineth every day. The revel of *Twelfth Night* hovers on the brink of tragedy. It opens with Olivia mourning her dead brother and Viola also mourning a lost brother. Over and over again in this comedy, we hear of the sad flow of time. The Duke calls for a song.

> Oh, fellow, come, the song we had last night.
> Mark it, Cesario; it is old and plain.
> The spinsters and the knitters in the sun,
> And the free maids that weave their thread with bones,
> Do use to chant it. It is silly sooth,
> And dallies with the innocence of love,
> Like the old age.
>
> (II. iv. 41–47)

Like the golden age, that is, the "good old days." When the priest comes at the end of the comedy to testify to Olivia and Sebastian's marriage, he says that it took place a little while before,

> Since when, my watch hath told me, toward my grave
> I have travelled but two hours.
>
> (V. i. 156–157)

Suddenly in the moment of festivity, there is this sudden, sharp reference to death. What is it the prayerbook says? "In the midst of life we are in death." And we sense that in this play; it creates a gay feeling of flow and change and movement, but a feeling, too, that life is flowing away in "the whirligig of time."

Another bittersweet element in the play is the sense of madness. The word occurs in this comedy as often as in any of the tragedies with real mad people. Still another bittersweet element is separation; Viola separated from Sebastian; Orsino separated from Olivia; Antonio separated from his friend Sebastian; Sir Toby banishing Sir Andrew at the end. The comedy draws fine lines somehow between madness and folly, and folly in the play edges over to a kind of madness.

Love and death, as in Wagner's *Liebestod,* come close together in *Twelfth Night*—another fine line the comedy draws. Olivia has lost a brother and yet by the end of the play, she has recovered a brother, Viola's brother, Sebastian. In Elizabethan times, the word "die" had a distinctly sensual sense to it; it meant to have sexual ecstasy, as in *Romeo and Juliet* or *Antony and Cleopatra* where the lovers "die together" at the end of the play. In this play, too, love and death are closely linked.

The world of *Twelfth Night* is a comic world, and it would grossly falsify the play to suggest that it is tragic, but we should recognize that there is tragedy on the brink of this comic world. A world of the sea, with its battles in which Orsino's nephew lost his leg, that harsh world of the sea and tempests, hovers always at the edges of the play. The play begins with music against which the second scene poises Viola's account of the tempest in which she lost her brother. In other words, the play begins with the contrast of tempest and music. The play ends with a tempest *in* music—"the rain it raineth every day." And in that final song of Feste, virtually all the themes of the play come together.

"When that I was and a little tiny boy" suggests the miraculous child of Twelfth Night while "the wind and the rain" reminds us of that world of the sea and tempests which awaits the ending of the revel, *Twelfth Night.* "A foolish thing was but a toy"—it makes a very neat statement of the theme of fancy in the play, the ambiguous thing on which we project our hopes. When we are children, toys are but toys, but as Feste found,

> But when I came to man's estate,
>
>   .   .   .
>
> 'Gainst knaves and thieves men shut their gate.
>
> (V. i. 382–383)

That is, foolish things are not just toys when you're a man; people take them very, very seriously. When Feste became a man, there was, alas, that defeat of expectations which happens so often in this play. A character like Malvolio or Olivia projects his or her wishes on some ambiguous object, and then it turns out to be just a trap, a trick which overwhelms them.

> But when I came, alas, to wive,
>
>   .   .   .

> By swaggering could I never thrive.
> (386–388)

The theme of the stanza is, in a somewhat garbled way, love as against authority or "swaggering." Somehow, in love, the ordinary rules and certainties of rank don't apply. And perhaps the other meaning of "swaggering,"—partying, roistering—applies in this play of partying. Then the cryptic fourth stanza,

> But when I came unto my beds
>   With hey, ho, the wind and the rain,
> With tosspots still had drunken heads,
>   The rain it raineth every day.
> (390–393)

That should remind us of Olivia's question, "What's a drunken man like, fool?", and the answer, "Like a drowned man, a fool, and a madman. One draught above heat makes him a fool, the second mads him, and the third drowns him." In this comedy there is an irresistible progression from simple folly and drinking to madness and drowning, to a world of shipwreck and piracy, a world in which time flows away, and folly becomes madness. Then, in the final stanza, Feste gives us his theme of entertainment:

> A great while ago the world begun
>   With hey, ho, the wind and the rain;
> But that's all one, our play is done,
>   And we'll strive to please you every day.
> (394–397)

He, in effect, asks from us, the audience, that we, having projected our hopes on this ambiguous, shifting, flowing thing we have watched, *Twelfth Night,* or, for that matter, his ambiguous song, that we will pay him his due of applause. And we will.

Twelfth Night gives us a chance to do homage to Shakespeare's comic imagination. In the two tragedies of the preceding chapters, *Julius Caesar* and *Hamlet,* we found that at the most basic level of the imagination, Shakespeare was dealing with the theme of separation. In *Julius Caesar,* it was the separation of Caesar into his body and his spirit, into the private, physical man, on the one hand, on the other, into the public, symbolic figure. The essence of the tragedy lay in the act of separating these two parts of Caesar, and in the fact that the two men who do the separating, Brutus and Cassius, each a half of Caesar, are two men, not one. Similarly, in *Hamlet,* perhaps the ultimate statement of Shakespeare's tragic imagination, the tragedy was again one of separation. Hamlet combined the man of thought and the man of action, but this combination would not function (except in "play"), and the tragedy regretfully, as it were, gave us the separated figures of Horatio and Fortinbras as an alternative. In other words, Shakespeare's mind confronts in *Hamlet* an ultimate tragedy, namely, that the combination of good qualities somehow does not work. In *Twelfth Night,* Shakespeare's theme is just the opposite of separation or fragmentation, as in the tragedies. His theme is combination, bringing everything together. He pours things into one another, even his audience getting mixed into the entertainment. It's rather like a Charlie Chaplin movie—one scene in particular comes to mind; it occurs, I think, in *The Bank.* Anyway, Charlie, playing the janitor in a bank, walks into a room in the basement. He's carrying a mop and a pail. There's a secretary sitting at the desk with a lot of papers. There's an electric fan cooling off the room, and one thing leads to another. The mop hits the secretary, and somehow the fan gets started going, and the papers blow around, and then the mop swings around and hits the bank executive, and he jumps up and stamps around and puts his foot in the pail of water, and suddenly everything in the room has come alive: everything in the room is flowing into everything else in the room. It's what we who study the matter call "comic combinability," the idea that comedy is like a great big ball of gum: you start it rolling and everything it touches gets attached and hooked onto the ball, mixed in together. Something of the sort goes on in *Twelfth Night.* Shakespeare's imagination works in patterns of flow and projection—the more things flow around, the more people project on them; the thing just cumulates and cumulates, culminating in those hilarious slapstick duel scenes between Sir Andrew and Viola-Cesario, until finally, everybody gets married, even Sir Toby marries Maria. It is as though the whole play just wanted to build up into a miraculous, overwhelming multiplication.

In a way, then, when we look at *Twelfth Night* as against *Julius Caesar* and *Hamlet,* we see in sharp relief, as it were, the difference between Shakespeare's tragic world and his comic world. Shakespeare's comic world is a world of combination and union; Shakespeare's tragic world is a world of separation and fragmentation. The tragic elements in *Twelfth Night* all tend to be associated with separation: Viola separated from her brother Sebastian; Orsino from Olivia; Sir Andrew from his money, and so on. At the end of the play, Malvolio rushes out, separating himself, saying, "I'll be revenged on the whole pack of you." The same thing was true of *The Merchant of Venice.* Shylock asks at the end of the play to be excused, to separate himself from the rest of the group; the tragic elements were, again, separation, Jessica's running away from her father or the effort to separate Antonio from a pound of his flesh.

Shakespearean comedy has always a tragic edge, but *Twelfth Night,* even with a bittersweet brink, is undeniably comic and it gives us a wonderfully comic vision of man. Man is a creature who looks on the fluid, ambiguous world of his experience and projects onto it what he would like to find; then he is overwhelmed and engulfed by the world of experience he has misunderstood—it splashes over him, almost drowning or maddening him. In much the same way, critics used to look at the rather ambiguous chronology of Shakespeare's plays and project onto it what they wished to find, namely, a deep, serious, solemn tragic period from 1600–1606, for, to the true critic, tragedy is always a more serious and worthwhile enterprise than comedy. But alas, this period of true, romantic "high seriousness" seems more mixed than pure. *Julius Caesar* and *Hamlet, Twelfth Night* and its companion levity, *As You Like It,* all seem to come about the same time. Instead of looking for a period of depression, the critic should accept the fact that with Shakespeare, there never really is pure tragedy or pure comedy, but always a dash of one in the other.

Nevertheless, there is a distinct difference between Shakespeare's comic imagination and his tragic vision. His tragedy is the tragedy of separation; his comedy the comedy of union and acceptance. Shakespeare's comic imagination accepts, even welcomes the confusion and hurly-burly, the combinations, the flow implicit in that phrase, "the whirligig of time." Shakespeare's tragic imagination sees tragedy as a kind of separation or breaking apart or fragmentation. At the beginning of *Twelfth Night* we have the tempest separated from the music, and the beginning of *Twelfth Night* is the saddest, most melancholy part of it. At the end of *Twelfth Night,* we have the tempest *in* music; we have them combined, reconciled, as in the late, great romances. The end of *Twelfth Night,* like the end of all Shakespeare's comedies, is an acceptance of even the most tragic parts of our experience, the passing of time, death, the rain. Even these have the power to entertain us.

> A great while ago the world begun,
>   With hey, ho, the wind and the rain;
> But that's all one, our play is done,
>   And we'll strive to please you every day.

OTHELLO

IF *Twelfth Night* IS THE COMEDY OF FANCY, THEN SURELY *Othello* IS ITS TRAGEDY. If *Twelfth Night* shows us the comic consequences of projecting onto reality what we wish or fear to find there, then *Othello* shows us the tragic consequences—not only for the protagonists of the play, but also for its critics. Many critics project onto a Shakespearean play a modern, or more properly, a late nineteenth-century novel, which describes people and places in exact, realistic detail. Instead, I have been arguing, we should look in Shakespeare for another kind of truth. The issue is, really, whether we are going to look in Shakespeare for a story truth, a truth of character and motivation and plot, or whether we are going to look in Shakespeare for a poetic or psychological truth, a truth that resonates in our minds perhaps because it is not literal, factual realism. Of all Shakespeare's major plays, the one that raises this question most directly, that *has* raised this question in the minds of most of its critics, is *Othello*. The chief problem is Iago. He just doesn't seem to make sense as a human being or the literal portrayal of a human being. In Coleridge's classic phrase, he seems a "motiveless malignity," an inhuman monster with no real reason for the terrible vengeance he wreaks.

There are problems, though, even more fundamental than Iago, notably the time scheme of the play. What time elapses between the various events of the tragedy? The first thing we see is Othello's marriage, the consummation of which is interrupted when Iago awakens Desdemona's father and when the emissaries come from the Senate to send Othello off to Cyprus. He and Desdemona leave for Cyprus right away, but since Othello and Cassio and Desdemona travel in three separate ships, nothing of importance to the tragedy happens.

The first night after they arrive, Othello bids his officers and the people of Cyprus goodnight and goes off to consummate his marriage to Desdemona.

> Come, my dear love.
> The purchase made, the fruits are to ensue;
> That profit's yet to come 'tween me and you.
> (II. iii. 8–10)

That very evening (140 lines later), Cassio gets drunk and starts a brawl which gets Othello up. Angrily, he dismisses Cassio from his post as lieutenant. The very next morning, Cassio sends to Desdemona asking her to intercede for him, and then begins the great temptation scene, Act III, scene iii. The very moment when Othello sees Cassio leave Desdemona, Iago begins his temptation and for five hundred lines of continuous dialogue Iago creates and then plays on Othello's fears: Othello is momentarily reassured; then, unknowing, he himself causes the loss of Desdemona's handkerchief; Iago continues his temptation, finally kneeling at the end of that scene to pledge his vows with those of the now-convinced Othello "to wronged Othello's service." From there on, the action moves continuously through the afternoon when Othello sees Cassio with the handkerchief, to the feast for the visitors from Venice, until Othello that night kills Desdemona in her bed. In other words, all the important action of the play seems to take place in something like twenty-four hours. Iago performs the superhuman feat of persuading Othello, who admittedly is not terribly bright, that within twenty-four hours after the consummation of his marriage —indeed, we are never quite sure whether it is consummated—his wife has deceived him. Iago has even convinced Othello "that she with Cassio hath the act of shame a thousand times committed." Obviously, something has gone radically wrong.

Further to confuse the matter, there are just as many indications of time in the play that prove the action takes place over a period of several weeks. One, obviously, is Iago's statement and Othello's belief that Cassio has made love to Desdemona "a thousand times." Even in the temptation scene itself, Othello says,

> What sense had I of her stol'n hours of lust?
> I saw't not, thought it not, it harmed not me;
> I slept the next night well, fed well, was free
> and merry.
> (III. iii. 338–340)

What next night? says the impudent critic. There is none. And yet there is still other evidence that there was such a night: Iago tells us that he "lay with Cassio lately," that is, shared his rooms with him. That is a night that somehow has to be fitted into the time scheme. How about the time when Bianca, that lady of little virtue who gives what little she has to Cassio, comes up to him and says,

> What, keep a week away? Seven days and nights?
> Eightscore eight hours? and lovers' absent hours,
> More tedious than the dial eightscore times?
> O weary reck'ning!

> (III. iv. 173)

It is indeed a weary reckoning—because we've just seen Cassio disembark at Cyprus, and we know that only a day has gone by in which he could have seen Bianca.

Othello is a man—or a figure of a man—who lives in two totally inconsistent time schemes. What sense, then, does it make to talk about his character or his motivation under such circumstances? Can we say that Othello is too easily jealous, when we do not know how long it takes him to become jealous? We would have to say that Othello is a lunatic for believing that his wife deceived him when there were not hours enough in the day for her to do it.

No. Something else is going on. Shakespeare has stepped out of time and space, and, as always, he is using the theater of our imagination. The key to his technique lies in those very words of Bianca's: "Lovers' absent hours [are] more tedious than the dial eightscore times." Shakespeare is trafficking in psychological or poetic time, not real time. He is dealing with an emotional time, a time in our minds, which makes "lovers' absent hours" seem longer than regular time, and this is, after all, a play about interrupted love. In a psychological or emotional sense, revenge is swift; Othello demands "some *swift* means of death for the fair devil." As in the style of the medieval and (English) Renaissance paintings Shakespeare knew, he has lifted his subject up out of real time and space. Shakespeare has stepped out of the physical world into the theater of our minds. He has gone beyond real time and real space into a psychological—or allegorical—or poetic time and space. We do Shakespeare's art a wrong if we fancy his plays tell us stories about real events and real people. Instead, his plays are appealing directly to the stranger forces of our minds. People do not, after all, live in clock time, as any student looking at his watch in a classroom lecture can tell you. The hours in the office seem shorter at ten o'clock in the morning than they do at four-thirty, and lovers' absent hours are indeed more tedious than the dial eightscore times. We ourselves live in a world of subjective, psychological time, as Shakespeare's plays do, and this transcending mere realism is why Shakespeare is a greater dramatist than those modern playwrights who try to give us a literal representation of reality. The events and the people in Shakespeare are psychological, allegorical, and poetic—and that observation brings us to Iago, and all the rivers and oceans of critical ink that have been spilled trying to account for him.

On the basis of just a first glance at the play, Iago seems not to need any explaining. He gives us motives, plenty of them. In his opening speech with Roderigo, he complains very bitterly that Cassio has been appointed Othello's lieutenant over Iago's head, while he, Iago, is left to be Othello's "ancient" or ensign. This is his materialistic motive; then, in his great speech at the end of Act II, scene i, he gives us his motives of jealousy:

> That Cassio loves her, I do well believe it;
> That she loves him, 'tis apt and of great credit:
> The Moor, howbeit that I endure him not,
> Is of a constant, loving, noble nature,
> And I dare think he'll prove to Desdemona
> A most dear husband. Now I do love her too;
> Not out of absolute lust, though peradventure
> I stand accountant for as great a sin,
> But partly led to diet my revenge,
> For that I do suspect the lusty Moor
> Hath leaped into my seat; the thought whereof
> Doth, like a poisonous mineral, gnaw my inwards;
> And nothing can or shall content my soul
> Till I am evened with him, wife for wife;
> Or failing so, yet that I put the Moor
> At least into a jealousy so strong
> That judgment cannot cure. Which thing to do,
>
>   . . .
>
> I'll have our Michael Cassio on the hip
> Abuse him to the Moor in the rank garb
> (For I fear Cassio with my nightcap too),
> Make the Moor thank me, love me, and reward me
> For making him egregiously an ass
> And practicing upon his peace and quiet
> Even to madness. 'Tis here, but yet confused:
> Knavery's plain face is never seen till used.
>
>   (280–306)

Iago gives us motives galore. He tells us that he believes Cassio loves Desdemona and she him; he claims that he himself loves Desdemona, not so much out of lust, he says, but because he suspects that the lusty Moor has cuckolded him with his wife, Emilia. And then he tells us that he fears Cassio with his nightcap, too. So that by the end of the speech we have four, four! motives for Iago's actions: his resentment of Cassio's promotion, his jealousy of Othello, his jealousy of Cassio, and the fact that he himself loves Desdemona.

And none of them sounds very convincing. Coleridge called it, "the motive-hunting of motiveless malignity" and decided Iago was a kind of devil. What bothered Coleridge, what bothers us, I think, is that there is a disproportion between Iago's motives and the terrible vengeance he wreaks. After all, the fact you didn't get the job you thought you were entitled to is not reason enough to cause the deaths of two innocent people and a third to lose his leg. Also, Iago tells us that he only *suspects* the Moor, he only *suspects* that Othello and Cassio have deceived him with Emilia, and he tells us that he doesn't really love Desdemona. There is a disproportion between the motives he gives and the crime he commits. And that disproportion matches another: the disproportion between Othello's actions and the evidence on which he bases those actions. The whole tragedy depends on these two disproportions, on Iago's failure and Othello's failure: Iago's failure, a failure in moral sense; Othello's failure, a failure in intellect. This parallel suggests that we need to look, then, not at Othello and Iago as individuals but as they combine together. The key to the tragedy lies neither in Iago alone nor in Othello alone, but in their combination and interaction.

We might begin by recognizing that Iago's name is suggestive, if not downright symbolic. His name comes from Santiago or San Diego—St. James—who is the patron saint of Spain and whose cult was associated with driving the Moors out of Spain, just as the essential thing about our Iago is his triumph over Othello. The real relationship between Othello and Iago is that Othello is the general and Iago the lieutenant or ensign. Their real relation is that of superior to subordinate, but Iago turns this around. He becomes, for example, Othello's doctor, and Othello the patient whom Iago himself has poisoned.

> Look where he comes! Not poppy nor mandragora,
> Nor all the drowsy syrups of the world,
> Shall ever med'cine thee to that sweet sleep
> Which thou owedst yesterday.
>
> (III. iii. 330–333)

In effect, Iago prescribes for Othello but denies his own prescription. Nothing will ever medicine Othello to sweet sleep again. Later on, Iago calls out, "Work on, my medicine, work!" He has become the physician, the false physician while Othello is the wounded patient into whose ear Iago pours pestilence. Iago the physician is also Iago the dramatist who sets up scenes and lines and images so as to manipulate the lives of his characters, Othello, Desdemona, and Cassio. Like other Shakespearean villains, Iago seems possessed by a kind of creative energy which runs away with him. He manipulates his characters, steering them and guiding them until they themselves take over his plan and act it out for him.

In short, Iago has reversed the natural relationship between himself and his commander. Up until the great scene, Act III, scene iii, when Iago's deadly words take hold of Othello, we always see Othello in the position of a commander. We see him first breaking up what promises to be a street fight between his own friends and the partisans of Desdemona's father: "Keep up your bright swords, for the dew will rust them." He shows a wonderful kind of majesty then and before his accusers at the council of Venice. In Act II, scene iii, we see Othello entering and putting down the street fight that Iago has gotten Cassio into. At the opening of Act II, we see him, Desdemona, and Cassio arrive at Cyprus. First, Cassio makes an entrance to the excited, expectant Cypriotes. Then Desdemona sweeps in, her entrance topping Cassio's; he announces her:

> Ye men of Cyprus, let her have your knees,
> Hail to thee, lady! And the grace of heaven
> Before, behind thee, and on every hand,
> Enwheel thee round!

> (II. i. 84–87)

Finally Othello makes his grand entrance, the last of the three and the most majestic, as all the people on the stage kneel to his arrival. It is as though he had commanded the very elements of the storm to subside.

Shakespeare always gives us Othello towering over the rest, calming, subduing, commanding, until Iago's suspicions begin to take hold of his mind. At the end of Act III, scene iii, there is a deadly parody of Othello's earlier role when Iago says of him, "Let him command." It is precisely then that Othello no longer commands and that Iago takes over. We see the terrible effects in Act IV, scene i, after Othello's insane "goats and monkeys" speech when the perplexed visitor from Venice asks:

> Is this the noble Moor whom our full Senate
> Call all in all sufficient? Is this the nature
> Whom passion could not shake? whose solid virtue
> The shot of accident nor dart of chance
> Could neither graze nor pierce?

> (IV. i. 257–261)

Iago is no commander himself but a persuader. When Othello appears monumental, masterful, Iago appears as cajoling, wheedling, petty, as, for example, at the opening of Act I, scene i, where he wins to his scheme the fool Roderigo, while Othello is winning the divine Desdemona. Just before Othello is to make his great entrance onto the dock of Cyprus, Shakespeare gives us Iago making a series of witty but slimy and smutty jokes. You might compare these two, Othello and Iago, to a great captain of industry (instead of war) and his public relations counselor or his advertising manager, and maybe the comparison to Madison Avenue is not so farfetched at that, because over and over again Iago's speech converts moral values, the values of faith and love and honesty into money or valuables or a jewel, as in his famous speech:

> Good name in man and woman, dear my lord,
> Is the immediate jewel of their souls.

> Who steals my purse steals trash; 'tis something, nothing;
> 'Twas mine, 'tis his, and has been slave to thousands;
> But he that filches from me my good name
> Robs me of that which not enriches him
> And makes me poor indeed.
>
> (III. iii. 155–161)

It's typical of Iago to take good name and convert it into a commodity, much the way an advertising agency might speak of a company's "image."

The commander as against the hidden persuader—that is one relationship between Othello and Iago. There is a much more important one, though: the relationship between the believer and the doubter. Othello is above all a believer. His attitude toward love is romantic, idealistic, even naïve. Whenever he speaks of war he speaks of it as a kind of romance and in terms of his own romantic history. In the same way, he takes all the mumbo-jumbo about that handkerchief so seriously. In the same way, he trusts Cassio; even more—he trusts Iago. Othello's essential quality is his great faith (or belief or pride) in the validity and nobility of human action. It is precisely this quality which undoes him, because it makes him trust Iago. Iago knows this quality in Othello and seizes on his advantage:

> The Moor is of a free and open nature
> That thinks men honest that but seem to be so;
> And will as tenderly be led by th' nose
> As asses are.
>
> (I. iii. 393–396)

Over and over in the temptation scene, Othello affirms his trust in Iago:

> I know thou'rt full of love and honesty
> And weigh'st thy words before thou giv'st them breath,
> Therefore these stops of thine fright me the more;
> For such things in a false disloyal knave
> Are tricks of custom; but in a man that's just
> They are close dilations, working from the heart
> That passion cannot rule.
>
> (III. iii. 118–124)

And again:

> This honest creature doubtless
> Sees and knows more, much more, than he unfolds.
>
> (242–243)

And again:

> This fellow's of exceeding honesty,
> And knows all qualities, with a learnèd spirit
> Of human dealings.
>
> (258–260)

"Honor," "honest," "honesty" are key words in *Othello*. They occur more often in this play than in any other of Shakespeare's by far. "Honest," to the Elizabethans, meant, first, of course, what we mean by "honest," that is, truth-telling, paying one's debts, and the like. It also meant what we mean by "honorable." Finally, there was a third sense to the word, when it was applied to a woman: it meant "chaste." It was the opposite of the word "light," meaning a "loose" woman. All through the tragedy, there is a constant questioning. Who is honest? Who is honorable? Who is chaste?

These questions are the doubts that Iago raises, for if Othello is a believer, Iago is, above all, a doubter. Just as he suspects Emilia with Cassio, suspects her again with Othello, he sees all the world in harsh, crude, cynical terms, and so he counsels Roderigo:

Virtue? A fig! 'Tis in ourselves that we are thus or thus. Our bodies are our gardens, to the which our wills are gardeners. . . . If the balance of our lives had not one scale of reason to poise another of sensuality, the blood and baseness of our natures would conduct us to most preposterous conclusions. . . . I say, put money in thy purse. It cannot be that Desdemona should long continue her love to the Moor—put money in thy purse—nor he his to her. It was a violent commencement, and thou shalt see an answerable sequestration—put but money in thy purse. These Moors are changeable in their wills—fill thy purse with money. The food that to him now is as luscious as locusts shall be to him shortly as bitter as coloquintida. She must change for youth: when she is sated with his body, she will find the error of her choice. [She must have change, she must.] Therefore put money in thy purse.

(I. iii. 319-350)

And at a later point:

Roderigo.   I cannot believe that in her; she is full of most blessed condition.
Iago.   Blessed, fig's-end! The wine she drinks is made of grapes. If she had been blessed, she would never have loved the Moor. Blessed, pudding! Did'st thou not see her paddle with the palm of his hand? Did'st not mark that?
Roderigo.   Yes, that I did; but that was but courtesy.
Iago.   Lechery, by this hand! an index and obscure prologue to the history of lust and foul thoughts. They met so near with their lips that their breaths embraced together. Villainous thoughts, Roderigo!

(II. i. 245-255)

In one of his most terrifyingly "honest" gestures, Iago confesses that this doubting, suspicious quality is a trait of his:

It is my nature's plague
To spy into abuses, and oft my jealousy
Shapes faults that are not.
(III. iii. 146-148)

Late in the play, just as Iago and Roderigo are about to kill Cassio, or try to, the motive behind Iago's feeling comes out: "If Cassio do remain, he hath a daily beauty in his life that makes me ugly." Iago thinks himself somehow dirty, filthy, base—this is in Iago, as in so many other people, the motive for his hatred and suspicion of others. Cassius was the same type: a man who hated himself and therefore could not live to be in awe of such a thing as himself.

When we put Othello and Iago in combination and see them as patient and doctor, character and dramatist, persuader and commander, but above all, as doubter and believer, as two who project sharply contrasted desires on the world, we begin to recognize, I think, something we have seen in Shakespeare before: the theme of fragmentation. In *Hamlet,* different aspects of Hamlet's character were projected outward onto Horatio, the man of thought, and Fortinbras, the man of action; the tragedy was that these two things were combined in Hamlet but could not work together. All the way back in *Romeo and Juliet,* different aspects of the two lovers were projected outward onto Mercutio and Rosaline and the Nurse and Friar Laurence. The same kind of thing goes on with Othello and Iago: that is, Othello seems to be the pure idealist, uncontaminated by any impulse of cynicism, while Iago seems to be pure cynic, uncontaminated by any impulse of idealism. We have somewhat the same thing in Desdemona and Emilia. The divine Desdemona, as she is called, seems a figure of perfect virtue, of perfect righteousness. In fact, we are given a whole scene, Act IV, scene iii, in which Desdemona's innocence and virtue are contrasted with the worldly wisdom of Emilia. I think we have the feeling, as we see this tragedy, that if somehow Othello and Iago could be mixed, if somehow the idealism could be tempered with a little speck of wisdom, if somehow Desdemona's perfect virtue could be tempered with a little of Emilia's worldly wisdom, the tragedy would not have taken place. These figures, Othello, Desdemona and Iago, become almost allegorical, almost unreal, in the pureness of their good and evil. There is something unnatural about it, as Iago points out:

> Who has a breast so pure
> But some uncleanly apprehensions
> Keep leets and law days and in session sit
> With meditations lawful?
> (III. iii. 138–141)

This tempering, however, is not the answer to the tragedy. We have, in the play, two rather instructive figures, people who do mix idealism and cynicism. They are Roderigo and Emilia. Both of them have idealistic impulses, particularly a faith in Desdemona, but both of them are corrupted by the cynicism of Iago. Both of them balance idealism and cynicism, but at the end of the play, they are both just as dead as the pure idealists, Othello and Desdemona. There seems to be no hope in this tragedy. We start out with the noblest of men, Othello, the purest of good, Desdemona, and the purest of evil, Iago. And evil triumphs. At the end of the play all the other principals are wounded or dead—only Iago is alive. In fact, in all of Shakespeare's tragedies there are only two villains who survive to the final curtain, and Iago is one of them. There seems to be no hope in this tragedy, and perhaps that is why it and the people in it seem a little unreal to us, because, after all, hope is a part of life.

Perhaps that is the reason that, more than any other of Shakespeare's major plays, *Othello* has an allegorical quality, a quality of unreality, a sense that the characters are more like spirits or abstractions than ordinary dramatic characters. Mostly, we get this feeling about Iago, who seems to be a "motiveless malignity," a spirit of doubt who can be understood only in relation to Othello, not as a separate being. In this sense, the tragedy is a psychological tragedy, in which we are seeing acted out before us two aspects of a single human being. In fact, we see Othello and Iago go through a kind of marriage in Act III, scene iii, the great temptation scene, when, at the end of the scene, they kneel together and exchange vows:

> *Othello.*   My bloody thoughts, with violent pace,
>   Shall ne'er look back, ne'er ebb to humble love,
>   Till that a capable and wide revenge
>   Swallow them up. (*He kneels.*) Now, by yond marble heaven,
>   In the due reverence of a sacred vow
>   I here engage my words.
> *Iago.*   Do not rise yet. (*Iago kneels.*)
>   Witness, you ever-burning lights above,
>   You elements that clip us round about,
>   Witness that here Iago doth give up
>   The execution of his wit, hands, heart
>   To wronged Othello's service! Let him command,
>   And to obey shall be in me remorse,
>   What bloody business ever.

(457–469)

This "marriage" (for what else is the kneeling and exchanging of vows?) brings together the divided halves of a single sensibility: Othello, the romantic, the idealist, the believer; Iago, the cynic, the doubter, in short, the villain—as he says of himself, "I am nothing if not critical."

Folklorists have turned up a lot of stories similar to *Othello*. They call the plot or motif "the calumniated wife," or "the calumniator believed." In Shakespeare's *Cymbeline,* one of the plots is based on this motif, which occurs also in the Man of Law's Tale in *The Canterbury Tales,* or, if we reverse the sexes, it is essentially the story of Joseph and Potiphar's wife. This motif, "the calumniator believed," is a way of making into a story two competing impulses, the impulse to trust, and the impulse to distrust. Such stories also act out the way in which, in our minds, thoughts we wish to keep secret, thoughts we do not wish to face, thoughts we repress, find their way deviously into consciousness. A psychologist would speak of "the return of the repressed." When we refuse to recognize certain thoughts, we tend, unconsciously, to project them onto the world outside our minds, particularly the thoughts and looks and words of other people. This is essentially what has happened in *Othello*. Othello, whose mind is so pure he will not allow an impulse of doubt, receives those impulses of doubt from the dark side of himself, Iago. Perhaps that is why Othello feels Iago "knows all qualities, with a learnèd spirit of human dealings"—because Iago knows the things Othello himself has tried to repress and deny.

One of the folk motifs in this tragedy is the theme of the calumniator believed; another is the traditional battle between black man and white. Incidentally, if you browse around among the criticisms of *Othello,* you will find a red herring occasionally drawn across the trail, namely, the question whether or not Othello was actually black, because Moors are not. Shakespeare, though, didn't know very much geography, and the two Moors in his works, Aaron the Moor in *Titus Andronicus* and Othello, are both quite explicitly described as Negroes. In fact, the drawing of a scene from *Titus Andronicus* (see Fig. 7) shows the Moor as black. We have to put down the designation "Moor" as simply one more of Shakespeare's geographical mistakes, like that mid-Atlantic seacoast of Bohemia.

Othello is a tragedy about the struggle, traditional in folklore, between black, dark, evil and fair, white, goodness—but the colors are reversed here. Where in traditional Greek mythology the black man (*Melanthos*) would stand for the forces of death or winter and the white man (*Xanthos*) for spring and rebirth, or, in our own Westerns, where the man in the black hat would be the "bad guy" and the man in the white hat the "good guy," these relations are reversed in *Othello*. That very reversal suggests one of the most basic themes of the tragedy, how difficult it is to know, as it were, black from white. Iago looks honest; everybody in the play, at one time or another, calls him "honest." And yet he is not. On the stage, this theme of what is black being actually white, and what is white being actually black, is often fudged. Iago is too often played as a moustache-twirling villain; the effect is to make the tragedy foolish, for any fool can see—or at least we in the audience can—that this Iago is a bad apple. No. Iago should be blond; he should project an air of goodness and honesty and sincerity far more than Cassio, who is usually the blond ingénue in most productions. To give credit to the deception of Othello, Iago must be, in the words of an eighteenth-century critic, "an open-hearted, frank, plain-dealing souldier, a character constantly worn by them for some thousands of years." Let us by all means, then, have blond Iagos to carry out this curiously reversed contrast of black and white.

There is another folk theme in the play, that of the shapeshifter. By the shapeshifter, folklorists refer to the trickster of American Indian stories, or such characters as Loki from Norse mythology, or Hermes from the Greek—characters whose essence is a series of tricks and clevernesses. Shakespeare would have known this folk character as the Vice, the villain, of the old morality plays. The shapeshifter is a character who travels by his wits, who by schemes and stratagems achieves his ends, usually triumphing over big, strong, monumental figures like Othello. The shapeshifter's stories project another human wish, one that I've noticed is most devoutly held by children and college professors, namely, that brains will somehow triumph over brawn. Back in the psychological depths, I suppose it is the child's hope that by being clever and witty he can somehow triumph over the superior strength and power of his parents. At any rate, Iago is one more in a long line of these characters of folklore and mythology, the shapeshifters.

There is still another great mythic theme in *Othello,* the juxtaposition of love and war, or, as in *Romeo and Juliet,* sex and fighting. Othello woos Desdemona by telling her of his exploits in war, as Iago calls it, "bragging and telling her fantastical lies." Othello tells us that, when Desdemona heard his history,

> She wished she had not heard it; yet she wished
> That heaven had made her such a man.
>
> (I. iii. 162–163)

Then, when Othello greets her in his magnificent entrance onto the docks of Cyprus in Act II, scene i, he cries out to Desdemona, "O my fair warrior!" Male and female, love and war, these are the dimensions of Othello and Desdemona. She finds the man in herself in Othello and he finds the woman in himself in Desdemona. The opening scenes of the play bring together Othello's marriage and the war with the Turks as simultaneous and related events, and when in Act III, scene iii, the scene of the temptation, Iago's trickery takes hold, Othello immediately and magnificently translates the loss of his love into the loss of his military occupation.

> O, now for ever
> Farewell the tranquil mind! farewell content!
> Farewell the plumèd troop, and the big wars
> That make ambition virtue! O, farewell!
> Farewell the neighing steed and the shrill trump,
> The spirit-stirring drum, th' ear-piercing fife,
> The royal banner, and all quality,
> Pride, pomp, and circumstance of glorious war!

> And O you mortal engines whose rude throats
> Th' immortal Jove's dread clamors counterfeit,
> Farewell! Othello's occupation's gone!
>
> (III. iii. 347–357)

As in *Romeo and Juliet,* love and fighting go together. They are the world of action and against that world of action stands the thought, the criticism, of Iago. The contrast is rather like that in *Hamlet,* a sense that somehow thought interferes with action. Doubting is the natural enemy, the antagonist, of action. "The native hue of resolution is sicklied o'er with the pale cast of thought." Here again, just as in juxtaposing love and fighting, there is a psychological truth. We all wish, I suppose, that we could act directly, forcefully, effectively, without hesitations, doubts, or thoughts—but there is an Iago in each of us.

There is still another level to *Othello,* a religious level. *Othello* is a tragedy that operates, in Emilia's phrase, at the level of "heaven and men and devils." Desdemona is divine, heavenly; Iago is devilish, hellish; and Othello is man, Everyman. Othello says of Desdemona, "If she is false, O, then heaven mocks itself!" Even Iago, who denies her "blessed condition," nevertheless recognizes that she can "play the god" with Othello. Indeed, Cassio greets her like a goddess when she comes ashore at Cyprus:

> Tempests themselves, high seas, and howling winds,
>
> . . .
>
> As having sense of beauty, do omit
> Their mortal natures, letting go safely by
> The divine Desdemona.
>
> . . .
>
> O, behold!
> The riches of the ship is come on shore!
> Ye men of Cyprus, let her have your knees.
> Hail to thee, lady! and the grace of heaven,
> Before, behind thee, and on every hand,
> Enwheel thee round!
>
> (II. i. 68–87)

If Desdemona is heavenly, Iago is hellish. At the end of the tragedy, in those terrible moments when Othello realizes the truth, he cries out:

> I look down towards his feet—but that's a fable.
> If that thou be'st a devil, I cannot kill thee.
>
> (V. ii. 287–288)

And indeed, he does not kill Iago. In despair, Othello asks,

> Will you, I pray, demand that demi-devil
> Why he hath thus ensnared my soul and body?
>
> (V. ii. 302–303)

Ludovico, the emissary from Venice, who pronounces the final words of the play, promises to torture "this hellish villain."

If Desdemona is heavenly and Iago hellish, Othello is Everyman choosing between them. He identifies himself with the earth in his language, by telling Desdemona stories,

> Of anters vast and deserts idle,
> Rough quarries, rocks, and hills whose heads touch heaven,
>
> (I. iii. 140–141)

of "Cannibals . . . Anthropophagi, and men whose heads do grow beneath their shoulders." He speaks of Arabian trees, of marble, of alabaster, of the rocks and stones of the earth. He compares his bloody thoughts,

> Like to the Pontic sea,
> Whose icy current and compulsive course
> Ne'er feels retiring ebb, but keeps due on
> To the Propontic and the Hellespont,
> Even so my bloody thoughts. . .
>
> (III. iii. 453–457)

When, after he has murdered her, he thinks of Desdemona, he thinks of her as a world, an earth

> Nay, had she been true,
> If heaven would make me such another world
> Of one entire and perfect chrysolite,
> I'ld not have sold her for it.
>
> (V. ii. 144–147)

Othello is earthly man, man of this world, and a good man. He tries to do the right thing, and that is the essence of his fall. Othello tries to do God's justice:

> It is the cause, it is the cause, my soul.
> Let me not name it to you, you chaste stars!
> It is the cause. Yet I'll not shed her blood,
> Nor scar that whiter skin of hers than snow,
> And smooth as monumental alabaster.
> Yet she must die, else she'll betray more men.
>
> (V. ii. 1–6)

Othello tries to do justice, but he chooses wrong. Instead of having faith in heavenly Desdemona, he with seeming reason takes Iago, the devil, for an honest man, and calls Desdemona the devil. "Devil!" he shouts at her, and again, "Oh, devil, devil!" He goes to get "some swift means of death for the fair devil." He takes her hand and says, "Here's a young and sweating devil here that commonly rebels," a moist hand speaking a liberal, sexual heart. At the end, when he has come to the terrible realization that Iago was the devil and Desdemona the angel, he speaks of himself as like Judas Iscariot, as

one whose hand,
Like the base Judean, threw a pearl away
Richer than all his tribe.

(V. ii. 345-348)

(The image, alas, is one of those terrible textual cruxes in Shakespeare. The Folio reads "Judean," apparently referring to Judas Iscariot, or, in general, the Pharisees and Levites who threw the pearl of Christ away. The quarto reads "Indian," and if you write them in an Elizabethan hand they look almost alike. "Indian" perhaps refers to Othello's Oriental, eastern background, but "Judean" fills out this Christian imagery.)

Image after image associated with Othello comes together in the first of his great speeches after he realizes the terrible error in what he has done. He thinks of himself as Man, and sees himself as helpless in the face of fate. His military occupation does not help him now, but he still thinks of a sea voyage; he is still Othello the traveler, the man who identifies himself with the earth. He speaks of heaven and men and devils:

But O vain boast!
Who can control his fate? 'Tis not so now.
Be not afraid, though you do see me weaponed.
Here is my journey's end, here is my butt,
And very seamark of my utmost sail.
Do you go back dismayed? 'Tis a lost fear.
Man but a rush against Othello's breast,
And he retires. Where should Othello go?
Now, how dost thou look now? O ill-starred wench!
Pale as thy smock! When we shall meet at compt,
This look of thine will hurl my soul from heaven,
And fiends will snatch at it. Cold, cold, my girl?
Even like thy chastity.
O cursèd, cursèd slave! Whip me, ye devils,
From the possession of this heavenly sight!
Blow me about in winds! roast me in sulphur!
Wash me in steep-down gulfs of liquid fire!
O Desdemona, Desdemona! dead!
O! O! O!

(V. ii. 265-283)

Calumniators believed, tricksters, shapeshifters, black man and white, love and fighting, heaven and men and devils—*Othello* is so rich in myth, there is scarce room to speak of its magnificent poetry. The poetry, the imagery, raises the same question that the patterns of action in the play ask: "Who can control his fate?" The poetry of the play sets off two worlds, a world in which there are values and a world in which there are only facts. The Elizabethan world-picture carried with it a belief that values were implicit in facts. Desdemona talks that way, and Othello talks that way, but for Iago the world is a positivist's world, a world in which there are only facts, observables. Iago is a kind of progressive seventeenth-century, or even twentieth-century, thinker when he makes such remarks as, "Virtue? A fig! 'Tis in ourselves that we are thus or thus." Iago manages to impose his positivistic view on the rest of the people in the play—at least until his tricks are revealed. The tragedy, then, builds in language and action on the tension between Othello's romantic view of man's wars and loves, and Iago's view that man is little more than an animal preying on other animals. He compares himself to a spider trapping a fly and he says, "With as little a web as this will I ensnare as great a fly as Cassio." That word "web"—as Iago uses it, it is simply a spider's web; but when Othello uses the word "web" he speaks of the mysterious handkerchief on which so much of the plot depends: "There's magic in the web of it." Othello's world is—or should be—the world of magic and witchcraft, the witchcraft of Desdemona's beauty and innocence, an innocence symbolized by the strawberries on that handkerchief, for strawberries were a traditional symbol for perfect righteousness (a handy bit of information for seeing Ingmar Bergman movies with). Iago's is another kind of world, a world where animals prey on one another and breed. Iago describes Othello's marriage as "an old black ram topping a white ewe," and when Othello is under Iago's spell, he thinks of Desdemona as "a cistern for foul toads to knot and gender in." Iago conjures up the picture of Desdemona and Cassio making love, "as prime as goats, as hot as monkeys," and the image turns up again in Othello's maddened cry, "Goats and monkeys!" Just as Iago converts the world of men to a world of animals, so he converts Othello's world of values, of faith, of magic and witchcraft, into money values. Iago's speech is filled with references to stealing, filching, robbing. He converts his good name, his "image," into a purse that someone might steal; he repeats over and over to Roderigo, "Put money in thy purse." "Go, make money." "Go, provide thy money." "Put money enough in your purse." In the same way, Iago untunes the musical and harmonious world of Othello, "the spirit-stirring drum, the ear-piercing fife." Iago promises himself, "Oh, you are well-tuned now! But I'll set down the pegs that make this music."

In general, Iago converts the ordered world of the Elizabethan world-picture, a world of divine harmony, a world in which facts and values go together, into a world of moral disorder, where there are only the basest, most animal elements of man. The images of the sea show the conflict. We are told, in the great mass of sea images at the arrival in Cyprus, that the tempests themselves cease and that the howling winds, the rocks and sands are like mortal natures. In a sense, man can make himself over into a stormy, natural force, as Othello does when he compares himself to "the Pontic sea" with its icy current and compulsive course. But man does better, or, at least, he does a more rational thing when he navigates his course. Thus Iago speaks of himself as being "belee'd and calmed" when Cassio is promoted ahead of him; when his plots are going well, Iago says, "My boat sails freely, both with wind and stream." Othello at the end of the play, when he realizes the tragic mistake he has made, speaks of his life as a voyage: "Here is my journey's end, here is my butt and very seamark of my utmost sail," and he speaks so immediately after he has asked the central question of the play, "Who can control his fate?" Man's life, in a sense, is a voyage which he controls. If he reduces himself to an animal, naturalistic level, he gives over that most human of functions, navigation.

That most human of functions, navigation, depends upon eyes and ears, upon our human senses, which, unfortunately, can be deceived. Othello asked for an "ocular proof" which turns out to be the handkerchief falsely stolen. Anyone but the romantic, idealistic Othello would know our eyes can be deceived by seeming. As Iago says,

> When devils will the blackest sins put on,
> They do suggest at first with heavenly shows,
> As I do now.
>
> (II. iii. 334–335)

Sight recalls the ideas of light and dark, which are obviously of great importance in the play: Othello being black, apparently evil; Iago, our Iago, anyway, being blond, apparently good. Earlier, Brabantio, Desdemona's father, insisted that she must have been drugged, "for nature so preposterously to err," that is, to marry this black man.

> Being not deficient, blind, or lame of sense,
> Sans witchcraft [she] could not
>
> (I. iii. 63–64)

have married the black Othello, unless he had deceived her with witchcraft. The same word, as in Othello's description of the handkerchief, "witchcraft" in this tragedy implies, not something bad, but that almost-supernatural magic of values which transfigures man. As Desdemona says, "I saw Othello's visage in his mind." In other words, she looked through his black skin, to the man and the mind within. But later, Iago manages to twist these values around so that Othello, doubting his wife, cries out,

> Her name, that was as fresh
> As Dian's visage, is now begrimed and black
> As mine own face.
>
> (III. iii. 386–388)

Othello, when he is about to do the terrible murder which is the tragedy, cries out, "Put out the light, and then put out the light," surely one of Shakespeare's most grim puns, for to the Elizabethans, "light" meant a light woman, an un-chaste woman. Desdemona—an unchaste woman? Or the light of heaven?

Even more important than this theme of sight with its imagery of light and dark is the idea of report, of *hearing* facts. The opening words of the play are, "Tush, never tell me!" and the last words are,

> Myself will straight aboard, and to the state
> This heavy act with heavy heart relate.
> (V. ii. 371–372)

Report dominates the opening scenes: Brabantio hears of his daughter's mar-riage through Iago's words and jumps to the wrong conclusion, just as later Othello will hear about his marriage from Iago and also jump to the wrong conclusion. Again Othello wooed Desdemona by report, by telling her stories of his life. In the opening scenes, juxtaposed against that wooing by reports of battles are the reports of the Turkish invasion. Iago, being a sort of Madison Avenue type, acts in the play through words, through reports. Emilia says, "Your reports have set the murder on."

The dying words—or the last words—of the three major characters, all con-cern report. Othello begins his last great speech with, "Soft you! A word or two before you go," and he asks them,

> When you shall these unlucky deeds relate,
> Speak of me as I am. Nothing extenuate,
> Nor set down aught in malice.
> (V. ii. 342–344)

He asks again—and finally—for a true report. Desdemona is smothered, revives briefly to lie, to give a false report and say that Othello is innocent: "Commend me to my kind lord, oh, farewell!" The best of all, though, are Iago's final words:

> Demand me nothing. What you know, you know.
> From this time forth I never will speak word.
> (V. ii. 304–305)

He—who's been doing all the talking! And it is irony on top of irony that the visitor from Venice asks so foolishly at this point, of this demidevil, "What, not to pray?" With a possible other grim pun on *pray, prey?* Surely our ears are deceived as Othello's are, for we, too, in hearing this play are hearing a "report."

Othello, perhaps more than any other of Shakespeare's plays, is played in the theater of the mind, with its characters representing almost abstract, spiritual essences, either religious or psychological. There is Othello the believer and Iago the doubter. There is Desdemona as heaven or faith; Iago as the devil of reason; Othello as man who must choose between them and who chooses wrongly because he trusts his reason instead of his faith. Confronted with a world of values married to a world of facts, Othello divorces them. He follows his senses, his eyes, and his ears, the reports he gets, and he is deceived. He takes the wit (wisdom) of Iago instead of the witchcraft of Desdemona. *Othello,* in the last analysis the most "psychological" of the great tragedies, is a play about the limitations of man's mind. Rather like *Macbeth,* it speaks of our ultimate inability, through our senses or our reason, to perceive moral values. *Othello,* in the final scenes, gives Desdemona's father the grim and grisly proof he had asked for:

> Words are words. I never yet did hear
> That the bruised heart was piercèd through the ear.
> (I. iii. 218–219)

By the end, the tragedy has pierced all our hearts through the ear.

MEASURE FOR MEASURE

Measure for Measure IS WHAT PROFESSIONAL SHAKESPEAREANS TERM "A PROBLEM comedy"; clearly a problem to the reader, perhaps it was a problem to the writer as well. *All's Well That Ends Well* and *Measure for Measure*—these are Shakespeare's so-called "problem comedies." They seem to have been written between 1601 and 1605, during the time when Shakespeare wrote the great tragedies. *All's Well* and *Measure for Measure* are queasy comedies, bitter, ironical, nasty; they deal with moral problems and issues in a complex, near-tragic way. These moral questions even become a little like those of a soap opera: Will Claudio be executed for getting Juliet pregnant? Will Isabella give herself to Angelo to save her brother's life? Will Angelo marry Mariana? Will the Duke return in time—and who is the mysterious friar? Tune in to Act V and find out. Such questions hardly spell out a cheerful, gay, romantic comedy like *Twelfth Night*. Rather, they define a bitter comedy dealing with moral issues.

The question, though, is, *What* issues? What problem does this problem comedy deal with?—Not an easy question to answer, because this is a comedy written in the rich style of the major tragedies. Not only is its style complex, it has the complexities that all comedies have, which make comedy so much more difficult a thing to understand than tragedy. In addition, the characters have a peculiar kind of complexity in that very often they do quite contradictory things.

The most obvious example, of course, is Angelo. As the Duke says,

> Lord Angelo is precise,
> Stands at a guard with envy; scarce confesses
> That his blood flows, or that his appetite
> Is more to bread than stone.
>
> (I. iii. 50–53)

So staunchly upright is he that the Duke, on leaving Vienna, puts Angelo in charge, even entrusts to him the sudden enforcement of "the drowsy and neglected act," the statute against fornication.

> He doth with holy abstinence subdue
> That in himself which he spurs on his power
> To qualify in others. Were he mealed with that
> Which he corrects, then were he tyrannous,
> But this being so, he's just.
>
> (IV. ii. 76–80)

But of course he *is* tyrannous, because he *is* "mealed with," that is, stained with (and perhaps "maled with") the fornication that he is trying to curb in others. Arresting Claudio for having gotten his sweetheart Juliet pregnant, Angelo responds, when Claudio's sister Isabella pleads for mercy, with a proposition: if she will sleep with him, he will pardon her brother's crime. Angelo is scarcely a model for judicial probity. Then, too, for all his high and mighty virtue, we learn that he had been engaged to marry a girl named Mariana and had jilted her. The most shocking aspect of Angelo's attempt on Isabella's virtue is that she was about to become a nun, and it is her very modesty that starts up Angelo's lust; he soliloquizes:

> Can it be
> That modesty may more betray our sense
> Than woman's lightness?
>
> (II. ii. 168–170)

In this respect—or lack of it—Angelo is exactly the opposite of the lowest character in the play. Lucio is a rake and libertine, but confronted with Isabella, he says,

> Though 'tis my familiar sin
> With maids to seem the lapwing and to jest,
> Tongue far from heart, play with all virgins so,
> I hold you as a thing enskied and sainted,
> By your renouncement an immortal spirit,
> And to be talked with in sincerity
> As with a saint.
>
> (I. iv. 31–37)

Toward Isabella, Lucio behaves in contradiction to his customary way; so does Angelo.

So does Isabella herself. When we first see her, she is about to enter a nunnery and "wishing a more strict restraint upon the sisterhood." Even the rules of a convent are not strict enough to suit her own very strict temperament. Yet later on in the comedy, we see her behaving essentially like a bawd, slipping Angelo a girl. To spare Isabella from having to sleep with the judge to save

Claudio's life, the Duke dredges up "Mariana in the moated grange," Angelo's jilted fiancée, to be slipped in to the lustful judge by Isabella in the dark of their midnight meeting. Now, it is true, as the Duke points out to Mariana,

> He is your husband on a pre-contract;
> To bring you thus together, 'tis no sin,
> Sith that the justice of your title to him
> Doth flourish the deceit.
>
> (IV. i. 71–74)

Even so, midnight rendezvous and bringing girls for seduction seem a sort of hanky-panky that no right-thinking *nun* would engage in.

Just as Isabella and Angelo do quite contradictory things, so the Duke himself seems to embody various opposites. First of all, he is a Renaissance Prince, the ruler of Vienna; but in Act I, he leaves Vienna, and throughout the middle of the play we see him disguised as a friar, a religious figure working to counteract with mercy the hard justice dealt out by his own deputy. In his disguise as a friar, he becomes a kind of dramatist, moving around behind the scenes, putting characters here and there, arranging plots and miraculous escapes. In Act V, when he returns to Vienna, he sets up (now in his character as Prince) an elaborate, dramatic ritual in which he has Isabella and Mariana plead publicly against Angelo. As Duke, he seems to take Angelo's side; then he appears as a friar; then there is a dramatic unmasking. He has Isabella, who believes that Angelo has murdered her brother despite her apparent compliance with his importunities, plead forgiveness for the corrupted judge. The Duke condemns just about everybody within reach to death, then, on Isabella's plea, forgives them all. In short, it is as though the Duke were trying to dramatize for his citizens the idea of justice or government. As he says, and you could say this very much of the play as a whole, " 'Tis a physic that's bitter to sweet end."

The Duke is both ruler and dramatist; but there is something more, something in the Duke of Providence, a Godlike or Christlike quality. Angelo says of him at the end,

> I perceive your grace, like power divine,
> Hath looked upon my passes.
>
> (V. i. 365–366)

"Like power divine," and yet, when he explains to Friar Thomas his reasons for appointing Angelo his deputy, Friar Thomas's first thought is that the Duke is on some amatory escapade. The Duke says, oh, no, it's not that, but the reasons he gives for appointing Angelo correspond to some of the rules for cruel and clever governing that Machiavelli, of all people, set up. In fact, his appointment of Angelo to enforce an unpopular law bears a fairly close likeness to the stimulus for one of the grislier acts of Cesare Borgia. In short, just as Isabella and

Angelo embody opposites, so the Duke himself seems a very strange and contradictory combination of Prince and friar; dramatist, God, and Borgia.

Not only do the characters embody contradictions; the language does, too. Over and over again, we hear how a single thing contains in itself a pair of opposites:

> Thus can the demigod Authority
> Make us pay down for our offense by weight
> The words of heaven; on whom it will, it will;
> On whom it will not, so: yet still 'tis just.
>
> (I. ii. 116–119)

—thus Claudio, ruefully on his way to prison, noting that authority seems to have in it a duality, paying down on some, not on others, "yet still 'tis just." His friend Lucio asks him,

> Why, how now, Claudio? Whence comes this restraint?
> *Claudio.* From too much liberty, my Lucio, liberty.
> As surfeit is the father of much fast,
> So every scope by the immoderate use
> Turns to restraint.
>
> (I. ii. 120–124)

Liberty seems to lead to its opposite, restraint; surfeit to fast; scope to limitation. The Duke explains why he himself cannot enforce the law against fornication:

> Sith 'twas my fault to give the people scope,
> 'Twould be my tyranny to strike and gall them
> For what I bid them do: for we bid this be done
> When evil deeds have their permissive pass
> And not the punishment.
>
> (I. iii. 35–39)

The Duke both forbade and encouraged sexual license. Now, by appointing Angelo, he must seem not to forbid it, but not to encourage it, either. The same sense of contradiction occurs in the description of the rules of the convent:

> Then, if you speak, you must not show your face,
> Or, if you show your face, you must not speak.
>
> (I. iv. 12–13)

Angelo's assistant, Escalus, pronounces a fine judicial maxim:

> Mercy is not itself, that oft looks so;
> Pardon is still the nurse of second woe.
>
> (II. i. 267–268)

Isabella finds within herself a contradiction as she pleads with Angelo for her brother's life:

> There is a vice that most I do abhor,
> And most desire should meet the blow of justice,
> For which I would not plead, but that I must,
> For which I must not plead, but that I am
> At war 'twixt will and will not.
>
> (II. ii. 29-33)

> I something do excuse the thing I hate
> For his advantage that I dearly love.
>
> (II. iv. 119-120)

And again, two opposites in a single thing, Isabella cries out:

> O perilous mouths,
> That bear in them one and the selfsame tongue,
> Either of condemnation or approof,
> Bidding the law make curtsy to their will,
> Hooking both right and wrong to th'appetite,
> To follow as it draws.
>
> (II. iv. 172-177)

The most massive, most famous of all these speeches binding opposites into a single thing in *Measure for Measure* (is not the title itself a pair of opposites?) is, of course, the Duke's magnificent speech of advice to young Claudio; acting as a friar, giving him religious counsel, he denies all the virtues we might attribute to life or to ourselves, even to the point where, "Thou art not thyself":

> Be absolute for death: either death or life
> Shall thereby be the sweeter. Reason thus with life:
> If I do lose thee, I do lose a thing
> That none but fools would keep; a breath thou art,
> Servile to all the skyey influences
> That dost this habitation where thou keep'st
> Hourly afflict; merely, thou art death's fool,
> For him thou labor'st by thy flight to shun,
> And yet run'st toward him still. Thou art not noble,
> For all th'accommodations that thou bear'st
> Are nursed by baseness. Thou'rt by no means valiant,
> For thou dost fear the soft and tender fork
> Of a poor worm; thy best of rest is sleep,
> And that thou oft provok'st, yet grossly fear'st
> Thy death, which is no more. Thou art not thyself,
> For 'thou' exists on many a thousand grains
> That issue out of dust. Happy thou art not,
> For what thou hast not, still thou striv'st to get,
> And what thou hast, forget'st. Thou art not certain,
> For thy complexion shifts to strange effects,
> After the moon. If thou art rich, thou'rt poor,
> For, like an ass whose back with ingots bows,
> Thou bear'st thy heavy riches but a journey,

And death unloads thee. Friend hast thou none,
For thine own bowels, which do call thee sire,
The mere effusion of thy proper loins,
Do curse the gout, serpigo, and the rheum
For ending thee no sooner. Thou hast nor youth nor age,
But as it were an after-dinner's sleep,
Dreaming on both, for all thy blessed youth
Becomes as agèd, and doth beg the alms
Of palsied eld: and when thou art old and rich,
Thou hast neither heat, affection, limb, nor beauty,
To make thy riches pleasant. What's yet in this
That bears the name of life? Yet in this life
Lie hid moe thousand deaths; yet death we fear,
That makes these odds all even.

(III. i. 5–41)

And after all these paradoxes, Claudio, who, after all, is the one going to die, not the friar, drily replies,

> I humbly thank you.
> To sue to live, I find I seek to die,
> And, seeking death, find life.

(41–43)

And in those words of Claudio's, we find the special and peculiar tonality of the opposites in *Measure for Measure*. We have seen opposites many times before, beginning with *Macbeth* and *Romeo and Juliet*, but in *Measure for Measure*, they give the world of the play a special tonality, and Claudio tells us what it is:

> To sue to live, I find I seek to die,
> And, seeking death, find life.

The special thing about opposites in *Measure for Measure* is that we are discovering them, finding them out, seeking them. We seek one thing and find its opposite. We seek a just magistrate in Angelo and find a corrupt one. We seek a strictly restrained nun in Isabella and we find a bawd. We seek a ruler in the Duke and find a friar. Isabella expects to find in her brother a man of honor indignantly rejecting the notion that his sister should prostitute herself to save his life. Instead, in one of the most pathetic moments of the play:

> Sweet sister, let me live.
> What sin you do to save a brother's life,
> Nature dispenses with the deed so far
> That it becomes a virtue.

Isabella.   O you beast,
O faithless coward, O dishonest wretch!
Wilt thou be made a man out of my vice?
Is't not a kind of incest, to take life
From thine own sister's shame? What should I think?

> Heaven shield my mother played my father fair,
> For such a warpèd slip of wilderness
> Ne'er issued from his blood. Take my defiance,
> Die, perish.

(III. i. 133–144)

The special relation between opposites in *Measure for Measure* is that first we see one thing, and then its opposite becomes visible. First we see an honorable brother, then a dishonorable one; first, a legitimate son, then a creature of illegitimacy or incest. In the final scene, we see a friar; then, the Duke's disguise as a friar is suddenly ripped off, and we see a Prince, the opposite of a friar. We could call this the theme of "inside and outside" or of things becoming visible. It comes out in the very opening speech of the play, "Of government the properties to unfold," or the last two lines of the play, when the Duke says,

> We'll show
> What's yet behind, that's meet you all should know.

We can see these unfolding opposites again in the Duke's great speech as he confers his office on Angelo.

> Angelo,
> There is a kind of character in thy life,
> That to th' observer doth thy history
> Fully unfold. Thyself and thy belongings
> Are not thine own so proper, as to waste
> Thyself upon thy virtues, they on thee.
> Heaven doth with us as we with torches do,
> Not light them for themselves; for if our virtues
> Did not go forth of us, 'twere all alike
> As if we had them not. Spirits are not finely touched
> But to fine issues.

(I. i. 26–36)

There is in *Measure for Measure* a sense of things unfolding, issuing, going forth. You can see the same theme in the idea of the relationship between Claudio and Juliet becoming visible as her pregnancy:

> The stealth of our most mutual entertainment
> With character too gross is writ on Juliet.

(I. ii. 149–150)

Perhaps most of all, we see the theme in Angelo's futile prayer:

> When I would pray and think, I think and pray
> To several subjects: heaven hath my empty words,
> Whilst my invention, hearing not my tongue,
> Anchors on Isabel: heaven in my mouth,
> As if I did but only chew his name,
> And in my heart the strong and swelling evil

Of my conception. The state, whereon I studied,
Is like a good thing, being often read,
Grown sere and tedious; yea, my gravity,
Wherein, let no man hear me, I take pride,
Could I, with boot, change for an idle plume
Which the air beats for vain. O place, O form,
How often dost thou with thy case, thy habit,
Wrench awe from fools and tie the wiser souls
To thy false seeming! Blood, thou art blood;
Let's write 'good Angel' on the devil's horn,
'Tis not the devil's crest.
                                                    (II. iv. 1–17)

Angels, devils; gravity, frivolity; words, thought; all opposites—first we see one thing; then we see its contradiction—all are "false seeming" as in Isabella's statement "this outward-sainted deputy . . . is yet a devil." Or in the Duke's similar description of Angelo:

O, what may man within him hide,
Though angel on the outward side!
                                    (III. ii. 254–255)

This interest in outside-and-inside opposites comes very close to imagery, and as you would expect, a lot of the imagery in *Measure for Measure* refers to clothing. We hear about a thief stealing clothing, about the fact that the hangman was entitled, as one of his perquisites, to the clothing of the man he executed. We hear about the friar's robe, and the nun's habit. Clothing seems to suggest in *Measure for Measure* as in *Macbeth* the roles that we human beings play. Angelo, when he is propositioning Isabella, says to her, if you be a woman show it now, by putting on "the destined livery," that is, by putting on the robe appropriate to your role. Isabella, in one of her speeches, gives us the play's great image of man, proud man, in terms of clothing.

                                    Man, proud man,
Dressed in a little brief authority,
Most ignorant of what he's most assured—
His glassy essence—like an angry ape
Plays such fantastic tricks before high heaven
As makes the angels weep; who, with our spleens,
Would all themselves laugh mortal.
                                    (II. ii. 117–123)

The play associates with clothing the idea of words. To Elizabethan theorists of language, words clothed thoughts (as opposed to our modern theory that words *are* thoughts). Thus we hear in Angelo's prayer,

When I would pray and think, I think and pray
To several subjects: heaven hath my empty words,

> Whilst my invention, hearing not my tongue,
> Anchors on Isabel; heaven in my mouth,
> As if I did but only chew his name,
> And in my heart the strong and swelling evil
> Of my conception.
>
> (II. iv. 1–7)

Angelo speaks of his "empty" words, empty of their substance, which is the strong and swelling evil of his thought. Yet words can themselves become a kind of action, as in Isabella's long persuasion scene, when she tries to persuade Angelo to forgive her brother. Again, words become action when they are a pre-contract, such as the one by which Claudio bedded with Juliet. In general, in law as in contracts or commands or statutes, words can be themselves a kind of action. Another kind of words is Lucio's "slander of the state," interesting because Lucio is the only character punished in the final denouement. In another sense, though, words are to be contrasted to action. That is, words represent only intentions, as when in the finale Isabella asks for Angelo's forgiveness,

> His act did not o'ertake his bad intent,
> And must be buried but as an intent
> That perished by the way. Thoughts are no subjects,
> Intents but merely thoughts.
>
> (V. i. 447–450)

Words, then, hover between action and mere potential action; they are something pregnant with action, ready to issue forth, unfold. Words and clothing are thus associated with the theme of "outside" and "inside."

At the same time, a good deal of the play is concerned with probing, with testing, with poking through the surface to find out what is really underneath. As the Duke says when he describes his plan to put Angelo in charge,

> Hence we shall see,
> If power change purpose, what our seemers be.
>
> (I. iii. 53–54)

In the final scene, Isabella begs the returned Duke,

> Let your reason serve
> To make the truth appear where it seems hid,
> And hide the false [that] seems true
>
> (V. i. 65–67)

This juxtaposition of seeming, clothing, and words, on the one hand, and probing and testing on the other, these classes of images themselves constitute one of the pairs of opposites in the play.

Another pair of opposites is the contrast between heaven in particular, or religion in general, as against what the play calls "our gross selves." On the side of heaven, there are all those characters who are bound up with the religious life, Isabella and the nuns associated with her, the Duke becoming a friar, associated with other friars, and Angelo, who is described as "this outward-sainted deputy." There is a great deal of talk in the play about religion, as in the last act, when Angelo compares the Duke to "grace," "power divine," looking on his sins, or in the Duke's early statement of the need for virtue to be an active, outgoing, unfolding virtue: "Heaven doth with us as we with torches do."

As against heaven, the play sets off "our gross selves" manifested, for example, in images of animals. Isabella describes man as "like an angry ape [who] plays . . . fantastic tricks before high heaven." The comic bawd Pompey describes Claudio's getting Juliet pregnant as "groping for trouts in a peculiar river." Food is another way of describing "our gross selves," as when the friar-Duke says that in Vienna,

> I have seen corruption boil and bubble
> Till it o'errun the stew,
>
> (V. i. 316–317)

"stew" being a cant term for a brothel. Also, oddly enough, the word "nunnery" was, as in Hamlet's "Get thee to a nunnery," a cant term for a brothel. In a sense, as between the convent to which Isabella belongs, one kind of nunnery, and the brothel run by the clowns, Mistress Overdone and Pompey, another kind of nunnery, we have the clearest statement of this theme of heaven as against our gross selves.

All these images of food, animals and the like seem to touch on the idea of breeding or sexuality, which, I suppose, is of sufficiently obvious importance in *Measure for Measure* that no critic's finger is needed to point it out. Still another way of describing "our gross selves" is in terms of money. There is an irony in the fact that Angelo, when he is first appointed deputy, asks,

> Let there be some more test made of my mettle
> Before so noble and so great a figure
> Be stamped upon it.
>
> (I. i. 48–50)

Angelo is punning on "mettle" and the "metal" that you would make coins out of. But later he speaks of coining in another way when he says to Isabella,

> It were as good
> To pardon him that hath from nature stol'n
> A man already made, as to remit
> Their saucy sweetness that do coin heaven's image
> In stamps that are forbid: 'tis all as easy
> Falsely to take away a life true made,

> As to put mettle in restrainèd means
> To make a false one.

(II. iv. 42-49)

Isabella offers her prayers as a bribe, and Elbow, the clownish sheriff, accuses the bawd, Pompey, of buying and selling men and women like beasts. Money seems to be associated with our gross selves; it also seems to be associated with another important theme in the play, breeding.

Measure for Measure is in large part concerned with the control of breeding by two different kinds of restraints, those of law and those of religion. We see breeding most obviously in Juliet's pregnancy.

> Your brother and his lover have embraced;
> As those that feed grow full, as blossoming time
> That from the seedness the bare fallow brings
> To teeming foison, even so her plenteous womb
> Expresseth his full tilth and husbandry.

(I. iv. 40-44)

The play associates breeding and sexuality with the low parts of ourselves. We hear about different kinds of usury: " 'Twas never merry world since, of two usuries, the merriest was put down," the joke being, as in *The Merchant of Venice,* that usury consists in breeding barren metal; sex offers a merrier usury. We hear of breeding also in terms of food, when the Duke, disguised as the friar, says of Vienna, "I have seen corruption boil and bubble till it o'errun the stew." Breeding is also associated very distinctly with venereal diseases, which are discussed in some detail in Act I, scene ii. Breeding, sexuality, and giving birth seem, in short, to be aspects of our gross selves, our low selves, the part of ourselves that is associated with food or animals or diseases or money.

There is a kind of paradox, then, in the fact that the Duke, by appointing Angelo his deputy, expects Angelo's virtue somehow to breed outwards, to spread through the city of Vienna.

> If our virtues
> Did not go forth of us, 'twere all alike
> As if we had them not.

(I. i. 33-35)

In the nature of the case, it is our low selves that tend to multiply, not our virtues, as the Duke seems to recognize when he confesses that one of his motives for appointing Angelo is to see "if power change purpose."

Our low selves seem naturally to tend to breed, to run away with our higher selves. To prevent this happening, there are legal and religious restraints on our actions, restraints that largely take the form of words, which seem to be a very special force in *Measure for Measure.* One of the key words is "die." As we have seen before, all the way back in *Romeo and Juliet*, or in John Donne's love poems or *Antony and Cleopatra*, the Elizabethans had some complicated meanings for the word "die." One of these was the ordinary meaning, to suffer physical death. A second was to have a sexual ecstasy, and the third was "die" in the sense of "dying to this world," having a religious ecstasy, or entering on a religious life, dying to be born again. *Measure for Measure*, in a sense, plays on all three meanings of the word. Claudio is threatened with death in the physical sense, as at various points in the play are Lucio, Angelo, Barnardine, and others. Then, there is dying in the various sexual encounters in the play, Claudio's affair with Juliet, or Angelo's with Mariana. Thus, the provost in charge of the prison speaks of Claudio as "a young man more fit to do another such offense than die for this," with a hidden pun on "die" in its sexual sense. Finally, there is the religious sense of "die," as when the Duke becomes a friar or when Isabella tries to enter the convent of St. Clare.

We see in the prison two senses of "die" contrasted. That is, in the course of the play, two people in prison are reprieved, Claudio and Barnardine. Claudio was condemned to a physical death for having indulged in sexual death. Barnardine, however, is a more mysterious figure, "A man that apprehends death no more dreadfully but as a drunken sleep: careless, reckless, and fearless of what's past, present, or to come; insensible of mortality, and desperately mortal" (IV. ii. 138–142). He is apparently an atheist, a man dying a fourth kind of death, a death of his religious sense:

> Sirrah, thou art said to have a stubborn soul,
> That apprehends no further than this world.
> (V. i. 476–477)

At the end of the play the Duke gives him his life and tells him to "Take this mercy to provide for better times to come." Claudio, about to die a physical death; Barnardine, about to die in a spiritual sense, to suffer death of the soul— both of them are reprieved.

The prison is apparently one of the important buildings in the Vienna of *Measure for Measure*, a building where people "die" in a physical sense. Two other buildings that we hear about are the nunnery, the convent of St. Claire, and Mistress Overdone's brothel in the suburbs, both places where people "die" in the other senses of the word. There is, too, that other verbal ambiguity, "nunnery" as a slang term for brothel, so that in a sense, the holiest, the highest and the basest, the lowest places in the play are all one, separated only by the differences in meaning of the word, "die."

We see our multiple meanings of "die" in yet another situation, the scene where the bawd, Pompey, is retrained into an executioner. A bawd is a man who make assignations for sexual purposes; the executioner, a man who arranges encounters with death. But, since death has a sexual meaning as well as its ordinary meaning, in still another sense, the bawd and the executioner, as the Provost says, "weigh equally; a feather will turn the scale."

These meanings of words come up in still another context, the comic scenes involving Elbow, who mixes up all kinds of words. "Do you hear how he misplaced," asks the justice, Escalus. And indeed he does misplace. He mixes up "use" and "abuse," "benefactor" and "malefactor," "carnally" and "cardinally," and with perhaps a very special application to Angelo, "respected" and "suspected." At one point he mixes up the legal actions of battery and slander, a kind of capsule way of catching one of the more important themes in *Measure for Measure,* the contrast between words and action, between slander and causing actual physical harm.

That paronomasia brings us to Lucio, a very puzzling figure in the play. He is described in the cast of characters at the end of the First Folio text as "a fantastique." To translate that into modern terms, we could say he is something between a beat and a fop. That is, he cuts himself off from normal social relations, professing a kind of indifference and impulsiveness, like a beatnik, but instead of expressing his impulsiveness in sloppy clothing, he expresses it in fantastic, foppish, overdone clothing. He plays a curious role in the play, almost a kind of opposite to the Duke. He cries out against the law in Act I, scene ii, but with total indifference, he seems to turn over his old friends Pompey and Mistress Overdone to that law. He insults the Duke in his absence to the friar who, as it turns out, is the Duke. In the final scenes he unmasks the friar to reveal the Duke. Oddly enough, Lucio is the only person really punished at the end of the play. Claudio is forgiven, the provost is forgiven, and Angelo is made to marry Mariana, and this, presumably, is no punishment. But Lucio is forced to marry a punk, a prostitute. His crime is, to quote the words of the play, "slandering a prince," a verbal action. And as we come again to words, through Lucio, we come very close to the heart of the play.

Measure for Measure is preeminently that play of Shakespeare's which deals most explicitly with the idea of government, a play that, in the words of its opening speech, seems designed "of government the properties to unfold." Yet there is a near-tragic discrepancy between theories of government, its "properties," and the actual unfolding or working out of government. We see in the course of the comedy two kinds of government: first, a legal government represented by Angelo, and second, a religious government, represented by Isabella. These two kinds of government, legal and religious, come together in the figure of the friar-Duke. First of all, he is a Renaissance Prince, the ruler of Vienna, but throughout the rest of the play we see him as a friar, as a religious man, almost counteracting his own legal deputy.

The thing that is governed in the play, both in the high plot involving Claudio, Juliet, Isabella, and Angelo, and in the low plot involving the bawds, punks, and fancy men, Pompey and Mistress Overdone and Kate Keepdown, the thing that is being governed at all these levels is sexuality. It comes in several different forms. The low characters give us sex at its most animal. Then there are the romantic lovers, Claudio and Juliet, who give us sex and love, and their shadow, as it were, is Angelo's hidden relationship with Mariana, herself hidden away. Finally, at the very highest level, there is the fact that Isabella, in becoming a nun, is about to become a bride of Christ. It is symbolic, I suppose, that at the end of the play, she (apparently) becomes the bride of the Duke instead, the Duke being a kind of God or Christ-figure in the play.

Sexuality in *Measure for Measure* takes a distinctive form, the precontract. Most introductions to the play explain what a precontract is: in effect, a legal, as opposed to a religious, marriage. A man and a woman agreeing to marry each other before a third person, usually a priest, by that very act made a binding contract to marriage. The process was not really complete until the church ceremony, but it was binding: neither party could contract another marriage while the contract was in force. In fact, it is quite possible that Shakespeare married Anne Hathaway on such an arrangement and then followed it up with a religious ceremony when she became pregnant. Sexuality in *Measure for Measure* occurs in the form of precontracts. Most obviously, there is the precontract between Claudio and Juliet:

> Upon a true contract
> I got possession of Julietta's bed.
> You know the lady, she is fast my wife
> Save that we do the [declaration] lack
> Of outward order.
>
> (I. ii. 140–144)

Then there is the precontract between Angelo and Mariana: "She should this Angelo have married, was affianced by her oath, and the nuptial appointed; between which time of the contract and limit of the solemnity," Angelo broke it off (III. i. 209–211). Then, Isabella, who is a novice, is about to become a nun or bride of Christ; in a sense, she, too, is involved in a precontract. Law and religion are put side by side. That is, the precontract is essentially a legal arrangement, which is not complete until it has been carried out one step further as a religious arrangement.

In fact, a marriage is not really complete (that is, it can be annulled) until it has been consummated. What I'm saying is that the marriage ceremony itself has the tripartite structure that the action of *Measure for Measure* has. The marriage ceremony begins with the betrothal, or, as we have been calling it, the precontract. "And thereto I plight thee my troth." The second step in the marriage ceremony is the strictly religious one, the actual ceremony of marriage: "With this ring I thee wed." The final step is the consummation. In *Measure for Measure,* law and religion govern sexuality. At the beginning of the play, we see legal actions taken to restrict sexuality. Then as the Duke becomes the friar, we have more and more religious action. Finally, in the last scenes, we find a kind of consummation in which the Duke arranges for the marriages of Juliet and Claudio, Angelo and Mariana, Lucio and Mistress Kate Keep-down. In those final scenes, death is always hovering next to sexuality. As so often in Shakespeare he is reaching for a kind of psychological truth. We speak, for example, of "dying of love." The marriage of Romeo and Juliet is, in effect, consummated by the act of dying together, as is the "marriage" of Antony and Cleopatra. Death becomes a symbol for sexuality. In fact, in Eliza-bethan times, as we have seen, the word "die" often meant "to have a sexual ecstasy."

All through the final scene in which the Duke metes out justice, then, there is a constant hovering between sexual consummation and the consumma-tion of death. For example, the Duke orders Angelo to marry Mariana, and to be beheaded, the beheading then being remitted. Lucio is sentenced to marry a punk, then to die, but his death, too, is forgiven, though he protests, "marrying a punk, my lord, is pressing to death." In Act IV, scene ii, when the bawd, Pompey, takes up the trade or "mystery" of being an executioner, we are told that a bawd and an executioner are about the same thing. That is, in a sense, each of them consummates a precontract, one a contract to death, the other a contract to sexuality. This balancing off of law and religion, death and sexuality, suggests in yet another way that *Measure for Measure* is a play about opposites, perhaps ultimately about the wedding of those most fundamental opposites, male and female.

This is a difficult play, one of the hardest of Shakespeare's plays to under-stand, partly, I suppose, because it is a play of contradictions and opposites, and contradictions that are never fully resolved; perhaps they never can be. In the most obvious sense, *Measure for Measure* is a play about justice, the art of government, the art of ruling ourselves. In another sense, insofar as the Duke is a representative of divine grace, it is a play about providence, about the way some divine purpose gives form and shape to our lives. In still another sense, insofar as the Duke is a dramatist arranging plots and characters and scenes, it is a play about dramatic creation. In fact, there is even a character called "Escalus." Within this play about authority, providence, and dramatic creation, the action seems to be the reconciling of opposites. That is, we are shown our low selves, our breeding selves, associated with food and animals and diseases and money, and these low selves, which have a tendency to breed and grow, are to be held in by legal and religious restraints, the legal restraints of justice, corrected (another pair of opposites) by mercy; breeding is to be contained also in the religious restraint of marriage. The play sets up a kind of principle of growth, our low selves, which breeds, unfolds, and then against this principle of growth a principle of "government," represented by legal restraints or religious abstinences. Conversely, we seek one thing and find its opposite. What we see of other people is their outer restraints, roles, robes, words, and manners; inside is the raw animal self. You could put the contrast in psychological terms: we see in others the restraining government of ego or superego; inside is the drive of the primitive id. These two opposed principles, the principle of growth or drive and the principle of restraint, are brought together and reconciled in the larger unity of self-government, political government, God's government (providence) or even in artistic creation.

The thing that seems to mediate between these two great opposites of growth and restraint is words. Words mediate as the precontract which turns low fornication into high marriage; words mediate as the laws which are applied to govern and moderate our gross selves. The governing powers operate by means of words: reports and commands and messages. In the comic scenes, words are perverted and distorted by the ridiculous statements of Elbow or perverted and distorted in a more serious way by Lucio, the fantastique.

In a sense, then, *Measure for Measure* gives us a comic, though not very funny, view of those opposites and contradictions which make up the great tragedies of this period. The interest in words in this play is like that in *Hamlet,* and the sense of the Duke as a dramatist makes him a kind of benevolent Iago. Think back to the multiplication and breeding in *The Merchant of Venice,* where we saw that the bad world of Venice was a world of division, while the good world of Belmont was a world of multiplication. Something does seem soured in Shakespeare's imagination, for multiplication and breeding have become, in this play, our low selves to be controlled and restrained by law and religion. Somehow breeding, love, has become dirty and distasteful as in Hamlet's diseased imagination. And yet, *Measure for Measure* is, after all, a comedy. It is built upon the mingling of opposites, and those same opposites that have made the tragedies tragic: the contrast between our gross selves and our heavenly selves, between Iago and Desdemona, for example. Where Iago is a dramatist who writes a tragedy, our Duke in *Measure for Measure* is a dramatist who sets up scenes, plots, and characters to write a comedy. This contrast brings us again to a conclusion we have come to before and will come to again about the Shakespearean imagination. In Shakespeare's mind, tragedy seems associated with division, fragmentation, splitting, opposites pitted against each other. His comic imagination suggests to us a world in which opposites are reconciled, brought into harmony in the larger purposes of a kind of ultimate government or art, an art, by the way, of words. Hamlet was interested in words and language, but there, words did not serve to bridge and reconcile; instead, they became a poison that entered the ear. In *Measure for Measure,* words serve the purpose that we would expect them to serve for a man like Shakespeare. They are a way of reconciling growth and restraint, artistic invention and artistic judgment, sexuality and government by law and religion. The essence of Shakespeare's comic imagination seems to be that things somehow find a unity, even the most opposite of things: "Like doth quit like, and Measure still for Measure."

KING LEAR

THIS IS THE GREAT PLAY. TO LOVERS OF SHAKESPEARE, HIS TWO GREATEST WORKS
are *Hamlet* and *King Lear,* and to the most sophisticated lovers of Shakespeare
I know, *King Lear* is the greater. Yet, oddly, it is often said *King Lear* cannot
be staged. Charles Lamb, the Romantic essayist and critic, started the idea. Lamb
asked whether, when we hear Lear in that great cosmic storm in Act III,
which troubles the heavens even as Lear's kingdom is troubled, even as his
mind is troubled, whether we can bear to know the storm is only a man
backstage shaking a sheet of tin to make the thunderclaps. Lamb felt
we could not, and indeed, in this day and age, *King Lear* is not, it's true, as
often staged as the other great tragedies. Shakespeare's imagination in *King
Lear* seems more sublime, more poetic, more cosmic, somehow bigger than
any stage can hold. Personally, I have always felt that *King Lear* would make
a marvelous movie, but it seems rather doubtful that the people who make 77
Sunset Strip or *Gunsmoke* are likely to leave off long enough to make a movie
of *King Lear.* Even so, only the film, or perhaps the radio, are media big
enough to hold the vasty reaches of this tragedy.

King Lear, like *Hamlet,* looks at man, but it looks at him in a different
and special way. *Hamlet* looks inside man. *Hamlet* the play, like Hamlet the
character, is introspective, a looking inside ourselves to find out what kind
of thing we are. *Lear* also looks at man, but it looks with man at the world
that contains man. *Lear* looks at man-in-nature. The later tragedy does not
have the perplexing enigmas of character that *Hamlet* did; what we find instead
is a far more vast, more cosmic, more universal poetry, a poetry that asks
over and over again, What is man's place in the universe? Does man stand at
the center, ranked around and above him the angels and the animals and the

planets, all, in a sense, pivoting upon him, on what happens on "this great stage"? Or is man simply another animal among animals, squatting on a tiny ball of dirt spinning around an aged sun, one of a billion such suns, one of a billion such balls of dust spinning in an endless, purposeless galaxy in a vast and indifferent universe?

Shakespeare, being of a traditional cast of mind, did not think man the creature of a vast and indifferent universe, though some of the characters seem to, and, of course, we do. The characters who think of man that way are the villains, Goneril, Regan, and Edmund. We, the modern audience, agree with them, not with the good people in the play. Our thought patterns have little, if any, room in them for people like Kent or Cordelia. Though we might like to be associated with the good people in the play, not the villains, we really cannot be. The reason, purely and simply, is that we live on the side of the seventeenth century that we do; Shakespeare lived on the other side of that great intellectual watershed, and it makes a difference.

The seventeenth century saw into being the scientific view of the world, the view that all of us to a greater or lesser extent live by now. The technical name for it is "naturalism"; people in the Renaissance spoke of it as "new philosophy," as expressed in politics by Machiavelli, in the world of letters by Montaigne, in philosophy by Descartes, in science by Galileo. In all these spheres, new philosophy took a quite skeptical, scientific view of man and his relation to the world around him; John Donne, the poet, wrote sadly how "new philosophy calls all in doubt." In the astronomical universe, man was held no longer to be at the center of things. In the political world, power became the crucial fact, not responsibility. In a philosophical sense, the things that are real and important are the things that we can measure and weigh and number, not the things of the spirit which seem to be only matters of custom, in Edmund's phrase, "the curiosity of nations," the odd customs that different peoples will live by. This was the great age of discovery, when, for the first time, really, man in Western Europe was forced to face the fact that there were people scattered all over the globe who lived differently from the way he did, who believed in different gods, and who seemed in many ways to be making a better job of it than he himself was. This is always an unsettling feeling, to find out that there are people who are basically different from you, and just as anthropology has had a profoundly disturbing effect on twentieth-century values, so this unsettling awareness of other cultures became a part of Renaissance naturalism.

As against this skeptical, scientific view of man in nature, this "modern" view, there was the older, traditional, medieval notion. Historians of ideas have a saying that, if you scratch a Renaissance man, you find a medieval. From this point of view, there really was no such thing as the Renaissance:

there was a medieval way of looking at things and thinking about them; there was the eighteenth-century way, the rationalist's way; and, in between, there was a transition period which we call the Renaissance. At any rate, in Shakespeare's day, balanced off against the naturalistic view of the universe, there was the traditional medieval view that man was at the pivot point of the universe; that the universe existed in a great chain of being; that everything in the universe had its proper rank in that chain; that there was a natural way of ordering political groups, namely, monarchy, with the king taking his title and his responsibility from God.

The central issue of *King Lear* is the conflict between these two different ways of looking at man in the universe, the naturalistic way and the medieval way. In a sense, you could consider *King Lear* the one play that Shakespeare wrote about the central intellectual issue of his day, indeed, of his century. To say that, though, would make *King Lear* simply a period piece, an interesting document in seventeenth-century intellectual history, and *King Lear* is much, much more than that. It is a play about one of the most enduring of all human problems, the problem of values, as a look at the tragedy itself will show.

One of the key words in *Lear* is "nature" and its derivatives, "natural," "unnatural," "disnatured." There are other synonyms: "monstrous" (meaning unnatural); "kind" (a dictionary will tell you that, in Shakespeare's day, "kind" still held its original meaning derived from "kin"; it meant what we are related to or born to, the kind of thing we naturally are, as we use the word "kind" in "mankind"). All these words, "nature," "disnatured," "natural," "unnatural," "monstrous," "kind," "unkind"—together, they occur more often by far in *King Lear* than in any other of Shakespeare's plays and they bear, in a way, the heart of the tragedy.

"Nature" and the related words carry much of the time the notion of the fixed medieval universe, with fixed relations and values among people and things. For example, when Lear thinks Cordelia is not showing enough love for him, he calls her "a wretch whom *nature* is ashamed almost t' acknowledge hers." France, who is wooing Cordelia, is puzzled by Lear's suddenly turning against her: he expresses his puzzlement as,

> Sure her offense
> Must be of such *unnatural* degree
> That monsters it.
>
> (I. i. 218–220)

Later, when Lear repents of his anger to Cordelia, he thinks of himself as having behaved unnaturally, not with a father's "nature":

> O most small fault,
> How ugly didst thou in Cordelia show!

> Which, like an engine, wrenched *my frame of nature*
> From the fixed place.
>
> (I. iv. 257–260)

He turns to curse Goneril with an unnatural child—

> If she must teem,
> Create her child of spleen, that it may live
> And be a thwart *disnatured* torment to her.
> (I. iv. 272–274)

In short, just as the father who does not love his daughter is out of nature, so the daughters who do not love their father are, "You *unnatural* hags!" They drive their father to madness and cursing:

> And thou, all-shaking thunder,
> Strike flat the thick rotundity o' th' world,
> Crack *Nature*'s moulds, all germains spill at once,
> That makes ingrateful man.
>
> (III. ii. 6–9)

This is the curse Macbeth made, to crack nature's molds, spill all the germains, the seeds or genes that guarantee that humans will have human children and not monsters. Lear's curse wishes the destruction of "nature," "kind," the very texture of an ordered world.

These words, notably "unnatural," come up over and over again in the Gloucester plot, parallel to the Lear plot. Gloucester, when he thinks his son Edgar has turned against him, cries out, "Oh villain, villain! . . . Abhorred villain, unnatural, detested, brutish villain; worse than brutish!" Later, "He cannot be such a monster," and then Gloucester muses on what has happened:

These late eclipses in the sun and moon portend no good to us. Though the wisdom of nature can reason it thus and thus, yet nature finds itself scourged by the sequent effects. Love cools, friendship falls off, brothers divide. In cities, mutinies; in countries, discord; in palaces, treason; and the bond cracked 'twixt son and father. This villain of mine comes under the prediction, there's son against father; the King falls from bias of nature, there's father against child. We have seen the best of our time.

(I. ii. 101–110)

Gloucester's astrological musings conjure up the whole traditional world-view in which cosmos, kingdom, family are bound in parallel orders. Edmund, pretending to be honest, pretends to think traditionally as his father does, "The effects [of these eclipses] succeed unhappily: as of unnaturalness between the child and the parent; death, dearth, dissolutions of ancient amities; divisions in state, menaces and maledictions against king and nobles; needless diffidences, banishment of friends, dissipation of cohorts, nuptial breaches, and I know not what."

Then, as against that kind of nature in which there are divinely ordained relationships between the king and his kingdom, the father and his children, against that traditional, medieval nature, the play poses a new kind of nature, represented by Edmund, when he is behaving like his own nasty self: "Thou, nature, art my goddess . . ." And even as Edmund addresses his goddess, we realize that he doesn't mean a goddess at all; he means a very physical, earthy kind of nature, a nature red in tooth and claw where only the fittest survive, very much a Darwinian or nineteenth-century kind of nature:

> Thou, Nature, art my goddess; to thy law
> My services are bound. Wherefore should I
> Stand in the plague of custom, and permit
> The curiosity of nations to deprive me,
> For that I am some twelve or fourteen moonshines
> Lag of a brother? Why bastard? Wherefore base
> When my dimensions are as well compact,
> My mind as generous, and my shape as true,
> As honest madam's issue? Why brand they us
> With base? with baseness? Bastardy base? Base?
> Who, in the lusty stealth of nature, take
> More composition and fierce quality
> Than doth, within a dull, stale, tirèd bed,
> Go to th' creating a whole tribe of fops
> Got 'tween asleep and wake?
>
> (I. ii. 1–15)

In Edmund's "nature" there is no difference between legitimate and illegitimate —there is only the fact of parenthood. And this view produced one of our twentieth-century social reforms. We have finally gotten around to erasing on birth certificates the distinction between legitimate and illegitimate children, and most of us would agree that's a good thing to do, because, as I've said, most of us think like Edmund: there is no reason to think an illegitimate child somehow less "natural" than a legitimate one.

Edmund goes on to scoff at his father's belief in astrology:

This is the excellent foppery of the world, that when we are sick in fortune, often the surfeits of our own behavior, we make guilty of our disasters the sun, the moon, and stars; as if we were . . . drunkards, liars, and adulterers by an enforced obedience of planetary influence. . . . An admirable evasion of whoremaster man, to lay his goatish disposition on the charge of a star.

(I. ii. 115–124)

Do you believe in astrology? Probably not, because you tend to think the way Edmund does. Even Lear, in his despair, takes Edmund's point of view: "Man's life is cheap as beast's." That is exactly the Edmundian or post-Darwinian kind of nature, naturalistic nature, in which man is only another animal, as we see him in the twentieth century, and as Lear sees the naked beggar:

> Is man no more than this? Consider him well. Thou ow'st the worm no silk, the beast no hide, the sheep no wool, the cat no perfume. . . . Thou art the thing itself; unaccommodated man is no more but such a poor, bare, forked animal as thou art.
>
> (III. iv. 97–102)

In effect, the difference between the two kinds of nature, chain-of-being nature and naturalistic nature, lies in divine intervention. In the animal nature of Edmund, the gods take no real part. In the traditional nature which Lear and Gloucester (seem to) support, the gods are working all the time. As Albany says, horrified at the daughters' mistreatment of Lear,

> If that the heavens do not their visible spirits
> Send quickly down to tame these vile offenses,
> It will come,
> Humanity must perforce prey on itself,
> Like monsters of the deep.
>
> (IV. ii. 46–49)

Albany is speaking of justice, and we hear a great deal in this tragedy about justice.

Basically, there are two kinds of justice—Aristotle originally drew the distinction. One kind is the kind we administer in the modern court, retributive justice, a justice that pays people back. If you slip and break your leg on my banana-peel-strewn sidewalk, I have to pay you back and make you as well off as you were before. This paying-back justice is the justice Lear calls on when he cries,

> Let the great gods
> That keep this dreadful pudder o'er our heads
> Find out their enemies now. Tremble, thou wretch,
> That hast within thee undivulgèd crimes
> Unwhipped of justice.
>
> (III. ii. 49–53)

That is retributive justice, and Lear calls on the gods to administer it as Albany had done, while Edmund, Goneril, and Regan are indifferent to retributive justice. There is another kind of justice, though, distributive justice, that right-winged people might call welfare justice. This is the justice that concerns itself with the way the goods of society are distributed in the first place, while retributive justice concerns itself with keeping that arrangement intact. In the realm of distributive justice, to Edmund, them that can, gets:

> Let me, if not by birth, have lands by wit;
> All with me's meet that I can fashion fit.
>
> (I. ii. 176–177)

Edmund, Goneril, and Regan, the positivists of the play, do not believe in any distributive justice, but the more tragic victims discover it, as Lear does, when he says to his Fool:

> In boy; go first. You houseless poverty—
> Nay get thee in. . . .
> Poor naked wretches, whereso'er you are,
> That bide the pelting of this pitiless storm,
> How shall your houseless heads and unfed sides,
> Your looped and windowed raggedness, defend you
> From seasons such as these? O, I have ta'en
> Too little care of this! Take physic, pomp;
> Expose thyself to feel what wretches feel,
> That thou mayst shake the superflux to them
> And show the heavens more just.
>
> (III. iv. 26–36)

And Gloucester has a parallel, though not so magnificent, speech:

> Heavens, deal so still!
> Let the superfluous and lust-dieted man,
> That slaves your ordinance, that will not see
> Because he does not feel, feel your pow'r quickly;
> So distribution should undo excess,
> And each man have enough.
>
> (IV. i. 66–71)

One of the things the victims in this tragedy learn is justice, both retributive and distributive.

Another is authority. At the beginning of the tragedy, we see a Lear proud and strong in his kingly authority. In his despair, in his madness, when he speaks the hard truths that Edmund knows, he has a different image of authority: "Thou hast seen a farmer's dog bark at a beggar?" "And the creature run from the cur. There thou mightst behold the great image of authority—a dog's obeyed in office" (IV. vi. 152–156).

Justice, authority, nature and un-nature, the medieval view and the naturalistic, seventeenth-century view, all these things develop the massive dualism of *King Lear*. The tragedy balances off against each other two great conceptions of man-in-nature. One, that man is just another animal, that there are no natural values; the other, that man is something special, that there are gods who are interested in him, who help him or perhaps treat him as wanton boys do flies, "kill us for their sport." But at least there are gods and they do take some kind of an interest. Right in the middle of these two conceptions come Cordelia's cold words, "I love your Majesty according to my bond, no more nor less." Cordelia has brought in that whole, wonderful, traditional view of man and the universe, that there are bonds, bonds supported by divine intervention, by God's love, and that these bonds are the most precious thing in the world. When she says, "I love your Majesty according to my bond, no more nor less," she has said a tremendous thing. Lear, it turns out, does not really believe in that traditional conception, *really* believe in it. Instead he wants to hear the same kind of fine, fancy, phony speech that he has heard from Goneril and Regan. Cordelia's word, "bond," which Lear thinks is "nothing," "untender," is exactly the right word. In the very next scene, Gloucester complains that the "bond" is cracked betwixt son and father in the general description of nature. Lear himself uses that very word "bond," when he speaks to the false Regan:

> No, Regan, thou shalt never have my curse.
>
> .   .   .
>
> Thou better know'st
> The offices of nature, bond of childhood,
> Effects of courtesy, dues of gratitude.
>
> (II. iv. 165–174)

In other words, Cordelia's word "bond" represents exactly what should be the relationship between parent and child in the traditional, medieval, one might almost say, fairy-tale view of the universe.

Yet Cordelia seems a little stiff-necked, cold, a little proud. Here is her poor, dear old father, about to go into retirement, and he's asking for a little speech of appreciation. Will she give it to him? Oh no! She is going to be very true, and virtuous, and a bit of a cold fish. Looking at *King Lear* that way is looking at it as though it were a naturalistic play, a modern play giving a rather realistic picture of things and people. You certainly can look at the play that way, though. The tragedy becomes an in-law problem, a Paddy Chayefsky-style television play about an old man who tries to sponge off his married daughters: the big executive, who's used to throwing his weight around, now has become very old and difficult (as the girls point out, "He hath ever but slenderly known himself"); now he is full of crotchets and fits and rages, but he expects to be obeyed just as if he were still in office running his gigantic corporation. As Regan points out to him, quite reasonably:

> How in one house
> Should many people, under two commands,
> Hold amity? 'Tis hard, almost impossible.
>
> (II. iv. 235–237)

A very reasonable, very Elizabethan point of view. But Lear flies into a rage. Again, Regan points out quite reasonably,

> To willful men
> The injuries that they themselves procure
> Must be their schoolmasters.
>
> (II. iv. 297–299)

If the old man is going to behave in this crotchety, infuriated way, he is simply going to have to learn. Then what does Lear do but get mixed up with a foreign invader, a terrible thing: even Albany, who is the moral spokesman in the play, feels that he has to resist this foreign invasion. Edmund, too, is, in a modern way, rather reasonable. He finds that his father is a traitor to his country, helping the foreign invader, and he turns him in. Wouldn't many people today praise a son who turned in his communist father to the F.B.I.? Of course. All good twentieth-century naturalists should really agree with Edmund, Goneril, and Regan.

King Lear, though, is not a Paddy Chayefskyan television drama: rather it has almost the quality of folktale. "Once upon a time there was a very old King and he had three daughters. The older two were spiteful and hard and bad, but the youngest was fair and good." Even in there being two different ways we can look at the tragedy, there is the basic dualism between the two kinds of nature: one nature, red in tooth and claw, realistic, guided only by the survival of the fittest, and another kind of nature, a traditional, folkloric, medieval kind of nature.

King Lear is the tragedy of man-in-nature, two kinds of nature. If you looked in *King Lear* just at the references to the gods, you would think that man is somehow in a specially favored position, that the gods in that traditional, medieval view of nature are constantly mixing into his affairs. We hear of revenging gods, blessed gods, gods that we adore, great gods, kind gods, mighty gods, clearest gods, ever-gentle gods; and we hear on the other side of devils. There is a whole list of the devils that have been afflicting poor Tom o' Bedlam: Obidicut, Hobbididence, Mahu, Modo, Flibbertigibbet. There is, too, a choicely graphic description of the devil that supposedly tempted Gloucester over the cliff,

> His eyes
> Were two full moons; he had a thousand noses,
> Horns whelked and waved like the enridgèd sea.
>
> (IV. vi. 69–71)

Even Edmund, the most naturalistic character in the play, cries out, "Now gods, stand up for bastards," though I suppose he is just making a joke. Lear, too, cries out, "You heavens, give me that patience, patience I need." Gloucester, in the depths of his despair, sees the gods as hostile, interfering, playfully sadistic,

> As flies to wanton boys are we to th' gods;
> They kill us for their sport.
>
> (IV. i. 36–37)

For the most part, though, we hear of the gods as revengers, as when Edgar speaks his father Gloucester's epitaph. He thinks back to the very opening words of the play when Gloucester explained how and where he begot the bastard, Edmund, and Edgar muses on the fact that it was this illegitimate child, this moment of sport, that cost Gloucester his sight,

> The gods are just, and of our pleasant vices
> Make instruments to plague us.
>
> (V. iii. 171–172)

Albany hears of the death of his wife and her sister, trapped in the coils of their devious relationship, and says,

> This judgment of the heavens, that makes us tremble,
> Touches us not with pity.
>
> (V. iii. 232–233)

Earlier, Albany, when he heard of Gloucester's eyes being torn out and Cornwall being killed in the act, spoke of,

> You justicers, that these our nether crimes
> So speedily can venge.
>
> (IV. ii. 79–80)

But then he adds,

> But, O poor Gloucester,
> Lost he his other eye?
>
> (80–81)

A curious juxtaposition, it suggests ironically that somehow, despite the big guns of heaven's justicers, Gloucester still lost both his eyes. In that grim irony is the curious thing about all these references to gods and to the devils. In spite of the dozens of references and invocations to them, at no point do the gods or devils *ever actually intervene*. The tragedy gives us in every case a perfectly naturalistic reason for any acts of justice or punishment that may take place. For all the justice of heaven, Cordelia, the most innocent character in the tragedy, is killed perfectly pointlessly at the end. If there be gods in *King Lear*, they don't live up to their reputation. Man in *King Lear* is a man whom the gods forgot.

In the last analysis, then, the gods in this tragedy seem to be either indifferent or superfluous. Justice becomes only a human abstraction. And even on that limited basis, how grimly it is presented in the play! There is the horrible parody of a trial in which Gloucester's eyes are torn out; that trial is itself immediately preceded by another horrible parody of justice in which Lear, and the beggar Edgar, and the Fool preside over an imaginary court, trying the false daughters. Lear describes human justice to the blind Gloucester:

> Thou rascal beadle, hold thy bloody hand!
> Why dost thou lash that whore? Strip thy own back.
> Thou hotly lusts to use her in that kind
> For which thou whip'st her. The usurer hangs the cozener.
> Through tattered clothes small vices do appear;
> Robes and furred gowns hide all. Plate sin with gold,
> And the strong lance of justice hurtless breaks;
> Arm it in rags, a pygmy's straw does pierce it.
> None does offend, none—I say none!
>
> (IV. vi. 157–165)

The play is full of abstract discussions of such things as "justice," "authority," or "suffering." For example, Edgar tells us in a general way about suffering,

> Who alone suffers suffers most i' th' mind,
> Leaving free things and happy shows behind.
>
> (III. vi. 102–103)

And again,

> The lowest and most dejected thing of fortune,
> Stands still in esperance, lives not in fear.
> The lamentable change is from the best;
> The worst returns to laughter.
>
> (IV. i. 3–6)

And yet again,

> O, our lives' sweetness!
> That we the pain of death would hourly die
> Rather than die at once.
>
> (V. iii. 185–187)

Is it any wonder with all this musing that Lear calls Edgar "this philosopher"?

"Philosopher," however, meant something different in Shakespeare's day; it meant approximately what we mean by a scientist, that is, one who studies "natural philosophy." Thus, Lear can say to the Tom o' Bedlam Edgar:

> First let me talk with this philosopher.
> What is the cause of thunder?
>
> (III. iv. 145–146)

Though Lear never gets his abstract discussion of thunder, we hear a variety of abstract, "philosophical" discussions, Lear on justice, Gloucester and Edmund on astrology, Edgar on suffering, and so on. In short, in the course of the tragedy, we see a number of efforts to reason abstractions through.

Yet, at the same time, one thing we do not see very much of in this play is reason. On the contrary, the play is filled with madness and folly. We first see Lear's folly in dividing his kingdom and in holding his strange little love contest. We see Gloucester's folly in believing the worst of his good son without even speaking to that son. We see before us on the stage a madman, the Tom o' Bedlam beggar, played by Edgar. The custom in Shakespeare's merrie England was, when the big insane asylum in London, Bethlehem Hospital, or as it was called "Bedlam," became too crowded, for the authorities to discharge some of the harmless lunatics to make their way in the world as best they could by begging. Such a beggar was called, generically, Tom o' Bedlam, and this is the part that Edgar chooses to play, the part of a madman and a beggar.

We see before us, too, a Fool, perhaps the most interesting and enigmatic figure in the play. It was the custom in medieval times, and even earlier, for the great man to keep a fool, so that, looking at this figure seated at his feet, he might remember that he himself was only mortal like the fool. The fool was a way of keeping your perspective on things, of saying to yourself from time to time, no matter how big and important you were, you were still mortal. There were two kinds of fools, the court fool and the natural fool. A court fool we have already seen, Feste, in *Twelfth Night,* a man in perfect sanity, in fact, probably unusually intelligent, who makes his living by pretending to be a little wacky. The natural fool was someone who was, as it were, touched by God, someone not quite right in the head. And that is the kind of fool we have in *Lear.* And yet, for all his folly, he knows the truth, and, "all-licensed," he points it out to Lear cruelly, with a terrible, hard directness.

When we think of Tom o' Bedlam who pretends to be mad but is really sane and the Fool who seems to be foolish but is really wise, you should contrast them in your mind with Gloucester and Lear who seem old and wise, but are actually fools and mad. Both the Fool and the Tom o' Bedlam seem to be allied with the rightful order of things, that traditional nature in which things have their proper place, and it is part of the terror of *King Lear* that the good world, the world of traditional values, is identified with the Fool and the madman.

In yet another sense, the Fool seems to stand for Cordelia. He appears when she disappears, and when she returns, the Fool drops out of the play. Lear, to tell us that Cordelia has been hanged, says, "And my poor fool is hanged." He is literally referring to Cordelia, the word "fool" here being a term of endearment, but his use of the word makes us think back to that strange figure who accompanied him in the storm on the heath. The Fool may mean something even more; in a way, he could stand for Lear's sense, the unpleasant, hard truths which Lear will not face.

The poet, John Keats, had still another suggestion for the significance of the Fool. Keats said, "The Fool's words are merely the simplest translation of poetry as high as Lear's. The Fool gives a finishing touch to the pathos." Then, too, as Keats pointed out, the Fool gets the laughs; and he keeps us from laughing at Lear when he is mad and a little ridiculous. In other words the Fool's function is to siphon off, as it were, the potentialities of comedy in Lear's behavior, as when he says things like:

> No, you unnatural hags!
> I will have such revenges on you both
> That all the world shall—I will do such things—
> What they are, yet I know not; but they shall be
> The terrors of the earth.
>
> (II. iv. 273–277)

As this impotent rage of Lear's suggests, there is something a little ridiculous, a little childish about him, in this grotesque tragedy of folly and madness. Goneril tells him, "As you are old and reverend, [you] should be wise." But the Fool points out to Lear, "If thou wert my fool, nuncle, I'd have thee beaten for being old before thy time." Lear asks, "How's that?" And the Fool replies, "Thou shouldst not have been old till thou hadst been wise." In effect, Lear has become as a child again, expecting to be tended like a baby by his daughters. Goneril says, "Old fools are babes again," and the Fool tells Lear, "Thou mad'st thy daughters thy mothers; for . . . thou gav'st them the rod, and put'st down thine own breeches."

The imagery has taken us quite a way from man and his relation to the gods, from man with his abstractions like justice and authority and philosophy, down into the realm of madness and the Fool's folly. But the nadir is yet to come. As Lear says,

> The tempest in my mind
> Doth from my senses take all feeling else
> Save what beats there.
>
> (III. iv. 12–14)

In the imagery of *King Lear,* man loses not only his reason, but all his senses. Man can no longer believe in the words he hears, like the gilded words that Lear hears in the love contest, or that fabulous description of a cliff which Edgar gives to Gloucester, a cliff which isn't there at all. One sense in particular the play seems fascinated with, sight. There are over a hundred references to "eye" or "look" or "see" or "sight." In fact, Lear's very last words are, "Look there, look there." These references to sight are thick in irony. Goneril, in the opening love contest, says as her very first words in the play,

> Sir, I love you more than word can wield the matter;
> Dearer than eyesight . . .
>
> (I. i. 55–56)

"Dearer than eyesight"—and this is the woman who will later, when Gloucester is captured, cry, "Pluck out his eyes!" Gloucester himself is the living embodiment of these ironies associated with sight. He comes upon Edmund pretending to read a traitorous letter. Gloucester asks, "What paper were you reading?" and Edmund replies, "Nothing, my lord." And Gloucester says, "No? What needed then that terrible dispatch of it into your pocket? . . . Let's see. Come, if it be nothing, I shall not need spectacles." This is the man whose eyes will be torn out, who later will say,

> I have no way, and therefore want no eyes;
> I stumbled when I saw.
>
> (IV. i. 18–19)

If the senses are not torn out like Gloucester's eyes, they are tossed into a horrible jumble. Lear tells the blind Gloucester, "You see how this world goes." Gloucester drily replies, "I see it feelingly." "What, art mad?" says Lear. "A man may see how this world goes with no eyes. Look with thine ears."

In this jumble of the senses, however, one sense survives. As the Fool says, "There's not a nose among twenty but can smell him that's stinking." "Truth's a dog must to kennel; he must be whipped out, when the Lady Brach may stand by th' fire and stink." Lear says, stating perhaps the most unpleasant truth of all, "Thou know'st, the first time that we smell the air we wawl and cry" (a line useful for quoting to obstetricians). After Gloucester's eyes are torn out, Regan cries, "Let him smell his way to Dover." And when Gloucester tries to kiss Lear's hand, Lear says, "Let me wipe it first; it smells of mortality." It is as though, if we were blind, deaf, and without feeling, we could still *smell* an unpleasant truth.

The imagery in this play not only destroys and jumbles man's sense and his senses, it even tears off his clothing. Lear's original plan to retire, to abdicate from the kingship, he expresses first as wanting to "unburdened crawl toward death." He says "we will divest us both of rule, interest of territory, cares of state." "Divest" means literally to take off one's clothing, one's vestments, one's ceremonial robes. The girls do indeed divest him, take all his retainers away, take even the shelter from his head, until Lear cries out in his magnificent speech:

> O reason not the need! Our basest beggars
> Are in the poorest thing superfluous.

> Allow not nature more than nature needs,
> Man's life is cheap as beast's. Thou art a lady:
> If only to go warm were gorgeous,
> Why, nature needs not what thou gorgeous wear'st,
> Which scarcely keeps thee warm.
>
> (II. iv. 259–265)

Then Lear goes out onto the heath, naked to the elements, as it were, and when, in this nakedness, he feels for the first time pity for others, he feels it in the terms of clothing.

> Poor naked wretches, wheresoe'er you are,
> That bide the pelting of this pitiless storm,
> How shall your houseless heads and unfed sides,
> Your looped and windowed raggedness, defend you
> From seasons such as these?
>
> (III. iv. 28–32)

Things are even worse than Lear believes in that speech, given as he looks at his Fool, for in the next twenty lines Edgar's naked body is suddenly thrust onto the stage before us; Lear comments on that naked body,

Thou wert better in a grave than to answer with thy uncovered body this extremity of the skies. Is man no more than this? Consider him well. Thou ow'st the worm no silk, the beast no hide, the sheep no wool, the cat no perfume. Ha! here's three on's are sophisticated. Thou art the thing itself; unaccommodated man is no more but such a poor, bare, forked animal as thou art. Off, off you lendings! Come, unbutton here.

(III. iv. 96–103)

And he tries to tear his own clothes off. This is Lear mad; the first thing Cordelia does to bring him back to sanity is to change his clothing. When she is killed and Lear speaks his final words over her dead body, he says, "Pray you undo this button." It is as though clothes were the thing that linked man to that higher nature, that nature of ceremony and order; without his clothes man is nothing but a poor, bare, forked animal.

Throughout *King Lear* man is compared to animals. Lear cries out against "those pelican daughters." "Detested kite," he calls Goneril, and hopes that she will have an ungrateful child, "that she may feel how sharper than a serpent's tooth it is to have a thankless child." "O Regan, she hath tied sharp-toothed unkindness, like a vulture, here." In his madness, Lear's mind sees humans as animal-like in the act of love.

> Adultery?
> Thou shalt not die. Die for adultery? No.
> The wren goes to't, and the small gilded fly
> Does lecher in my sight.
>
> (IV. vi. 109–112)

We could go on and on. In the course of the tragedy, we hear about the dog, the horse, the cow, the sheep, the hog, the lion, the bear, the wolf, the fox, the monkey, the fitchew (polecat), the civet, the pelican, the owl, the crow, the chough, the wren, the fly, the butterfly, the rat, the mouse, the frog, the tadpole, the wall-newt, the water-newt, the worm, and so on, and so on. But perhaps the most pathetic reference to animals and the clearest in meaning is Lear's sentence over the dead Cordelia:

> No, no, no life?
> Why should a dog, a horse, a rat, have life,
> And thou no breath at all?
> (V. iii. 306–308)

It is as though the lowest attribute of man, mere living, mere animal spirits, even this gets taken away.

This set of images—gods, abstractions, clothing, sense and senses, animals—is stripping and anatomizing man, looking at his attributes one by one, from the highest to the lowest. The tragedy has stripped him of his gods, of all his pretensions, of his words, of his reason, his senses, his clothing. Now confronted with that naked, *animal* body, Lear asks for a naturalistic explanation of traditionally unnatural behavior: "Let them anatomize Regan. See what breeds about her heart. Is there any cause in nature that makes these hard hearts?" The central image of the play is a body being yanked and wrenched and tortured, dissected, pulled apart as wanton boys would pull apart flies. Lear tells us,

> I am bound
> Upon a wheel of fire, that mine own tears
> Do scald like molten lead.
> (IV. vii. 46–48)

He describes "a thousand [devils] with red burning spits come hizzing in upon 'em." We hear of Edgar, "whom the foul fiend hath led through fire and through flame, through ford and whirlpool, o'er bog and quagmire," "Poor Tom, that eats the swimming frog, the toad, the tadpole, the wall-newt and the water[-newt]." We hear Lear describe his body as tortured by disease,

> Thou art my flesh, my blood, my daughter;
> Or rather a disease that's in my flesh,
> Which I must needs call mine. Thou art a boil,
> A plague-sore, or embossèd carbuncle
> In my corrupted blood.
> (II. iv. 216–220)

Throughout the language, we hear of the human body being tugged, wrenched, beaten, pierced, stung, scourged, flayed, gashed, scalded, tortured in every way. We get the image not only in the language but on the stage before our very eyes. We see Kent trip up Oswald; we see Kent stuck in the stocks; we see Edgar's flesh naked to the storm; we see Lear bear in the dead Cordelia's body; we see Gloucester bound to a chair, his beard pulled and his eyes torn out. These torture images culminate in the words spoken as Lear dies,

> Vex not his ghost. O, let him pass! He hates him
> That would upon the rack of this tough world
> Stretch him out longer.
>
> (V. iii. 314–316)

Mere existence in the world, in time, is torture.

In this horrible torturing and dissection, the images take us back to the very place we were born, to woman. As Albany says, "Proper deformity seems not in the fiend so horrid as in woman." Woman, in a sense, is the most sacred but the most taboo and deadly of things in the world. Freud, in his essay on this play, saw in Cordelia a reversal. She, the youngest, the loveliest, and the most loving of the three daughters, Freud said, by her muteness, by her saying nothing, symbolizes death, Lear's death. But death is an ugly fact, and Shakespeare in his imagination, as we all often do in dreams, reverses this ugly fact into its lovely opposite, Cordelia. Cordelia, then, is the ultimate mother, Mother Earth, carrying the dead Lear in her arms. The image comes out reversed: Lear carries the dead Cordelia in his arms, but the idea is the same, that somehow our destiny, the place where we are born and the place where we die is a woman. As Friar Laurence said in *Romeo and Juliet*:

> The earth that's nature's mother is her tomb.
> What is her burying grave, that is her womb.
>
> (II. iii. 9–10)

But the womb in *King Lear*? That speech from *Romeo and Juliet* seems like a breath of fresh air when we hear what people in this play have to say about the womb. Edgar speaks of his father to his bastard brother, and says,

> The dark and vicious place where thee he got
> Cost him his eyes.
>
> (V. iii. 173–174)

"The dark and vicious place"—that is what woman has become in this play. Lear says of women:

> Down from the waist they are Centaurs,
> Though women all above.
> But to the girdle do the gods inherit,
> Beneath is all the fiend's.

There's hell, there's darkness, there is the sulphurous pit; burning, scalding, stench, consumption. Fie, fie, fie! pah, pah! Give me an ounce of civet; good apothecary, sweeten my imagination!

> (IV. vi. 123–130)

In *King Lear* Shakespeare's imagination seems to have hit a low point. The images strip man of everything. Heaven is taken away from him. His own abstractions like justice and authority are debased and destroyed. His reason is turned into madness and folly. His age becomes childishness, his childhood age. His sight is destroyed, and he is left with only stink and stench. His clothing is torn off until he becomes only a bare forked animal spawned in a "dark and vicious place." Then he is tortured and twisted, exposed to the elements, burned, stretched on the rack. In short, the image *King Lear* gives us of man is man tortured, racked between two natures, two ways of seeing man-in-nature, until man is left with "nothing."

That summary suggests that a most important something in *Lear* is, in fact, "nothing." The first time we meet nothing is in that foolish love contest that Lear sets up. Shakespeare makes it very clear to us, in the opening lines of the play, that Lear has already marked out the divisions of his kingdom. That itself, as any Elizabethan could have told you, was a very silly thing to do. A kingdom should not be divided, for dividing a kingdom can lead only to civil war. In fact, had not all the trouble started with Lear and the invasion from France, there quite likely would have been a civil war between the two men who get the two halves of Lear's kingdom, Albany and Cornwall. We hear about it,

> There is division,
> Although as yet the face of it is covered
> With mutual cunning, 'twixt Albany and Cornwall.
> (III. i. 19–21)

Dividing a kingdom was a foolish thing to do in the first place, but then Lear compounds his folly, by pretending that he is going to give away the parts of his kingdom according to which of his daughters "shall we say doth love us most." This is pure window-dressing, "nothing"; the division of the kingdom has already been made, and he gives Goneril who speaks first her part of the kingdom before Regan and Cordelia have even had a chance to speak. When Lear asks Cordelia to speak, he says, "What can you say to draw a third more opulent than your sisters?" In other words, Lear has already made up his mind, and the love contest really counts for nothing. It is precisely at this point, that we first hear in the tragedy of *King Lear* its key word, "nothing."

Lear.	What can you say to draw
	A third more opulent than your sisters? Speak.
Cordelia.	Nothing, my lord.
Lear.	Nothing?
Cordelia.	Nothing.
Lear.	Nothing will come of nothing. Speak again.
Cordelia.	Unhappy that I am, I cannot heave

> My heart into my mouth. I love your Majesty
> According to my bond, no more nor less.

> (I. i. 85–93)

"Nothing"—and yet what was Lear's love-contest but nothing, mere show, just as Goneril's and Regan's words of love were mere show, nothing. The word echoes again in this, the opening scene, when Lear insists he will give nothing in the way of a dowry with Cordelia, "Sir, there she stands. . . . And nothing more." In the next scene, when Edmund begins the treachery in the Gloucester plot, the word comes up again. Gloucester comes upon Edmund reading a letter:

Gloucester. Why so earnestly seek you to put up that letter?
Edmund. I know no news, my lord.
Gloucester. What paper were you reading?
Edmund. Nothing, my lord.
Gloucester. No? What needed then that terrible dispatch of it into your pocket? The quality of nothing hath not such need to hide itself. Let's see. Come, if it be nothing, I shall not need spectacles.

> (I. ii. 28–35)

This nothing, unlike Lear's or Cordelia's, is treacherous: it is the forged letter in which Edgar is made to seem to plot against his father; and, of course, his father does not "see" the trick. He is figuratively blind as he will be literally blind later. He sees "nothing."

The next interesting use of the word "nothing" crops up in the Fool's first dialogue with Lear:

Fool. Have more than thou showest,
Speak less than thou knowest,
Lend less than thou owest,
Ride more than thou goest,
Learn more than thou trowest,
Set less than thou throwest;
Leave thy drink and thy whore,
And keep in-a-door,
And thou shalt have more
Than two tens to a score.
Kent. This is nothing, fool.
Fool. Then 'tis like the breath of an unfee'd lawyer—you gave me nothing for't. Can you make no use of nothing, nuncle?
Lear. Why, no, boy. Nothing can be made out of nothing.
Fool [to Kent]. Prithee tell him, so much the rent of his land comes to; he will not believe a fool.

> (I. iv. 112–128)

First, there are the Fool's paradoxes (like those of France), then "nothing" and even an echo of Lear's earlier "Nothing will come of nothing." The Fool comes back to the idea when he tells Lear:

I had rather be any kind o' thing than a fool, and yet I would not be thee, nuncle: thou hast pared thy wit o' both sides and left nothing i' th' middle. . . . Thou wast a pretty fellow when thou hadst no need to care for her [Goneril's] frowning. Now thou art an O without a figure. I am better than thou art now: I am a fool, thou art nothing.

(I. iv. 176–185)

"Nothing," in the Fool's words, becomes a zero, a cipher with no numbers attached to it to give it value, and this arithmetical use of the word suggests that the play is in some sense preoccupied with counting and numbering.

Most obviously, this counting comes out in what we might call the "countdown scene," II. iv, where the girls count off Lear's hundred knights. Lear starts by assuming he can stay with Regan with his hundred knights, after Goneril has told him to cut the number to fifty. Regan says, "Fifty followers? . . . What should you need of more?" Then, a few lines later, "I entreat you to bring but five-and-twenty." So Lear turns back to Goneril who had bid fifty, but she replies, "What need you five-and-twenty? ten? or five?" And Regan drives in the final nail, "What need one?" Then Lear goes off into his magnificent speech,

> O reason not the need! Our basest beggars
> Are in the poorest thing superfluous.
> (II. iv. 259–260)

He begins to realize that somehow you can't value things that way, that the human world is not simply a world of numbers, of physical need, that ultimately you can justify "nothing" on that basis. "Man's life is cheap as beast's."

Number somehow fails to convey the most important things in human experience, and yet the play seems preoccupied with number and quantity. The very opening line of the play is, "I thought the King had more affected the Duke of Albany than Cornwall." "More affected," that is, he had loved one more than the other, an attempt to quantify, to state in terms of more and less. The very closing lines of the play also measure:

> The oldest hath borne most; we that are young
> Shall never see so much, nor live so long.

"See so much," "live so long"—this is the language of quantity, and the tragedy of King Lear seems to hinge on the problem of quantifying what you cannot quantify, the things in human experience like love, like suffering, sin, grace, loyalty, the relationship of father to daughter or father to son—these are things that even in this day of modern psychology, numbers tell us very little about.

Lear's problem is that he tries to quantify what cannot be quantified. In that opening love contest,

> Tell me, my daughters . . .
> Which of you shall we say doth love us most,
> That we our largest bounty may extend
> Where nature doth with merit challenge?
> (I. i. 48–53)

He tries to quantify love, to have love expressed in words of amount—I love you thus and thus much—and he in turn hopes to respond with giving a certain amount of land. Goneril realizes what he wants and gives it to him.

> Sir, I love you more than word can wield the matter;
> Dearer than eyesight, space, and liberty;
> Beyond what can be valuèd, rich or rare;
> No less than life, with grace, health, beauty, honor;
> As much as child e'er loved, or father found;
> A love that makes breath poor, and speech unable.
> (I. i. 55–60)

She describes her love in terms of amount, and this is an insane way of describing love. The madness of it all comes out in the countdown scene. Regan has gotten the number of Lear's knights down to twenty-five, and Lear says to Goneril:

> I'll go with thee.
> Thy fifty yet doth double five-and-twenty,
> And thou art twice her love.
> (II. iv. 253–255)

Trying to translate love into the number of knights that one of your daughters will allow you—there's something insane in it, the same kind of madness as when Lear describes Cordelia after he has rejected her, "Now her price is fallen." What a terrible thing for a father to say about his daughter, "her price is fallen," as if he were auctioning her off.

The word "price" in a sense reminds us of Cordelia's bond: "I love your Majesty according to my bond, no more nor less." The word "bond" in one sense is a commercial word. It is the word Shylock used about his loan to Antonio in *The Merchant of Venice,* but also the word "bond" is a word that brings in that whole medieval, traditional view of nature, held together by the bonds of value, of God's love, if you will, the whole "chain" of being. In that word, "bond," we find focused the two areas of experience of the play, the two kinds of nature, the two uses of value: value in a numerical sense, in the sense of price, and value in a sense that goes beyond numbers into a world of pure value or quality, a world of paradox. Thus France, when he accepts Cordelia, the daughter that Lear is throwing away, accepts her in paradoxes:

> Fairest Cordelia, that art most rich being poor,
> Most choice forsaken, and most loved despised!
> (I. i. 250–251)

France has caught the feeling of the thing, that value, loyalty, love, these are not things to be expressed in terms of money or numbers. Cordelia is most rich being poor. Values somehow go beyond numbers. Even Lear himself finds it out. In the scene in the storm, as he is about to huddle in a hovel, a king now become lower than the lowest beggar, we hear him say,

> The art of our necessities is strange,
> And can make vile things precious.
> (III. ii. 70–71)

Vile things become precious: things of no numerical worth suddenly acquire value. The problem is like that in *Othello,* where there were two totally inconsistent time schemes, which even so made a certain kind of sense, a psychological sense. There is a time that we tick off in the neat divisions around the face of a clock, scientific time, but there is a realer time, our own subjective time, the time we feel. So in *Lear.* You can count things off in a nice numerical, scientific way, but values, true values, are something that come from our own feelings, and cannot be described in numbers. In effect, Shakespeare is here showing us his tragic hero doing what in *Othello* the villain of the tragedy did. Iago turned moral values into money values—in *King Lear,* it is the hero, Lear, who does.

There is a second, lesser tragic hero in *Lear,* Gloucester. In a way, his situation parallels Lear's situation, but there are some important differences. Gloucester, too, is involved with trying to quantify human relations that should not be thought of in terms of quantity but in terms of quality. In the very opening little dialogue of the play, Gloucester introduces to Kent his illegitimate son, Edmund, but he points out in a rather crude and commercial way that he has another son, a legitimate son: "I have a son, sir, by order of law, some year elder than this who yet is no dearer in my account." Gloucester loves his sons equally, unlike Lear who loves his daughters unequally (he has always shown a preference for Cordelia). Yet Gloucester allows the order in which these two sons were born to determine the way he treats them. And his bad son, Edmund, responds in kind,

> Wherefore should I
> Stand in the plague of custom, and permit
> The curiosity of nations to deprive me,
> For that I am some twelve or fourteen moonshines
> Lag of a brother?
> (I. ii. 2–6)

Edmund seems to feel that he is being deprived of land by some sort of numerical hanky-panky. Where Lear divided the land more or less equally among his daughters, and allowed that division to be upset only because of their words,

Gloucester is giving all his land to the older son, the son who has a greater *number* of years. Edmund, not unreasonably, feels he is being deprived. Gloucester's foolishness is in a sense just the opposite of Lear's foolishness. Lear got into trouble because he asked his daughters which of them loved him most. Gloucester gets into trouble because he *doesn't* ask which of his sons loves him most. Edmund turns up with a forged letter which purports to show that Edgar is plotting against his father's life. His father turns on Edgar without ever confronting him. Lear judges falsely because he confronts his daughter; Gloucester judges falsely because he fails to confront his son.

A great deal of this play comes together in terms of a pun, a pun that Shakespeare had a lot of fun with in *Romeo and Juliet,* but in *King Lear,* the pun is hidden. It doesn't actually come out in the words, and yet it seems to have been floating around in Shakespeare's imagination. We can start with a number, the number that starts all the rest of the numbers, one. "One," the single, sole, and solitary self, a number that seems to hover between numbers in general and qualities, one or nothing. But "one" comes up in this play not so much as "one" but as "I," the individual. "I" leads us into a favorite Shakespearean pun on the letter "I" and the organ "eye." Gloucester loses his eyes, but Lear loses his "I" in the other sense, his self, his mind, the thing that makes him what he is. Then, there is still another sense of the sound "I": "aye," the affirmative, and both Lear and Gloucester get into trouble because they do not affirm by their actions what they seem to believe, namely, that medieval view of nature as an ordered and harmonious hierarchy. "One," "I," "eye," "aye"—this audio-visual pun, in a sense, underlies the whole of *King Lear.*

Armed with this grand pun and our insight about the importance of numbering and quantity in the play, we are in a position to look at the dynamics of the tragedy. The tragedy takes place in three movements. Some critics have compared them to the Inferno, the Purgatory, and the Paradise of Dante's *Divine Comedy* and called *King Lear* the *Divine Comedy* of the Renaissance. Maybe so, but, at any rate, *King Lear* does have three movements. The first is what might be called the movement of mistaking. Lear mistakes and banishes his one loyal daughter. Gloucester mistakes in believing his one false son. It is also a movement of division where the families of Gloucester and Lear are divided. But, more important in a way, Lear is trying to divide himself as a king into the real substantive power of the king and what he himself calls the "addition" to a king.

> Cornwall and Albany,
>
>   . . .
>
> I do invest you jointly with my power,
> Preeminence, and all the large effects
> That troop with majesty. Ourself, by monthly course,

With reservation of an hundred knights,
By you to be sustained, shall our abode
Make with you by due turn. Only we shall retain
The name, and all th' addition to a king. The sway,
Revenue, execution of the rest,
Belovèd sons, be yours; which to confirm,
This coronet part between you.

(I. i. 127–139)

That image of trying to divide an undividable crown suggests the foolishness of what Lear has done. He has taken the *power* of a king, the sway, revenue, execution, and tried to separate that from the symbolic and ceremonial qualities that surround kingship, the name and all the *addition to* a king. In other words, he is making the same kind of division that the play makes throughout, between man as a raw animal, having a certain physical power, and man as something special involved with words and abstractions and clothing.

After these mistakes, the play moves on into its second phase, the movement of paradox in which everything turns topsy-turvy. We hear the Fool talk about a man's brains being in his heels, and he delivers a prophecy, a strange, paradoxical prophecy and concludes, "This prophecy Merlin shall make, for I live before his time." Lear says, "We'll go to supper in the morning." And the Fool replies, "And I'll go to bed at noon"—his last words. The Fool, in a sense, is the living embodiment of this topsy-turvy quality of the middle section of the play.

Lear's madness also establishes it. "Look with thine ears. See how yond justice rails upon yond simple thief. Hark in thine ear. Change places and, handy-dandy, which is the justice, which is the thief?" This topsy-turvy quality seems to be associated, too, with the turns of Fortune's wheel. Lear says he is bound upon a wheel of fire, and Edmund, when retribution finally catches up with him, sadly decides, "The wheel is come full circle."

Even more than a world harassed by the storms of fortune, this middle world of the tragedy is a world of paradox. On the heath the madman is the wise man, and the Fool has real knowledge. The King is a beggar; the rich man is poor; the false man (the disguised Kent) is the true man. The blind see, the meek triumph, and the dead live. This middle section shows us two trials, two mockeries of justice. In Act III, scene vi, the three justices, the play-madman Edgar, the Fool, and the real madman Lear, pass justice on the two sisters. As against that trial of madness, a trial of pure value, there is the trial of pure power in the scene which follows, Act III, scene vii, when Cornwall tears out Gloucester's eyes. In the great scene where Edgar pretends to lead Gloucester to the edge of the cliff, Act IV, scene vi, we hear Edgar, in some of Shakespeare's loveliest poetry (which is nevertheless only words), conjure up the image of a great high cliff, a great height between man and man which exists only in words. Then, in the second half of the same scene we see Lear quantifying the idea of his own kingship: "Ay, every inch a king," an assertion merely words just like every inch of that cliff made up of nothing but words.

In the final scene of the play, Act V, scene iii, we see the third movement, the two natures working themselves out as they have all through the play. At first, Lear and Cordelia seem somehow to have risen above the world of fact into a world of pure value:

> No, no, no, no! Come, let's away to prison.
> We two alone will sing like birds i' th' cage.
> When thou dost ask me blessing, I'll kneel down
> And ask of thee forgiveness. So we'll live,
> And pray, and sing, and tell old tales, and laugh
> At gilded butterflies, and hear poor rogues
> Talk of court news; and we'll talk with them too—
> Who loses and who wins; who's in, who's out—
> And take upon 's the mystery of things
> As if we were God's spies; and we'll wear out,
> In a walled prison, packs and sects of great ones
> That ebb and flow by th' moon.
>
> (V. iii. 8-19)

Lear and Cordelia seem to have risen above that imperfect world, the world of things which ebb and flow by the moon. Curiously, this speech contains the one Christian reference in a play which purports, at least, to take place in a pre-Christian period of history. Lear says that he and Cordelia will watch like "God's spies." The world of raw animal power, though, catches up with them and Cordelia is hanged. Goneril, Regan, and Edmund die as they have lived, die in their own raw, snarling animality. There is a sublime irony in Edmund's words,

> Yet Edmund was beloved.
> The one the other poisoned for my sake,
> And after slew herself.
>
> (V. iii. 240-242)

Some love! which issues only in savagery and murder and suicide. Lear comes in carrying the dead body of Cordelia. He seems to have gone mad again, and he dies, looking on Cordelia's lips, as we saw him in Act I, scene i, looking on her lips for something, and he finds, again, "nothing."

In other words, we find in the last movement of the play the same ambiguity that we found in the opening scene. In one sense you could say that the final scene shows us hard facts, tough, animal people, winning out in the end over the world of values, which are only an illusion, only words, "nothing." In another sense you could say that the end of the play shows us the triumph of love, Gloucester, Cordelia, Lear, even Edmund, Goneril, and Regan, all dying at the height of love. In a sense, when Lear looks on Cordelia's lips, he does not see "nothing"; he sees, as in the old superstition, her soul in the moment of death, issuing from her lips, and he cries, "Look there, look there!" But there is nothing: faith, hope, love, these are the madnesses of an old deposed King: "He but usurped his life." It takes an unnatural madness to believe in traditional values; yet not to believe in them makes us simply animals, our lives meaningless, hopeless. They are "nothing," but, believed, everything. Shakespeare does not attempt to resolve the pull of these two demands, to believe and not to believe, and perhaps precisely in his not trying to resolve them lies the ultimate tragedy, the tragedy behind *King Lear*.

This is a tragedy that speaks to us. In a sense, Shakespeare is simply providing a document in seventeenth-century intellectual history; he is giving us two views of man-in-nature, an earlier, sixteenth-century view and a more tortured, naturalistic seventeenth-century view. One is what we called medieval nature, a traditional, Christian view of nature in which there is a rightful order or hierarchy or ranking of things. Everything has its place in that order, the mere existence of a thing, the mere fact of it, implies its value, just as in any other hierarchical system. The other kind of nature we called "naturalistic" nature. It is the nature that in a sense all of us since the seventeenth century live in, a nature of fact, of cause-and-effect, a nature of number, the nature that science tells us about. In *King Lear* there are not only these two kinds of nature, but also two styles to the play, two ways of looking at the action on the stage which correspond to these two kinds of nature. One way takes the tragedy as a kind of ritual, ceremonial, almost allegorical play, the kind of play that medieval theatergoers liked. Lear becomes the almost allegorical figure of the King, the greatest and therefore the most typical of men. Another way we saw of looking at the play is as a modern play, a kind of television drama dealing with the problem of in-laws, the old father trying to live with his married daughters. Depending on which way you look at the tragedy, you will have quite different feelings about what happens in it. If you consider the play from the point of view of traditional values, you will feel that Lear is, as he says, "A man more sinned against than sinning." If you look at the play as a modern television drama, you will feel that the senior citizen is refusing to accept the place he must necessarily occupy in society, and you will give your sympathy to the daughters, Regan and Goneril, and Edmund, who are "modern."

Man in *King Lear* is initially surrounded by the things that lift him above the animals, which set him in that medieval, traditional "nature": his relationship to gods; his abstractions like justice and authority; his clothing and food and shelter. In the course of the play these things are stripped off one by one until we are left with what Lear calls, "the thing itself; unaccommodated man is no more but such a poor, bare, forked animal as thou art." That poor, bare, forked animal body, even after all the distinctively human things have been stripped off, even then, that body is racked, tortured, loaded down with weights and cares. In other words, the image *King Lear* gives us of man is of man tortured between two natures (see Fig. E). Man, be he the King at the top of the

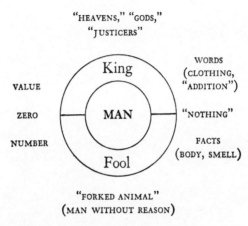

Fig. E. Tensions and choices in King Lear.

scale or the Fool at the bottom, is at the center of a series of tensions. He is torn between his links to heaven, the gods, perfect justice on the one hand and the fact he is a mere "forked animal" on the other. Only his reason, his "sense," seems to differentiate him from the animals; but reason alone will not justify his values. They seem merely words, "nothing," and it takes a kind of madness (or faith) to believe in them. As against these words—love, hope, faith—are the facts of his body, facts so real you can smell them, you can number them, examine them as a scientist would. As against such facts, values seem an illusion, "the curiosity of nations," that no rational man could hold. Yet, what are we without values? In short, *King Lear* shows us man wrenched and torn between conflicts and pulls that cannot be resolved. The seventeenth century could not resolve them; neither can the twentieth. In our century, as in the Renaissance, the central problem in philosophy (and outside of it) is the problem of values:

What are they? How can they fit into a scientific picture of the universe? How can you justify them? How can you even know them? *King Lear,* magnificently tragic, gives us no answer except to go on somehow and "the gored state sustain."

𝗟𝗟𝗟𝗟𝗟𝗟𝗟

14

𝗟𝗟𝗟𝗟𝗟𝗟𝗟

ANTONY AND CLEOPATRA

Antony and Cleopatra IS A MARVELOUSLY MIDDLE-AGED PLAY. SHAKESPEARE WAS IN middle age when he wrote it—about forty-three—and the play shows it. This ripe, voluptuous tragedy of two lovers is quite a different thing from his earlier tragedy of two lovers, *Romeo and Juliet,* written when he was about thirty-one. *Romeo and Juliet* is a tragedy of adolescent love, almost puppy love, while *Antony and Cleopatra* is a play of adulterous love and a love which is by no means a first love. Like all of Shakespeare's tragedies, these two love tragedies build on simple, realistic situations. *Romeo and Juliet* could take place in Levittown between two feuding neighbors: the son of one falls in love with the daughter next door, and so on. *Antony and Cleopatra* also has a simple situation at its core: a big butter-and-egg man from the Midwest comes to the wicked, wicked city, falls in love with a chorus girl, and deserts his wife. But *Antony and Cleopatra* is so much more than that.

It is a big play that deals with big kingdoms and empires, with mighty monarchs and powerful queens. While it does have this simple domestic relations problem at its core, this is a play which seems to involve the whole of the earth. "His face was as the heav'ns." "His legs bestrid the ocean; his reared arm crested the world," says Cleopatra of her dead lover. Antony sends a message to his love:

> *Alexas.* 'Say the firm Roman to great Egypt sends
> This treasure of an oyster; at whose foot,
> To mend the petty present, I will piece
> Her opulent throne with kingdoms. All the East
> (Say thou) shall call her mistress.'
>
> (I. v. 43-47)

And Cleopatra responds by saying,

> He shall have every day a several greeting,
> Or I'll unpeople Egypt.
>
> (I. v. 77-78)

"Great Egypt," "All the East," Shakespeare suggests bigness by these constant references to kingdoms, empires, the whole world. He suggests it, too, by having all through the play messengers like Alexas travel back and forth across the face of the earth. But these are not the only ways he suggests bigness.

> Nay, but this dotage of our general's
> O'erflows the measure

—the opening lines of the play. Not just kingdoms and empires are big; love is big:

> *Antony.*   Let Rome in Tiber melt and the wide arch
> Of the ranged empire fall! Here is my space,
> Kingdoms are clay: our dungy earth alike
> Feeds beast as man. The nobleness of life
> Is to do thus.
>
> (I. i. 33-37)

and he embraces his "space," Cleopatra.

Not only Antony's love for Cleopatra seems to have this wonderful bigness, but all kinds of love. When Antony thanks his soldiers, a great rank and mass of men, he says,

> I wish I could be made so many men,
> And all of you clapped up together in
> An Antony, that I might do you service
> So good as you have done.
>
> (IV. ii. 16-19)

Antony's great generosity to Enobarbus is part of this bigness. Enobarbus deserts him, goes over to Caesar; instead of abusing Enobarbus, Antony sends after him, "All thy treasure, with his bounty overplus." Our word "magnanimous" means "bigness of mind," and Shakespeare seems to be playing on this feeling that I suppose we all have, to some extent, that the big thing is somehow the splendid, the wonderful, the noble thing.

Even the dramaturgy of the play has this expansive quality. *Antony and Cleopatra* has no less than forty-two separate scenes. Some critics say this makes the play too choppy, too broken up; and it's true, if you are only reading the play, these forty-two scenes do get a bit confusing. On the stage, however, particularly on that 27½- by 43-foot scaffold on which Shakespeare played his plays, more scenes simply move faster. A film, for example, may have thousands of separate little shots, but we are not confused by them. Shakespeare's stagecraft is much closer to cinematics than that of a modern stage, where a curtain would have to go up and down forty-three times in the course of the play. On his stage, the sheer number of scenes carries out the expansive mood, the feeling that bigness is wonderful.

The tragedy seems to say the splendid thing about the love of Antony and Cleopatra is how big it is. Antony's followers can say, truthfully, "We have kissed away kingdoms and provinces." As this line suggests, part of the bigness of their love comes from the aura of splendor and riches and grandeur. We hear of an armor all of gold, chairs of gold, a shower of gold, an orient pearl, a hail of pearls, and treasure—Antony's treasure, Cleopatra's treasure, Enobarbus' treasure, with Antony's "bounty overplus."

As for Enobarbus, he has perhaps the richest and the most splendid speech of all, and that fact is very odd, for after all, Enobarbus is blunt, cynical, hard-headed. In the course of the play he is the one who makes most of the nasty, smutty jokes at Cleopatra's expense. Yet he can say of her:

> The barge she sat in, like a burnished throne,
> Burned on the water: the poop was beaten gold;
> Purple the sails, and so perfumèd that
> The winds were lovesick with them; the oars were silver,
> Which to the tune of flutes kept stroke, and made
> The water which they beat to follow faster,
> As amorous of their strokes. For her own person,
> It beggared all description: she did lie
> In her pavilion, cloth-of-gold of tissue,
> O'erpicturing that Venus where we see
> The fancy outwork nature.
>
> (II. ii. 192–202)

By giving the speech to Enobarbus, Shakespeare says, in effect, Cleopatra is so magnificent, she can transfigure even this stern, hard, cynical Roman. In a way, you could say that this speech is quite "out of character," quite "inconsistent" with the rest of what Enobarbus does. But realism of character gives way to a larger dramatic purpose. Shakespeare uses this inconsistency of character as part of his total dramatic idea; the fullness of Enobarbus' language suggests how Cleopatra transfigures people, how associated with her are not only magnificence and splendor and riches but, as in the continuation of Enobarbus' speech, food:

> Upon her landing, Antony sent to her,
> Invited her to supper. She replied,
> It should be better he became her guest;
> Which she entreated. Our courteous Antony,
> Whom ne'er the word of 'no' woman heard speak,
> Being barbered ten times o'er, goes to the feast,

> And for his [tavern meal] pays his heart
> For what his eyes eat only.
>
> (II. ii. 220–227)

Cleopatra seems associated not only with bigness and richness, but also with food and appetite. She says of herself that she was "A morsel for a monarch." At another point, when Antony is angry at her, he reminds her, "I found you as a morsel cold upon dead Caesar's trencher." Enobarbus pays her the lovely compliment:

> Age cannot wither her, nor custom stale
> Her infinite variety: other women cloy
> The appetites they feed, but she makes hungry
> Where most she satisfies.
>
> (II. ii. 236–239)

Cleopatra differs rather markedly from Octavia, the Roman wife: "Octavia is of a holy, cold, and still conversation. . . . Mark Antony . . . will to his Egyptian dish again" (II. vi. 119–123).

As this nasty remark about the "Egyptian dish" suggests, the Egyptian attitude toward food, or the Alexandrian attitude, is rather sharply different from the Roman. For example, the night before one of the big battles, Antony says things like,

> Come,
> Let's have one other gaudy night: call to me
> All my sad captains; fill our bowls once more;
> Let's mock the midnight bell.
>
> (III. xiii. 182–185)

And again,

> Call forth my household servants; let's to-night
> Be bounteous at our meal.
>
> (IV. ii. 9–10)

"Scant not my cups," he says, and, "burn this night with torches." "Let's to supper . . . and drown consideration" (IV. ii). That is Antony's Alexandrian attitude toward feasting. Octavius Caesar, the cold, hard Roman, says, that same night before battle, simply,

> Feast the army, we have store to do't,
> And they have earned the waste.
>
> (IV. i. 15–16)

Antony seems splendid, magnificent, magnanimous, and Caesar seems niggardly by comparison. At that strange banquet which is held on the boat with Pompey, Caesar never relaxes,

Pompey.   This is not yet an Alexandrian feast.
Antony.   It ripens towards it. Strike the vessels, ho!
Here's to Caesar!
Caesar.   I could well forbear't.
It's monstrous labor when I wash my brain
And it grows fouler.
Antony.   Be a child o' th' time.
Caesar.   Possess it, I'll make answer;
But I had rather fast from all four days
Than drink so much in one.

. . .

Pompey, good night. Good brother,
Let me request you off: our graver business
Frowns at this levity.

(II. vii. 95–120)

With Caesar, it is always business before pleasure; there seems to be no such thing for this man as the relaxed, casual kind of time that an Antony likes. Of Antony in Alexandria we hear, for example, of "Eight wild boars roasted whole at a breakfast, and but twelve persons there." By contrast, Caesar complains about such orgies:

Antony,
Leave thy lascivious wassails. When thou once
Was beaten from Modena, where thou slew'st
Hirtius and Pansa, consuls, at thy heel
Did famine follow, whom thou fought'st against
(Though daintily brought up) with patience more
Than savages could suffer. Thou didst drink
The stale of horses and the gilded puddle
Which beasts would cough at. Thy palate then did deign
The roughest berry on the rudest hedge.
Yea, like the stag when snow the pasture sheets,
The barks of trees thou browsed. On the Alps
It is reported thou didst eat strange flesh,
Which some did die to look on.

(I. iv. 55–68)

Where Antony likes plenty and magnificence and feasting, Caesar seems to regard it as much more noble to be involved with starvation and famine, with drinking the stale of horses instead of those luscious Alexandrian wines that Antony now enjoys.

As all this talk of drinking suggests, there are in *Antony and Cleopatra* (as in Shakespeare's other loving plays, *Twelfth Night,* for example) a lot of liquids, things flowing and melting into one another. The very opening line of the play says: "This dotage of our general's o'erflows the measure." We hear of tears, sweat, blood, wines, poisons, medicine, perfume, molten gold, the Nile, the Tiber, the ocean, and so on. A lot of these references to liquids are quite gratuitous, as when Antony describes Octavia being unable to make up her mind; she is like

>   The swan's down-feather
> That stands upon the swell at full of tide,
> And neither way inclines.
>
> (III. ii. 48–50)

Another one of these gratuitous references is Antony's lush description to the somewhat drunken Lepidus of the effect of the Nile on fertility:

>   They take the flow o' th' Nile
> By certain scales i' th' pyramid. They know
> By th' height, the lowness, or the mean, if dearth
> Or foison follow. The higher Nilus swells,
> The more it promises; as it ebbs, the seedsman
> Upon the slime and ooze scatters his grain,
> And shortly comes to harvest.
>
> (II. vii. 17–23)

Water seems to be associated with fertility and loving and in particular with Egypt, the Nile, and Cleopatra. When Antony is away, Cleopatra spends her time (when she is not playing billiards) fishing:

> Give me mine angle, we'll to th' river: there,
> My music playing far off, I will betray
> Tawny-finned fishes. My bended hook shall pierce
> Their slimy jaws; and as I draw them up,
> I'll think them every one an Antony,
> And say, 'Ah, ha! y' are caught!'
>
> (II. v. 10–15)

And one of her servants remembers a joke she played on Antony,

>   'Twas merry when
> You wagered on your angling, when your diver
> Did hang a salt fish on his hook, which he
> With fervency drew up.
>
> (15–18)

Enobarbus' description of Cleopatra, again, links her to water: "The barge she sat in, like a burnished throne, burned on the water." At the end of the play, in the final battles, Antony very foolishly abandons his Roman custom of fighting on land; instead he fights at sea with Cleopatra and loses, another kind of barge burning on the water.

All this interest in liquids hints that Shakespeare is in part playing with the four elements, earth, air, fire, and water. As usual, the Elizabethans had a nice commonsensical approach to these things. Nowadays, we tend to think there are a hundred or so elements with varying numbers of neutrons and protons and electrons and other mysterious mythical entities which may exist for a microsecond or two. The Elizabethans were very sensible—they realized that everything in the world was made up of the four elements, earth, air, fire, and water. In *Antony and Cleopatra,* Shakespeare uses these four elements to create the bigness of the tragedy: the play seems to have in it the makings of a whole universe. One of these four elements, water, or in general, liquids, has already turned up. There is a great deal, too, about earth in such phrases as, "The triple pillar of the world," or Antony's remark, "Kingdoms are clay: our dungy earth alike feeds beast as man." Antony himself is "the demi-Atlas of this earth," "the crown o' th' earth." By and large the element of fire is associated with spirit, battle, and with the Roman military virtues. Earth is associated with conquering empires and kingdoms, another Roman pastime. Water, by contrast, is associated with Egypt's love and fertility. The contrast comes clear in the battles at the end where the Romans tend to stick to the land, and the Egyptians fight —or run away—on the water.

Another thing, besides the references to liquids, that gives us this sense of the fluidity of things in Alexandria is a series of animals fusing, melting, and, indeed, mating.

> Sometime we see a cloud that's dragonish;
> A vapor sometime like a bear or lion,
> A towered citadel, a pendant rock,
> A forkèd mountain, or blue promontory
> With trees upon't that nod unto the world
> And mock our eyes with air. Thou hast seen these signs.
>
> .   .   .
>
> That which is now a horse, even with a thought
> The [cloud] dislimns, and makes it indistinct
> As water is in water.
>
> .   .   .
>
> My good knave Eros, now thy captain is
> Even such a body: here I am Antony,
> Yet cannot hold this visible shape.
>
> (IV. xiv. 3–14)

Antony is describing himself as disintegrating, melting under the effects of his defeats in Egypt. The drunken tourist, Lepidus, says, "Your serpent of Egypt is bred now of your mud by the operation of your sun: so is your crocodile." The image is one of animals spontaneously generating from the rich, fertile mud of Egypt. Cleopatra curses,

> Melt Egypt into Nile! and kindly creatures
> Turn all to serpents!
>
> (II. v. 78–79)

Again, the image is one of animals melting, transforming. Even Egypt itself melts, the earth sinking into water, as earlier Antony had cried, "Let Rome in Tiber melt."

One of the things that melts is horses, for example, in Antony's image of a cloud shaped like a horse that dissolves, dislimns, becomes indistinct. By contrast, when the Romans speak of horses, they are thinking pretty much in cavalry terms, and there, horses are fixed, constant. They speak, for example, of the "never-yet-beaten horse of Parthia," the Parthian cavalry. When people speak of horses in the Egyptian context, they are quite different. For example, when Cleopatra thinks of Antony when he is away:

> Where think'st thou he is now? Stands he, or sits he?
> Or does he walk? or is he on his horse?
> O happy horse, to bear the weight of Antony!
>
> (I. v. 19–21)

Naturally, confusion comes when these two attitudes toward horses get mixed. Enorbarbus suggests that it's probably not a good idea for Cleopatra to be present at Antony's battles:

> If we should serve with horse and mares together
> The horse were merely lost; the mares would bear
> A soldier and his horse.
>
> (III. vii. 7–9)

Horses in an Egyptian context become sexual, flowing, mating—hardly a suitable cavalry.

There may be a faint mythological overtone here. Cleopatra, in the course of the play, is compared to the great mother-goddesses, Isis and Venus; she is called "our terrene moon," "this great fairy." These mother-goddesses could take the form not only of the moon but also of great Demeter, the goddess of the harvest and grain. She was sometimes imaged as mare-headed Demeter, that is, a goddess shown in the form of a woman with a mare's head. The so-called "triple goddess" has come up before in connection with *The Merchant of Venice* and *King Lear*. For both those plays, we referred to Freud's essay in which he pointed out that in many ways man's fate seems bound up with three versions of woman. First, there is the woman he loves; then there is the woman who is a mother, either his fruitful wife or the mother from whom he was born; finally, there is the so-called ultimate mother, Mother Earth, death. In mythology we often find a combination of three goddesses or three aspects of one goddess that correspond to these three aspects of woman which seem so intimately bound up with man's destiny; the three Fates, for example, have this form. Curiously, in *Antony and Cleopatra,* we find three women that correspond roughly to these three fundamental aspects of woman. First of all, there is Cleopatra, the fruitful mother, the bountiful, loving charmer, the Venus or Isis. Then there is the virginal Octavia, "of a holy, cold, and still conversation," a Diana. Finally, there is the furious Fulvia, Antony's first wife, who rages like some revenging death-goddess or Persephone. Perhaps, then, the three women surrounding Antony make a faint echo of that famous figure of mythology, the triple goddess who was sometimes the mare-headed goddess. But perhaps this is all pretty fanciful and tangential.

What we've been doing, in effect, in all our talk about horses and food and the rest of it, is to define two worlds: the world of Rome and the world of Alexandria. Caesar embodies the spirit of Rome, Cleopatra the spirit of Alexandria. It is around these two poles that the action of the play orbits. Messengers go back and forth between these two places; Antony has a wife in Rome and a girl friend in Alexandria; and so on. Different in almost every way, these two worlds are alike in one respect. They are both big worlds, worlds peopled by kings and queens and rulers of the earth.

In every other way these worlds are sharply contrasted. Rome is associated with the solid, cold, hard earth while Alexandria is linked to the Nile, to warm, tropical, flowing water. The Roman world is a masculine world where women are subservient to their lords and masters: Octavia marries the man her brother tells her to. Alexandria, however, is a woman's world, ruled by a woman, Cleopatra, surrounded by her female attendants or her eunuchs; men are allowed in this goddess-woman's world only as lovers, in a sense, as suppliants. The Roman world is a world of politics in which men are busy building empires, establishing power and domination. Alexandria is a world of love, of feasting and reveling and enjoying oneself, lotos-land. In Rome, politics determines love relations; Octavia must marry Antony to make a kind of political love between Antony and her brother Octavius Caesar. In Alexandria, it is just the other way around: love takes over and confuses politics, in that Antony abandons his better judgment to fight by sea because his girl friend wants him to, or, in general, in the fact that Antony loses out in the political situation because of his amatory sidelines.

Finally, and most important, the Roman world seems to be a world that thrives on scarcity, as in Caesar's speech, praising Antony because "at thy heel did famine follow." "Thou didst drink the stale of horses and the gilded puddle." Like Spartans, these Romans encourage starvation and hardship; they seem to think it's a good thing to suffer. The Alexandrians, on the other hand, like luxury and comfort; theirs is a world of plenty, of fertility, of rich harvests

and growth; and they like it that way. The Roman world is a world of division.
Antony and Octavius seem to regard themselves as competitors. The victorious
Caesar says:

> I must perforce
> Have shown to thee such a declining day
> Or look on thine: we could not stall together
> In the whole world. But yet let me lament
>
>   .   .   .
>
>   that our stars,
> Unreconciliable, should divide
> Our equalness to this.
>
>   (V. i. 37–48)

Caesar feels he has to compete with Antony for the world; he has to divide it
with Antony, then fight him until he has it all to himself. When Caesar comes
to capture Cleopatra, he causes her to divide her treasure. In that very interesting little scene which is almost always omitted in performances, Act III, scene i,
we see two lieutenants of Antony describing how dangerous it is to do more for
Antony than might look good for Antony's reputation.

> Better to leave undone, than by our deed
> Acquire too high a fame when him we serve's away.
>
>   .   .   .
>
> Who does i' th' wars more than his captain can
> Becomes his captain's captain; and ambition
> (The soldier's virtue) rather makes choice of loss
> Than gain which darkens him.
> I could do more to do Antonius good,
> But 'twould offend him.
>
>   (III. i. 14–26)

The Roman world is a world of division where people hold back, are niggardly
with their courage or with their bounty, because they feel this is a world of
competition, a world of strife.

To the Romans, it's very important to show off, to have triumphal marches
which prove you are important and have succeeded in the competition. This is
Caesar's description of the way Antony has sent Octavia home:

> Why have you stol'n upon us thus? You come not
> Like Caesar's sister. The wife of Antony
> Should have an army for an usher, and
> The neighs of horse to tell of her approach
> Long ere she did appear. The trees by th' way
> Should have borne men, and expectation fainted,
> Longing for what it had not. Nay, the dust

> Should have ascended to the roof of heaven,
> Raised by your populous troops.
>
> (III. vi. 42–50)

As you hear that suffocating, dry, dusty description with its horses, remember the beautiful watery description of Cleopatra on her lovely, liquid, golden barge. In a way, the difference between Octavia's proposed triumphal entrance and Cleopatra's is the whole difference between the world of Rome and the world of Alexandria. One is the world of bounty flowing forth in plenty: the other is the world of dry scarcity in which men faint, longing for what they have not. In Rome you show your own bigness by depriving other people, by triumphing over them, as by parading Cleopatra in your triumphal march, shaming and humiliating her in "th' imperious show of the full-fortuned Caesar"; Octavia would acquire "honor" by demurely snooting her rival. Cleopatra refuses to go through with it:

> Know, sir, that I
> Will not wait pinioned at your master's court
> Nor once be chastised with the sober eye
> Of dull Octavia. Shall they hoist me up
> And show me to the shouting varletry
> Of censuring Rome?
>
> (V. ii. 52–57)

She describes that awful humiliation to her ladies-in-waiting:

> Saucy lictors
> Will catch at us like strumpets, and scald rhymers
> Ballad us out o' tune. The quick comedians
> Extemporally will stage us, and present
> Our Alexandrian revels: Antony
> Shall be brought drunken forth, and I shall see
> Some squeaking Cleopatra boy my greatness
> I' th' posture of a whore.
>
> (V. ii. 214–221)

(That was of course exactly what was happening: some squeaking boy was playing Cleopatra. Only a genius could afford to play with the dramatic illusion this way.) Cleopatra's worries about being borne in triumph to Rome show us the Roman way of life, establishing your own importance by humiliating and shaming other people. Contrast what Antony and Cleopatra do,

> To-night we'll wander through the streets and note
> The qualities of people.
>
> (I. i. 53–54)

Antony and Cleopatra want simply to enjoy life. In fact, one of Antony's last requests of Caesar is that he be allowed to live as a private citizen.

The world of Rome, however, is a world of iron military honor, which you can gain only by taking it away from someone else, a world very different from Alexandria, which is bountiful, plentiful, giving, with enough for all. The first words that Antony and Cleopatra speak are:

> Cleopatra.   If it be love indeed, tell me how much.
> Antony.   There's beggary in the love that can be reckoned.
> Cleopatra.   I'll set a bourn how far to be beloved.
> Antony.   Then must thou needs find out new heaven, new earth.
>
> (I. i. 14–17)

This dotage of our general's does indeed o'erflow the measure; for the world of Alexandria is expansive. It seems to cry out for great space, "new heaven, new earth,"

> Let Rome in Tiber melt and the wide arch
> Of the ranged empire fall! Here is my space,
>
> (I. i. 33–34)

says Antony, as he embraces Cleopatra. By contrast, the Roman world is a world of confinement: when Caesar comes to Egypt, a man brings him a message that Cleopatra is confined in her monument. Caesar's strategy is to limit and confine Antony's movements more and more. At the end of the play, the highest praise he can give the two tragic victims is that no grave will *enclose* a pair so famous.

In short, *Antony and Cleopatra* is the tragedy of two worlds, one bountiful, plenteous; the other competitive, stingy, confining. Of all the other plays we have considered, this play seems closest to *The Merchant of Venice;* there, too, the play juxtaposed two worlds, the world of Shylock's Venice, a man's world, harsh, hard-boiled, realistic, competitive, a scarcity economy; the world of Portia's Belmont, a woman's world, full of plenty, of giving, of love, and feasting. Critics and audiences often talk as though Antony were some sort of a flawed tragic victim, as though it were a flaw in him not to be tending to his warlike business, slaughtering people, starving himself, and fighting Caesar, instead of enjoying himself in Alexandria. Is pleasure wrong? Is it such a right and noble thing to be like Caesar? Somehow, I don't think so, and neither does Cleopatra:

> 'Tis paltry to be Caesar:
> Not being Fortune, he's but Fortune's knave,
> A minister of her will.
>
> (V. ii. 2–4)

Better by far to be the "knave" of the strumpet Cleopatra. By contrast with the generous, comfortable world Cleopatra offers, Caesar seems to me simply cold and nasty. It is really better to be a Spartan than an Athenian?

This play is morally complicated. Rather than think of Antony choosing between a way which is very, very right, the Roman way, and a way which is very, very sinful and wrong, the Alexandrian way, we should understand the tragedy as putting before us two ways the human being sometimes chooses to live, that hard-boiled Spartan, Puritan way, and the more relaxed way of Athens or Alexandria or Los Angeles. Which is more moral? Notice what happens to those cold unpleasant Romans when they have a banquet on Pompey's boat. It's rather like an American Legion convention; when all these sterling hard-boiled types from the Midwest get away from home, they behave disgracefully. By contrast, we never see Antony and Cleopatra behaving in so crude and sophomoric a way. Is it more moral to deny and inhibit natural impulses or to enjoy them? I don't know.

Anyway, the tragedy does operate between these two worlds, Caesar's world of Rome and Cleopatra's world of Alexandria. And Antony is the tragic victim; caught between these two worlds, he loses and dies. But beware, oh beware, of treating this tragedy as though it were simply the tragedy of Antony. Cleopatra dies, too, and the play is as much her tragedy as his. Her death contributes just as much to the meaning of the tragedy as Antony's; it images the way in which the comfort-loving world of Athens or Sunset Boulevard is likely to give way before the hard-driving world of Sparta or Rome. In a way, each of these two worlds makes the other die.

"Die," as in *Measure for Measure*, is likely to be a complicated word in an Elizabethan play, with meanings physical, sexual, and religious. In *Antony and Cleopatra*, with its two worlds of Rome and Alexandria, each of these two worlds kills the other, makes the other die. That is, Caesar makes Antony die in a physical sense. Cleopatra makes Antony die in a sexual sense. If you like, you can think of the whole tragedy as a play about the three meanings of the word "die." For example, Enobarbus' ribald jokes in Act I, scene ii, play on "dying."

> *Enobarbus.* Why, then we kill all our women. We see how mortal an unkind-
> ness is to them. If they suffer our departure, death's the word. . . .
> Under a compelling occasion let women die. It were pity to cast
> them away for nothing, though between them and a great cause
> they should be esteemed nothing. Cleopatra, catching but the least
> noise of this, dies instantly; I have seen her die twenty times upon
> far poorer moment. I do think there is mettle in death, which com-
> mits some loving act upon her, she hath such a celerity in dying.
> (I. ii. 130–141)

The whole, low, ribald joke lies in the multiple meanings of the word "die" (and also of "nothing"). Enobarbus' jokes about dying contrast with the jokes that the Egyptians make at the beginning of the scene. Where Enobarbus is sarcastic, where he sneers at their life in Egypt, Cleopatra's attendants, Charmian and Iras and Alexas, all make jokes not about dying but about life, about sexuality, about the oily palm that was supposed to indicate a warm heart, about the over-flowing Nile, about "an inch of fortune." In a sense, these two sets of ribald jokes show the essential difference between the Egyptians and the Romans. The same thing occurs in Act I, scene i, where a couple of Romans comment on "This dotage of our general's," while Cleopatra and Antony together dismiss the whole Roman way of life:

> Kingdoms are clay: our dungy earth alike
> Feeds beast as man. The nobleness of life
> Is to do thus,
>
> (I. i. 35–37)

and he embraces Cleopatra.

But what about the third meaning of the word "die," dying to the world? There is a lot in the tragedy about dying in the sexual sense, but what about dying in a religious sense? Dying in that third sense of the word brings us to the ending of the play, perhaps the most beautiful part of this essentially middle-aged tragedy. Toward the end of the play, we begin to find, not exactly religious references, but at least references to mythology. In Act IV, scene iii, the sentries hear music under the earth; they wonder about it and finally conclude,

> 'Tis the god Hercules, whom Antony loved,
> Now leaves him.

Antony becomes furious because the Egyptian fleet turned its back, because Cleopatra (in the Elizabethan phrase) was "false as water." He curses:

> Eros, ho!
> The shirt of Nessus is upon me; teach me,
> Alcides, thou mine ancestor, thy rage.
> Let me lodge Lichas on the horns o' th' moon
> And with those hands that grasped the heaviest club
> Subdue my worthiest self. The witch shall die.
>
> (IV. xii. 42–47)

Then, after he thinks Cleopatra has died in a physical sense, he promises her:

> Eros!—I come, my queen.—Eros!—Stay for me.
> Where souls do couch on flowers, we'll hand in hand,
> And with our sprightly port make the ghosts gaze:
> Dido and her Aeneas shall want troops,
> And all the haunt be ours.
>
> (IV. xiv. 50–54)

And with all this talk about death and love, it is interesting, too, that Antony is addressing a servant called Eros, the name of the god of love.

In connection with that third sense of the word "die," the end of the play brings a great many images of a body disintegrating, breaking up, leaving this world. Antony describes a cloud, like a dragon, a bear, a lion, a horse:

> Even with a thought
> The rack dislimns, and makes it indistinct
> As water is in water.
>
> . . .
>
> My good knave Eros, now thy captain is
> Even such a body: here I am Antony,
> Yet cannot hold this visible shape.
>
> (IV. xiv. 9–14)

Antony is describing death in a physical sense, but also a sort of dying to the world. He goes on when he plans suicide to speak of death in a sexual sense:

> I will be
> A bridegroom in my death, and run into't
> As to a lover's bed.
>
> (IV. xiv. 99–101)

Antony speaks of death in the physical sense and in the sexual sense, but really to find death in the religious sense of dying to this world, we must turn to the death of Cleopatra. In this joint tragedy, Antony dies first, but the big death scene is Cleopatra's. It is she who is transfigured in death. She becomes both more noble than we have ever seen her before—and more common. The lines leading up to her death bring together all the different parts of the play, almost like themes in a piece of music which come all crashing in together for the great coda at the end: bigness, the splendor and the feasting and the drinking and the liquids of the Alexandrian way of life; the martial, Spartan self-denial, the divisive quality, of the Romans; the four elements, particularly water; animals melting and flowing, particularly horses; but above all,

> *Cleopatra.*   Our size of sorrow,
> Proportioned to our cause, must be as great
> As that which makes it.
>
> (IV. xv. 4–6)

And that great, big cause, Antony, dying, is brought in to her.

> *Cleopatra.*   O sun,
> Burn the great sphere thou mov'st in, darkling stand
> The varying shore o' th' world!
>
> . . .
>
> *Antony.*   I am dying, Egypt, dying.
>
> . . .

Cleopatra.   How heavy weighs my lord!
          Our strength is all gone into heaviness.

                              . . .

                              Welcome, welcome! Die where thou hast lived,
          Quicken with kissing.

                              . . .

Antony.   I am dying, Egypt, dying.

                              . . .

                    A Roman, by a Roman
          Valiantly vanquished. Now my spirit is going,
          I can no more.

                              . . .

Cleopatra.   O, see, my women,
          The crown o' th' earth doth melt. My lord!
          O, withered is the garland of the war,
          The soldier's pole is fall'n: young boys and girls
          Are level now with men. The odds is gone,
          And there is nothing left remarkable
          Beneath the visiting moon.
                                        (IV. xv. 9–68)

"Royal Egypt! Empress!" Cleopatra's women call to her, fearing she, too, has died. But she revives, and denies such titles.

          No more but e'en a woman, and commanded
          By such poor passion as the maid that milks
          And does the meanest [chores]. It were for me
          To throw my sceptre at the injurious gods,
          To tell them that this world did equal theirs
          Till they had stol'n our jewel. All's but naught.

                              . . .

                              Ah, women, women, look!

                              . . .

                              What's brave, what's noble,
          Let's do't after the high Roman fashion,
          And make death proud to take us.

                              . . .

          Ah, women, women!
                                        (IV. xv. 73–90)

The scene is a rejection of this world. It begins with the great vastness always associated with Antony and Cleopatra and Caesar: "Darkling stand the varying shore o' th' world." "I am dying, Egypt, dying." Enormous images involve whole countries. Then, as Cleopatra lifts Antony up to her monument, "How heavy weighs my lord," and she urges him to die sexually, die on her lips as well as die physically; finally, of course, he dies to the world when he says, "Now my spirit is going, I can no more." Then something wonderful happens with Cleopatra. She tells us that everything is even on earth,

> The odds is gone,
> And there is nothing left remarkable
> Beneath the visiting moon.

The earth is just the earth and she is no longer a queen,

> No more but e'en a woman, and commanded
> By such poor passion as the maid that milks
> And does the meanest [chores].

And she decides to throw away the world in the "high Roman fashion." It is at the end of the play that Antony and Cleopatra cease being rulers of the world and become people, "no more but e'en a woman." This is why *Antony and Cleopatra* is a play that celebrates life, that finds the nobility of life in the simplest things, the poor passion of a milkmaid.

By contrast with this worldly wisdom, the tragedy gives us next that rather foolish Caesar still mixed up with his empires. He hears that Antony is dead and he says:

> The breaking of so great a thing should make
> A greater crack. The round world
> Should have shook lions into civil streets
> And citizens to their dens. The death of Antony
> Is not a single doom, in the name lay
> A moiety of the world.
>
> (V. i. 14–19)

Caesar can't seem to get over his own bigness, the fact that formerly he and Antony had ruled the world together. Now he rules it alone, and he pronounces over Antony a kind of epitaph that sums up the Roman way of competition, of dividing things, of struggle. He tells us how much he loved Antony and yet how necessary it was to drive him to death; he talks much like Brutus:

> O Antony,
> I have followed thee to this. But we do [lance]
> Diseases in our bodies. I must perforce
> Have shown to thee such a declining day
> Or look on thine: we could not stall together
> In the whole world. But yet let me lament
> With tears as sovereign as the blood of hearts
> That thou, my brother, my competitor
> In top of all design, my mate in empire,
> Friend and companion in the front of war,

The arm of mine own body, and the heart
Where mine his thoughts did kindle—that our stars,
Unreconciliable, should divide
Our equalness to this.

(V. i. 35–48)

Dividing, competing, killing (like two horses fighting over a stall, the whole world), this is the "high, Roman fashion"; and as the scene goes on we see Caesar in his lowest moments. He, the ruler of the entire world, insists that his men, his servants, follow him and let him justify himself, explain that it wasn't really his fault at all.

Go with me to my tent, where you shall see
How hardly I was drawn into this war,
How calm and gentle I proceeded still
In all my writings. Go with me, and see
What I can show in this.

(V. i. 73–77)

He becomes absurd and hypocritical and his ridiculous effort to assuage his guilt serves to set off the nobility of Antony and Cleopatra, especially the nobility of Cleopatra who, after all, hasn't seemed very noble so far in the play. But, by contrast with Caesar—

Cleopatra.   'Tis paltry to be Caesar:
Not being Fortune, he's but Fortune's knave,
A minister of her will. And it is great
To do that thing that ends all other deeds,
Which shackles accidents and bolts up change;
Which sleeps, and never palates more the dung,
The beggar's nurse and Caesar's.

(V. ii. 2–8)

She continues her earlier line of talk, that all the distinctions in the world are gone; now that Antony is gone, everything else is equal. She turns her back on the world of Caesar, the world of politics and empires. In fact, she turns her back on all the world, the dung, as she calls Mother Earth, the element earth. For the next fifty lines or so she exercises her old charms on Proculeius and Dolabella to try and find out what Caesar plans to do with her, and she refuses to be drawn into his triumphal procession. Surrounded with lies and trickery, she remembers Antony:

I dreamt there was an Emperor Antony.
O, such another sleep, that I might see
But such another man.

·   ·   ·

His face was as the heav'ns, and therein stuck

A sun and moon, which kept their course and lighted
The little O, th' earth.

. . .

His legs bestrid the ocean: his reared arm
Crested the world: his voice was propertied
As all the tunèd spheres, and that to friends;
But when he meant to quail and shake the orb,
He was as rattling thunder. For his bounty
There was no winter in't: an autumn 'twas
That grew the more by reaping: his delights
Were dolphin-like, they showed his back above
The element they lived in: in his livery
Walked crowns and crownets: realms and islands were
As plates dropped from his pocket.

(V. ii. 76–92)

Her words have the liberty she lacks. Though she tells of an Antony big as the whole solar system, Cleopatra is confined in her tomb, still subject to the mercies of Caesar. The play makes us feel how absurd this world is as against the universe of love toward which she is moving when Cleopatra tries to save her treasure from Caesar. Her trickery reflects the Roman ability to make everything divide and fight against itself, here, to make Cleopatra squabble with her treasurer. It suggests, too, how unimportant are these considerations of money and the real world, compared to the world of love she envisions. Cleopatra describes how she will not be a part of Caesar's triumphal procession, and her description suggests how petty and ugly a thing Caesar's triumph is.

Mechanic slaves
With greasy aprons, rules, and hammers shall
Uplift us to the view. In their thick breaths,
Rank of gross diet, shall we be enclouded,
And forced to drink their vapor.

(V. ii. 209–213)

Mechanic slaves, saucy lictors, squeaking boy actors, this is all that Caesar's triumph amounts to. Cleopatra turns to her suicide:

Show me, my women, like a queen: go fetch
My best attires.

. . .

My resolution's placed, and I have nothing
Of woman in me: now from head to foot
I am marble-constant: now the fleeting moon
No planet is of mine.

(227–241)

At this point—how marvelous is Shakespeare's imagination!—in comes a clown. What other dramatist could pull off a tour de force like this, bringing a comic in to highlight one of the most splendid and magnificent death scenes ever written. First, the baseness of Caesar, now, the foolishness of the clown serve as foils to Cleopatra and make her more noble, more wise, than we have seen her before.

The clown (or bumpkin), however, tells us even something more. As Kierkegaard, the Danish theologian, pointed out, when viewed from a direction looking toward the Idea (in a way, he means God), our apprehension of the discrepancy between the infinite and the finite is pathos. When viewed with the Idea behind us, the apprehension is comic. Shakespeare, by introducing a note of comedy at this point, is suggesting, in a way, an almost religious note, the profoundly comic attitude made possible by Cleopatra's almost religious rejection of this world, her "dying" in the third sense of that word. Coleridge said, "In humor the little is made great and the great little, in order to destroy both, because all is equal in contrast with the infinite." That is exactly what is happening in the tragedy at this point. All through the rest of the play we have been dealing with kings and queens and empires and monarchies, all the big things of this world. Then Antony dies, and Cleopatra tells us that all is equal now, there's nothing big or important left: the big and the little are the same, the clown and Caesar. Both she and Antony move on toward an infinite, toward a new kind of bigness, in which they can look back at the world and see it is all pretty small. In other words, the clown introduces a dying-to-the-world. His jokes are about death in all three senses.

> Cleopatra.   Hast thou the pretty worm of Nilus there,
>   That kills and pains not?
>
> (V. ii. 243–244)

"Worm" was a normal word for a small snake, but it also vividly, perhaps a little too vividly, suggests death, and as any good Freudian would be quick to point out, it is a phallic symbol as well—so the clown can joke on all three kinds of death.

Clown.   Truly I have him; but I would not be the party that should desire you to touch him, for his biting is immortal: those that do die of it do seldom or never recover.

Cleopatra.   Remember'st thou any that have died on't?

Clown.   Very many, men and women too. I heard of one of them no longer than yesterday; a very honest [that is, chaste] woman, but something given to lie, as a woman should not do but in the way of honesty—how she died of the biting of it, what pain she felt. Truly, she makes a very good report o' th' worm.

. . .

> Give it nothing [also ribald], I pray you, for it is not worth the
> feeding.
> *Cleopatra.* Will it eat me?
> *Clown.* Yes, forsooth. I wish you joy o' th' worm.
>
> (V. ii. 245–278)

A brilliant sequence! The jokes are about dying in the sexual sense—but also dying in the physical sense and, at the same time, dying in that third, religious sense. From this rich, low note rises a Cleopatra, purified, ennobled, ready to die in every sense you can imagine:

> Give me my robe, put on my crown, I have
> Immortal longings in me. Now no more
> The juice of Egypt's grape shall moist this lip.
> Yare, yare, good Iras; quick. Methinks I hear
> Antony call: I see him rouse himself
> To praise my noble act. I hear him mock
> The luck of Caesar, which the gods give men
> To excuse their after wrath. Husband, I come:
> Now to that name my courage prove my title!
> I am fire and air; my other elements
> I give to baser life.
>
> . . .
>
> [*She takes the asp.*]
>   Come, thou mortal wretch,
> With thy sharp teeth this knot intrinsicate
> Of life at once untie. Poor venomous fool,
> Be angry, and dispatch. O, couldst thou speak,
> That I might hear thee call great Caesar ass
> Unpolicied!
> *Charmian.*   O Eastern star!
> *Cleopatra.*   Peace, peace!
> Dost thou not see my baby at my breast,
> That sucks the nurse asleep?
>
> (279–309)

Something wonderful has happened to Cleopatra—she has become a woman. She had spoken before of being moved, "By such poor passion as the maid that milks and does the meanest chores." Now she cries out, "Husband, I come." In the opening scenes how contemptuous she had been of Octavia and Fulvia, "the married woman," but now she sees marriage as a title, an honor. She drops off all the heaviness, the heaviness, for example, represented by Antony's weight, and becomes fire and air, the lighter elements that will rise up. She becomes almost motherly, treating the asp, the deadly snake, as a baby nursing at her breast. Charmian speaks her epitaph,

> Now boast thee, death, in thy possession lies
> A lass unparalleled.
>
> (314-315)

Another brilliant touch—not the logical, sensible word that any other dramatist would have used, a *queen* unparalleled, but a *lass* unparalleled, simply—a woman.

After Cleopatra has died, that rather stuffy Caesar comes in puzzling about how she died, why, and solemnly says,

> Her physician tells me
> She hath pursued conclusions infinite
> Of easy ways to die.
>
> (352-354)

You can take that as a ribald remark if you like—it's not at all inappropriate because Antony and Cleopatra have died now in all three senses. In fact, you can think of this entire tragedy as one long treble-entendre on the word "die."

Yet despite that interest in the idea of dying, *Antony and Cleopatra* shows how much the last plays of Shakespeare are concerned with life. Shakespeare's imagination is passing from the third or tragic period to the fourth and final one, and we are seeing a rich transmutation of the two distinctive things we discovered about Shakespeare's imagination in his tragedies. First, he tended to see tragedy in terms of fragmentation or division. Second, he seemed to have a kind of distaste for the physical things of this world, the body, food, sex. Now, with *Antony and Cleopatra,* we come to the last phase of Shakespeare's writing. In this play, fragmentation, the disintegration of the body that we saw just before the final death scenes, this has suddenly become heroic, triumphant, practically comic. *Antony and Cleopatra* is almost not a tragedy at all. The atmosphere is expansive, sunny, casual. Food and sexuality have become signs of health. (Contrast *Hamlet* where food became garbage and sexuality was filthy and dirty.) Shakespeare wrote one tragedy after *Antony and Cleopatra,* the tragedy of *Coriolanus,* a final, vicious satire of that cold, Roman military hero who seems so busy with his wars and his battles and his empire building that he can't enjoy the simple and important things of life, like a wife and child.

In the last plays, Shakespeare moves away from the themes of politics and war that interested him when he was a younger man. His last plays are a celebration of life. He thinks tenderly of the physical things associated with living. He writes tenderly of the relationship between parent and child. In these last plays, Shakespeare's imagination is the imagination of a man older now, closer to death, a man who looks with great tenderness on life. He has come from the teen-age maunderings of *Romeo and Juliet* to the tender, mature, warm love of *Antony and Cleopatra.* In a sense, his imagination has run the whole gamut of a lifetime. And it is in *Antony and Cleopatra* that we most clearly see the transition toward the late romances: the tragedy of two sharply contrasted worlds, the hard, competitive one of Rome, the other, lush, liquid, of Alexandria. This is the essence of the tragedy: the tension between two possible kinds of life, a life that seeks honor and renown at the expense of others; and a life that multiplies and grows through love. For Antony and Cleopatra, for all of us, tragedy strikes because such an aggressive, divisive morality acts as though it must confine and destroy any and all impulses toward love and pleasure. Yet this tragedy is very nearly a comedy, its catastrophe very nearly a happy ending—because, for Antony, Cleopatra, and all of us, love can achieve a richness within itself that transcends competition or theft. The two figurative senses of "die" can overcome even physical death—almost. *Antony and Cleopatra* remains a tragedy for the two life-styles are two, not one, and we do die in an all-too-literal way.

ᒪᒪᒪᒪᒪᒪᒪ

15

ᒪᒪᒪᒪᒪᒪᒪ

THE WINTER'S TALE

WITH *The Winter's Tale,* WE COME TO THE LAST GRAND PHASE OF SHAKESPEARE'S imagination, the phase of romances, as they are often called—*Pericles, Cymbeline, The Winter's Tale, The Tempest.* Until about twenty years ago, people paid relatively little attention to these plays—except for *The Tempest.* The big plays, the important plays, were the great tragedies. But in the twentieth century, we have become more and more interested in these late plays for a variety of different reasons. For one thing, twentieth-century critics have stressed the importance of looking at a Shakespearean play as poetry, rather than—so the nineteenth-century critics tended to see verse drama—as story. Some of Shakespeare's loveliest poetry comes in the late plays, while these plays are somewhat less satisfactory on the story level than the tragedies. Apparently, Shakespeare's artistic interest—or that of his audience—had shifted. He—or they—seemed less interested in following the fall of great heroes such as Macbeth, or Othello, or Hamlet: they became more interested in stories which portrayed the tribulations of aristocratic lovers with, to put it crudely, happy endings. Sometimes these late plays are called tragicomedies, that is, plays which could end as tragedies. In *The Winter's Tale,* for example, Leontes, the jealous husband, is behaving much the way Othello does, but in this tragicomedy everything comes out more or less all right in the end. Further, Shakespeare's dramatic interest seems much more concentrated on the coming out all right than on the original tragic fall. In fact, he is really quite perfunctory about the source of trouble; he doesn't even bother to motivate Leontes' jealousy. He just gives us that jealousy, much the way he just gives us the love-contest in *Lear,* for which there is also no "adequate motivation." This tendency to slight matters of motivation makes these plays hard to stage for modern audiences. Today, when we go to the theater, we tend to expect a realistic representation of realistic people in realistic situations. These late plays give us anything but that. In *The Winter's Tale,* for example, Leontes, entertaining his fellow king and friend Polixenes, flies into a baseless jealousy and sentences his newly born daughter (whose legitimacy he doubts) to be exposed. Polixenes escapes back to Sicily; Leontes' wife and son die of grief. In the second half, sixteen years and many coincidences later, the daughter and Polixenes' son have fallen in love. Confronted with Polixenes' sudden and enraged disapproval, they flee to Sicily. There, identities are disclosed, and wonderful past all whooping! a statue of Leontes' wife Hermione turns out to be the genuine article—she has been hiding all that time. This is hardly the kind of realism that Inge and Miller and the other bards of Broadway have accustomed us to.

These late plays are often called romances; by that, critics mean they involve farfetched, fantastic happenings in far-off, exotic places. There seems to be a lot of rambling in these romances, traveling back and forth over sixteen years from Sicily to the seacoast of Bohemia, for example. The name "romances" also reminds us of the earliest novels, the Greek "romances," which often dealt with the relationships of parents and children, as these late plays do, and which often turned on some incident of a lost child's being suddenly rediscovered as by a birthmark or, as in *The Winter's Tale,* by some jewels, letters, and whatnot left with an abandoned baby. Now, this can be fairly trashy stuff, all things considered.

And yet not so, really. Such stories about discovering lost children are great favorites with human beings, and that makes us think there must be something to them. One of the reasons twentieth-century critics have become so interested in these late plays is that they seem involved with myth, with some of the great legends and stories, patterns of imagination, that haunt, create wonder in, human minds for generation after generation. Perhaps another thing that the word "romance" should suggest to us is that these plays are "wonderful" in a quite literal way: full of wonder. They are plays in which Shakespeare looks at life, at men and women, and wonders. He becomes almost like a child or a very young man again as he looks at the world around him and finds it somehow new and beautiful—wonderful.

He looks, for example, at the seasons. *The Winter's Tale* is much involved with summer and winter. In the opening scene, the courtier Camillo remarks, "I think this coming summer the King of Sicilia means to pay Bohemia the visitation which he justly owes him"; in the last scene Camillo admonishes his king,

> My lord, your sorrow was too sore laid on
> Which sixteen winters cannot blow away,
> So many summers dry.
>
> (V. iii. 49–51)

Earlier, the jealous Leontes was rebuked by Paulina:

> Therefore betake thee
> To nothing but despair. A thousand knees
> Ten thousand years together, naked, fasting,
> Upon a barren mountain, and still winter
> In storm perpetual, could not move the gods
> To look that way thou wert.
>
> (III. ii. 207-212)

But most of all we are made aware of the seasons through the lovely Perdita. Her name means "the lost one," and when she is found, Leontes says to her, "Welcome hither, as is the spring to the earth." It is she who presides over that lovely feast of the sheep-shearing, "No shepherdess, but Flora peering in April's front." She is Flora, the goddess of spring, who gives flowers to the people around her:

> *Perdita.*   Reverend sirs,
> For you there's rosemary and rue; these keep
> Seeming and savor all the winter long.
> Grace and remembrance be to you both,
> And welcome to our shearing!
> *Polixenes.*   Shepherdess—
> A fair one are you—well you fit our ages
> With flowers of winter.
> *Perdita.*   Sir, the year growing ancient,
> Not yet on summer's death nor on the birth
> Of trembling winter, the fairest flowers o' th' season
> Are our carnations and streaked gillyvors.
>
> (IV. iv. 73-82)

As all this talk of flowers would suggest, *The Winter's Tale* treats seasons mostly in terms of plants. Yet plants seem to be linked very closely to the people in the play. In the lines just above, Perdita is trying to give to the visitors at the feast the flowers which are appropriate to them, to their season of life. Earlier, when Perdita was being left in a basket like a foundling, the courtier who was doing it bade her farewell, "Blossom, speed thee well." In the opening scene when one of the courtiers is describing the relationship between the two kings, he says, "They were trained together in their childhoods, and there rooted betwixt them then such an affection which cannot choose but branch now," comparing the relationship between them to a tree. When young Florizel approves the plan of running away with Perdita to Sicily, he says, "There is some sap in this." The old crone, Paulina, speaks of Leontes' sick jealousy as,

> The root of his opinion, which is rotten
> As ever oak or stone was sound.
>
> (II. iii. 88-89)

In all these phrasings, human relations, human feelings are identified with plants—and also with animals.

When young Florizel asks Perdita to dance, he says,

> Our dance, I pray.
> Your hand, my Perdita. So turtles pair
> That never mean to part,
>
> (IV. iv. 153–155)

meaning, of course, not the reptilian kind of turtle, but turtledoves; so Paulina, when near the very end of the play, she says of herself,

> I, an old turtle,
> Will wing me to some withered bough and there
> My mate, that's never to be found again,
> Lament till I am lost.
>
> (V. iii. 132–134)

Then, too, there is the lovely description of the childhood of the two kings who were brought up together.

> We were as twinned lambs that did frisk i' th' sun,
> And bleat the one at th' other. What we changed
> Was innocence for innocence; we knew not
> The doctrine of ill-doing, nor dreamed
> That any did.
>
> (I. ii. 67–71)

And speaking of animals, let us not forget what is perhaps the most famous stage direction of all time, the one in the middle of Act III, scene iii, *"Exit, pursued by a bear."* The bear, like the other references to animals, images the human situation, here the unnaturalness, the savagery, of exposing the lovely daughter, Perdita, to die in a wilderness.

With animals, then, bears and turtledoves, and with plants and flowers, *The Winter's Tale* images the human relationships with which the play deals. Just as the play is much concerned with seasons, with the cycles and generations of plants and animals, so it is much concerned with generations of people. We see two neighboring kings, and we see their respective sons and the daughter of Leontes. Here again is one of Shakespeare's suburban stories, for all that these are kings and queens: one suburban householder becomes jealous of his wife with his neighbor, and the rift between them is patched up by the marriage of their children—rather like a comic *Romeo and Juliet*.

The thing about families that seems to play the most important part in this comedy is family likenesses. Mamillius, for example, Leontes' son, dies early in the play for mysterious and mythic reasons—Leontes looks at him and says, "They say we are almost as like as eggs."

> Looking on the lines
> Of my boy's face, methoughts I did recoil
> Twenty-three years, and saw myself unbreeched,
> In my green velvet coat, my dagger muzzled
> Lest it should bite its master and so prove,
> As ornaments oft do, too dangerous.
> How like, methought, I then was to this kernel,
> This squash, this gentleman.
>
> (I. ii. 153–160)

When Florizel, in the final act, turns up in Sicily, Leontes says of him,

> Your mother was most true to wedlock, prince,
> For she did print your royal father off,
> Conceiving you. Were I but twenty-one,
> Your father's image is so hit in you,
> His very air, that I should call you brother,
> As I did him.
>
> (V. i. 123–128)

When Leontes speaks of the way Florizel looks like Polixenes, he reminds us that this play, in effect, hinges on two likenesses of Hermione. Like so many Shakespearean plays, *The Winter's Tale* seems to have two movements, two great waves of action. The first wave begins with Leontes' strange jealousy, his punishment and humiliation of his queen, and continues to Act III, scene iii, where his servant Antigonus exposes his infant daughter and she is found by the shepherd and the clown in Bohemia. Then enter Time, the Chorus, and we pass over sixteen years. The second wave begins at Act IV, scene ii, with the romance between Polixenes' son Florizel and the now-grown-up Perdita and their trip back to Sicily. In other words, the action in the first wave moves from Sicily to Bohemia; in the second wave, from Bohemia to Sicily. In the first wave of action the child is lost; in the second wave of action the lost child is found. In the first wave of action we find a breach between Leontes and his childhood friend Polixenes; in the second wave of action this breach is healed by the marriage of their two children. As in *Hamlet* the Ghost marked off the two waves of action and in *Macbeth* the witches, in *The Winter's Tale* the two halves are marked off by likenesses of Hermione. Just before the servant Antigonus is to expose the child, he has a dream,

> I have heard, but not believed, the spirits o' th' dead
> May walk again. If such thing be, thy mother
> Appeared to me last night, for ne'er was dream
> So like a waking.
>
> (III. iii. 15–17)

That dream is one likeness of Hermione. The second likeness of Hermione is, of course, that miraculous statue which comes to life in the final scene:

> O, thus she stood,
> Even with such life of majesty—warm life,
> As now it coldly stands—when first I wooed her!
>   (V. iii. 34–36)

cries Leontes. These are two images of Hermione, Hermione in the dream, Hermione the statue, and yet, as Leontes' words contrasting the cold statue with warm life suggest, these are only likenesses, ultimately fakes.

The real likeness is the child, the lost child, a likeness of Leontes:

> Behold, my lords.
> Although the print be little, the whole matter
> And copy of the father—eye, nose, lip,
> The trick of's frown, his forehead, nay, the valley,
> The pretty dimples of his chin and cheek, his smiles,
> The very mould and frame of hand, nail, finger.
> And thou, good goddess Nature, . . . hast made it
> So like to him that got it.
>   (II. iii. 97–104)

"Good goddess Nature"—that takes us back to the seasons and the plants and the animals, and the specific sense of nature that *The Winter's Tale* has: nature as things changing but coming out like again, season after season, generation after generation, creating anew the forms of plants and animals. "Good goddess Nature," Paulina calls her, and in the lovely sheep-shearing scene, we hear of "great creating nature." This is a nature supported by heavenly influences, by the truth of the oracle, by the curse of sterility that the oracle carries against Leontes' unnatural jealousy, by the dream that comes to Antigonus, and simply by the outrageous coincidences that go with one of Shakespeare's later plays. Another heavenly influence is the sun, associated with the men in the play. Leontes, for example, playing on the idea of s-u-n, s-o-n, calls his son "the welkin's eye," that is the heaven's eye, the sun. We hear about Apollo the god of the sun; in fact it is Apollo who sends the oracle that reveals the truth of Hermione's innocence. Apollo was the god of the sun, the god of light in all senses, notably the light of reason, which Leontes, when he is being jealous, is sadly lacking. Another heavenly influence is the moon, intimately associated with woman and the processes of generation, but also here, the inconstant moon of *Romeo and Juliet,* the moon associated with change and changeability: Leontes' sudden jealousy, his casting Perdita away, with "nine changes of the watery star," an echo of the Elizabethan phrase, "false as water."

There seems to be a preoccupation in this play with the contrast between things being alike and things changing; constancy against things decaying, going to pieces. Florizel says to Perdita,

> What you do
> Still betters what is done. When you speak, sweet,
> I'd have you do it ever. When you sing,
> I'd have you buy and sell so, so give alms,
> Pray so, and for the ord'ring your affairs,
> To sing them too. When you do dance, I wish you
> A wave o' th' sea, that you might ever do
> Nothing but that, move still, still so,
> And own no other function.
>
> (IV. iv. 135–143)

A wave of the sea, ever different, ever the same, constant. Constancy seems to be achieved through growth and fertility, as when Leontes and Paulina describe how he might be kissing Hermione had he not so suddenly changed his affection:

> *Leontes.* I might have looked upon my queen's full eyes,
>   Have taken treasure from her lips—
> *Paulina.*   And left them
>   More rich for what they yielded.
>
> (V. i. 53–55)

There is a kind of never-ending plenty in this multiplication through great creating nature. It is as though Shakespeare were saying in the play what he says in one of the most lovely of his sonnets, Sonnet 116, "Love is not love which alters when it alteration finds." Constancy requires loyalty through the vicissitudes of growth and change.

In this contrast between likeness and constancy on one hand and change on the other, these two things take place in time. As that sonnet says,

> Love's not Time's fool, though rosy lips and cheeks
> Within his bending sickle's compass come.
> Love alters not with his brief hours and weeks
> But bears it out even to the edge of doom.

Hours and weeks—time is another important element in *The Winter's Tale*. Almost the last thing we hear about in the play—it occurs in the next to the last line—is "this wide gap of time." *The Winter's Tale* even has a character called Time, who appears as a chorus to mark the division between the two great movements of the play. He says:

> Impute it not a crime
> To me or my swift passage that I slide
> O'er sixteen years and leave the growth untried
> Of that wide gap, since it is in my power

> To o'erthrow law and in one self-born hour
> To plant and o'erwhelm custom.

(IV. i. 4–9)

Time, in *The Winter's Tale,* suggests not only the seasons and the repetitions, the recurrences of nature, but a kind of irretrievable decay, and also sudden, unnatural, artificial changes, such as Leontes' sudden jealousy, "this diseased opinion."

Just as Leontes' sudden jealousy starts the trouble of the first movement of the play, so the other king's, Polixenes', sudden rage starts the troubles of the second movement of the play. Both these rages are associated with the same kind of change. The first, Leontes' jealousy, is associated with the belief that his daughter is not his own child, is not like him, but is Polixenes' child. Similarly, Polixenes' rage comes about because he is afraid his princely son will marry a lowly shepherd's daughter and so change the family's nobility. He compares such a match to the gardener's art of grafting, which will marry

> A gentler scion to the wildest stock,
> And make conceive a bark of baser kind
> By bud of nobler race.

(IV. iv. 93–95)

In that speech, he is testing Perdita, seeing if she will agree to this artificiality, and she won't. A key speech, it brings together a number of the themes of *The Winter's Tale.*

> *Perdita.*   Sir, the year growing ancient,
> Not yet on summer's death nor on the birth
> Of trembling winter, the fairest flowers o' th' season
> Are our carnations and streaked gillyvors,
> Which some call nature's bastards. Of that kind
> Our rustic garden's barren, and I care not
> To get slips of them.
> *Polixenes.*   Wherefore, gentle maiden,
> Do you neglect them?
> *Perdita.*   For I have heard it said
> There is an art which in their piedness shares
> With great creating nature.
> *Polixenes.*   Say there be;
> Yet nature is made better by no mean
> But nature makes that mean. So over that art
> Which you say adds to nature, is an art
> That nature makes. You see, sweet maid, we marry
> A gentler scion to the wildest stock,
> And make conceive a bark of baser kind
> By bud of nobler race. This is an art
> Which does mend nature—change it rather—but
> The art itself is nature.

Perdita.   So it is.
Polixenes.   Then make your garden rich in gillyvors,
               And do not call them bastards.
Perdita.   I'll not put
               The dibble in earth to set one slip of them,
               No more than, were I painted, I would wish
               This youth should say 'twere well, and only therefore
               Desire to breed by me.

                                      (IV. iv. 79–103)

In effect, Perdita is saying she wants pure nature, purebred flowers; such tricks as a gardener's grafting flowers together are like a woman's using cosmetics to give herself a beauty that is only skin deep. Polixenes (following an argument of Montaigne's) seems to accept this kind of grafting, although, quite inconsistently, at the end of the scene, he accuses his son, "Thou a sceptre's heir, that thus affect'st a sheep-hook!" The dialogue between Polixenes and Perdita sets up the basic opposition in the play. So far, we have been calling it the difference between, on the one hand, natural growth and the passage of the seasons and, on the other, sudden change. In this little dialogue it becomes clear what Shakespeare means. He is contrasting art and nature. To the Elizabethan, the word "art" meant something more than it does to us today; "art" makes us think mostly of painting, but to the Elizabethan "art" meant all human activities, all activities which added to or in some way went beyond natural processes. In Tasso's phrase, "Nature is the art of God," that is, nature is to God as art is to man. This play sets off against the seasons, the stars, the plants, the animals of nature, all kinds of human contrivances.

We could call them all art or artifice, but as we look at them we recognize a cluster and complex of ideas that we have seen in Shakespeare many, many times before, starting with *Macbeth:* that cluster of things associated with ceremonies, with clothing, with words, with playacting, with all kinds of artificial formalities. When we've encountered it before we've spoken of it as the "outside" of what we called "the theme of inside-and-outside." Here, in *The Winter's Tale,* the cluster has the specific connotation of artifice as against nature.

The very opening lines of the play set the tone: two courtiers, Archidamus and Camillo, try to exchange courtesies, ceremonial words, but get all tripped up in their own involved, artificial forms of expression. Contrasted to the words they use is the living body of the young prince, Mamillius:

Camillo.   It is a gallant child—one that indeed physics the subject, makes old
             hearts fresh. They that went on crutches ere he was born desire yet
             their life to see him a man.

                                      (I. i. 35–38)

A nice compliment, but the other courtier, Archidamus, breaks in to show, laughingly, that it's really just words, formality:

Archidamus.   Would they else be content to die?
Camillo.   Yes—if there were no other excuse why they should desire to live.
Archidamus.   If the king had no son, they would desire to live on crutches
                 till he had one.

(39–43)

That first scene gives in miniature this contrast between a mere verbal ceremony
and a living heir. The second scene gives it in much more deadly earnest when
Leontes, who encourages his wife to be ceremonious to their visitors, because of
that very ceremony, her polite gestures, flies into a rage and forgets that Hermione is the mother of his child.

> O, that is entertainment
> My bosom likes not, nor my brows. Mamillius,
> Art thou my boy?

(I. ii. 118–120)

Linked to the idea of ceremonies and ceremonial visits are words, the conventional words of praise which are exchanged like money. Again, those two courtiers in Act I, scene i—

Archidamus.   We cannot with such magnificence—in so rare—I know not what
                 to say. We will give you sleepy drinks, that your senses, unintel-
                 ligent of our insufficience, may, though they cannot praise us, as
                 little accuse us.
Camillo.   You pay a great deal too dear for what's given freely.

(12–16)

The courtier is "paying" thanks. Again, Leontes says to Polixenes, "Stay your
thanks awhile and pay them when you part," treating words like money. Words
and money, moreover, start the trouble in the two movements of the play. The
problem in Sicilia, the thing that makes Leontes jealous is the kind words he
ordered his wife to give to his fellow King. In Bohemia, Polixenes flies into a
rage because his rich son, surrounded with the ceremonies of the princedom,
wishes to marry a mere shepherd's daughter.

As always in Shakespeare, linked to these ideas of words, ceremony, and state
are images of clothing which we associate particularly with that odd, odd character, Autolycus. There is a whole section in Act IV, scene iv, where this bal-
ladeer, this wordmaker, sells words in the form of ballads and songs, lying
ballads and songs, and sells ribbons, smocks, "inkles, caddises, cambrics, lawns,"
all fabrics, all surface things. Perdita, though, is so much more than these things:

Florizel.   She prizes not such trifles as these are.
               The gifts she looks from me are packed and locked
               Up in my heart.

(IV. iv. 350–352)

Another favorite image of Shakespeare's for this kind of artifice is playacting.
The immediate result of Polixenes' rage and his forbidding his son to see Perdita

again is that Florizel and Perdita, the two simplest, most direct and honest people in the play, are forced to disguise themselves.

Ceremony, words, money, clothing, playacting: these are the artifices that are set off against great creating nature in *The Winter's Tale*. Consider, then, the way the play ends up, with a statue that comes to life. What better symbol for this contrast between art and nature!

Leontes.	What was he that did make it? See, my lord,
	Would you not deem it breathed? and that those veins
	Did verily bear blood?
Polixenes.	Masterly done.
	The very life seems warm upon her lip.
Leontes.	The fixture of her eye has motion in't,
	As we are mocked with art.

(V. iii. 63–68)

And we are indeed "mocked with" art. All those human contrivances can lead us almost to nature, almost to a real woman, but alas, art can only create a statue. Real life belongs to "good goddess Nature," "great creating nature." This is the essence of *The Winter's Tale,* this contrast between art and nature, between the real, the growing, the creating, in short, life itself, and art.

Art falls far short of nature just as a statue falls short of the living woman. And that fact brings us to a third set of polarities in *The Winter's Tale:* first, likeness and change; second, art and nature; third, man and woman. It is necessary to note, I suppose, that it is the men who cause all the trouble in this play. Leontes flies into his baseless fit of jealousy; Polixenes objects to his son's marrying a shepherdess. The women in the play, Paulina, Hermione, and Perdita, all seem to be on the side of love and life, of children and friendship, the healthy, natural things. In fact, the play seems to turn on the figure of Perdita, the lost one.

She is a miraculous child; when she is first born, she stands for a fresh start, a kind of innocence,

> This child was prisoner to the womb and is
> By law and process of great nature thence
> Freed and enfranchised, not a party to
> The anger of the king nor guilty of,
> If any be, the trespass of the queen.

(II. ii. 59–63)

No sooner born but she is condemned to death, to be exposed on "some remote and desert place" "where chance may nurse or end it."

> Come on, poor babe.
> Some powerful spirit instruct the kites and ravens
> To be thy nurses. Wolves and bears, they say,
> Casting their savageness aside, have done

Like offices of pity.

(II. iii. 184–188)

Antigonus takes the child, carries it over the sea (always a grandly mythic thing to do), and leaves the "blossom" on the shore of Bohemia. He promptly is pursued by a bear; the ship is destroyed; but out of these "things dying" two shepherds take up the child, a "thing . . . newborn," a child born from the sea, as it were. The old shepherd comments:

Would any but these boiled brains of nineteen and two-and-twenty hunt this weather? They have scared away two of my best sheep, which I fear the wolf will sooner find than the master. If anywhere I have them, 'tis by the seaside, browsing of ivy. Good luck, an't be thy will! What have we here? Mercy on's, a barne, a very pretty barne!

(III. iii. 62–68)

That's an odd word, "barne." Obsolete today, it means simply a child. For Shakespeare, it occurs only in two other plays. The word is the old past participle of the verb "to bear." That is, a "barne," a child, is something "born," the past participle of "bear." And it is curious that we should just have had that most remarkable stage direction, *"Exit, pursued by a bear."* Is it possible that Shakespeare is playing on the word by a kind of visual image of a bear? He gives us a deadly savage form of the idea of bearing, and then a miraculous child which is born, a life-giving version of "bearing." The bear should remind us of the animal savagery of the King, and as the shepherd said, he was brought to the side of the sea because two of his best sheep have been scared away by a similar savagery. The two sheep remind us of the description of Leontes and Polixenes as children, as "barnes," "twinned lambs that did frisk i' th' sun." These two twin lambs, at the point when the shepherd or *pastor* is looking for his lost sheep, are themselves lost, estranged, separated by a bearlike savagery.

Perdita is a miraculous child, whose loss leaves Sicily a kind of Waste Land. As the oracle says, "The king shall live without an heir if that which is lost be not found." Perdita is lost and Hermione dies, and Paulina says to Leontes

Therefore betake thee

To nothing but despair. A thousand knees
Ten thousand years together, naked, fasting,
Upon a barren mountain, and still winter
In storm perpetual, could not move the gods
To look that way thou wert.

(III. ii. 207–212)

And Leontes agrees,

Once a day I'll visit

The chapel where they lie, and tears shed there
Shall be my recreation.

(236–238)

Perdita's loss leaves Sicily wintry, infertile, despairing, without an heir, a Waste Land. But miraculously, she makes Bohemia where she is reborn out of the sea a kind of "green world." This is a technical term that Shakespearean scholars use to refer to something that goes on in most of Shakespeare's comedies. The comic characters seem to leave the real world and go off into a kind of fairy-tale, legendary world of fertility and growth where matters somehow get straightened out. That "green world" is the source of the miraculous thing that will solve the problems of the play. Portia's Belmont in *The Merchant of Venice* is such a "green world" from which Portia, who solves the trouble of the play, comes, or one could think of the moated grange where Mariana in *Measure for Measure* stays, or the Forest of Arden in *As You Like It.* In *The Winter's Tale,* Bohemia is the green world. The whole point of Perdita's home among the shepherds is that it is so different from the court; the words the play associates with it are "rustic," "rural," "humble," "homely," "simple." Bohemia is above all a world of fertility, full of flowers, flocks, and loving couples. But the miraculous Perdita can carry this greenness even to the Waste Land of Sicily. When she arrives there, Leontes greets her, "Welcome hither, as is the spring to the earth." Perdita seems something rather more than just a good-looking sixteen-year-old girl. As Polixenes says of her,

> This is the prettiest low-born lass that ever
> Ran on the greensward. Nothing she does or seems
> But smacks of something greater than herself,
> Too noble for this place.

> (IV. iv. 156–159)

She is, of course, a princess, but she is more, even, than that. Florizel says she seems to become almost a goddess, in fact, the goddess of the flowers.

> These your unusual weeds to each part of you
> Do give a life—no shepherdess, but Flora
> Peering in April's front. This your sheep-shearing
> Is as a meeting of the petty gods,
> And you the queen on't.

> (IV. iv. 1–5)

And Leontes, when he welcomes her to Sicily, senses the same quality,

> Most dearly welcome!
> And your fair princess—goddess!
> (V. i. 129–130)

A servant tells him:

> This is a creature,
> Would she begin a sect, might quench the zeal
> Of all professors else, make proselytes

Of who she but bid follow.

Paulina.   How? not women?
Servant.   Women will love her that she is a woman
            More worth than any man; men, that she is
            The rarest of all women.

                                        (V. i. 106–112)

Perdita has the qualities of a goddess, but what goddess? In effect, she herself tells us, when she prays,

                            O, Proserpina,
            For the flowers now that, frighted, thou let'st fall
            From Dis's wagon.

                                        (IV. iv. 116–118)

Proserpina, or in her Greek name, Persephone, the goddess of the spring who was stolen by the god of the underworld (Dis, or Pluto): because she misbehaved slightly down there, she spends six months below the earth during which we have winter, a time of sterility, infertility, a Waste Land; then she returns and the spring comes. It is a curious detail that when Florizel wishes to give her an identity so as to introduce her to Leontes, he says,

Florizel.   Good my lord,
            She came from Libya.
Leontes.   Where the warlike Smalus,
            That noble honored lord, is feared and loved?

                                        (V. i. 155–157)

From Libya, a kind of underworld, a dark, African world like the underworld from which Proserpina or Persephone emerges to bring the spring, as indeed she does bring the spring to Sicily, which has been a Waste Land these past sixteen years.

                            O, Proserpina,
            For the flowers now that, frighted, thou let'st fall
            From Dis's wagon; daffodils,
            That come before the swallow dares, and take
            The winds of March with beauty; violets dim,
            But sweeter than the lids of Juno's eyes
            Or Cytherea's breath; pale primroses,
            That die unmarried, ere they can behold
            Bright Phoebus in his strength—a malady
            Most incident to maids; bold oxlips and
            The crown imperial; lilies of all kinds,
            The flower-de-luce being one. O, these I lack
            To make you garlands of. . . .

                                        (IV. iv. 116–128)

Proserpina or Persephone was a rather complicated figure in Greek and Roman mythology. She was, as it were, two parts of an old friend, the triple goddess.

We first met the triple goddess in *The Merchant of Venice,* in Freud's essay on that play. Freud pointed out that goddesses or choices among goddesses in mythology often tend to come in threes, the most famous example being Paris' choice among Hera, Athena, and Aphrodite. These triple goddesses represent the three relationships that man has with woman: first, woman the mother; second, woman the mate, the beloved; third, the ultimate mother, Mother Earth. Now Persephone or Proserpina combined the young, virginal, loving aspects of woman and the terrible death goddess. In fact, her name, "Persephone" means "the bringer of destruction." In one sense it is odd to make the goddess of spring also the bringer of destruction. In a deeper sense, though, putting these two into a single figure is a way of saying that it is precisely the processes of growth which are the processes of death. In any case, Persephone or Proserpina represented both. Curiously, in the speech we have just interrupted, Perdita is both. When she is at her most springlike, wanting to strew her lover with garlands, suddenly our Persephone becomes a goddess of death.

> *Perdita.*   These I lack
>   To make you garlands of, and my sweet friend,
>   To strew him o'er and o'er!
> *Florizel.*   What, like a corse?
> *Perdita.*   No, like a bank for love to lie and play on.
>   Not like a corse; or if, not to be buried,
>   But quick and in mine arms.
>
> (IV. iv. 127–129)

Not like a corpse, or if like a corpse, not to be buried, except living and in her arms—there she seems like the goddess of death, Mother Earth. But then she becomes the spring goddess again.

>   Come, take your flowers.
>   Methinks I play as I have seen them do
>   In Whitsun pastorals.
>
> (132–134)

(Whitsun pastorals were spring festivals with plays and other theatricals.)

When we look at this comedy as a whole, we find a full complement of triple goddesses. Except for this faint hint linking Perdita to death, she is for the most part the virginal stage of woman, the bringer of spring and life, Proserpina or Flora. Her mother, Hermione, who also goes through a kind of miraculous death and rebirth, is the Venus or Aphrodite figure, the fruitful mother Paulina, the old lady, who generally superintends and watches over the action, who sits there croaking like a deadly bird to remind the King of his sin, she is the third, deathly part of our triple goddess, the crone. In fact she is called a "crone." At the end of the play she says,

> I, an old turtle,
> Will wing me to some withered bough and there
> My mate, that's never to be found again,
> Lament till I am lost.
>
> (V. iii. 131–134)

Yet such is the power of the fertility that Perdita brings that even the goddess of death is married off at the end of the comedy.

The women in *The Winter's Tale* make up a triple goddess, but what about the men? What's left for them? The men occur, naturally enough, as fathers and sons, sons and lovers, the roles corresponding to the three aspects of woman represented by the triple goddess. First, there is a son, Mamillius, and later his reincarnation, as it were, Florizel. They are young, and they are, in their different ways, lovers. Then, there are fathers, Leontes and Polixenes, both, as it usually turns out in comedies, harsh and foolish fathers. Finally, we see old, wise counselors such as Antigonus or Camillo (in the course of the play, both are married to the crone Paulina).

In the case of the men, though, something special has been added. As we have already seen, the men in this play are associated with sudden change, with art as against nature, with ceremony and courtesies and words and money and clothing and playacting. All these things contrast with real life, the processes of generation that take place in nature and woman. And who in the play sums up all these different things associated with men? Who, when he first appears, tells us about stealing clothes, stealing money, about singing lying ballads? Autolycus, the strange, special, puzzling clown of the play. He tells us one of his ballads is about "How a usurer's wife was brought to bed of twenty money-bags at a burthen"—a grotesque parody of the processes of growth and procreation that are associated with women. As in *The Merchant of Venice* usury means making dead metal breed, and it is typical of the men in *The Winter's Tale* that they should take money, dead metal, more seriously almost than life itself.

Even more than money, Autolycus is associated with clothing. He first appears disguised in rags, playacting, pretending that his money has been stolen from him. It is he who provides the clothing with which Florizel and Perdita disguise themselves so they can escape to Sicily. They speak of "the outside of thy poverty," and tell him to hurry because the gentleman, that is, Florizel, "The gentleman is half-flayed already," speaking of clothing as though it were skin covering over the outside. In general, Autolycus is associated with the outsides, the superficial qualities of things. Three times in the course of the play, he changes his clothing, and it is he who threatens the old shepherd and his son with being flayed alive.

Not just Autolycus, though, but all the men in the play are associated with these superficial things. Florizel's father, for example, asks his son why he does not deal with the peddler Autolycus:

> Sooth, when I was young
> And handed love as you do, I was wont
> To load my she with knacks. I would have ransacked
> The pedlar's silken treasury and have poured it
> To her acceptance. You have let him go
> And nothing marted with him. . . .

Florizel.   Old sir, I know
> She prizes not such trifles as these are.
> The gifts she looks from me are packed and locked
> Up in my heart.

(IV. iv. 340–352)

Florizel, under the spell of Perdita, prefers the reality represented by inner nature, while Polixenes allies himself with the superficial things Autolycus sells. There is a further irony in that Polixenes' tyranny makes Perdita, who above all the others holds in herself the inner essence of nature, makes her disguise herself: "I see the play so lies that I must bear a part." Another pair of men associated with superficies are the old shepherd and his son, much concerned with their rise in rank. The son takes it as very important that he is now a gentleman born, "Ay, and have been so any time these four hours," as though his rank, his outside, his clothing could somehow change the natural fact of his own birth.

In short, all the men seem preoccupied with outsides, ceremonies, words, clothing; and all these things come together in the almost mythical figure of Autolycus:

My traffic is sheets; when the kite builds, look to lesser linen. My father named me Autolycus, who being, as I am, littered under Mercury, was likewise a snapper-up of unconsidered trifles. With die and drab I purchased this caparison, and my revenue is the silly cheat.

(IV. iii. 23–27)

Autolycus, born under the sign of Mercury, named after a famous thief in the *Iliad,* is another old mythical friend of ours, the shapeshifter or trickster like Mercury himself, and rather like Iago, although in this case a quite harmless Iago. The contrast between him and the women of the play comes out very neatly when Autolycus says, "Now, had I not the dash of my former life in me, would preferment drop on my head" (V. ii. 108–109). Autolycus is preoccupied with preferment, that is, his social rank, his position at the court. In the next scene, though, Hermione, the fruitful mother, says,

> You gods, look down,
> And from your sacred vials pour your graces
> Upon my daughter's head!
>
> (V. iii. 121–123)

It is with the woman, the mother, that true grace rests as against the false grace of court preferment.

As its very deepest and most basic level, then, *The Winter's Tale* is a play about man and woman, woman the repository of nature, man the creator of art. For example, the contrast comes out in the two dances that take place in the sheep-shearing scene. The first one, coming after Perdita's great speech about the flowers, about nature, about Proserpina, is a dance of shepherds and shepherdesses. The second dance comes after Autolycus has appeared to sell his ballads, his words, and it is a dance of satyrs, classic symbols for lust. Associated with woman we have the mating of man and woman, the act of procreation: associated with man alone we have only animal lust. In a way, Autolycus himself is a kind of spirit of fertility or spring. When he first appears he comes singing a song as a pagan spirit, a Pan, would:

> When daffodils begin to peer,
>   With heigh! the doxy over the dale,
> Why, then comes in the sweet o' the year,
>   For the red blood reigns in the winter's pale.
>
> (IV. iii. 1–4)

But Autolycus does not carry the rich sense of spring and harvest, of fertility, that Perdita, the true spring goddess, seems to bring. As he sings,

> But shall I go mourn for that, my dear?
>   The pale moon shines by night.
> And when I wander here and there,
>   I then do most go right.
>
> (15–18)

He wanders here and there; he seems trivial, superficial, here today and gone tomorrow.

Isn't Shakespeare getting here at a fundamental truth about man and woman? That is, woman is the bearer of new life and in that process man plays, while an essential part, a somewhat distant one. The facts of fatherhood are learned rather late in our development toward civilization. It takes a long time for primitive man to connect the birth of a child with the act of fathering it nine months previously. Woman bears the child in her body, while man seems much less close to the whole process. Often in mythology, the idea is imaged in the sun fertilizing the earth. The earth is very real, very solid, very much here. Sunbeams are by comparison abstract, ephemeral. As an old proverb has it, it's a wise father that knows his own child. Indeed, there might be a mistake about a child's father, but it would be difficult indeed to mistake its mother. It is in this sense that *The Winter's Tale* images to us woman as close to nature, to growth and harvest; man as preoccupied with ceremonies, clothing, words, in short, with art.

The comedy closes with art—the statue; indeed, we are even told the name of the artist, "that rare Italian master, Julio Romano." In actuality, Julio Romano was the man who illustrated the splendidly bawdy sonnets of Aretino; perhaps, then, we should link him, with the other men of the play, to animal lust. In any case, the statue he is said to have made comes to life—all through the scene we hear Paulina talk about art:

> Her dead likeness, I do well believe,
> Excels whatever yet you looked upon
> Or hand of man hath done.
>
> (V. iii. 15-17)

But the real art is not "the hand of man," but the woman's art which creates real life, a mysterious art that Paulina keeps as her secret:

> *Polixenes.* Make it manifest where she has lived,
> Or how stol'n from the dead.
> *Paulina.*   That she is living
> Were it but told you, should be hooted at
> Like an old tale; but it appears she lives.
>
> (V. iii. 114-117)

Woman offers life itself; man, the mere telling of lies, "an old tale," in fact, *The Winter's Tale.*

It is, then, a comedy about the ways men interfere with and women restore the processes of "great creating Nature." In these last plays, Shakespeare turns away from the "big" themes of the tragedies, good-and-evil, fact-and-value, and turns to art and nature. The plot contrasts the sterility of man's creativity (his jealousies and ambitions, his songs, statues, and bargains, his bearish cruelties) with the fertility that women offer: "bearing" children, bringing even statues to life. In tone, the comedy balances its contrived, artificial form (tragicomedy, romance) with the richly natural birth, copulation, and death which are its subject matter. As for imagery, there is a great deal in *The Winter's Tale* (even its title) about the seasons, which go round and round in time, always changing, but always coming out the same. The play is much concerned with cycles and generations, with plants, for example, and harvests—we are even shown a summer festival for the sheep-shearing. The play is concerned, too, with animals: those sheep again, even that grand stage direction, *"Exit, pursued by a bear."*

In this comedy, Shakespeare seems to be thinking of nature as essentially re-curring forms; the play has a version of that fearful curse of Macbeth and Lear: Florizel says, if he break his faith with Perdita, then

> Let nature crush the sides o' th' earth together
> And mar the seeds within,
>
> (IV. iv. 471–472)

"the seeds within," which guarantee that the forms of nature, plants, animals, men, will recur. Thus, *The Winter's Tale* is also much concerned with family likeness. In the course of the play we learn that Mamillius looks like Leontes, Florizel like Polixenes, Perdita like her father. As always in Shakespeare, this orderly, harmonious, recurring nature is supported by various heavenly influ-ences: Apollo and his oracle; the dream in which Hermione's first "likeness" appears; the sun and moon. Change and likeness (these recurring forms): this pair is one of the major contrasts in the play. As against the normal recurrences of nature in time, we have the unnatural, sudden changes in time of Leontes and Polixenes. In particular, there is Leontes' sudden breaking away from his natural love for his wife, his friend, his newborn daughter, into a baseless jealousy; at the end of Act III, scene ii, he changes back again, just as suddenly, unnaturally, unnaturalistically. Another great contrast in the play is that between nature and unnature, or, in another sense, nature and art. Women are concerned with, have, "the seeds within"; man is concerned with the art without. Thus, in the open-ing scenes, men show a great deal of interest in ceremony, royal state and pomp, courtesy, visits, reputation. Later on, the men concern themselves with words and money and clothing and playacting, all focused in the outlandish figure of Autolycus.

The Winter's Tale is Shakespeare near the end of his career. He must have known that he was going to retire within a year or so, and he takes this chance to look back on his own art, an art of disguise, an art which dresses people up into costumes and creates a cold and sterile reality, a "winter's tale," as fake as the lies and the confidence stories and the ballads of Autolycus. Shakespeare looks back on his art and pays a beautiful tribute to nature. He looks back on his own man's life and pays a beautiful tribute to woman. Man creates art, in-vents philosophies and musics, makes money, sets up courts and ranks and cere-monies, writes plays, publishes criticism; man does all these things, but woman does the really important thing—she has babies.

ᏞᏞᏞᏞᏞᏞᏞ

16

ᏞᏞᏞᏞᏞᏞᏞ

THE TEMPEST

WITH *The Tempest,* WE COME TO SHAKESPEARE'S LAST PLAY—OR MORE OR LESS his last play. After *The Tempest,* he apparently had a hand in *Henry VIII* and *The Two Noble Kinsmen,* collaborating on these two plays with young John Fletcher, who succeeded him as the leading dramatist for the King's Men. *The Tempest* is, though, Shakespeare's last solo performance, the last play he wrote entirely himself before he retired to Stratford. Indeed, in 1611, when this play was probably written, he may already have left London. We have noticed before how meager Shakespeare's stage directions are, scarcely more than an "enter" or an "exit." They didn't need to be very elaborate, because he was either directing his plays himself or present when they were being directed. In *The Tempest,* the stage directions are unusually elaborate: we can guess—and it's only a guess—that Shakespeare was not present, that he had already gone back to Stratford.

This is, in effect, Shakespeare's last play, and for that reason people like to think it in some way represents his farewell to the stage, that this play is somehow more autobiographical than the others. Of course, none of his other plays shows any signs at all of being autobiographical: there is very little in his plays which refers to contemporary doings and gossip and nothing at all that explicitly refers to his own life. Shakespeare did not "express himself" in that crude romantic sense of spewing out one's emotions all over the landscape. Then, if he is not autobiographical in his other plays, why should he be so in *The Tempest?*

It is interesting, though, that this play follows on *The Winter's Tale,* in which Shakespeare was thinking like an older man, thinking about life and art, making his most eloquent and exquisite tribute to the life-giving powers of woman. Then comes *The Tempest,* a play in many ways about men, and the doings of men, particularly the magical arts of one man, Prospero. Legend has it that Shakespeare was famous for his acting the parts of old men; it is possible that he, if he was still in London, acted Prospero.

It is curious, too, that Shakespeare in this play turns back to one of his favorite themes; we've seen it in *Romeo and Juliet, Othello, Antony and Cleopatra:* the theme of love as against war and politics, or, in general, the contrast between the world of love and the practical world of business and affairs, as in *King Lear, The Merchant of Venice,* or *Hamlet.* In a way, one can trace Shakespeare's development and growth by the ways in which love comes to outweigh the practical world. In this play, the last unalloyed Shakespearean writing, from its start almost to its finale, the love of Miranda and Ferdinand dominates all the other actions. *The Tempest* seems the diametric opposite of *Romeo and Juliet.* Where, in *Romeo and Juliet,* the lovers were defeated by the war between the rival houses of Montague and Capulet, in *The Tempest,* the love of Ferdinand and Miranda unites the formerly hostile houses of Milan and Naples. The political plot, moreover, Shakespeare manages with his left hand; it is almost brushed off in contrast to the love plot. The original usurpation when Antonio stole Prospero's throne from him takes place long before the play begins, and we only hear about it in narration. There is a political revolt in the play, but by Stefano, a drunken butler, Trinculo, a jester, and that wonderful half-man half-animal, Caliban. Except for a brief bit when Sebastian and Antonio plot to usurp the throne of the King of Naples, political rebellion is relegated to the low comic scenes. Love has almost entirely outweighed in this last play the world of practical affairs.

The contrast between love and political rivalry is an old theme of Shakespeare's. *The Tempest* also has a new theme, or at least one that does not seem so important in the earlier plays, the theme of freedom as against confinement or servitude. We hear, for example, how Ariel was confined,

> Into a cloven pine; within which rift
> Imprisoned thou didst painfully remain
> A dozen years.
>
> (I. ii. 277-279)

and how Prospero released Ariel,

> It was mine art,
> When I arrived and heard thee, that made gape
> The pine, and let thee out.
>
> (291-293)

Throughout, Ariel seeks freedom, and in the very last line of the comedy, Prospero bids him, "To the elements be free, and fare thou well!"

Another character who is concerned about servitude and freedom is Caliban. He seems almost an intellectual construct, modeled from early accounts of American Indians—his name is an anagram of "cannibal." Caliban is the "natural man" (in a Renaissance, not a Romantic, sense), that is, man in an animal way but unimproved by what (to the Renaissance) really made a man, the graces of Christian civilization. Caliban, less than Ariel who was confined into a tree, was confined into a rock; again, unlike Ariel, Caliban rebels against his lord, Prospero, and sings his strange little song,

> 'Ban, 'Ban, Ca—Caliban
> Has a new master: get a new man.
> Freedom, high-day! high-day, freedom! freedom,
> high-day, freedom!
>
> (II. ii. 179–181)

That is one kind of freedom, the license the natural man seeks. Another kind is the ideal state Gonzalo, the old courtier, describes in a speech which Shakespeare borrowed from Montaigne's essay on (oddly enough) cannibals:

> I' th' commonwealth I would by contraries
> Execute all things; for no kind of traffic
> Would I admit; no name of magistrate;
> Letters should not be known; riches, poverty,
> And use of service, none; contract, succession,
> Bourn, bound of land, tilth, vineyard, none;
> No use of metal, corn, or wine, or oil;
> No occupation; all men idle, all;
> And women too, but innocent and pure;
> No sovereignty.
>   . . .
>
> All things in common nature should produce
> Without sweat or endeavor. Treason, felony,
> Sword, pike, knife, gun, or need of any engine
> Would I not have; but nature should bring forth,
> Of it own kind, all foison, all abundance,
> To feed my innocent people.
>
> (II. i. 143–160)

That is one kind of freedom, as against the confinements suffered by Ariel or Caliban. But even Prospero himself is confined, as he tells us in the Epilogue, speaking now as an actor:

> I must be here confined by you,
> Or sent to Naples.
>   . . .

> Release me from my bands
> With the help of your good hands.
>
> . . .
>
> As you from crimes would pardoned be,
> Let your indulgence set me free.

Prospero, as was customary in epilogues, has thrown off, partly, his role in the play, and is now addressing the audience as himself, as an actor. He is thinking of being confined in the wooden theater, and that's rather curious, because wood in *The Tempest* seems to be intimately associated with the ideas of confinement and servitude.

Ariel was confined in a cloven pine, and the essence of Caliban's service is,

> He does make our fire,
> Fetch in our wood, and serves in offices
> That profit us.
>
> (I. ii. 311-313)

But then, when Caliban plots his revolt, he plans to get his co-conspirators to "with a log batter his skull, or paunch him with a stake," or, alternatively, "thou mayst knock a nail into his head." Caliban seems to want to reverse his own servitude by treating Prospero as wood. Another case of confinement in wood comes when the King, Alonso, and his followers, the wicked politicians, are "Confined together . . . in the line grove which weather-fends your cell," that is, the grove of "line" or linden trees. The boatswain and seamen were "dead of sleep and (how we know not) all clapped under hatches," that is, confined in their wooden boat. The essence of the servitude which Ferdinand must endure to win Miranda is wooden,

> I must remove
> Some thousands of these logs and pile them up.
> (III. i. 9-10)

> I am, in my condition,
> A prince, Miranda; I do think, a king
> (I would not so), and would no more endure
> This wooden slavery than to suffer
> The fleshfly blow my mouth. Hear my soul speak!
> The very instant that I saw you, did
> My heart fly to your service; there resides,
> To make me slave to it; and for your sake
> Am I this patient log-man.
>
> (III. i. 59-67)

Wood, wooden, logs—they seem to be important words in this play, perhaps because, in Shakespeare's time, "wood" was a homonym. "Wood" could have its modern meanings associated with trees, but "wood" (sometimes spelled "wode" in this second sense) could also mean mad or bestial. Shakespeare plays upon the two meanings of the word when he has one of the distraught lovers in *Midsummer Night's Dream* cry, "Here am I . . . wood within this wood." Similarly, "woodman" could mean, in Shakespeare's day, either a savage or someone who lived in a forest and provided wood—in short, Caliban. The two meanings of the word "wood" come together in his single brutish figure.

In fact, Caliban is called a "savage" and, in an older spelling, "salvage"; the word comes from Latin *salvaticus,* from *silva,* wood, and means "of the woods, wild, uncivilized." Quite literally, then, in the figure of Caliban, we have a savage, a "woodwose" or "woodman" in the old sense of wildman. The word "wooden" always in Shakespeare seems to carry with it connotations of brutishness, senselessness, dullness, doltishness. At the same time, Shakespeare twice uses the word "woodman" to suggest a hunter—of women. Thus, *The Tempest*'s recurring references to wood serve as a way of exploring the play's interest in man's enslavement to such passions as lust for power or for money or for women.

One aspect of that brutishness is Caliban's attempt to rape Miranda. A violent, savage lust contrasts with the far more civilized and graceful love of Ferdinand and Miranda. Where Caliban's lust is an attempt to break through his servitude, Ferdinand's love, his willingness to carry wood, represents an acceptance of servitude within freedom. After he has confessed his love to Miranda, explained why he is "this patient log-man," she says:

> I'll be your servant,
> Whether you will or no.
> *Ferdinand.* My mistress, dearest,
> And I thus humble ever.
> *Miranda.* My husband then?
> *Ferdinand.* Ay, with a heart as willing
> As bondage e'er of freedom. Here's my hand.
> (III. i. 85–89)

Ferdinand accepts the freedom-in-bondage of civilized love, the duty not to violate Miranda's chastity before their marriage.

In return, he is shown the promise of fertility. In the beautiful harvest masque of Act IV, scene i, Ceres, the goddess of grain, promises fertility; Iris, the rainbow, the covenant between heaven and earth, promises the blessing of the gods; Juno, the goddess of marriage, blesses the match. Prospero puts on a harvest masque with a dance of nymphs and reapers. Like so many Renaissance studies of love, *The Tempest* links the idea of chastity to justice. In the Renaissance, both these words had a larger meaning than they tend to do for us today. For us today, justice tends to mean that if I bang up your fender,

I have to pay for it and put you back in the condition you were in before I banged up your fender. To the Renaissance, justice meant almost all of human action directed to a rightful, a fit end. For us, chastity tends to have a Sunday-school or *Reader's Digest* connotation of "thou shalt not neck." For the Renaissance, the idea was much richer. It was a restraint on natural impulses, not restraint for the sake of restraint, but for the sake of ultimate fertility—as in this play. Ferdinand and Miranda swear chastity, not for chastity's sake so much as that the marriage shall be blessed with "sweet aspersion" from the heavens "to make this contract grow."

To Shakespeare's Renaissance audience, both chastity and justice meant restraints on human action toward some greater end; both were forms of government (as in *Measure for Measure*). Chastity in *The Tempest* is represented in the relationship of Ferdinand to Miranda. Justice is represented in Prospero's forgiveness of the men who have wronged him, Alonso and Sebastian and Antonio. In both cases, chastity and justice involve forbearance. As Prospero says,

> The rarer action is
> In virtue than in vengeance. They being penitent,
> The sole drift of my purpose doth extend
> Not a frown further. Go, release them, Ariel.
>
> (V. i. 27–30)

That word, "release," reminds us again how important the ideas of freedom and servitude (or confinement) are in this play; reminds us, too, that both justice and chastity (in their Renaissance senses) are restraints in the service of some greater end. But they are self-imposed restraints against the wildness of the "woodman" or savage, not crude confinements in pine or oak or rock.

What Prospero is asking Ariel to release his prisoners from is the linden-grove—in a traditional symbolism, the "wood of error," where they are "distracted," "spell-stopped." Over and over again in this play, Prospero puts people to sleep: he seemingly hypnotizes Miranda (I. ii), Alonso and Gonzalo (II. i), and he has put the whole crew of the ship to sleep. In that sleep, the characters are visited by dreams, dreams which reveal to them their own faults, the knowledge of their own past, dreams which lead them through this mysterious island. This sleep, these dreams become images for Prospero's control over these people, as for example, when Ferdinand says, "My spirits, as in a dream, are all bound up." Life itself in this play seems a kind of dream, as Prospero points out in a very famous sentence,

> We are such stuff
> As dreams are made on, and our little life
> Is rounded with a sleep.
>
> (IV. i. 156–158)

Life itself becomes an illusion, a show of some kind, a dream enslaving us, and that leads us to yet another theme in *The Tempest,* the familiar one of inside-and-outside. When Shakespeare's imagination dwells on the appearances of this world, he tends to think of them in terms of clothing. When Prospero asks Miranda:

> Lend thy hand
> And pluck my magic garment from me. So,
> Lie there, my art,
>
> (I. ii. 23–25)

he identifies his art with his cloak, just as in *Macbeth* titles and honors were described as clothing. Again, the conspirators, when they are washed up on shore, find to their surprise that their clothes have not been damaged by the sea, but are as rich as they ever were. (Maybe this was just an economic necessity in Shakespeare's Globe Theatre: nobody wanted to spoil a lot of good costumes by making them look as though they were stained with the sea, but, economic necessity or no, it all adds to the magical, wonderful quality of *The Tempest* as well as to the interest in clothing.) Clothes are important at the end of the play as well, when the clowns Stephano and Trinculo and Caliban become all involved with the frippery, the wardrobe, hanging outside Prospero's cell, instead of getting about their business of rebellion. At the end, Prospero regards it as important that he show himself as he was when he was Duke of Milan.

> Ariel,
> Fetch me the hat and rapier in my cell.
> I will discase me, and myself present
> As I was sometime Milan.
>
> (V. i. 83–86)

Clothing is one way Shakespeare develops the contrast between inner and outer man.

Acting is another. Ariel has to play the part of a harpy, and spirits are brought in to play Iris and Ceres and Juno. Along with acting goes the really quite surprising amount of music we find on this desert island (music which, quite coincidentally, gratified the tastes of 1611). Music and song, like Prospero's magic, restrain us with their spell. As Ferdinand comments:

> Where should this music be? I' th' air or th' earth?
> It sounds no more; and sure it waits upon
> Some god o' th' island. Sitting on a bank,
> Weeping again the King my father's wrack,
> This music crept by me upon the waters,
> Allaying both their fury and my passion
> With its sweet air.
>
> (I. ii. 388–394)

Again, he uses the image of music to describe the way he felt about former loves,

> Full many a lady
> I have eyed with best regard, and many a time
> Th' harmony of their tongues hath into bondage
> Brought my too diligent ear.

(III. i. 39–42)

Not only the high characters like Ferdinand hear music, but even Caliban hears it in his lovely, strange little speech,

> Be not afeard: the isle is full of noises,
> Sounds and sweet airs that give delight and hurt not.
> Sometimes a thousand twangling instruments
> Will hum about mine ears; and sometime voices
> That, if I then had waked after long sleep,
> Will make me sleep again; and then, in dreaming,
> The clouds methought would open and show riches
> Ready to drop upon me, that, when I waked,
> I cried to dream again.

(III. ii. 132–140)

Voices in the air, dreaming, clothing and costumes, music, acting—*The Tempest* is a play about plays. We hear of Ariel pretending to be fire, pretending to be invisible music; we see shapes bringing in a banquet which Sebastian calls "a living drollery," a phrase one could apply to this whole play. Ariel and Prospero drive spirits about like dogs. Caliban is described as a monster, a freak that could be shown in a sideshow. There is that wonderful masque of Iris, Ceres, and Juno. The masque was a common and popular form in Shakespeare's day and still more after: a little playlet, one might even call it a pageant, with rather formal verse, a good deal of music and dancing, and allegorical characters among whom are usually some wild men, like Caliban, who made up something called an antimasque. *The Tempest* is full of shows like that masque.

Even more, it is full of telling and teaching. Prospero, for example, is an English teacher: Caliban reminds him, "You taught me language, and my profit on't is, I know how to curse." Prospero explicitly describes himself as a schoolmaster to Miranda, but in the course of the play he teaches a lot of people a lot of things: Ferdinand the importance of love; Alonso, Sebastian, and Antonio honesty in political dealings. Indirectly, he teaches Caliban what a fool he is to follow such men as Stephano and Trinculo, and indirectly, he teaches Ariel, who is only an elemental spirit, the meaning of emotion. Not just Prospero though, but others are also involved in teaching. "I'll teach you how to flow," says Antonio, trying to persuade Sebastian to political assassination. And even Caliban says that he will teach Stephano and Trinculo:

> I prithee let me bring thee where crabs grow;
> And I with my long nails will dig thee pignuts,
> Show thee a jay's nest, and instruct thee how
> To snare the nimble marmoset; I'll bring thee
> To clust'ring filberts, and sometimes I'll get thee
> Young scamels from the rock.
>
> (II. ii. 163-168)

But these are bad teachings as well as minor teachings. The important one is Prospero's teaching the sinister nobles.

All this teaching suggests it is a fundamental concern of the play. The teaching in *The Tempest,* moreover, has a special quality. It seems associated always with wonder and amazement, with putting people to sleep, making them think that what they have seen and heard is almost a dream. In Act I, scene ii, Prospero explains to Miranda who she is and how he and she came to be imprisoned on the island; then she sleeps: "The strangeness of your story put heaviness in me." This all begins to have a kind of familiar ring. People being put to sleep, being made to wander through a maze on the island, being, in effect, blindfolded, unable to see those who are playing tricks on them, made to do unpleasant tasks like carrying logs, led finally to a secret place, Prospero's cell, and shown miraculous dreamlike visions which reveal secrets—isn't this an initiation ritual just such as you might find in a college fraternity? For that matter, we could go all the way back to Stone Age times when the young men who were to be initiated into the tribe were taken apart from the rest of the people, given drugs, put to sleep, made to undergo various ordeals, often including a walk through a maze, then shown in some womby cave the religious rituals and secrets of the tribe, and brought back to the tribe as fully accredited members. *The Tempest* is that kind of initiation ritual. As Gonzalo says, "Here's a maze trod indeed," and Alonso:

> This is as strange a maze as e'er men trod,
> And there is in this business more than nature
> Was ever conduct of. Some oracle
> Must rectify our knowledge.
>
> (V. i. 241-244)

Alonso is quite accurate: the ultimate aim of treading the mazes of initiation is the acquiring of new understanding, finding one's self. Gonzalo says, at the finale,

> O, rejoice
> Beyond a common joy, and set it down
> With gold on lasting pillars: in one voyage
> Did Claribel her husband find at Tunis,
> And Ferdinand her brother found a wife

> Where he himself was lost; Prospero his dukedom
> In a poor isle; and all of us ourselves
> When no man was his own.
>
> (V. i. 206–213)

Or as Prospero notes of his prisoners—or audience,

> Their understanding
> Begins to swell, and the approaching tide
> Will shortly fill the reasonable shore,
> That now lies foul and muddy.
>
> (V. i. 79–81)

Originally, initiation rituals represented attempts to simulate an experience of death and rebirth. The initiate was put to sleep or put through some sort of ordeal as an approximation to death. *The Tempest,* too, gives us a pattern of death and rebirth. Ferdinand believes his father dead, and his father believes that he is dead. The courtiers believe the mariners have perished. Then, they are all brought to life again, reborn from their immersion in the amniotic sea, or in the case of Stephano, Trinculo, and Caliban, in that "filthy mantled pool."

The Tempest, in short, has that same ritual and mythic quality that we found in *The Winter's Tale,* which was also a play about the relationship of art and nature, also a play based on a kind of death and rebirth, and a play in which the myth of Proserpina was very important. That same myth turns up in *The Tempest,* though in a rather hidden and obscure way. The event that got Alonso, Sebastian, and company out on the ocean in the first place was the King of Naple's marrying his daughter Claribel to the King of Tunis. As Sebastian says:

> Sir, you may thank yourself for this great loss,
> That would not bless our Europe with your daughter,
> But rather loose her to an African,
> Where she, at least, is banished from your eye
> Who hath cause to wet the grief on't.
>
> .   .   .
>
> You were kneeled to and importuned otherwise
> By all of us; and the fair soul herself
> Weighed, between loathness and obedience, at
> Which end o' th' beam should bow.
>
> (II. i. 119–127)

Africa, somehow a dark, strange, fearsome place, and Claribel, whose name means "beautiful and bright," married to a dark African king, echo the legend of dusky Dis ravishing and abducting down to Hades the daughter of Ceres, Proserpina, the bright goddess of spring. Miranda, however, whose name means "she who is to be wondered at," replaces Proserpina and brings back fertility to the earth; her marriage with Ferdinand creates not a year half fertile, half sterile, but a year of perpetual growth and plenty, as the goddesses promise:

> Spring come to you at the farthest
> In the very end of harvest.
> Scarcity and want shall shun you,
> Ceres' blessing so is on you.
> (IV. i. 114–117)

But the Proserpina theme which bulked so large in *The Winter's Tale* is quite minor in *The Tempest*. *The Winter's Tale* was a play about woman, the wonderful creating power of woman. *The Tempest* is a play about man, and man's wonderful creating power, not now in the sense of giving birth, but as his ability to teach, to show, to put on plays, if you will, which will somehow initiate people.

But initiate them into what? The new life *The Tempest* gives its characters is really a new sense of life: a sense of the newness and freshness of things, a sense of wonder. As Ariel says,

> I boarded the King's ship: now on the beak,
> Now in the waist, the deck, in every cabin,
> I flamed amazement.
> (I. ii. 196–198)

Miranda looks at Ferdinand, and says,

> I might call him
> A thing divine; for nothing natural
> I ever saw so noble.
> (I. ii. 418–420)

And Ferdinand looks on her:

> Most sure, the goddess
> On whom these airs attend! Vouchsafe my prayer
> May know if you remain upon this island,
> And that you will some good instruction give
> How I may bear me here. My prime request,
> Which I do last pronounce, is (O you wonder!)
> If you be maid or no?
> (422–428)

And again he says:

> Might I but through my prison once a day
> Behold this maid, all corners else o' th' earth
> Let liberty make use of. Space enough
> Have I in such a prison.
> (491–494)

In the last act, the final revelation, old Gonzalo says of the island,

> All torment, trouble, wonder, and amazement
> Inhabits here.
>
> (V. i. 104–105)

And then, of course, there are Miranda's famous words:

> O, wonder!
> How many goodly creatures are there here!
> How beauteous mankind is! O brave new world
> That has such people in't!
>
> (V. i. 181–184)

"O brave new world." The phrase is famous because Mr. Aldous Huxley made it the title of a famous science-fiction novel. *The Tempest* itself is very like science fiction. After all, Shakespeare based the play in part on voyagers' and discoverers' descriptions of the New World, a world that seemed just as strange and new and wonderful to Renaissance men as the moon and Mars and Venus seem wonderful to twentieth-century men. In fact, some years ago the Yale Dramatic Society put on a science-fiction production of *The Tempest* and there is even a science-fiction movie called *Forbidden Planet*, which is based on a sort of Freudian reading of *The Tempest*. You can see how it would go: Prospero is the mad scientist ruling over his lonely planet with a beautiful daughter. He sees on his telescreen, or what you will, a rocket ship foundering in the Van Allen belt around the planet, and by his scientific powers he brings down the ship with a handsome young Air Force captain in it. The film even had an Ariel, a friendly robot called Robbie. *The Tempest* would make very good science fiction, having what most science fiction today lacks, a sense of wonder at the newness of things. At the same time that *The Tempest* seems to have this affinity with the most modern of modern writing, it seems to reach back into "The dark backward and abysm of time," and follow the pattern of an initiation ritual such as we would find among Stone Age cave-dwellers, man in his earliest, most primitive form, leading people through a maze culminating in a miraculous vision in a cave.

The Tempest resembles not only Stone Age and modern drama, but also Roman drama, specifically, the practice of the unities, and the use of the basic themes of Roman comedy. The "unities" were a set of three rules derived from Aristotle, though Aristotle himself didn't invent them—his Renaissance commentators did by extrapolating some of his ideas and codifying the practice of Roman comedies. These rules held that a play should have three unities, the unity of time, the unity of place, and the unity of action. The unity of time meant that a play should take place in one day (approximately). The unity of place demanded that a play should take place entirely within the confines of one city or its suburbs or something of similar size. The unity of action held that a play should have but one story line. Now, Shakespeare never paid very much attention to these rules. In *The Winter's Tale*, for example, there is that "great gap of time," sixteen years, in the middle of the play, and the scene moves from Sicily to Bohemia. In *Macbeth*, the play moves from Scotland to England. There are only three plays in which Shakespeare obeyed the unities, and oddly enough, they are his first and his last comedies. The first two are *Love's Labour's Lost* and *The Comedy of Errors*, which Shakespeare wrote at the very beginning of his career, when he was finding his own style by imitating other writers; in the case of *The Comedy of Errors*, the Roman comedies of Plautus; in *Love's Labour's Lost*, the Italian *commedia dell'arte*. Finally, in his last comedy, *The Tempest*, he again obeys the unities. It's an odd coincidence.

If you look at Roman comedies, you will find they have almost unanimously three elements: there is a contest between a young man and an older one, usually over a girl; the play ends with a marriage; and at the end of the play a slave is freed. These elements, if you take them back into that "dark backward and abysm of time," go all the way to prehistoric Greek fertility dramas in which a divine hero struggled against an adversary, was killed, and then was miraculously reborn, freeing the village from the spell of winter or its past sins or what-have-you. These "archetypal" elements of the fertility dramas became fore-shortened, as it were, civilized, into the elements of Roman comedy. And lo and behold, those same elements occur in *The Tempest*. In *The Tempest* we have a struggle between a younger man and an older one, between Ferdinand and Prospero, over the possession of a girl, Miranda. The play ends with the betrothal of Ferdinand and Miranda. At the end of the play a slave, Ariel, is freed.

I think we can fairly say that Shakespeare in *The Tempest* is being a little self-conscious about his role as a dramatist. Perhaps these Roman elements, the unities and the themes of Roman comedy, got in because Shakespeare was trying to place himself in a dramatic tradition, perhaps the tradition Ben Jonson advocated. A friend of Shakespeare's, a playwright like Shakespeare, but a great student of the classics, Jonson maintained that the English popular drama of his day should copy Roman drama in such matters as the unities and the satire of contemporary manners. Jonson was not as popular or successful a playwright as Shakespeare was, though he was a playwright the bright young literati admired. The older Shakespeare may well have seemed to the young intellectuals of the day a slicker sort of popular writer. There is not the slightest evidence for this story, but I like to imagine it anyway—that Jonson and Shakespeare were sitting in the Mermaid Tavern one Friday night, and Ben was crying up the Romans. Will looked at him and said, "Ben, I'm going to write you a comedy that follows all these Roman rules you've been pushing for so long, and you'll see that it doesn't look like any Roman comedy you've ever seen. It isn't the rules that are important, it's the spirit of the thing." And the result was *The Tempest.* Well, it's a nice story, *ben trovato,* and there is, no doubt, not a word of truth in it. Nevertheless, *The Tempest* does follow these Roman rules, and it is a singularly un-Roman comedy.

The thing, I think, that makes it seem un-Roman is the sense of wonder, of the newness and strangeness of things, the way all the characters seem to feel that they have fallen into a brave new world. At the same time, the unities and the Roman elements combine with the sense of revelation to set the play in a dramatic tradition reaching from the science-fiction film of today back into the fertility drama and the initiation rituals of prehistoric times. But if *The Tempest* represents an initiation of its characters—and its audience—what is the special revelation, the almost religious vision, which comes at the end of the initiation? It is the game of chess in the sacred confines of Prospero's cell.

Prospero.	Pray you look in.
	My dukedom since you have given me again,
	I will requite you with as good a thing,
	At least bring forth a wonder to content ye
	As much as me my dukedom.

Here Prospero discovers Ferdinand and Miranda playing at chess.

Miranda.	Sweet lord, you play me false.
Ferdinand.	No, my dearest love,
	I would not for the world.
Miranda.	Yes, for a score of kingdoms you should wrangle,
	And I would call it fair play.
Alonso.	If this prove
	A vision of the island, one dear son
	Shall I twice lose.
Sebastian.	A most high miracle!
Ferdinand.	Though the seas threaten, they are merciful.
	I have cursed them without cause [*Kneels.*]
Alonso.	Now all the blessings
	Of a glad father compass thee about!
	Arise, and say how thou cam'st here.
Miranda.	O, wonder!
	How many goodly creatures are there here!
	How beauteous mankind is! O brave new world
	That has such people in't!
Prospero.	'Tis new to thee.

(V. i. 167–184)

New, miraculous, wonderful—this is the ultimate teaching of *The Tempest*, that somehow the people in the play approach the world anew and find it fresh and wonderful after this strange initiation.

The chess game is a magnificent symbol. For one thing, chess is a game of war, of political fighting; here wildness has been transmuted into a game, into a civilized pastime, just as the war of the sexes between Ferdinand and Miranda has been clothed and sanctified in the rules of matrimony. Ferdinand and Miranda have risen above playing each other false. They have come to a kind of love within the rules, a playing together that transcends worldly affairs. Also, Ferdinand is now carrying wood in a way rather different from carrying logs. Those crude raw logs have somehow become metamorphosed and transformed into wooden kings and bishops and knights, entire kingdoms, now seen as only "play."

That leads us to still another aspect of this very rich symbol, the chess game, a traditional value so often repeated it is well known even to such an innocent as Sancho Panza:

"Tell me [said Don Quixote], have you not seen some comedy in which kings, emperors, pontiffs, knights, ladies, and numerous other characters are introduced? One plays the ruffian, another the cheat, this one a merchant and that one a soldier. . . . Yet when the play is over and they have taken off their players' garments, all the actors are once more equal."

"Yes," replied Sancho, "I have seen all that."

"Well," continued Don Quixote, "the same thing happens in the comedy and intercourse of this world, where some play the part of emperors, others that of pontiffs—in short, all the characters that a drama may have—but when it is all over, that is to say, when life is done, death takes from each the garb that differentiates him, and all at last are equal in the grave."

"It is a fine comparison," Sancho admitted, "though not so new but that I have heard it many times before. It reminds me of that other one, about the game of chess. So long as the game lasts, each piece has its special qualities, but when it is all over they are all mixed and jumbled together and put into a bag, which is to the chess pieces what the grave is to life."

The chess game is a symbol for "play" and *The Tempest* is a play about "play." Even more, the chess game is a symbol for life itself and a certain attitude toward life—that life is but a game, "play," just as that favorite Shakespearean idea, "All the world's a stage," implies a certain relaxed acceptance of the foibles of life, most of all a willingness to accept its end.

The Winter's Tale and *The Tempest,* these two last plays, bear an intimate relation to each other. *The Winter's Tale* was about the wonderful creating power of woman. *The Tempest* deals with the wonderful creating power of man. In these two last plays, Shakespeare seems to be comparing art to nature, thinking of nature as the art of God, thinking of men's arts as imitating and fulfilling God's art, nature, yet ultimately not quite equaling it. *The Tempest* turns away from political rivalry and the business of the world toward love and procreation. It builds on the contrast between freedom and servitude or confinement: Prospero and Miranda confined to the island, then freed; Ariel seeking his freedom; Caliban trying to rebel against his ruler; that discussion of an ideal state in which everything is free—Gonzalo's speech from Montaigne. In the Epilogue Prospero himself, now throwing off his part, asks us as an actor to set him free through applause. The image *The Tempest* uses for servitude over and over again is wood, which seems to have overtones of dullness, brutishness, but also wildness and savagery. The comedy seems to create a feeling that the truly free man is the one in control, not the slave of his own passions and lusts, be they for power or women. The truly free man is not the "woodwose," but the man who knows "All the world's a stage."

The Tempest is a play about play, playing plays and playing chess, and the way play can work transformations: turn greed for political power into political responsibility; transform lust into love and, ultimately, marriage. The comedy builds on that special Renaissance sense of justice and chastity as forms of *decorum* (in its rich classical sense), human actions in the world of affairs and in the world of private relationships leading to the greater end of the good life.

The Tempest is a play of sleep and dreams, miraculous visions, masques, illusions, imaginings. Clothing is important, acting, sound effects, music, and shows: the disappearing banquet, the mysterious music of the island, the beautiful harvest masque that celebrates the betrothal of Ferdinand and Miranda—these shows are for a purpose, to transform people, to teach them things. The people of the play, except, of course, Prospero himself, greet these transformations and informations with wonder and amazement, like a new and beautiful dream. A miraculous quality runs through the play. It initiates its characters—and its audience—into a sense of the wonder, the freshness deep down things. The characters are made to wander a maze, to do tasks, suffer ordeals, die and be reborn to see miraculous visions like the game of chess. Finally, they return to the world better men.

They have been transformed by a man, Prospero, who controls the world they have entered. He is very much its master, and to him there is nothing new about it. Contrast his hard-boiled attitude with Miranda's,

> *Miranda.*   O brave new world
>   That has such people in't!
> *Prospero.*   'Tis new to thee.
>   (V. i. 183–184)

Prospero throughout the comedy is the master of it. We see him as an authority-figure in all kinds of dominant roles. He is the king, the ruler of the island, just as he was Duke of Milan. He is a father, and a rather stern father at that. He is an English teacher and a schoolmaster. He is a magus, that is, a magician or sage. And he is, above all, a dramatist. He has turned his island into a theater, and those who come there are shown miraculous shows which somehow teach them more than any mere words could the right way to live in justice and chastity. Notice how close this blithe, sunny comedy is to that crabbed, difficult problem comedy, *Measure for Measure*. There, too, there was an authority-figure who dominated the action, the Duke. He, too, was like a dramatist or playwright, setting up scenes and moving characters here and there in order to teach his subjects about chastity and justice. Prospero is a happier, sunnier version of that Duke of dark corners. He is a happier dramatist, but also a dramatist about to give over his art.

> Ye elves of hills, brooks, standing lakes, and groves,
> And ye that on the sands with printless foot
> Do chase the ebbing Neptune, and do fly him
> When he comes back; you demi-puppets that
> By moonshine do the green sour ringlets make,
> Whereof the ewe not bites; and you whose pastime
> Is to make midnight mushrumps, that rejoice
> To hear the solemn curfew; by whose aid
> (Weak masters though ye be) I have bedimmed
> The noontide sun, called forth the mutinous winds,
> And 'twixt the green sea and the azured vault
> Set roaring war; to the dread rattling thunder
> Have I given fire and rifted Jove's stout oak
> With his own bolt; the strong-based promontory
> Have I made shake and by the spurs plucked up
> The pine and cedar; graves at my command
> Have waked their sleepers, oped, and let 'em forth
> By my so potent art. But this rough magic
> I here abjure; and when I have required
> Some heavenly music (which even now I do)
> To work mine end upon their senses that
> This airy charm is for, I'll break my staff,
> Bury it certain fathoms in the earth,
> And deeper than did ever plummet sound
> I'll drown my book.

> (V. i. 33–57)

Is that Shakespeare's farewell to the theater? "This rough magic I here abjure." "I'll break my staff." "I'll drown my book." In medieval times, stage directors carried a book, the promptbook or text of the play, and also a staff or wand with which they pointed out positions for the actors. Perhaps Shakespeare himself carried that book and staff, and in this speech he is giving them over, bidding farewell to his career as a dramatist. Perhaps.

Prospero, at any rate, is a dramatist. He is also a man, very like Adam. He lives on an island rather like an earthly paradise. And he fell from Milan, as Adam fell, through the search for knowledge.

> At that time
> Through all the signories it [Milan] was the first
> And Prospero the prime duke, being so reputed
> In dignity, and for the liberal arts

> Without a parallel; those being all my study,
> The government I cast upon my brother
> And to my state grew stranger, being transported
> And rapt in secret studies.
>
>   . . .
>
> I thus neglecting worldly ends, all dedicated
> To closeness, and the bettering of my mind
> . . . but by being so retired,
> . . . in my false brother
> Awaked an evil nature.
>
>   (I. ii. 70–93)

Like Adam, Prospero fell through his search for knowledge, yet Prospero is not simply like Adam, but this authority-figure, king, father, magus, schoolmaster, an authority so powerful that

> Graves at my command
> Have waked their sleepers, oped, and let 'em forth
> By my so potent art.

Prospero is a kind of god, and *The Tempest* is his Nature; this comedy pays a good deal of attention to the four elements, earth, air (there is even a character named Ariel who is associated with the air, as Caliban is associated with the earth), fire (Ariel flaming amazement), and water, notably the sea. Prospero manipulates the island and its four elements like a kind of theater to teach his characters—and his audience. This is Prospero's art. But what about Nature? Nature, we have seen, is, in a Renaissance cliché, "the art of God." In other words, Prospero manipulates his island like a theater in the same way that God, in a Christian view of things, manipulates all nature, the theater of this world, to tutor men into the newness and freshness of Paradise: "Destiny," Ariel notes, "hath to instrument," has as its means, "this lower world and what is in it." Prospero, then, becomes a play-version of God or destiny. As Ferdinand says when he hears invisible music:

> Where should this music be? I' th' air or th' earth?
> It sounds no more; and sure it waits upon
> Some god o' th' island.
>
>   (I. ii. 388–390)

And later, when he comes to explain how he has met Miranda, he says, "By immortal providence she's mine," but it was really the old setter-up of scenes, Prospero, who played "immortal providence." When they are finally betrothed, Ferdinand casts himself as Adam in Prospero's Eden:

> Let me live here ever!
> So rare a wond'red father and a wise
> Makes this place Paradise.
>
>   (IV. i. 122–124)

The Tempest seems to be saying that Prospero the dramatist is a play version of God the dramatist; his stage is not all the world, but this island, which he uses to teach the men of "this lower world," what is fitting, just, and chaste.

Is *The Tempest,* then, Shakespeare the dramatist's farewell to the stage? A long farewell to all his greatness? It is not really right to read Shakespeare's plays as though they were autobiography, as though he were a Romantic poet like Shelley or Byron telling us about all the intricate delicacies of his soul. *The Tempest* stands very much on its own two beautiful feet as a wonderful comedy about the interaction of art and nature, man and God. We don't need to think of it as Shakespeare's farewell. Yet, it is almost an answer to *The Winter's Tale:* women make babies, but dramatists are like gods. Its theme seems to be so much a theme about drama and the kind of teaching that drama does, how the dramatist imitates God, that we do the play no violence if we choose to hear in it Shakespeare's adieu. There is no real evidence that it is Shakespeare's farewell, but if it makes you feel good as it makes me feel good, if it gives you a warm sentimental feeling in your abdomen as it gives me a warm sentimental feeling in my abdomen, then let us by all means think of it as Shakespeare's long farewell, and particularly when Prospero looks at the little play he has just put on, and breaks it off, because reality calls, and says:

> Be cheerful, sir.
> Our revels now are ended. These our actors,
> As I foretold you, were all spirits and
> Are melted into air, into thin air;
> And, like the baseless fabric of this vision,
> The cloud-capped towers, the gorgeous palaces,
> The solemn temples, the great globe itself,
> Yea, all which it inherit, shall dissolve,
> And like this insubstantial pageant faded,
> Leave not a rack behind. We are such stuff
> As dreams are made on, and our little life
> Is rounded with a sleep.
>
> (IV. i. 147–156)

When Prospero looks and gestures at the world around him, "the great globe itself," does he mean the Globe? I'd like to think so, partly, I suppose, because I am basically a sentimentalist, but partly because it gives us our cue to exit. In Prospero's closing words,

> As you from crimes would pardoned be,
> Let your indulgence set me free.

17

AFTERTHOUGHTS

THERE REMAINS BUT TO ANSWER A QUESTION THAT WAS ASKED AND ANSWERED AT the outset, but should be asked and answered again and again. What have we been doing with this mélange of triple goddesses and clothing images and Oedipus complexes? In essence, we have been asking of the several plays, "What is it that makes this play the way it is?" In each play, we have made a number of observations about structure, parallelisms, recurring images, themes, characterizations (sometimes), and out of these separate observations, we have tried to make a statement of the special quality of each play, what informs and shapes the action, events, people, and language, what, in short, makes the play the way it is: a *Macbeth*-principle ("the tragedy of our uncertainty about the way supernature penetrates nature") or a *Tempest*-principle ("how the dramatist imitates God"). Such statements are not "morals" or messages, nor do they in any sense substitute for the play itself, any more than a map moralizes about or substitutes for a landscape.

Critics speak of the organic unity of a work of art, meaning, I take it, our feeling that there is something distinctive in the work or behind it that makes it the way it is. At least one of the critic's—or reader's—obligations is to find out and at least feel, maybe formulate, those "seeds within," the *Macbeth*-principle or the *Tempest*-principle. This is an organic perception, one analogous to our understanding of nature: there are "the seeds within" of snail-ness that make snails snail-like. In the same way, we perceive in other human beings their distinctive quality and respond to it. In this sense, the perception of the organic unity of art shades over into the perception of life itself, one reason why art is morally and intellectually important. My target as a critic has been your perception (and, incidentally, my own), and I suspect it was Shakespeare's target as a playwright,

> To work mine end upon their senses that
> This airy charm is for.

It is a customary piety in Shakespearean circles, however, to say that the only way really to perceive, to understand and enjoy Shakespeare is to see him in the living theater. I, for one, dissent. We speak of Shakespeare as being "immortal," but surely this is merely a figure of speech and a crude one at that. No one, I suppose, would claim that Shakespeare's jokes are all immortal, as "alive" as when they first forced a guffaw out of those garlicky groundlings. How often do we hear a modern audience laugh at anything but the sight gags in a Shakespearean production? In a more precise sense, Shakespeare's plays are two-thirds or slightly more than two-thirds dead.

It takes three things to make drama: an actor working from a script; a theater; an audience. Shakespeare's audience, of course, is long gone, and we are not a very happy substitute. We are far less sensitive to language than they were, and we no longer think in the semimedieval way that they did. Necessarily, many Shakespearean attitudes (toward monarchy, for example) will be alien to us. At best we can don them like an intellectual costume and masquerade as Elizabethans for the purposes of the play. Shakespeare's theater, too, has long since crumbled into dust. Admirable as are the many modern efforts to reintroduce the platform stage into Elizabethan productions, they nevertheless play to an audience for whom the conventions and customs of that stage are odd, faintly unnatural, perhaps merely quaint.

To a twentieth-century audience, the theater that is most congenial to us, the one we see most often, discuss most avidly, feel most comfortable and natural in is not, despite all middlebrow homage to it, the "legitimate stage," but the screen of film or television. Lamentable as much of the material is, it is, nevertheless, the theater we see in this day and age. Unfortunately, it is a theater ill suited to Shakespeare. His was a verbal art; film and television, when properly handled, are visual arts. In the best screened Shakespeares, Sir Laurence Olivier's *Henry V,* for example, the director manages to wed visual and verbal elements. In the less successful ones, they are at war, and usually the verbal elements lose. The director becomes so involved with creating pictures, moving characters from here to there, staging horse-opera style battles (as in Olivier's later *Richard III*), that the play has to be drastically and disastrously cut. Nevertheless, a twentieth-century reader or listener, simply hearing Shakespeare's language, will almost inevitably imagine performance in screen terms, not those of the legitimate stage, and naturally so, and those terms are far from Shakespeare's verbal art.

Shakespeare's real theater, moreover, was not the half-timbered Globe, but the imagination of his audience, and here, indeed, the twentieth century can deliver a living Shakespeare. Through the many fine recordings of Shakespearean plays, a modern audience can have a performance which is imagined in the theatrical ("screen") terms which are natural to us but which does no violence to the essential nature of the play. The next best thing to hearing a recording is simply to read the text imaginatively; then, too, imagination, though less assisted, will necessarily create the real Shakespeare, true to the play itself, yet conceived in a production natural to its new audience. It is for this reason that I, as a critic, have concentrated on the text of the plays rather than on the plays as events on a stage: reading or hearing the play, these are really performances "in the quick forge and working-house of thought," whereas actual stage performances of Shakespeare these days as often come between us and the play as lead us into it.

> Think, when we talk of horses, that you see them
> Printing their proud hoofs i' th' receiving earth,

the Prologue (of *Henry V*) tells us—and we can do it. But can we do so watching the usual modern production?

That is the third member of the triad that makes up drama: important as audience and theater are, there is no drama without an actor working from a script, the actual production of a play. Here, indeed, the twentieth century fails us. I can count on the toes of one foot the productions of Shakespeare that have really been exciting and wonderful experiences in the theater, and I suspect most Shakespeareans would, if pressed, admit no more. This is truly an astonishing situation—as though, to shift arts, there were not an orchestra in the country that could play a Beethoven symphony properly. And is that so farfetched an analogy? Surely, Shakespeare is as elementary an item in an acting company's repertory as Beethoven in an orchestra's. Is producing a play so different a thing from performing a symphony?

There is the crux of the matter; we can call it the cult of novelty. The twentieth-century director and actor want—or need—to be "original"; they seem (generally) unwilling to settle on a good performance of Shakespeare and then sensitively and skillfully perform it with minor variations, as a conductor of a symphony would. Rather, each production must be something new, must have its special, novel gimmick, even if the gimmick has nothing to do with the play or positively violates it. The play becomes a cardboard cake on which the playcook can show off the really important thing, his ingenious icing. It was, I suppose, Orson Welles's famous production of *Julius Caesar* in the thirties that set the fashion for this century; that production itself worked a curious transmutation on the play, substituting our twentieth-century attitude toward dictators for the Renaissance emotions toward a prince that the play itself seeks to stir.

Welles's "modern dress" method has prompted a host of imitators, not all of them by any means bad. For example, the Old Vic production of *Troilus and Cressida,* in the costumes of 1910 or so, nicely caught the almost Viennese over-ripeness of the play; the various productions of *Much Ado* in Spanish or Mexican settings (despite a tendency to bog down in fandangos and castanets) bring out the crucial importance of honor in its old sense.

Novelty, itself, then, is not the evil, but rather novelty which shows no respect or understanding of the play into which it is being thrust. I remember a production of *Macbeth* in which Malcolm's soldiers supposedly carrying "leavy screens" from Birnam Wood carried bits of driftwood (driftwood, I suppose, being far more artsycraftsy); but a major point of the Birnam Wood business is that the forces of fertility and procreation are arrayed against the sterile, wintry tyrant. Driftwood hardly conveys the feeling. In that same production, Jason Robards, Jr., as Macbeth, on learning "The Queen, my lord, is dead," shuffled off backstage to return with Siobhan McKenna (Lady Macbeth) in his arms and croon (somewhat winded) the "To-morrow and to-morrow and to-morrow" as a sorrowful love-lament over his dead bride. But the whole point of the "To-morrow" speech is that the Macbeths have cut themselves off from natural processes in time, the cycles of birth and death and love that unite husband and wife; they are, must be, loveless—"unnatural" is the word the play uses—in the second phase of the action. One could list dozens of such oddments from stage productions long since and rightly forgotten. Film productions have the doubtful virtue of preserving their eccentricities indefinitely. For example, in *Julius Caesar,* Shakespeare takes some pains to give us the final strategy in which the armies of Brutus and Cassius, divided, image the fatal dualism of the two conspirators. The M-G-M *Julius Caesar* (except for this, an excellent production) showed Antony and Octavius' troops firing down on Brutus and Cassius' armies together in a narrow defile. The basic pattern of the play thus thrown aside, what was gained was a sort of *Gunga Din* climax plus a fine zinging of arrows and bowstrings like the one that had proved such a success in Olivier's *Henry V.* A classic slip occurs in the rococo Anglo-Italian *Romeo and Juliet:* Laurence Harvey (Romeo) sits stolidly on a bench while the Friar and Nurse address a Romeo "There on the ground, with his own tears made drunk." Even an Italian director could have found out the simple sense of the line.

These are matters of props, blocking, and the like, the director's means for realizing imagery and structure on a stage. Acting itself is both a far more important and far more difficult part of production. My own limited and amateur experience as an actor gives me little ground for avuncular counsel; nor does the tendency of actors and theater departments to cultivate ignorance like a rich uncle give me much hope my counsel would be heeded. One curious fact, though, may help, namely, that amateur and semiprofessional companies are so often

327 Afterthoughts

more successful with Shakespeare than more famous groups with (probably) better actors. For one thing, the amateur company is less likely to have a star whose part must be built up at the expense of the rest of the play. The amateur group is also less likely to feel the need of startling novelty, is more willing to settle for simply a good, competent performance. Most important, the acting style of the modern amateur often comes far closer to the Shakespearean style than that of many modern professionals. Shakespeare wrote for a specific acting and production style, as any playwright does; another style violates a play of his as much as it would a comedy of Molière. That "Globe" style is, in Bernard Beckerman's excellent formulation, "ceremonious." That is, the actor types the character, imitating the ideal rather than the specific, and stresses the language rather than the business. Within this type-characterization, the actor should give himself fully to the overwhelming passions that are the "big" sections of the part, passion being, from the point of view of Elizabethan psychology, eo ipso, motivation. The amateur's limited skills will typically come out with this style of acting quite naturally; the professional's greater range and sense of consistency will often prove his undoing. Almost certainly, the much-vaunted "method," suggesting Pleistocene depths, repressed and rather sinister drives churning under the torn T-shirt, is utterly alien to the Shakespearean character. A really skilled and tactful practitioner of "The Method" will recognize that understanding the character also involves understanding the distinctive world of the play, including its quite limited conception of human psychology. But this is to demand an almost scholarly understanding, more the province of a learned journal than a property in a theater.

From the point of view of actor and producer, the beginning of wisdom for Shakespearean production is to recognize that it cannot be done. Given the changed theater and audience, the finest performance will fall short of the mark, an imagined re-creation from text or recording. Once an acting company recognizes this limitation, they can arrive at the best possible performance by letting the play itself control and inform its production, perhaps by means of the kind of "map" we have been developing.

Our maps so far have been of individual plays. What can we conclude about Shakespeare himself? In a strict sense, nothing. Shakespeare was a popular artist, a writer responsive to the conventions of his theater and the tastes of his audience. Just from looking at the plays themselves, there is no way to tell whether Shakespeare really believed the things the plays seem to say. Neither is there any way to tell whether Shakespeare put something in the text consciously or unconsciously. And in any case, we've been talking about only thirteen plays out of the canonical, say, thirty-seven. For all these reasons, it is presumptuous to look back over the path we have traveled and say anything about Shakespeare. And yet we have been in contact with the greatest imagination the world has ever known; even if, in a strict sense, we have no right to conclude anything about Shakespeare himself, I think we feel that we do in some sense know him, through the recurring patterns in his plays.

The one theme that seems to run through all of Shakespeare's plays is: the contrast between the private, inner world and the outer, public world, between the world of love and the world of affairs, the world of the family and the world of politics and business. We have seen it as the contrast between private man and public man in, say, *Julius Caesar* or *Macbeth,* or as the contrast between sex and fighting in *Romeo and Juliet,* between love and empire in *Antony and Cleopatra,* or the tension between King Lear's relations to his daughters and to his kingdom, or the two aspects of Prince Hal: Falstaff and Hotspur. In a sense, this contrast between private and public, inner and outer, is a contrast between a life force, the force of love, and a death force, the force of worldly ambition. We could approximate them in the two great terms of Freud, Eros and Thanatos. When Shakespeare looks at the public world, the world of wars and politics and commerce, he tends to see it in a distinctive way, as divisive and competitive. The harshness of Shylock's mercantile world, for example, is imaged as a false breeding or multiplication, the taking of interest, really a kind of division. Similarly, in *Julius Caesar,* the essence of the tragedy was the splitting of Caesar into public spirit and private body.

This sense of fragmentation and splitting seems to be the essence of Shakespeare's tragic imagination. In *Hamlet,* the hero was split among Horatio and Fortinbras, Laertes and Ophelia, split into the man of thought and the man of action. In the tragedies, the public world and the ambitions of people in that public world seem to take over and corrupt the private world, break it apart, be it the world of the lovers in *Romeo and Juliet* or *Antony and Cleopatra,* or the household of the Macbeths, or the family of King Lear. The comedies turn this action around. The private world of love and marriage and family outweighs and overcomes the public world. The private world seems to create an atmosphere in which things breed and multiply, in which there is plenty and bounty, creation and fertility. For example, one of Shakespeare's favorite comic themes is the theme of projection or fantasy, where in the comedies, *Twelfth Night,* for instance, a person projects his inner wishes on the outer world, deludes himself, and thus gives rise to all kinds of comic consequences, mostly laughter. In the tragedies, the situation is the other way round: tragic consequences result when an Othello projects his inner thoughts, while a Malvolio or a Leontes produces comic results. But more typically in the tragedies, a man projects wishes taken from the public world onto his own or someone's private life and so corrupts it. Iago's ambition destroys the marriage of Othello; Macbeth and Lady Macbeth kill together in a political crime, but die separately as man and wife.

In *King Lear,* the political lusts of the daughters destroy their private relation with their father. A political assassination corrupts a family in *Hamlet.*

The private world, the world of love and creativity, seems most often associated in Shakespeare with woman; and the idea of woman itself seems to go through three stages in his career. In the early plays, as in Portia's Belmont, woman seems to be bountiful, merciful, giving, the source of harmony and wealth. In Shakespeare's two middle periods, in the great histories and tragedies, woman seems to be a disturbing influence, for example, Lady Macbeth, or Lear's daughters; think of Hamlet's feelings about his mother, or Angelo's sudden lust for Isabella in *Measure for Measure.* In Shakespeare's last period, the period of the romances, woman seems to be thought of as the life-giver, the fertile, creating mother, good goddess nature, great creating nature, as in *The Winter's Tale.*

Woman seems naturally drawn to the inner, private world. Man, in Shakespeare, seems drawn to the outer, public world. Man is associated with ambition, with politics, with war, with words. Like Hotspur or Brutus or Antony, men tend to leave love behind them to pursue political will-o'-the-wisps. The contrast between Autolycus in *The Winter's Tale* and Perdita sums it up. Perdita is the image of woman as a life-giving goddess; Autolycus is the image of man, a kind of satyr, given to sex and lust, concerned with clothing and titles and honors and all kinds of externals. Autolycus is much concerned with words as men almost always are in Shakespeare, most notably in the windy, rhetorical world of *Julius Caesar,* that Roman man's world.

Words, words, words seem to have been important to Shakespeare, not unsurprisingly. Mostly, he seems to image language as a garment; he held the traditional idea of words as clothing thoughts or meaning. He seems to think of language as a kind of artificial covering, and this is most clear in the early plays, like *Romeo and Juliet,* when the language is artificial and formal. As Shakespeare moves into the middle period of his career, the language becomes looser, more natural, but at the same time more complex; in a manner of speaking, there are more figures of speech per inch. Along with this development of his language, there is a greater skill and interest in motivation and characterization. Then, as he moves into the final period of his career, he seems to lose interest in carefully motivating people; we get instead the artificiality of Leontes' jealousy in *The Winter's Tale* and the almost allegorical quality of such figures as Ariel and Caliban in *The Tempest.* Yet these final plays retain the rich language of his middle period, combining much of Shakespeare's most beautiful poetry with the sense that "this is only a play."

And what did Shakespeare think of plays? What did he think of his own art? Like all the other male arts, he seems to regard plays as a not quite satisfactory substitute for life. When Shakespeare wishes to insult life or run it down, he calls it a play or a dream, as in Macbeth's "Life's but a poor player that struts and frets his hour upon the stage," or in *King Lear* where life becomes "This great stage of fools." *The Tempest* and *The Winter's Tale* both give over art in favor of nature.

Shakespeare is often playful about plays—he seems to regard them first and foremost as entertainment—yet he also seems to subscribe to that Renaissance belief that drama, being an untruth, is immoral unless it justifies itself by teaching. There is even something faintly sinister in playwriting. The scene-setting Duke in *Measure for Measure* is a mysterious duke of dark corners; and Shakespeare's greatest playwright is—Iago. Almost as if to compensate for the element of untruth, those characters in Shakespeare's middle and late plays who seem closest to dramatists and playwrights invariably use their plays to teach. Hal reminds himself of kingly duty in his little playlet with Falstaff. Hamlet uses the play-within-the-play to teach himself his uncle's guilt. Iago—even as false and perverted as Iago is—uses the little scenes and episodes he conjures up to teach Othello. The Duke in *Measure for Measure* sets up scenes and events to teach his subjects about justice and chastity. Prospero stages the harvest masque in *The Tempest* to instruct Ferdinand and Miranda about marriage. In these late romances, plays present the characters with an image of life which makes them realize the ways in which "all the world's a stage," a sentence that seems to be the distinctive wish that informs and characterizes Shakespeare's work.

Though it is rather ridiculous to try to characterize in so brief a space "myriad-minded Shakespeare," even so brief a sketch as this suggests how deeply down the roots of his plays reach. Man as concerned with the outer world, woman with the inner; tragedy as fragmentation, amputation; comedy as bringing man and woman together—Freud was quite right when he said, "Not I but the poets discovered the unconscious," and Shakespeare was his favorite poet. Shakespeare seems to have had *par excellence* that ability which modern psychology tells us is the essence of artistic creation: the power to reach to the most archaic layers of his experience and re-create the essentials of our own.

The true poet, Keats said, "has no Identity." He "will have as high an imagination that he will be able to throw his own soul into any object he sees or imagines, so as to see, feel, be sensible of, and express all that the object itself would . . . he will speak out of that object, so that his own self will, with the exception of the mechanical part, be 'annihilated.'" Keats himself could "conceive of a billiard Ball that it may have a sense of delight from its own roundness, smoothness and [the] very volubility . . . of its motion." One of the passages from Shakespeare that Keats took especial delight in was the little description in *Venus and Adonis* of

> the snail, whose tender horns being hit,
> Shrinks backward in his shelly cave with pain,
> And there, all smoth'red up, in shade doth sit,
> Long after fearing to creep forth again.

Shakespeare, in effect, has gotten inside the snail itself, and perhaps it suffices to say that poetry was for him a way of entering, not just the snail, but all his characters, the world of nature, and, in some kind of ultimate comic gesture, us as well.

INDEX

act-and-scene divisions, 9–10, 262–263
acting: naturalistic, 10, 27–28, 328; Shakespearean, 9–10, 326–327; *see also* images, themes
actors: boy, 8–9; hired, 8
Adam, 320–321
Aeschylus, 28
All for Love, 18
All's Well That Ends Well, 216
ambition (in *Macbeth*), 60
anachronism, 57
analogy, language of, 38–42
animals, 36; *see also* images
anti-semitism (in *Merchant of Venice*), 91–93
anti-Stratfordian theories, 1–2, 25–26
antithesis, *see* figures of speech
Antony and Cleopatra, 132, 193, 227, 230, 261–283, 305, 328, 329
Antony and Cleopatra (Dryden), 18
Aretino, 302
Aristophanes, 92
Aristotle, 18–19, 21, 34, 44, 89, 238, 315
Armstrong, Louis, 31
As You Like It, 6, 25, 196, 296
Athenians, 272–273
audience, Elizabethan, 11
authorship question, 1–2, 25–26
Autolycus, 299, 329; *see also Winter's Tale*

Bacon, Delia, 26
Bacon, Sir Francis, 26
bardolatry, 22–26
"barne," 295

Barrymore, John, 156
Beaumont, Francis, 2
Beckerman, Bernard, 327
Bergman, Ingmar, 14, 165, 212; *see also* cinema
Bethlehem Hospital, 244
Betterton, Thomas, 154, 161
Bible, 64, 70, 100
biblical plays, 92
birds, 36; *see also* images
Blake, William, 28
blood, *see* images
body, *see* images, themes
Booth, Edwin, 156
Borgia, Cesare, 218–219
Boswell, James, 155
Bowdler, Thomas, 20
boy actors, 8–9
Bradley, A. C., 42
British Critic, 20
Burbage, Cuthbert, 8
Burbage, James, 6, 8
Burbage, Richard, 8, 14, 157
Byron, 322

Caesar, 38, 137–140; *see also Julius Caesar*
Calderón, 28
Cambridge Shakespeare, 20
Capell, Edward, 20
Carlyle, Thomas, 22, 24
Cassius, 205; *see also Julius Caesar*
Cervantes, 318
chain of being, 34–42, 130–132, 145, 235, 238, 253, 258